Controllership Fourth Edition
1995 Cumulative Supplement

# SUBSCRIPTION NOTICE

This Wiley product is updated on a periodic basis with supplements to reflect important changes in the subject matter. If you purchased this product directly from John Wiley & Sons, Inc., we have already recorded your subscription for this update service.

If, however, you purchased this product from a bookstore and wish to receive (1) the current update at no additional charge, and (2) future updates and revised or related volumes billed separately with a 30-day examination review, please send your name, company name (if applicable), address, and the title of the product to:

Supplement Department
John Wiley & Sons, Inc.
One Wiley Drive
Somerset, NJ 08875
1-800-225-5945

For customers outside the United States, please contact the Wiley office nearest you:

Professional & Reference Division
John Wiley & Sons Canada, Ltd.
22 Worcester Road
Rexdale, Ontario M9W 1L1
CANADA
(416) 675-3580
1-800-567-4797
FAX (416) 675-6599

John Wiley & Sons, Ltd.
Baffins Lane
Chichester
West Sussex, PO19 1UD
UNITED KINGDOM
(44) (243) 779777

Jacaranda Wiley Ltd.
PRT Division
P.O. Box 174
North Ryde, NSW 2113
AUSTRALIA
(02) 805-1100
FAX (02) 805-1597

John Wiley & Sons (SEA) Pte. Ltd.
37 Jalan Pemimpin
Block B #05-04
Union Industrial Building
SINGAPORE 2057
(65) 258-1157

# Controllership
## The Work of the Managerial Accountant
## Fourth Edition
## 1995 Cumulative Supplement

**JAMES D. WILLSON**

*Senior Vice President—Finance (Retired)*
*Northrop Corporation*


**JANICE M. ROEHL-ANDERSON**

*Principal*
*Ernst & Young, Denver, Colorado*

JOHN WILEY & SONS, INC.
New York • Chichester • Brisbane • Toronto • Singapore

This text is printed on acid-free paper.

Copyright © 1995 by John Wiley & Sons, Inc.

All rights reserved. Published simultaneously in Canada.

*Library of Congress Cataloging in Publication Data:*

Willson, James D.
    Controllership, the work of the managerial accountant/James D.
  Willson and James P. Colford—4th ed.
        p.     cm.
    Rev. ed. of: Controllership, the work of the managerial
  accountant. 3rd ed. c1981.
    Includes bibliographical references and index.
    ISBN 0-471-63278-3
    1. Controllership.   2. Managerial accounting.   I. Colford, James
  P.  II. Willson, James D.   Controllership, the work of the
  managerial accountant.   III. Title.
  HG4026.H43 1991
  658.15'1—dc20                                        90-12215
    ISBN 0-471-63278-3
    ISBN 0-471-09411-0 (Supplement)

Printed in the United States of America

10 9 8 7 6 5 4 3 2 1

# PREFACE

The thrust of *Controllership, Fourth Edition,* as well as the preceding editions, is to provide suggestions and guidance to the accounting-trained financial executive so that he or she can use the technical background and experience in assisting the development and growth of a business entity on a sound financial basis. The book encourages the evolution of the controller from the financial fact recorder to the strategic financial analyst or business adviser involved in the planning and control of the business enterprise.

This supplement continues this effort by identifying some of the changes in the business environment that may dictate a change in emphasis or direction in some aspects of business management. Thus, this 1995 supplement includes, among other matters, limited comments on the recent developments in the evolution of the controllership function (Chapter 2), changes in accounting standards and the role the controller might play (Chapter 4), an outline of some of the new computer software that can assist the controller (Chapter 5), the cash flow ratios relating to cash sufficiencies and efficiencies (Chapter 8), some suggested changes in emphasis of internal control and the internal audit function (Chapters 9 and 10), and some suggestions on the planning and control of sales (Chapter 20), research and development (Chapter 24), cash and short-term investments (Chapter 27) as well as management of liabilities (Chapter 33) and shareholders equity (Chapter 34).

Then, relatively more space is devoted to these important current topics:

- The importance of business ethics, and how to promote and enforce ethical business behavior (Chapter 1)
- Some observations about effective cost determination, including activity-based costing and its application to both manufacturing and non-manufacturing functions (Chapter 4A)
- An overview of the growing globalization of business and the related impact upon an organization's structure, strategies, and the financial functions (Chapter 11A)
- In the context of investor relations, some financial market objectives are suggested which the controller might pursue, as well as some methods of maintaining a successful investor relations program (Chapter 13)
- Conditions to monitor in a program of successful acquisitions, including the evolution of multinational operations (Chapter 18)
- The relationship of detailed performance standards to entity profit goals and a discussion of time-based standards and benchmarking as part of a balanced system of performance measures (Chapter 19)

- The role of the controller in productivity improvement (Chapter 26A)
- In the context of planning and control of plant and equipment, some comments are made regarding foreign investments, the new manufacturing environment, and suggestions to explain the impact of generally accepted accounting principles on capital expenditures (Chapter 32)
- Commentary on the increased activity to improve financial accounting and reporting (Chapters 35A and 36)
- Some of the important changes taking place in computer technology, including its impact on the controllership function (Chapters 46–53)

These topics range from selecting a financial information system to software package implementation; as well as popular new subjects such as a description of groupware, and an overview of client/server computing.

To help assure that the information systems discussion is relatively accurate and up-to-date, our co-author, Janice M. Roehl-Anderson, together with some of her co-workers in the firm of Ernst & Young and elsewhere, who have been involved in information systems selection, installation, and implementation, have provided a great deal of data on this important area. In addition to authoring several chapters dealing with financial information systems, Jan Roehl-Anderson has coordinated the selection of knowledgeable contributing authors and their chosen topics. These contributing authors are identified in the Acknowledgments.

These topics, and others, are addressed so that the controller is kept aware of developments in the financial/accounting field and maintains his or her viewpoint as a broad-gauge business executive.

JAMES D. WILLSON
JANICE M. ROEHL-ANDERSON

*Los Angeles, California*
*Denver, Colorado*
*September 1994*

# ACKNOWLEDGMENTS

Our contributing authors, listed alphabetically, are responsible for updating or writing the chapters indicated:

**David M. Bassett,** Senior Consultant
Ernst & Young, Denver Office
    Chapter 5 (updating), Role of the Computer in Business and Financial
       Analysis
    Chapter 47, Computer Hardware Trends
    Chapter 53, A Brief Introduction to Client/Server Computing

**Sandra Borchardt,** Senior Manager
Ernst & Young, Boston Office
    Chapter 47A, Management Techniques for Software Package Integration
    Chapter 47AA, Software Package Integration
    Chapter 49, Automated Financial Accounting Systems

**Melissa W. Breeze,** Information Systems Consultant
Denver, Colorado
    Chapter 47C, Graphics in Business

**Tim Cranston,** Senior Manager
Ernst & Young, Cleveland Office
    Chapter 48, Financial Forecast Modeling: Converting Decisions and Plans
       to Cash and Value

**Hans Hultgren,** President
Integrated Systems Group, Denver, Colorado
    Chapter 47B, Groupware

**Jeffrey L. Sturrock,** Account Executive
Texas Instruments, Dallas, Texas
    Chapter 50, Electronic Data Interchange (EDI)

Jan Roehl-Anderson would like to thank God for His unending blessings. Additionally, she would like to thank Nelma Mannes for her outstanding administrative skills and June Moyer for her superb editing talents, which they have demonstrated in preparing this supplement. Additionally, and most importantly, thanks should be given to Fritz Anderson for his unending patience and moral support.

We are indebted to the Wiley editorial and production staffs, especially Sheck Cho, Mary Dobday, and Chris Sampson for their assistance in guiding this supplement through the publishing process.

# SUPPLEMENT CONTENTS

**Note to the Reader:** Materials new to *this* supplement are indicated by an asterisk (*) in the left margin of the contents listed below and throughout the supplement. Sections not in the main text are indicated by a (New) after the title.

# CHAPTER 1

# Accounting and Its Relation to Management

**p. 16.** *Add at the end of section 1-10:*

## 1-10A ETHICS IN BUSINESS (NEW)

Section 1-10 discusses standards of ethical conduct for management accountants, but the interest of the controller, as a member of top management, in ethical conduct does, or should, extend to the entire business and not merely to the accounting function. In today's environment, he or she probably would want to *know* that his or her company is doing business in a highly ethical manner. Just as the mission statement of an entity explains what the company intends to achieve, and the annual business plan describes how the annual objectives will be attained, so also the ethics statement—if one exists—indicates the kind of ethics acceptable in accomplishing the mission.

But why is more attention now being paid to business ethics? Is the moral basis on which business is conducted any less acceptable than, say, five years ago? There are several answers to these questions. An increasing number of public reports describe fraudulent acts on Wall Street, or in government contracts, and elsewhere. Moreover, with the globalization of business, competition has become more intense and the ethical basis of meeting it may have deteriorated. Some managers may feel under increased pressure to achieve the annual business plan or to meet other short-term business objectives. Also, attempts at corporate takeovers, downsizing, and the sale of entire segments of divisions have exerted an influence on executives to "look good."

Before discussing what steps are desirable to maintain an acceptable level of ethical conduct, it may be helpful to look at some typical questions that might arise in a business. These are not the more easily answered questions of whether something is black or white, or whether it is clearly honest or dishonest. Further, the answers relate in large part to the integrity of the individual employee, and to a desire to be guided by a high level of values.

### THE MORALITY OF "MANAGING" EARNINGS

Businesspeople from the CEO down to the department managers typically are under pressure to meet the monthly budget, or to achieve the planned sales, or reach the net income target for the year.

Here are some representative actions that *operating* managers might consider in an attempt to reach an operating plan result or a net income goal for the month, quarter, or year:

- Grant special discounts at year end to stimulate sales
- Offer special credit terms of deferred payments until the next calendar year in an effort to increase yearend sales
- Sell surplus plant and equipment, at a profit, in order to increase the quarterly net income
- Sell unwanted or surplus inventory to secure cash, and to increase net income to the planned level
- Defer needed, but not essential, repairs and maintenance until the next fiscal year to stay within the budget level of expenses
- Accelerate year end shipments through the use of overtime
- Record as a shipment on December 31, a load of material that did not leave the factory until January 2. (The fiscal year ends December 31.)

Are these unethical actions? In the normal sales cut-off procedures, the accountants would identify the improper dating on the advanced shipment mentioned in the last item above. But if the controller knew of the impending operating decision on the other transactions, should he or she have taken any action? Is there anything wrong with decisions made to achieve plan if the action was not illegal or dishonest, or if human life was not at stake? There are some who might consider many of the above actions unethical.

A survey concerning the acceptability of some selected business practices, both operating and accounting, resulted in these generalizations.[1]

- The respondents generally viewed the management of short-term earnings by *accounting* methods as significantly less acceptable than attaining the same ends by changing *operating* decisions or procedures.
- Materiality was a factor in the decision. Short-term earnings management was judged less acceptable if the earnings impact of the action was large rather than small.
- The direction of the effect on earnings makes a difference. *Increasing* earnings was judged less acceptable than reducing profits.
- The time period of the impact may influence ethical judgements. Managing the short-term earnings at the end of an interim quarterly reporting period was

---

[1] William J. Bruns, Jr. and Kenneth A. Merchant, "The Dangerous Morality of Managing Earnings," *Management Accounting,* Aug. 1990, p. 23. The William Taylor article mentioned in the Selected Reference (*Harvard Business Review,* March/April 1989) contains a copy of the ethics test.

viewed as somewhat more acceptable than taking comparable action at the end of an annual reporting period.

- Finally, the *method* of managing earnings influenced the test response. Thus, increasing profits through the use of extended credit terms was seen as less acceptable than accomplishing the same results by selling excess assets, or using overtime to accelerate the shipment.

Most of the decisions listed earlier in this segment (except that involving the sales cut-off) would have been regarded as acceptable. The ethics test results indicate that there are greatly varying opinions among operating managers as to what constitutes unacceptable ethical conduct. It can be understood, therefore, that any attempt to develop a written code of ethics to deal with such specific and detailed transactions, would require careful thought.

## DEFINING UNETHICAL BEHAVIOR

Deciding what is proper conduct is rather straight forward when the acts are unlawful or illegal, or when the choice is moral versus immoral, and when the important relevant facts are known. But in many cases all the facts are not known and/or we operate in grey areas. Moreover, with the passage of time, what was once considered unacceptable behavior becomes acceptable. How, then, should the top management of a company determine what is acceptable or unacceptable conduct? Some suggested steps in such a procedure might include:

- Hold discussions among the higher levels of management to identify various points of view.
- Clearly recognize the implications of any ethical decision of an action on the employees, investors, the public and the competition.
- Balance any tentative ethical decision against the company's self interest versus some of the broader interests.
- Finally, weigh the ethical decisions against what is perceived as the traditional values espoused by the company.

If the above procedures do not result in more or less generally accepted decisions as to ethical conduct, then the chief executive will need to make the choices, based on his or her training and judgment.

## PROMOTING AND ENFORCING ETHICAL BEHAVIOR

Assuming the management has reached general agreement about what constitutes ethical business conduct, how are these decisions made known and enforced? Any such program probably would encompass these three steps:

1. *A code of ethics and standards of conduct should be developed and reduced to writing.*

    The code should explain the basic viewpoint of top management about unethical conduct. It should also define those actions that are expected to occur, and should be equally explicit about unacceptable conduct. It should not consist of general platitudes, which merely sound good.

Guidance about types of conduct should be subdivided according to the important kinds of activities. Some illustrative topics included in some codes contain such matters as:

- Code of ethics
- Standards of conduct
- Conflicts of interest
- Bidding, negotiating, and performing under U.S. government contract
- Meals and entertainment
- Use of company car (and other assets)
- Gifts and payments of money
- Complete and accurate books, records, and communications
- Preservation of assets
- Compliance with anti-trust laws
- Political contributions
- Year-end and accounting adjustments
- Year-end operating activities
- Attaining annual business plan objectives
- Cost consciousness
- Workplace safety
- Product safety
- Employee discrimination (religion, race, sex, nationality, etc.)
- Hazardous waste disposal
- Political activities
- Compliance with SEC and other securities laws and regulations
- Restrictive trade practices
- International boycotts
- Leave for military or other federal service
- Corporate ethics office (ombudsman)

2. *The code of ethics and standards of conduct must be communicated to all employees.*

The employees should understand the attitude of management about unethical conduct and have clear knowledge about specific acts. The means of communicating with employees could include group meetings, training and development programs, newly hired employee orientation sessions, videotapes, and employee handbooks.

3. *The code must be enforced and monitored.*

In many cases, relevant procedures may be reviewed by the internal auditors, independent accountants, or the staff of corporate counsel. The corporate ethics office (the ombudsman) may be the device to receive complaints of alleged violations and investigate them. One rule is paramount: Uniform enforcement is essential. If employees perceive that executives are dealt with leniently, and lower level employees harshly, then code enforcement becomes difficult.

One available guideline for monitoring the business ethics and conduct of almost any company is the Defense Industry Questionnaire on Business Ethics and Conduct developed by a group of defense contractors.[2]

Another enforcement technique is to require all managers and certain key professionals to affirm annually in writing (a standard form) that each (1) is aware of the company code of conduct and (2) has adhered to it.

## 1-11   SELECTED REFERENCES

**p. 16.**   *Add these references:*

Andrews, Kenneth R., "Ethics in Practice," *Harvard Business Review,* Sept.–Oct. 1989, pp. 99–104.

Bruns, William J., Jr., and Kenneth A. Merchant, "The Dangerous Morality of Managing Earnings," *Management Accounting,* Aug. 1990, pp. 22–25.

Bhide, Amar, and Howard H. Stevenson, "Why be Honest if Honesty Doesn't Pay," *Harvard Business Review,* Sept.–Oct. 1990, pp. 121–129.

Cohen, Jeffrey R., "Ethics and Budgeting," *Management Accounting,* Aug. 1988, pp. 29–31.

Gellerman, Saul W., "Why 'Good' Managers Make Bad Ethical Choices," *Harvard Business Review,* July/Aug. 1986, pp. 85–90.

Hennessy, Edward L., Jr., "Business Ethics—Is It a Priority for Corporate America?," *Financial Executive,* Oct. 1986, pp. 14–19.

Lander, Gerald H., Michael T. Cronin, and Alan Reinstein, "In Defense of the Management Accountant," *Management Accounting,* May 1990, pp. 54–57.

Rich, Anne J., Carl S. Smith, and Paul H. Mihalek, "Are Corporate Codes of Conduct Effective?," *Management Accounting,* Sept. 1990, pp. 34–35.

Skeddle, Ronald W., "Business Ethics: Dealing in the Gray Areas," *Financial Executive,* May–June 1990, pp. 9–13.

Sweeny, Robert B., and Howard L. Siers, "Survey: Ethics in Corporate America," *Management Accounting,* June 1990, pp. 34–40.

Taylor, William, ed., "The Gray Area—Ethics Test for Everyday Managers," *Harvard Business Review,* March–April 1989, pp. 220–221.

Verschoor, Curtis C., "Readers Respond to Accounting Ethics Case Study," *Management Accounting,* July 1990, pp. 53–55.

---

[2] See Official Releases, *Journal of Accountancy,* August 1987, pp. 152–162 for the Questionnaire and selected questions and interpretations about it.

# CHAPTER 2

# The Controllership Function

## 2-12  A CONTINUING EVOLUTION

**p. 26.**  *Add at the end of section 2-12:*

In many companies, the controller is the CFO and, as the duties of the CFO change, a corresponding change takes place in the role of the controller. A recent survey of chief financial officers of multinational corporations conducted by KMPG Peat Marwick and Business International provided further evidence of evolution in the financial function. This list summarizes the responses to questions about how the CFO role is changing.[1]

|  | *Affirmative Response (%)* |
|---|---|
| CFO's influence over operating decisions has increased. | 67 |
| CFO is moving beyond traditional financial areas to activities more closely related to CEO. | 52 |
| CFO has been elevated in the corporate hierarchy. | 36 |
| CFO position has not changed or has decreased in influence. | 16 |

Percentages do not total 100 due to multiple responses.

The survey sends the message to all financial executives that top management expects the CFO to play an expanded role in assisting the enhancement of corporate profitability as well as competitiveness.

---

[1] Lawrence S. Maisel, "Proactive and Powerful—The New CFO," *Financial Executive,* July/Aug. 2 1990, p. 14.

## 2-16  QUALIFICATIONS OF THE CONTROLLER

**p. 31.**  *Add after the listing of qualifications:*

Compare the listed qualifications of the controller with the skills needed to be a successful CFO as revealed in a recent survey of CFOs.[2]

|  | *Affirmative Response (%)* |
|---|---|
| Business sense/understanding of operations | 84 |
| Problem-solving ability | 50 |
| Integrity | 49 |
| Innovativeness | 43 |
| Vision of the "big picture" | 43 |

Percentages do not total 100 due to multiple responses. As noted, more than half rated a business sense and understanding of operations, problem-solving ability, or integrity as a needed skill. But innovativeness and having a vision of the "big picture" were not far behind. Essentially, the CFO and other major executives must view the CFO as a business person (and not just a figure person) and part of the business management group before the financial executive can be effective in helping to shape the strategy and direction of the business. Mr. Controller, prepare for the future!

**p. 31.**  *Add at the end of section 2-16:*

## 2-16A  THE NEW TYPE OF MANAGER (NEW)

Having discussed the controller's task and his/her desired qualifications, it may be useful to mention briefly a related change taking place in business—one that can profoundly influence how the controller can be effective.

In this 1992–1993 period, competition is becoming more brutal. As a result, customers are more demanding, investors expect better performance, and even corporate directors are becoming more independent and are asking tougher questions. The World War II type of manager, perhaps one of the most successful and powerful business groups ever, is passing from the scene. Witness what has happened recently at IBM, General Motors, Westinghouse Electric, and American Express. Today's chief executive simply can't be to wedded to the past. Times often call for a shake-up.

The old-time autocratic manager very often told people what to do, when to do it, and how to do it. But a new type of manager and a new organizational structure are coming onto the scene, and this scene includes the controller's department. Some of the trends include flattened hierarchies, self-managed teams, and pay-for-performance systems. These new managers want to be seen as leaders, sponsors, and facilitators—anything but managers. They seek to *empower* their people—to ask questions that will help the staff solve the problems and make decisions on their own. Under the old system, decisions were perhaps made faster; under the new system, where "the team"

---

[2] *Ibid.*, p. 15.

shares in the decision, the inclination is to get the decision into operation faster. However, occasions will still arise when the leader must direct a decision.

The two types of managers can be illustrated by the following comparison:

| Old-Type Manager | New-Type Manager |
| --- | --- |
| Follows the chain of command | Deals with whoever is necessary to get a job done |
| Thinks of self as manager or boss | Thinks of self as a team leader, an internal consultant, or a teacher |
| Makes most of the decisions alone | Invites the other members of the group to share in decision making |
| Keeps information to self | Shares information |
| Tries to master a single discipline, such as accounting or marketing | Seeks to master a broad band of managerial disciplines |
| Demands long hours | Demands results most of all |

This new type of manager requires effort. Yet this aggressive, entrepreneurial management style may be not only the key to the growth and success of the business, but also the new way of advancing his/her career.

## 2-17  SELECTED REFERENCES

**p. 31.**  *Add these references:*

Byrne, John S., "Requiem for Yesterday's CEO," *Business Week,* Feb. 15, 1993, pp. 32–33.
Dumaine, Brian, "The New Non-Manager Managers," *Fortune,* Feb. 22, 1993, pp. 80–91.

# CHAPTER 4

# Accounting Principles and Practices

## 4-2  FINANCIAL ACCOUNTING STANDARDS BOARD (FASB)

**p. 59.** *Delete sentence, "A list of the statements issued to date is set forth in Figure 4-6" and add:*

A list of the statements issued through February of 1992 is set forth in Figure 4-6. However, with the greater frequency in which standards of the FASB are promulgated, as well as the more numerous pronouncements of the other rule-making bodies, it seems impractical to detail them in any future supplement. The reader can keep up to date with such developments through reading each issue of the *Journal of Accountancy*. Moreover, the rule-making bodies can be contacted directly at the addresses for each, as listed in the Selected References. Then, too, the reader may secure information through the independent accountant working with his or her company, or other independent accountants. Finally, through its Technical Information Service, the AICPA technical hotline may answer inquiries about specific audit or accounting problems. The organization may be called toll-free at (800) 223-4158 (except New York) or (800) 522-5430 (New York only).

**p. 62.** *Add to Figure 4-6 the following standard:*

| | |
|---|---|
| No. 106—Employers Accounting for Post-retirement Benefits Other Than Pensions | 12/90 |
| No. 107—Disclosure about Fair Value of Financial Instruments | 12/91 |
| No. 108—Accounting for Income Taxes—Deferral of the Effective Date of FASB Statement No. 96 | 12/91 |
| No. 109—Accounting for Income Taxes | 2/92 |

## 4-4  OTHER ACCOUNTING RULE MAKERS

\* **p. 70.** *Add this sentence to the end of the section, "International Accounting Standards Committee (IASC)":*

With the increase in frequency expected for IASC standards, no further additions will be made to Figure 4-9.

**p. 71.**   *Add to Figure 4-9 the following two standards:*

IAS 30   Disclosures in the Financial Statements of Banks and Similar Financial Institutions

IAS 31   Financial Reporting of Interests in Joint Ventures

**p. 72.**   *Add to Figure 4-10 the following under Statements and Interpretations:*

| | | |
|---|---|---|
| *Statement No. 9,* | "Reporting Cash Flows of Proprietary and Non-Expendable Trust Funds and Governmental Entities That Use Proprietary Fund Accounting" | 9/89 |
| *Statement No. 10,* | "Accounting and Financial Reporting for Risk Financing and Related Insurance Issues" | 11/89 |
| *Statement No. 11,* | "Measurement Focus and Bases of Accounting—Governmental Fund Operating Statements" | 5/90 |
| *Statement No. 12,* | "Disclosure of Information on Postemployment Benefits Other Than Pension Benefits by State and Local Governmental Employers" | 5/90 |
| *Statement No. 13,* | "Accounting for Operating Leases with Scheduled Rent Increases" | 5/90 |
| *Statement No. 14,* | "The Financial Reporting Entity" | 6/91 |
| *Statement No. 15,* | "Governmental College and University Accounting and Financial Reporting Models" | 10/91 |

\* **p. 73.**   *Add in the second paragraph after "A listing of GASB Pronouncements is shown in Figure 4-10.":*

Given the frequency of GASB Pronouncements, no further additions will be made to Figure 4-10.

**p. 73.**   *Add at the end of section 4-4:*

## 4-4A   THE HIERARCHY OF GENERALLY ACCEPTED ACCOUNTING PRINCIPLES (GAAP) (NEW)

There are so many bodies providing standards and interpretations for accounting and reporting by U.S. companies, that it may be helpful for a corporate controller to view them in order of accepted authoritative force.

1st level:   FASB Statements and interpretations, APB Opinions and AICPA Accounting Research Bulletins.

2nd level:   FASB Technical Bulletins, AICPA Industry Audit and Accounting Guides and AICPA Statements of Position.

3rd level:   Consensus positions of the FASB Emerging Issues Task Force and AcSEC Practice Bulletins.

(These items have achieved more significance and authority than AICPA accounting interpretations and prevalent industry practices which have for many years been considered 2nd level GAAP.)

4th level:   AICPA accounting interpretations, uncleared AICPA guides and position statements. Q's and A's published by the FASB staff and prevalent and recognized industry practices.

5th level:   Other accounting literature which includes International Accounting Standards Committee Statements, FASB Concept Statements, GASB Statements and Interpretations, AICPA Issues Papers, APB Statements, and pronouncements of professional associations, regulatory agencies and accounting textbooks and articles.

## 4-4B   ROLE OF THE CONTROLLER IN ACCOUNTING STANDARDS SETTING (NEW)

With at least five standard-setting bodies, FASB, AICPA, CASB, IASC, and SEC, (and the GASB and EITF for some unique situations) working to develop accounting rules, the controller of an American company can be overwhelmed by the amount of "standards" work-in-process at any given time. Combine this theoretical detail with the implementation procedures needed for approved standards and it is easy to see that keeping current on accounting principles development is a monumental task. However, it is one that the controller must be involved in and the earlier the involvement, the more effective he or she will be in the process. This participation is needed not only for the development of usable and representative accounting principles but also for the planning and control of the business. For example, many standards (e.g., Pensions, Income Tax, Other Post Employment Benefits) affect the timing of revenue and/or costs and can have a significant effect on the reported financial results of a company. The sooner such a potential result can be analyzed and a range of the dollar impact sized and reported to top management, the more helpful it is to the long-range planning of the business. For example, once the amount of expense associated with retirement benefits other than pensions became known, certain companies took steps to cap, reduce, or control these costs. The benefits of knowing the effects of such an accounting change five to ten years early, gave some companies the opportunity to *plan* a transition rather than having to react *after* the standard was released.

Because most controllers are too busy to handle this work themselves, a knowledgeable professional can be assigned the responsibility to establish liaison with the standard-setting bodies. This person would know what subjects were being considered by each of the regulators, what Discussion Memorandums and Exposure drafts were released, what changes they included, and what schedule the program was on. He or she would keep the controller informed of these developments and have any dollar impact sized. In addition, he or she would develop a company position on each matter, using knowledgeable accounting and operating managers as needed, and present it to the controller. Approved company analyses can then be transmitted to the regulators at all stages of the standards development process, providing important input and helping influence the final product. The controller should also make higher management aware of possible changes and the estimated impact or range of impact on future financial statements of the company. Such regular briefings keeps top management from having to deal with unpleasant surprises when new standards must be implemented.

p. 73. *Add new chapter:*

# CHAPTER 4A

# Effective Costing Practices: The Cost System (New)

The controller, as the chief accounting executive of the company, has the responsibility to design, install, and maintain the general and cost accounting systems for the entity—at all levels, including corporate, divisional, plant, department, or unit. This is in addition to other major responsibilities related to financial planning, control, and reporting.

---

Sections 4A-5 and 4A-6 in this chapter have been adapted and reprinted with the permission of Warren, Gorham, and Lamont, Inc., from Chapter 38B, Cost Systems vs. Effective Cost Determination in *Budgeting and Profit Planning Manual,* 2nd edition, 1991 Cumulative Supplement, by James D. Willson. Copyright 1984, 1990, 1991 by Warren, Gorham, and Lamont, Inc., 210 South Street, Boston, Massachusetts 02111. All rights reserved.

The accounting principles and practices, and the related standards, which are critical to the proper operation of the general accounting system in an entity are reviewed in a general way in Chapter 4 of the main volume. The chief movers in developing the accounting principles and the sources for the information on the subject are discussed. Similarly, this chapter reviews some of the current issues concerning cost accounting systems and cost determination, without delving into the complex details of various costing systems. Several excellent texts and the Selected References provide useful information on the design complexities and operation of the various existent cost systems. The authors focus on those areas needing current attention, without getting involved in long discourses on costing principles.

## 4A-1    INTRODUCTION

This is a period of change and stress for many U.S. manufacturers as they strive to compete in a global market plan. Among other things, customers are demanding improved quality, faster delivery, and perhaps a greater variety of product. Then, too, competitors are adjusting quickly to marketplace changes, are finding improved material and supply sources, relocating factories and distribution centers to secure the benefits of lower labor costs and permissible working conditions, changing manufacturing methods to reduce costs, and taking advantage of U.S. trade policies and loopholes. Service companies face many of the same problems in both United States and foreign markets. Inflation can make the problem even more difficult. This competitive pressure increases the need for good cost information. Business managers must know the cost of each product so it can be properly and competitively priced, to produce a profit. Moreover, the management must have timely and accurate data for cost planning and cost control.

In such a competitive environment cost control and cost determination have been impacted in these ways:

- In this age of advanced technologies, *manufacturing* methods and processes have changed, and proper costing procedures should reflect these changes.
- In many businesses, the *nonmanufacturing expenses* have significantly increased, so that greater care must be exercised in the application of these expenses— research and development, advertising, selling, and general and administrative expenses—to each product or product line.
- In general, the cost accountants are being forced to take a more analytical or questioning viewpoint in examining the applicability of costs to products, functions, organizational subdivisions or other cost objects.

In this chapter, we examine some of the costing practices and the need, as well as the ways and means, to make them more specific. This background should be helpful to the reader when examining the planning and control functions in his or her company as related to each type of cost or expense, or asset, as discussed in later chapters of this book.

Another reason for writing this chapter is to place before the reader some of the alleged weaknesses outlined in recent critical articles about the "obsolete cost systems" being employed in U.S. industry. He might test the cost systems and cost determination methods under his cognizance against the criticisms. Most of us are aware that the quality of the cost systems or management accounting systems, or cost determination methods—call them what you will—usually depends on the professional astuteness of the CFO, or controller, or chief accountant, and the accounting staff. Today's alert management accountant seeks to provide management with timely and relevant planning and control information. And in our more aggressive and more competitive larger companies, he usually succeeds.

Finally, much of the controversy about cost accounting relates to the method of allocating either indirect manufacturing expenses or service and general and administrative expenses to cost objects. These are extensively discussed, along with the excellent and relevant Statements of Management Accounting (SMA) in Chapters 23 and 26 of the main volume. The review in this earlier chapter will make you more alert to costing implications as you read the many later sections on sales, expense, and cost planning and control.

These subjects are discussed in the balance of this chapter:

- Uses of the "cost accounting" system
- Changes in the manufacturing environment
- A few stated weaknesses in some cost systems
- Activity-based costing
- Selecting the proper cost system.

## 4A-2   USES OF THE COST ACCOUNTING SYSTEM

In exploring just how cost accounting systems, (or management accounting systems) in some U.S. companies might be improved, it may be helpful to review typical uses of such cost accumulation methods. But even in defining a cost accounting system there is a certain looseness of terms. To many accountants, a cost accounting system refers only to those accounts and accounting functions in which are recorded the outlays and usage of assets pertaining to *manufacturing* operations, that is, to costs related to the movement of products between the raw material stage and the finished goods status. In a broader sense, the term "cost accounts" applies to that group of accounts in which are assembled the expenditures related to either manufacturing, or engineering, or research and development, or selling and distribution, or general and administrative activities, in such a manner that the costs of these separate activities are revealed in terms of some unit that has been selected as a yardstick.[1]

Applying the broader concept of costs, most knowledgeable individuals would agree that cost systems are employed principally for these three purposes:

- Inventory valuation
- Product cost determination
- Cost and expense management and control.

Some persons might make a finer distinction in applications and add these uses:

---

[1] Theodore Lang, ed., *Cost Accountants Handbook* (New York: Ronald Press, 1945) p. 218.

- Short-term and long-term (strategic) planning
- Justifying capital expenditures
- Motivating and measuring managers.

A few comments are made on each of these purposes.

## INVENTORY VALUATION

One widely used purpose of a cost system is to value inventories. Using generally accepted accounting principles, current period production or manufacturing costs must be allocated to current production. Then, the costs of current production must be segregated between those products sold and those products in inventory. Typically, manufacturing costs are accumulated in three primary classes: direct material, direct labor, and manufacturing overhead. A discussion about the proper cost allocation of these three categories is contained in Chapters 22 and 23 of the main volume; and the valuation of inventories is reviewed in Chapter 30. Suffice it to say here that such valuations and allocations are used by most public companies, in conjunction with generally accepted accounting principles, for the determination of monthly, quarterly, and annual operating results as well as the periodic financial position.

With respect to the use of the cost system for determining inventory values, these additional comments may be useful:

1. Under generally accepted accounting principles, the full production cost base may be adjusted to the lower of cost or market.
2. Quite often, the emphasis on inventory valuation is on the *aggregate* value for profit or loss determination purposes—and not necessarily on the specific value for each product.
3. Originally, when direct labor content was a major cost element, manufacturing overhead was allocated on this basis. Now, with increased automation, and so on, direct labor typically represents perhaps 15% or less of total production cost. Under such circumstances, another allocation basis may be more applicable.
4. Quite often, in the context of controlling manufacturing labor or overhead, changes are made in manufacturing method. While appropriate adjustments may be made in departmental operating budgets for such changes, because of their individual small size, often no change is made in the costing base used for inventory valuation. Accordingly, some cost differences arise, but are treated as "accounting adjustments" and create no significant problem. When *major* changes occur in manufacturing processes, or when the individually small changes become important in the aggregate, then the cost basis for inventory valuation should be adjusted.
5. Only manufacturing costs normally are used as the base for product inventory valuation. R&D, selling and general and administrative expenses, and so on are excluded.
6. With the trend to just-in-time (JIT) techniques, and resulting lower or nonexistent inventories, the inventory valuation application has lost some of its importance.

## PRODUCT COST DETERMINATION

Correct product costs are a critical element in the survival and growth of an enterprise. Why? Among other reasons, they very often are the basis for setting the selling price of products in general, and for proper tactical business decisions in particular. Prices are a major determinant of profitability.

The manufactured cost of a product as developed by the cost system (employed for inventory valuation) often is the *starting point* used by the sales or manufacturing staff in making product pricing decisions—often the wrong decision. Why? Many times those who use such costs do not understand the basis of calculation or the limitations in usefulness. Some of the reasons why such a cost should not be used for marketing decisions without adjustments are these:

1.  The manufactured cost of a product usually represents historical costs, and it may not be indicative of future costs.

2.  The manufacturing cost typically contains a significant element of indirect or allocated costs. If the basis of manufacturing cost allocation is too general, that is, is not product specific, then the resultant cost is simply wrong or inaccurate.

3.  For many pricing and marketing decisions, the *total* cost of the product, including engineering, research and development, advertising and sales promotion, selling, and general and administrative expense, are the relevant costs. (See pp. 506–517 in the main volume.)

4.  For a great number of tactical business decisions, *total* costs, including full manufacturing costs, as well as all other costs, may not be the relevant or applicable cost base. As an example, for some short-term decisions (such as securing the initial sale) perhaps the direct or variable out-of-pocket costs, plus a small margin, is the proper cost basis. (See Chapter 20.) As a general statement, for different purposes or applications a different type of cost may be needed.

5.  In those instances, where total real costs are applicable, using average percentages of manufacturing costs or of the selling price for some of the indirect expenses may be improper. A particular product or product line may have its unique specific functional cost, for example, selling or advertising, which should be recovered, and which must be reflected in the cost basis used for setting the selling price.

In general then, the type of cost used should be relevant to the decision to be made. Such product manufacturing cost, or total product cost, need not be calculated every month—but only as required for a particular answer. And the costing systems should provide the basis for rather quickly determining the proper relevant cost. This is a field in which use of the combined talents and experience of the management accountant and the marketing representative, as well as the manufacturing executive, is highly desirable.

## COST AND EXPENSE MANAGEMENT AND CONTROL

The third purpose for which the output of the "cost system" is employed is the management and control of both costs and expenses. To be sure the same "system" that accumulates actual costs for inventory valuation also may be used for cost planning and control. But the application is quite different. For control purposes, actual costs or expenses are compared with a budget or other standard, and corrective action is taken to bring the expenditures in line with what is expected. This is the type of control discussed throughout the main volume.

But these differences in the control application should be noted as compared to the once-a-month cost accumulation for inventory valuation purposes:

- *Timely* data are needed for control purposes. Accordingly, some costs may be reported on a real time basis as incurred using a computer. In other instances, after the fact costs are adequate, some being provided on an hourly, daily, weekly, or monthly basis. (This contrasts with the monthly accumulation and reporting for financial purposes.)

- In the context of *control,* a manager cannot, or should not, be held accountable for those costs he cannot control. Hence, arbitrary allocations are to be avoided. If service costs are charged to the using departments, the charge should be based on actual usage at a standard rate. For inventory valuation, manufacturing costs are accumulated in the service department then allocated to the using department, and then to the product.

- Expense behavior under conditions of varying business volume is treated differently for inventory valuation purposes as contrasted to cost management. Thus, for inventory valuation, the concept of normal capacity—(see p. 601 of the main volume)—is used. Under this basis, the fixed standard manufacturing expenses are divided by the units or productive hours for the average volume over the period of the business cycle, to secure the average unit fixed manufacturing expense for inventory valuation. In contrast, for planning and control purposes, costs and expenses may be viewed as either variable, semi-variable, or fixed, (see pp. 99–103 of the main volume) and measured for the specific applicable time horizon. And while some costs, for example, direct labor, may be viewed over the very short term as variable, for planning purposes it may be regarded as semi-variable. Or supervisory costs may be regarded as fixed over the short term, but for planning purposes may be regarded as managed (semi-variable).

- Finally, where unexpected events occur beyond the control of the department manager, for example, a hurricane work stoppage, and damage, special adjustments may be made to the departmental budget so that the department manager is not penalized in his monthly or weekly budget performance report. Such events basically may be disregarded in inventory valuation.

## SHORT-TERM AND LONG-TERM (STRATEGIC) PLANNING

For the preparation of the short-term or annual business plan, the existing cost level of every department, function, activity, or product usually is the starting point in calculating cost or expense levels. These costs are then adjusted for any expected change in such matters as: volume of business activity, organization structure, functions, and such related subjects as inflation rates, price changes, raw material costs, salary and wage increases, process changes and product mix. (See Chapter 16 of the main volume.) In this way, the final business plan is a realistic view of what is expected to happen. Every opportunity is provided for the necessary adjustment to realistic cost levels. The managers typically prepare their own departmental plans, using guidelines approved by the CEO and

CFO (with the assistance of the controller). The controller's department furnishes him or her with the historical cost or expense data on which the plan is constructed.

With respect to the strategic plan, which deals with broad classes of data, and is less detailed than the annual plan, while the "cost systems" provide much of the basic information, this is substantially adjusted to reflect expected revenue or cost levels five or ten years or more in the future. (See Chapters 14 and 15 of the main volume.)

In the context of business planning, ample opportunity is given to adjust revenues and cost data, as well as asset, liability and net worth data, to fit realistic expectations or alternative scenarios. The cost system output, or historical cost accumulation, is only a starting point.

## JUSTIFYING CAPITAL EXPENDITURES

In most businesses, capital investments in plant and equipment usually must be justified by the expected rate of return. Often, this is measured by the estimated cash flow produced by the investment over its expected life. (See Chapter 32 of the main volume.) If it meets a minimum rate, if funds are available, and if it is consistent with the strategic plan, the proposal usually is approved. In this application also, the starting point may be the output of the cost systems. Cost estimates for determining profitability (cash flow) must be relevant to the specific products to be produced. This is another instance where averages simply may not be applicable. The data collected in the "cost systems" usually are adjusted, as in the planning application discussed earlier, to reflect expected operating/financial conditions and, hence, the anticipated profit or return on the investment.

## MOTIVATING AND MEASURING MANAGEMENT

Another stated application of cost system output is to motivate and judge performance of the various segments of business management. A very common measure is comparison of actual cost or expense levels with a plan or budget or standard. Another often used measure is the return on assets or return on equity achieved by the entity, or division. The net income or operating income used as the numerator, and the related investment (inventories and fixed assets, etc.) used for the denominator is that produced directly or indirectly by the cost system. In some instances, these latter general (book accounting) measures of entity performance may be adjusted for inflation or other factors. (See pp. 131–134 of the main volume.) Moreover, to financial performance factors may be added other noncosts, nonfinancial factors (for example, market share, quality standards, share of on-time deliveries). In any event, the institution of suitable or appropriate measures requires study. A measure wrongly applied, such as volume growth or departmental throughput, can cause a manager to take actions not in the best interest of the company. See the later discussion in this chapter.

## 4A-3   CHANGES IN THE MANUFACTURING ENVIRONMENT

One important impetus for examining cost systems and cost determination methodology is the major changes which are, and have been, taking place in the manufacturing environment. To some, the advent of the advanced manufacturing technologies are a cause for concern as to the degree that management accountants are and should be assisting U.S. manufacturers become and stay competitive in the world economy. A good understanding as to just how the factory is changing is an important first step in evaluating the reliability of manufacturing cost systems in the U.S. generally, and in any one entity in particular.

Two knowledgeable writers have classified the changes being made in manufacturing in this fashion.[2]

- Higher quality
- Lower inventories
- Flexible flow lines
- Automation
- Product line organization
- Effective use of information.

These six major changes are indicative of a commitment to produce high quality at the lowest practical cost with on-time delivery. These developments are also signs of a different management philosophy from that which prevailed in the 1960s and 1970s. High quality is no longer viewed as an alternative to lower costs; rather, it is seen as consistent with such a condition. Further, high labor utilization and its related overhead absorption is no longer, alone, necessarily considered an indication of efficiency. Such a manufacturing level might be counterproductive in that it could be the cause of overproduction as well as excess inventories and attendant write-offs.

A few expanded comments on the six areas of manufacturing change follow.

## HIGHER QUALITY

Attention has focused on quality for two reasons: (1) U.S. manufacturers recognized that if they did not improve quality, then foreign competitors in many instances simply would drive them out of the marketplace. (2) Business managers began to realize that poor quality was a significant cost driver. It was recognized that improved quality, secured through the use of good materials, with a highly trained labor force, together with well-maintained equipment simply reduces the costs of nonquality: scrap, rework, equipment breakdowns, higher field service, and greater warranty failures.

## LOWER INVENTORIES

Many managements are reducing company inventories while still maintaining delivery schedules and satisfactory customer service. They have begun to realize that:

1. The carrying of inventories requires added capital; and that the cost of such capital is much higher than it was in the recent past.

2. Aside from the interest on capital, these costs related inventories can be substantially reduced: the higher moving and handling costs; a higher level of spares,

---

[2] Robert A. Howell and Stephen R. Soucy, "The New Manufacturing Environment: Major Trends for Manufacturing Accounting," *Management Accounting,* July 1987, pp. 13–19.

increased obsolescence, as well as the higher insurance and tax expenses on inventories.

3. Finally, management has come to recognize that many Japanese businesses have become eminently successful in meeting customer needs despite increased inventory turns and the reduced inventory levels.

## FLEXIBLE FLOW LINES

A substantial number of manufacturers are redesigning the factory flow lines in order to shorten the product cycle time and to permit an increase in the variety of product.

Under the flexible flow line concept the various pieces of equipment needed in the product manufacturing process are brought together in one location. Accordingly, large groups of identical pieces of equipment are split up, and multiple "mini" product lines are formed. The results are: less material handling, reduced inventory, shorter cycle time, and the ability to manufacture more than one product on the production line.

## AUTOMATION

In the minds of many, automation may be the most visible change in the manufacturing environment. When the management has redesigned the factory layout and has introduced flexible flow lines, together with other operational improvements, then it can leverage these moves through the introduction of automation.

Automation can be at any one of three levels: (1) a stand-alone piece of equipment, such as a computer-controlled lathe; (2) a production cell, such as a flexible flow line; or (3) a fully automated factory.

In justifying such capital investments, formerly only the savings in direct labor and the related fringe benefits, together with economies of smaller inventories, were considered. Now, the justification process also includes estimates of the benefits arising from improved quality, quicker delivery, and, in general, a higher level of customer satisfaction.

## INCREASED EMPHASIS ON PRODUCT LINE ORGANIZATION

In general, the typical manufacturing organization structure was characterized by a large number of central service departments such as: quality control, maintenance, production control, inspection, and engineering. This structure was based on the theory that the scale of operations would justify the economics. Very often this result did not happen.

The product line organization resulted in a reassignment of specialized service skills to the product lines and the consequent reduction of the service organizations. Among other benefits, this structure identified the resource with the using product. The result was better product costing and improved pricing.

## IMPROVED INFORMATION TECHNOLOGY

When the new information technology is adopted, combining electronic mail, fax machines, and personal computers in a thoroughly integrated information system, the usual result is faster and better communication, including real-time data. As a consequence, manufacturing control is improved: the factory manager can observe performance via computer as it is happening. For example, he need not wait for a month-end scrap report, comparing actual and standard scrap generation. He can discern rather quickly the exact status of raw material or work-in-process inventories. In some applications, computers can monitor and control operations—often with better results and less expense. (Machines don't get tired and need not be paid overtime.)

## THE IMPACT ON COSTS

So what is the impact of these, and the many other changes in the manufacturing environment, on manufacturing costs and cost management? Here are a few of them:

- Increased attention being paid to engineering and product design since product cost of manufacturing often is largely determined in this early stage.
- A decrease in the direct labor cost component.
- An increase in equipment-related costs, such as depreciation, power, and equipment repair.
- A change in manufacturing costs structure, for example, use of units of production depreciation rather than straight line (or accelerated) depreciation.
- Recognition of the need to re-examine the method of allocating manufacturing overhead to departments and products.
- A decrease in some service department personnel costs, such as repair and maintenance costs.
- An increased need for real-time performance information or computer-generated data, instead of long after the fact manual data.
- An increase in the information cost component of the business.
- The need for more nonfinancial performance measures, such as the number of customer complaints, number of on-time deliveries, relative share of defect-free units—all of which are critical to quality control and customer service.

## 4A-4  SOME VIEWS ON WEAKNESSES IN "COST SYSTEMS"

In the last five years or so, not only has there been a number of significant changes in manufacturing methods as well as costing practices, but also an increase in the number of articles in business periodicals that are highly critical of existing cost systems or costing practices. Some of these criticisms, in no particular order, and from various sources, include:

- Existing cost systems were meant primarily to value inventories and provide data for the statements of income and expense. They really were never designed to discriminate between product lines or products within those lines.
- Most cost management systems are historical financial reporting oriented and do not adequately measure operational performance.
- Traditional accounting systems fail to provide proper information for strategic decisions.

- The internal management accounting function has now become subservient to the external reporting function in U.S. firms. Contemporary U.S. practice is characterized by the internal use of accounting conventions that have been developed or mandated by external reporting authorities; and management accounting practices are now driven by an external reporting mentality.

- Management accounting reports are of little help to operating managers attempting to reduce costs and improve productivity.

- The management accounting system fails to provide accurate product costs.

- Today's cost systems measure the segment of a product's life that begins at the time it enters production.

- We are not capturing and allocating research and development costs so that management can determine the true profitability of a product over its lifetime.

- Unfortunately, managers' horizons contract to the short-term cycle of their monthly profit or loss statements.

- The control emphasis differs as between advanced manufacturing technologies (AMTs) on the one hand and accounting systems on the other. Accounting systems are basically feedback arrangements, and the expectation is that corrective action will be taken after the reporting period—a day, week, month, or year. In contrast, most AMT systems are designed to function in an opposite manner. Basically, they are primarily preventive in nature, with on-line, real-time responses often required.

- The majority of cost accounting systems are work-order oriented and do not adequately identify the impact of cost drivers (those conditions, activities, or factors that cause costs to change) on the manufacturing cost of specific operations or products.

- The new management methods stress the need for focusing on not only costs, but also on quality and flexibility. Management accounting, therefore, must look beyond transaction-based cost information to know if decisions will deliver increased profits.

Consider whether there is a weakness which should be corrected in your company. Do any of these opinions echo ones expressed by your management? Some of the opinions expressed are correct, and others are only partially correct. Some fail to distinguish between the cost accumulations for inventory valuation only, and the cost determinations individually made for specific purposes, for example, product pricing. Some focus on the manufacturing accounting system for accumulating costs and ignore the integrated management reporting practice which compares actual cost performance with a budget or standard, developed with the assistance of the operating department manager, specifically designed to measure departmental performance (regardless of the treatment of costs for inventory valuation).

# 4A-5   ACTIVITY-BASED COSTING (ABC)

On to the currently popular subject—activity-based costing . . . First, what is it? A basic definition developed by the Computer Aided Manufacturing—International (CAM-I), a nonprofit industry sponsored consortium that deals with contemporary industry problems, defines activity-based costing as "the collection of financial and operation performance information tracing the significant activities of the firm to product costs."[3] The significance of this definition will become clear as you read the following sections on activity-based costing.

But ponder, as a starting point, how important perception and the degree of analysis is to properly solving a problem—the allocation of expenses to a product.

For example, look at receiving, handling, and storage costs in a representative factory. It is a relatively simple matter to accumulate the departmental costs under the control of the foreman. These expenses are routinely gathered for planning and control purposes. But what about assigning such costs to a product? Very often a single basis, such as weight or value, might be used to allocate expenses to a product or component. But more in-depth analysis might reveal that different product groups required varying times and volume in storage. Hence, it is prudent to segregate storage and handling costs into those that were *transaction-related* and those that were *storage time* related. Consequently, the transaction related expenses may be assigned to parts based on the frequency of handling (received, counted, moved, and issued). The time related expenses (utilities, taxes, insurance) each being governed by actual time stored, should be charged to products accordingly.

This analysis of storage costs is an example of the need to sometimes refine the costing method to reflect the value consumed at differing rates by different parts or components. And this same principle may be what is at the heart of many differences of opinion as to how activities and costs must be managed.

Costs are caused by activities. If these activities can be reduced, then the related costs also should be lowered. Those involved with activity-based costing soon realize that most nonmaterial costs do not vary directly with labor volume, but rather, vary with product diversity and operational complexity.

Any attempt to develop activity-based product costs and to manage all costs properly, should include attention to these various steps:

- Analysis of the processes involved (Process Value Analysis-PVA)
- Development of activity-based process costing
- Development of activity-based product costing
- Analysis to assure that responsibility accounting is being followed
- Re-examination of desirable performance measures, including some nonfinancial components
- Relate investment decisions to improved efficiency and value-added activities, together with profitability.

Brief comments on each of these steps follow.

## PROCESS VALUE ANALYSIS (PVA)

Total cost management (TCM) is a business philosophy of managing all company resources as well as the activities that consume those resources. Managing costs in a TCM

---

[3] Norm Raffish, "How Much Does That Product Really Cost? Finding Out May Be as Easy as ABC," *Management Accounting,* March 1991, p. 37.

environment means focusing on the factors that cause or "drive" these cost consuming activities. The initial step in the entire procedure is process value analysis (PVA) which method defines each process, examines the need for the activity, determines the cost "drivers," and isolates those that do or do not add value; and plans corrective action. One set of suggested steps for the entire review is this:

1. *Define the process*
   - Document the process flow
   - Define the input requirements for each process step
   - Define the output of each step
   - Identify customer (both internal and external) requirements
   - Compare customer requirements with the input/output requirements
   - Identify or define the required (full-time equivalent) staff level for each process

2. *Analyze the activities*
   - Identify each activity within each process
   - Using customer requirements, identify each activity as value adding or non-value adding
   - Determine the cycle time for each activity
   - Calculate for each process the cycle efficiency—the value-added time as related to total time
   - Cumulate the efficiency through the entire business chain

3. *Analyze the cost drivers*
   - Identify the cost drivers—the cause and the effect
   - Analyze the effect of eliminating the nonvalue adding drivers

4. *Plan improvements*
   - Determine, by activity, the costs of both the value-adding and nonvalue-adding activities
   - Select methods to eliminate any nonvalue factors and optimize the value-adding ones
   - Chart performance and progress by appropriate performance measures

Aside from the detailed analytical study necessary in PVA, these few remarks are made about the key functions or segments in a fully integrated ABC system that relates product costs to performance measurement and to asset investment.

## ACTIVITY-BASED PROCESS COSTING

First comes activity-based *process* costing, and after that comes activity-based *product* costing. This is to say that, according to sound costing methodology, most nonmaterial costs are first accumulated by department, which essentially is by process or activity. These activity-based process costs are next identified by product. Logically, it follows that if business management is to secure accurate product costs, it must first develop reliable *process* costs. Moreover, any reliable process costs should be related to activities. They should not be based on a somewhat arbitrary allocation of expenses which originated, for example, in some service department. Each departmental manager should be held accountable only for those costs he can control. Thus, a charge from one department to another should be based on a level of activity. For example, the power charge should be based on the amount of electricity used (at standard or predetermined rates) and not on some allocation based on arbitrary assumptions.

It should be recognized that if the units of activity can be reduced, then the departmental processing costs should be lower. But this condition will not be realized unless the excess resources at the originating spot (services) are either reduced or rerouted to more productive areas.

## ACTIVITY-BASED PRODUCT COSTING

For the optimum profitability of the business, accurate product costs are mandatory, whether for long-term strategy determination, or the annual business plan, or tactical decisions, or day-to-day product pricing. The preferred priority of product cost determination is that shown in Figure 4A-1. The first choice is to identify costs, such as material or labor costs, by direct attribution. If this is possible, there can be little argument about the relevance of the cost. The second preferred avenue is through cost assignment

**Figure 4A-1**   Preferred Assignment of Costs.

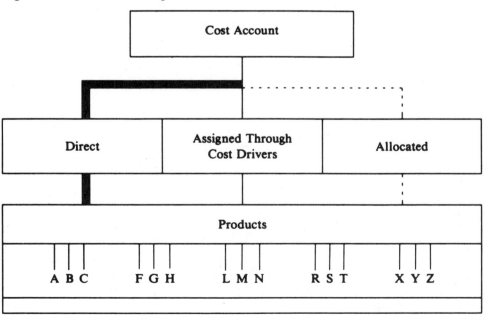

Preferred
Second Preference
Last Preference

which is based on the use of cost drivers. If a product can be charged for the resources it consumes, then, if the bases are correct, the costs should be regarded as acceptable. Finally, to the extent these two relationships are unknown, then the third and least desired cost assignment technique is used—cost allocation.

An excellent illustration of a matrix of costs for a computer manufacturer is reflected in Figure 4A-2. This illustration shows not only production costs, but also engineering, research and development, marketing, and other expenses. Sound activity-based costing would attempt to relate these latter functional costs to specific products, and not rely solely on arbitrary allocations. One product, for example, may require substantially more sales effort than another, and such activity requirement should be reflected in the selling price.

Much of the discussion about proper product costing relates to the treatment of the indirect costs—whether manufacturing or service, or general and administrative. As previously commented, the Statements of Management Accounting (SMA) No. 4G contained in Chapter 23, and No. 4B included in Chapter 26, of the main volume can be valuable guides on the subject.

## RESPONSIBILITY ACCOUNTING

Another basic element related to proper costing and cost control is responsibility accounting. This key tool, one of several in sound financial planning and control, is discussed and illustrated in Chapter 6 of the main volume. Suffice it to state here that the concept requires that the revenues, or costs, or transactions should be recorded in such a fashion that they are identified with the supervisor or manager in the organization who controls the activity and can be held accountable for it.

To highlight the problem, a concrete example can be given. There is a tendency in some companies to charge using departments or process groups for some service costs, such as heat and power, maintenance, or computer department services, or accounting services, and so on through *general* allocations based on area, payroll, or head count. Such arbitrary allocations usually do not reflect actual consumption of the service. Hence, both process costs and product costs are distorted. In the review of activity-based costing, the objective should be to ascertain if a true activity-based method of making charges exists, and if not, can it be installed. Again, a producing department should be charged only for the activity requested or received so that the entity has true responsibility costing.

## PERFORMANCE MEASURES

In any well-managed company, performance measures can be one element of a sound planning and control system. Basically, performance measures should represent the mix of financial and nonfinancial operating measures that advance the business objectives, and are consistent with the level of business responsibility to which they are applied. These clarifying comments are made:

1.  Chapter 7 of the main volume discusses measures of *overall* business performance, including Statement on Management Accounting (SMA) 4D, entitled, "Measuring Equity Performance."

**Figure 4A-2**   Input-Output Cost Matrix.

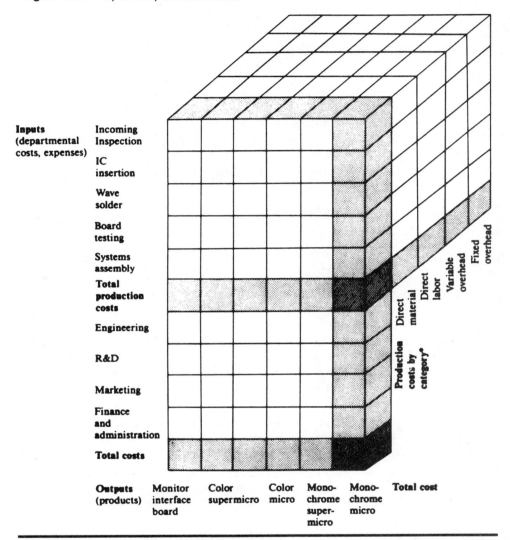

**Inputs**
(departmental
costs, expenses)

Incoming Inspection

IC insertion

Wave solder

Board testing

Systems assembly

**Total production costs**

Engineering

R&D

Marketing

Finance and administration

**Total costs**

**Outputs**
(products)

Monitor interface board    Color supermicro    Color micro    Monochrome supermicro    Monochrome micro    **Total cost**

Direct material    Direct labor    Variable overhead    Fixed overhead

**Production costs by category***

*These categories can be shown in considerably more detail, such as machine overhead, labor overhead, or material overhead.

*Source:* Reprinted by permission of *Harvard Business Review.* An exhibit from "What Kind of Cost System Do You Need?" by Michael J. Sandretto, Jan.–Feb. 1985, Copyright 1985 by the President and Fellows of Harvard College; all rights reserved.

2. In the middle management area, current wisdom is to focus on nonfinancial measures, such as quality, customer satisfaction, on-time deliveries, and so on, as well as the usual financial yardsticks. Such measures, and related financial gauges, should be such that they do not maximize the performance of the individual area, department, or function, at the expense or injury of the total entity—building excess inventory to decrease unit production costs, but creating added costs elsewhere in the value chain (through faulty product), placing responsibility elsewhere.

3. The performance measures should be consistent with the process value analysis just discussed in (a) providing visibility to progress in elimination of nonvalue adding activity, and optimizing value adding activity; (b) assisting in cost reduction by measuring the real driver of activity; and (c) measuring in an appropriate way the reduction in product unit costs (not merely functional costs).

**INVESTMENT MANAGEMENT**

The final segment of this circle of business decisions based on activity management is that related to investments. Chapter 32 of the main volume and this Supplement reviews the fundamentals of making sound judgments regarding capital investments (and related project or working capital investments) in some detail.

Here are three pertinent observations:

1. A preferred way of evaluating a capital investment is by the discounted cash flow method. It should be obvious that if activity-based costing is desirable for product pricing and strategy planning, then this same methodology should be employed in calculating the true net cash inflow from any proposed capital investment. This requires recognizing the cash flow from each product or product line which benefits from the expenditure, and not a cash flow based on broad-brush averages.

2. Aside from net cash flow calculations based on product costs, the examination of the real cost drivers may focus attention on potential competitive activity as it may impinge on these factors.

3. In today's environment, the attention being directed to the many nonfinancial factors that influence the customer—quality, on-time delivery, and so on—should encourage estimates of their impact on the return on assets.

## 4A-6  ACTIVITY-BASED NONMANUFACTURING COSTS

In the 1985–1991 time span, many articles were written about traditional cost systems. In the opinion of the authors, there are at least two common themes prevalent in a great number of the writings: (1) they tend to be critical of costing practices because a proper "cost driver" is not used to assign costs to a cost object; and (2) the focus seems to be on manufacturing costs to the exclusion of other functional costs.

The authors wish to make a couple of simple observations on these two subjects before proceeding to the main thrust of this section—attention to costing for nonmanufacturing functions. In the first instance, many articles stress that the "cost driver"— the force that should regulate the costs to be incurred—must be discovered, much as though it were a new thought. Yet, the term "cost driver" may be viewed as a modern word for "measure of activity," or "factor of variability" for the function under discussion. In some instances, as manufacturing methods changed, little attention was directed by the controller or others to the need for a new base against which a variable cost should be measured. But a great deal of accounting literature stressed the proper concept—the need for an activity base that would be a fair indicator of how the cost should vary. In discussing the relationship of costs to volume, a key step is "the selection of the activity measure or factor of variability for each function and/or cost."[3.1]

The second common characteristic—emphasis on manufacturing or production costs—may be explained on the basis that formerly a large share of the costs of a product were related to the cost to manufacture, and that perhaps more analysis was done on manufacturing costs than, say, marketing costs. Yet, some authors many years ago stressed the need for proper analysis of distribution costs in view of the relatively high proportion of costs of this function in some companies. One source made this statement: "Yet it is sometimes forgotten that distribution costs are probably just as important as production costs in determining what price the consumer must pay for an article."[3.2] In the 1990s distribution costs, which include marketing expenses as well as physical distribution costs, have assumed an even greater significance.[3.3] Proper analysis of distribution costs, as well as any other significant nonmanufacturing costs, is essential to assist management in making informed decisions which affect profitability. Included would be such matters as product pricing, adding or dropping production product lines, terms of sales in different territories, quantity discounts, size-of-order pricing, and many more similar decisions.

On the subject of proper costing practices, the authors probably can be most helpful to the reader by identifying the steps in a cost and profit analysis which extends to all functions of a business. First, the general procedure is outlined, followed by specific illustrative analyses relating to products and territories. This analysis identifies several significant profit subtotals for arriving at different types of decisions. Similar steps would be required in making any of the distribution cost analyses outlined in Chapter 21 of the main volume. The degree in which the elements of each major functional cost (manufacturing, engineering, marketing, research and development, financial, and general administrative) are variable, and the factors of variability may differ by industry and company.

The general procedure for a meaningful analysis of costs or expenses would be as follows:

1. Determine the activities performed under each major function, for which costs or expenses should be identified or segregated, based on responsibility reporting principles, and identifiable activity measures.

   Thus, for the marketing function, the identified activities might be:

   Advertising

   Sales promotion

---

[3.1] J. Brooks Heckert and James D. Willson, *Business Budgeting and Control, 2nd ed.*, New York: The Ronald Press Company, 1955, p. 57.

[3.2] *Ibid.*, p. 232.

[3.3] See Sections 21-3 and 21-8 of the main volume. In the suggested analyses, the term "semi-direct" costs has the same meaning as costs assigned through cost drivers.

Direct selling

Warehousing

Packing and shipping

Order handling

Marketing administration

2. Accumulate the direct costs for each activity, by type of cost (hourly labor, fringe benefits, supplies, travel expenses, depreciation, etc.) and tentatively segregate each into the fixed, programmed, or variable cost components. (See Chapter 6.) Which costs are direct may depend on the type of analysis to be made. Thus, in a territorial analysis, the costs of territory A would be direct as to that territory; warehousing could be assigned by a cost driver; but district supervisory expense would be indirect.

3. Select the appropriate cost drivers for the activity. Often a single basis will suffice, such as weight might apply to storage costs, for example; but a time factor also may be appropriate for those time-related costs such as depreciation or property taxes. (See Section 4A-5 earlier in this chapter.) For direct selling costs, gross sales may be an appropriate base, or number of sales calls might apply. Order handling could relate to number of orders.

4. Calculate the unit cost for each activity. Basically, this will represent the total cost of the activity divided by the quantity of the cost driver selected. Where no specific cost driver can be determined, then some general allocation basis, such as gross sales, must be selected. In some instances, it may be more practical to calculate the percentage distribution of the cost driver—say percentage of engineering manhours for allocation to product lines, in lieu of the unit cost for the cost driver.

5. Where no suitable cost driver can be found, then a less desirable basis must be used for cost allocation purposes. (See Figure 4A-2A.)

6. Perform the contribution margin and total margin analysis when direct costs, costs assigned through cost drivers, and the residual allocation costs can be determined through application of the appropriate base. (See p. 524 of the main volume.) Thus, these different margin levels might be calculated:

- Contribution margin after direct variable costs
- Contribution margin after variable costs assigned by cost drivers
- Contribution margin after allocated variable costs
- Margin after programmed costs
- Margin after direct fixed costs
- Margin after allocated fixed costs
- Net income after taxes on income.

In making the contribution margin analysis, one key objective is to identify those costs that would discontinue if the product were discontinued, from those continuing

**Figure 4A-2A**   Product Line Data.

## The Johnson Company
SELECTED PRODUCT LINE DATA
FOR THE YEAR 19XX

| | Product Line | | |
|---|---|---|---|
| Description | X | Y | Z |
| Unit selling price (gross) | $75 | $20 | $100 |
| Unit manufacturing cost | | | |
|   Direct material (variable) | $15 | 2 | $ 1 |
|   Assigned through cost drivers (variable) | 5 | 3 | 1 |
|   Allocated (fixed) based on square footage of | | | |
|     manufacturing area | 1.50 | .90 | .33 |
| | $21.50 | $ 5.90 | $ 2.33 |
| Quantity of units sold (net) | 100,000 | 50,000 | 30,000 |
| Unit weight of product (lbs.) | 5 | 2 | 1 |
| No. of orders handled | 400 | 200 | 500 |

fixed costs which would be a burden until the causative factor (such as a building) was either written off or was devoted to other uses and products.

The profitability analyses are reflected in Figures 4A-2C and 4A-2D—one by product line and one by sales territory. By use of direct assignment of certain costs, and by application of the proper cost driver, management has a great deal of confidence in the costs and expenses applicable to each product (and thence to territory). It also is of the opinion that were a product (or territory) to be discontinued, the variable costs assigned to that product or cost object would cease. Further, although the programmed costs are fixed by management decision, that share applicable to a particular product could be eliminated. As a result of the product analysis, management can understand that product Y is unprofitable, but does provide enough profit margin to cover all but $14,000 of the fixed costs assigned to the product. A review probably should be made for possible sales price adjustments or the lowering of variable costs, and the impact on other products of dropping the line, before deciding to discontinue the product. The management is also made aware of the high profitability of product Z and the relatively low profit contribution by product X.

The income and expense analysis by territory reveals that the company, although located in the southwest of the United States earns 60% of its net income in the northwest, among other reasons, because of the high proportion of product Z sales in that area. Perhaps a further subanalysis of product profitability by territory, and an examination of detailed costs, can provide further useful information for the management.

Profitability analysis requires a great variety of detailed calculations. Some of supporting data for the product line and territorial analysis are shown in Figures 4A-2A and 4A-2B. The computer can be of great assistance in gathering, as well as sorting and re-sorting, the data into various desired subcategories.

**Figure 4A-2B**   Territory and Product Data.

**The Johnson Company**
SELECTED DATA BY TERRITORY AND PRODUCT
FOR THE YEAR 19XX

| Description | | Total | Territory Northwest | Territory Southwest |
|---|---|---|---|---|
| Unit Sales | | | | |
| Product | | | | |
| X | | 100,000 | 30,000 | 70,000 |
| Y | | 50,000 | 25,000 | 25,000 |
| Z | | 30,000 | 20,000 | 10,000 |
| Orders Handled | | | | |
| Product | | | | |
| X | | 400 | 120 | 280 |
| Y | | 200 | 100 | 100 |
| Z | | 500 | 333 | 167 |

| Pounds Shipped | Unit Weight | | | |
|---|---|---|---|---|
| Product | | | | |
| X | 5 | 500,000 | 150,000 | 350,000 |
| Y | 2 | 100,000 | 50,000 | 50,000 |
| Z | 1 | 30,000 | 20,000 | 10,000 |

| Engineering Hours & Cost | % Total | ($000) | | |
|---|---|---|---|---|
| Product | | | | |
| X | 65 | $101 | $ 30 | $ 71 |
| Y | 3 | 4 | 2 | 2 |
| Z | 32 | 50 | 33 | 17 |
| Total | 100 | $155 | $ 65 | $ 90 |

| Research and Development | % Professional Hours | Cost ($000) | | |
|---|---|---|---|---|
| Product | | | | |
| X | 39 | $199 | $ 60 | $139 |
| Y | 2 | 10 | 5 | 5 |
| Z | 59 | 301 | 199 | 102 |
| Total | 100 | $510 | $264 | $246 |

**Figure 4A-2C** Statement of Income and Expense by Product.

## The Johnson Company

STATEMENT OF INCOME AND EXPENSE FOR THE YEAR 19XX BY PRODUCT LINE ($ IN 000)

| Description | Total | Product Line X | Y | Z | Assigned Cost Driver or Allocation Base |
|---|---|---|---|---|---|
| *Gross Sales* | $11,600 | $7,600 | $1,000 | $3,000 | |
| Less: | | | | | |
| Returns and Allowances | 120 | 110 | 10 | — | Direct as to product |
| Freight—Out | 150 | — | — | 150 | Direct as to product |
| Total | 270 | 110 | 10 | 150 | |
| *Net Sales* | 11,330 | 7,490 | 990 | 2,850 | |
| *Cost of Sales* | | | | | |
| Direct—Variable | 1,630 | 1,500 | 100 | 30 | Direct as to product |
| Assigned thru Cost Drivers (Variable) | 680 | 500 | 150 | 30 | (Various cost drivers determined by manufacturing process or department) |
| Total | 2,310 | 2,000 | 250 | 60 | |
| *Gross Margin After Variable Manufacturing Costs* | 9,020 | 5,490 | 740 | 2,790 | |
| *Other Costs and Expenses—Variable* | | | | | |
| Marketing | | | | | |
| Selling | 1,160 | 760 | 100 | 300 | 10% of gross sales |
| Advertising | 700 | 500 | 50 | 150 | Units sold |
| Warehousing | 630 | 500 | 100 | 30 | $1 per lbs. shipped |
| Packing and Shipping | 180 | 100 | 50 | 30 | $1 per unit sold |
| Order Handling | 55 | 20 | 10 | 25 | $50 per order handled |
| Total | 2,725 | 1,880 | 310 | 535 | |
| Engineering | 462 | 400 | 50 | 12 | 20% of variable manufacturing expense |
| Research and Development | 1,133 | 749 | 99 | 285 | 10% of net sales |
| General and Administrative | 1,133 | 749 | 99 | 285 | 10% of net sales |
| Total Variable | 5,453 | 3,778 | 588 | 1,117 | |

(Continued)

33

**Figure 4A-2C** *(Continued)*

| Description | Total | Product Line | | | Assigned Cost Driver or Allocation Base |
| --- | --- | --- | --- | --- | --- |
| | | X | Y | Z | |
| *Margin After Variable Costs* | 3,567 | 1,712 | 182 | 1,673 | |
| *Programmed Costs (Fixed)* | | | | | |
| Engineering | 155 | 100 | 5 | 50 | Engineering manhours—direct as to product |
| Research and Development | 510 | 200 | 10 | 300 | Manhours on each project—product oriented |
| Total Programmed Costs | 665 | 300 | 15 | 350 | |
| *Margin After Programmed Costs* | 2,902 | 1,412 | 167 | 1,323 | |
| *Fixed Expenses* | | | | | |
| Manufacturing | 205 | 150 | 45 | 10 | Square footage |
| Marketing | 260 | 180 | 30 | 50 | % of variable marketing expense |
| Engineering | 31 | 20 | 1 | 10 | 20% programmed engineering costs |
| Research and Development | 105 | 40 | 5 | 60 | 20% programmed research and dev. costs |
| General and Administrative | 1,160 | 760 | 100 | 300 | 10% of gross sales |
| Total Fixed Costs | 1,761 | 1,150 | 181 | 430 | |
| *Margin (Loss) After Fixed Costs* | 1,141 | 262 | (14) | 893 | |
| Taxes Based on Income (38%) | 434 | 100 | (5) | 339 | |
| *Net Income (Loss)* | $ 707 | 162 | (9) | $ 554 | |
| % Net Sales | 6.2% | 2.2% | (.1%) | 19.4% | |

34

**Figure 4A-2D** Statement of Income and Expense by Territory.

## The Johnson Company

STATEMENT OF INCOME AND EXPENSE BY TERRITORY FOR THE YEAR 19XX ($ IN 000)

| Description | Total | Territory Northwest | Southwest | Assigned Cost Driver or Allocation Base, etc. |
|---|---|---|---|---|
| *Gross Sales* | $11,600 | $4,825 | $6,775 | |
| Less: | | | | |
| Return and Allowances | 120 | 38 | 82 | |
| Freight-out | 150 | 150 | — | |
| Total | $ 270 | $ 188 | $ 82 | |
| *Net Sales* | 11,330 | 4,637 | 6,693 | |
| *Cost of Sales* | | | | |
| Direct (material)—Variable | 1,630 | 520 | 1,110 | Direct as to product; by product to territory |
| Assigned Through Cost Drivers—Variable | 680 | 245 | 435 | Various cost drivers determined by process and department |
| Total | $ 2,310 | $ 765 | $1,545 | |
| *Gross Margin After Variable Manufacturing Expenses* | 9,020 | 3,872 | 5,148 | |
| *Other Costs and Expenses—Variable* | | | | |
| Marketing | | | | |
| Selling (Direct) | 1,160 | 483 | 677 | Direct as to territory |
| Advertising | 700 | 275 | 425 | Units sold |
| Warehousing | 630 | 220 | 410 | Lbs. shipped |
| Packing and Shipping | 180 | 75 | 105 | Units sold |
| Order Handling | 55 | 28 | 27 | Cost per order handled |
| Total | $ 2,725 | $1,081 | $1,644 | |
| Engineering | 462 | 153 | 309 | 20% of variable manufacturing costs |
| Research and Development | 1,133 | 464 | 669 | 10% of net sales |
| General and Administrative | 1,133 | 464 | 669 | 10% of net sales |
| Total Variable | 5,453 | 2,162 | 3,291 | |

(*Continued*)

35

**Figure 4A-2D**  (Continued)

| Description | Total | Territory Northwest | Territory Southwest | Assigned Cost Driver or Allocation Base, etc. |
|---|---|---|---|---|
| *Margin After Variable Costs* | 3,567 | 1,710 | 1,857 | |
| *Programmed Costs (Fixed)* | | | | |
| Engineering | 155 | 65 | 90 | Engineering hours direct as to product |
| Research and Development | $ 510 | $ 264 | $ 246 | Manhours on each project—product oriented |
| Total Programmed Costs | $ 665 | $329 | $ 336 | |
| *Margin After Programmed Costs* | $ 2,902 | $1,381 | $1,521 | |
| *Fixed Costs—Allocated* | | | | |
| Manufacturing | 205 | 74 | 131 | Square footage |
| Marketing | 260 | 104 | 156 | % of variable marketing expense |
| Engineering | 31 | 10 | 21 | 20% of programmed engineering costs |
| Research and Development | 105 | 43 | 62 | 20% of programmed research and development costs |
| General and Administrative | $ 1,160 | $482 | $ 678 | 10% of gross sales |
| Total Fixed Costs | $ 1,761 | $ 713 | $1,048 | |
| *Margin After Fixed Costs* | 1,141 | 668 | 473 | |
| Taxes Based on Income (38%) | $ 434 | $ 254 | $ 180 | |
| *Net Income* | $ 707 | $ 414 | $ 285 | |
| % Net Sales | 6.2% | 8.9% | 4.3% | |

## 4A-7  SELECTING THE PROPER COST SYSTEM

As stated earlier, the controller has a major responsibility for the design, installation, and maintenance of the cost systems of the entity. Among the reasons for providing a background on the uses of a cost system, some of the environmental changes which impact the cost system, some of the actual or alleged weaknesses in many cost systems, and commentary on activity-based costing is to motivate you to think about answers to such questions as these:

- Does the cost system or costing practices in my company have the weaknesses described?
- Does the management really know the true total unit cost for each of our major products (research and development, engineering, manufacturing, selling, advertising, distribution, and general and administrative expenses) and its real margin (over the probable life cycle as well as at the present time)?
- Is the economic justification for the company capital expenditures based on product-specific costs, or merely on averages for the nonmanufacturing elements?

The survival and long-term growth of the company may depend on positive responses to these questions. This should bring the controller and the chief cost accountant to ask themselves, "Just what kind of cost system or cost determination procedure is proper for my company?" We are not concerned solely with the cost system for inventory valuation, but with the broader task of proper cost determination including the relevant costs of all functions—not just manufacturing.

A number of factors need to be considered when designing or selecting (or updating) a cost system. These include:

- Nature of the product
- Competitive posture of the company or product
- Type of manufacturing process
- Extent to which costs are needed for planning purposes
- Degree of control desired by management
- Size of the company
- Nature and demands of the distribution system (for nonmanufacturing cost determination)
- Nature of analyses required by management.

The cost matrix shown in Figure 4A-2 provides an indication of both the input (departmental expenses, labor and material) and the output (product costs and functional costs) possibilities of a total cost system. Typically, management wants to know costs by type of cost, by department, and by product, for each activity and type of input and for a designated time period. Where the product has only a single or few material components and is made in a high-volume automated process, the cost system can be simple. Where there are many components of material (each important) and many operations, the cost system is much more complex. However, the advent of the computer now makes a detailed, complex cost system economically feasible.

Some managements may need little *control* information in a continuous standardized process. They can see the waste or slippage, and can check the speed of machinery, as a result, little cost control information may be needed. Or, in a small plant, the manager may be so knowledgeable about the product and process that by observation he can see if costs are in line. For *planning* purposes, the scope of cost determination or analysis and the availability of alternative scenarios probably will be the feature getting most management attention when selecting the system.

There are practical limits to the amount of data that can be accumulated or calculated under a cost system. In a high volume simple product environment, such as petroleum refining, it is relatively easy and unobtrusive to collect cost data. At the other extreme, consider a low volume multifunctional job such as that of a doctor or nurse in a general hospital. Can anyone imagine a system wherein the doctor or nurse records the time spent with each patient—perhaps 3 or 4 minutes for each event, and perhaps 30 events per day? Patients would be annoyed; and the service staff would need to be expanded substantially. It logically follows that in any cost system, installation and operating costs must be considered, as well as interruption of the basic process.

It is generally known that a number of types of cost systems are in use. Some provide detailed and accurate costs; others may provide only estimated or average costs. Some may produce actual or historical costs; in other cases, a predetermined cost plus variances may be the output. For the manufacturing function, cost systems may be classified as follows:

A.  *Actual costs*
   (1)  Job order costs
   (2)  Process costs
B.  *Predetermined costs*
   (1)  Standard costs
      (a)  Job order
      (b)  Process
   (2)  Estimated costs
      (a)  Job order
      (b)  Process

A job order system is one which collects separately each element of cost for each job or order on which work is being done. Hence, the ability to identify or segregate quantities of product going through the plant is a requisite. This system will be found in plants manufacturing to customer order or doing special jobs.

A process cost system is one which accumulates costs for continuous or mass production, wherein the output consists of like units with each unit being processed in a similar manner. This system would be applicable where the product is manufactured in bulk or as a homogeneous total, making a differentiation of articles difficult. Thus, process costs are applicable where there is:

**1.** A continuous or mass production
**2.** A loss of identity of individual items or lots
**3.** A complete standardization of product and process exists.

A process cost system is based on average costs and can be applied on an actual cost or standard cost basis.

Predetermined costs are costs calculated in advance of manufacture, based on specified future conditions. They may be standard costs or estimated costs. Management is interested in what the costs should be. Actual costs are accumulated for comparison with the predetermined costs, and the *variances* are reported.

In a standard cost system, scientific estimates are made of the quantity as well as the cost of material, labor, and manufacturing expenses which should be incurred in making the article. Analyses of variations from standard are made as they occur.

Estimated costs are, as the name indicates, mere estimates of what the costs should be. They are less accurate than standard costs. This method may supplement the financial accounting in firms that have incomplete or inadequate cost systems. Again, as in a standard cost system, actual costs may be compared with the estimated cost, and the variances reported for investigation.

The previous discussion of cost systems has been limited to *manufacturing* cost systems. In addition to a manufacturing cost system, provision needs to be made to accumulate and properly classify the nonmanufacturing expenses (research and development, advertising, selling, distribution, as well as general and administrative). Such expenses probably need to be segregated and identified:

1.  By nature of expense (salaries and wages, fringe benefits, supplies, travel, and so on).
2.  By function or department (selling, etc.).
3.  By expense behavior, that is, fixed, variable, or semi-variable.

The proper cost identification facilitates a grouping of the relevant costs for the decision under consideration.

These cost systems have been described only in a very general way. While many managers may think a cost system is very simple in nature, in actuality it may be very complex. To become familiar with the many complications and variations, the reader may wish to review some of the excellent texts on cost systems and costing techniques as well as the Selected References.

The nature of the product and the manufacturing process are the important determinants in selecting a manufacturing cost system. These two factors often will influence management as to the amount of planning or control data required. Figure 4A-3 identifies eight groups of products and companies, classified according to input and operating characteristics, by the type of cost system probably most applicable.

The purpose for which the costs are used will be a factor in the *manner of cost segregation* required, and the frequency needed. Thus, for *planning* purposes it may be desirable to segregate costs into their variable, semi-variable and fixed components, and perhaps to distinguish incremental costs from full costs. Moreover, such data will be needed only when a planning exercise is underway—perhaps once a year or once a quarter—and not every month.

In contrast, for *control* purposes, costs and expenses should be classified as controllable or uncontrollable (for certain short-term decisions). The nature of the product and process and the relative importance of each cost element will largely determine which detailed cost elements need to be monitored, and the frequency of review. Here are some examples:

**Figure 4A-3**   A Framework for Cost Systems.

| | Job-order process | Batch process | Assembly process | Continuous process |
|---|---|---|---|---|
| Discrete-part products, many materials inputs | Machine shop<br>Construction<br>Shipbuilding<br>Oil well drilling | General purpose machine tools<br>Medium-volume industrial products | Automobiles<br>Electronics<br>Household appliances | |
| Single or few materials inputs | Printing | Utility poles<br>Bakery goods<br>Cutting tools—drill bits, grinding wheels, etc. | Canned goods<br>Household utensils<br>Simple tools | Paint<br>Glass<br>Simple chemicals |
| Services | | Department store<br>Large daily newspaper<br>General hospital<br>Electronics repair | Fast-food restaurant<br>Tabloid newspaper<br>Dialysis clinic<br>Muffler repair | |
| Joint products | | ← Meat packer   Integrated circuits manufacturer* →<br>Sawmill | | |
| | | ← Integrated wood products company   Chemical plant†   Oil refinery → | | |

\* Few products, little choice of output.
† Many products, wide choice of output.

*Source:* Reprinted by permission of *Harvard Business Review.* An Exhibit from "What Kind of Cost System Do You Need?" by Michael J. Sandretto, Jan.–Feb. 1985, Copyright 1985 by the President and Fellows of Harvard College: all rights reserved.

- A low-margin, high-volume product where price is the primary factor for customer selection, probably will require a detailed and precise cost system. In contrast, it may not be as critical for a high-margin unique product of low volume.
- The cost structure of the product may dictate what cost elements must be closely controlled. If material costs are 95% of the cost, then little attention need be directed to labor or overhead.
- The size of the producing company will influence the cost system design. When it is small, perhaps personal observation is sufficient. When it grows, and must rely

on reporting methods, a formal cost system may be required—especially if the product or process is complex.

- The product cycle is a consideration. In the early product life, the article may be unique and command such a high margin that cost control is not important. When the product matures and margins become smaller, then cost control may be the center of attention.

- Market position may be the key factor in selecting the degree of cost control. If one company dominates a market where volume is crucial, then a detailed cost system may be necessary to control costs and be more reliable when changing prices.

Often the unique qualities of the product, and related demand, will set the price— not costs. But in those instances where costs are the determinant of market strategy and price, then accurate product cost determination is critical.

## 4A-8  SUMMARY

The controller has the basic responsibility for the proper design, installation, and operation (and revision when required) of the basic cost determination methods of his or her company. The term "cost determination methods" encompasses the costs or expenses of every department, function, activity, or product of the entity. This expression is intended to be all inclusive, and not restricted to the "cost system," which may be interpreted by many as only the manufacturing cost system.

While the controller has responsibility for the methods used to accumulate costs, to be effective he or she must take into account the information needs of all members of management. The "system" should be composed of the proper building blocks (see, for example, Figure 4A-2) so that the management can be provided with most of the required financial and related data on an economical basis. Properly done, especially in this age of computers, the need for many exhaustive and lengthy manual cost studies, or the tendency of the engineers to develop their own systems, should be held to a minimum.

Such information systems envision the following:

1. Provision of cost data for *planning* purposes, including information for alternative scenarios, on a timely basis and in a usable format. Recognition would be given to cost behavior—whether fixed, variable, or semi-variable—and to the costs *relevant* for the decision. These cost segregations would apply, as may be applicable, to each department or organizational unit or product or other cost object.

2. Provision for *control* purposes, on a timely basis and in usable format, embodying the principle of responsibility accounting, the required monetary data and other quantified data (manhours, machine hours, scrap generation percentages, on-time deliveries, etc.). Much control data may be furnished on a repetitive basis, but provision should be made for a reasonable amount of special analyses.

3. Provision for required inventory valuation data and other financial information for monthly (or sometimes more frequently) income and expense and financial position determination.

4. As may be appropriate, the cost data should be compiled to recognize the impact of the cost drivers and other appropriate measures of cost activity.

**5.** The various segments should be regularly audited or monitored so that they reflect existent operating procedures.

The excellence or suitability of the cost accumulation procedures and reports will depend in large part on the astuteness of the controller and the staff who deal with the cost accounting practices.

## 4A-9   SELECTED REFERENCES

Ames, B. Charles, and James D. Hlavacek, "Vital Truths About Managing Your Costs," *Harvard Business Review,* Jan.–Feb. 1990, pp. 140–147 (HBR Reprint No. 90102).

Brimson, James A., "How Advanced Manufacturing Technologies Are Reshaping Cost Management," *Management Accounting,* Mar. 1986, pp. 25–29.

Cheatham, Carole, "Updating Standard Cost Systems; Making them better tools for today's manufacturing environment," *Journal of Accountancy,* Dec. 1990, pp. 57–60.

Cooper, Robin, "You Need a New Cost System When . . . ," *Harvard Business Review,* Jan.–Feb. 1989, pp. 77–82 (HBR Reprint No. 89102).

Cooper, Robin, and Robert S. Kaplan, "Measure Costs Right: Make the Right Decisions," *Harvard Business Review,* Sept.–Oct. 1988, pp. 96–103 (HBR Reprint No. 88503).

———, "How Cost Accounting Distorts Product Costs," *Management Accounting,* April 1988, pp. 20–27.

Dearden, John, "Measuring Profit Center Managers," *Harvard Business Review,* Sept.–Oct. 1987, pp. 84–88 (HBR Reprint No. 87503).

Dilts, David M., and Grant W. Russell, "Accounting for the Factory of the Future," *Management Accounting,* April 1985, pp. 34–40.

Dudick, Thomas S., "Why SG&A Doesn't Always Work," *Harvard Business Review,* Jan.–Feb. 1987, pp. 4–7 (HBR Reprint No. 87106).

Foster, George, and Charles T. Horngren, "JIT: Cost Accounting and Cost Management Issues," *Management Accounting,* June 1987, pp. 19–25.

Ferrara, William L., "More Questions than Answers. Is the Management Accounting System as Hopeless as the Critics Say?," *Management Accounting,* Oct. 1990, pp. 48–52.

Howell, Robert A., and Stephen R. Soucy, "Cost Accounting in the New Manufacturing Environment," *Management Accounting,* Aug. 1987. pp. 42–48.

———, "Operating Controls in the New Manufacturing Environment," *Management Accounting,* Oct. 1987, pp. 25–31.

Johnson, H. Thomas, "A Blueprint for World Class Management Accounting," *Management Accounting,* June 1988, pp. 23–30.

Kaplan, Robert S., "One Cost System Isn't Enough," *Harvard Business Review,* Jan.–Feb. 1988, pp. 61–66 (HBR Reprint No. 88106).

Lewis, Ronald J., "Activity-Based Costing for Marketing," *Management Accounting,* Nov. 1991, pp. 33–38.

McIlhattan, Robert D., "How Cost Management Can Support the JIT Philosophy," *Management Accounting,* Sept. 1987, pp. 20–26.

McNair, C. J., and William Mosconi, "Measuring Performance in an Advanced Manufacturing Environment," *Management Accounting,* July 1987, pp. 28–31.

O'Guin, Michael, "Focus the Factory with Activity-Based Costing," *Management Accounting,* Feb. 1990, pp. 36–41.

Ostrenga, Michael R., "Activities: The Focal Point of Total Cost Management," *Management Accounting,* Feb. 1990, pp. 42–49.

Raffish, Norm, "How Much Does That Product Really Cost?" *Management Accounting,* March 1991, pp. 36–39.

Sandretto, Michael J., "What Kind of Cost System Do You Need?" *Harvard Business Review,* Jan.–Feb. 1985, pp. 110–118 (HBR Reprint No. 85113).

# CHAPTER 5

# Role of the Computer in Business and Financial Analysis

## 5-5 CORPORATE MODELS

**p. 82.** *Add at end of section:*

Extensive commentary on modern computer-based financial models is contained in Chapter 48.

**p. 95.** *Add at the end of Section 5-16:*

## 5-16A  A REPRESENTATIVE SOFTWARE LIBRARY (NEW)

Large companies have skilled information systems professionals who are knowledgeable about the many software packages available for business use. In order to help the controller of a smaller business establish a software library that will handle his/her financial needs the following summary is provided.

| Application | Software Package | |
|---|---|---|
| I.  Essential Functions | | |
| • Data Base Management | PARADOX (DOS/Windows) | |
|    Used for collecting all business | DBase IV | |
|    information, both financial and | Microsoft Access (Windows) | |
|    nonfinancial | | |
| • General Accounting | Peachtree Complete | Great Plains |
|    Used for general ledger and | ACCPAC Plus/BPI | State of Art— |
|    sub-ledger recording | Access to Platinum/ | MAS/90 |
|    | Platinum Series | Macola |
|    | Cima | Solomon |
| • Graphics | PowerPoint (Windows) | Charisma |
|    Used to prepare statements and | Harvard Graphics | Aldus |
|    reports from data files | Persuasion (Windows) | Persuasion |

*(Continued)*

---

This chapter was updated by David M. Bassett, Senior Consultant, Ernst & Young, Denver.

| Application | Software Package | |
|---|---|---|
| (See Chapter 47C for a complete discussion of Graphics and Business) | Freelance Graphics<br>Delta Graph Professional | |
| II. Other Basic Functions | | |
| • Word Processing<br>  Used to prepare correspondence, reports, etc. | Word Perfect<br>Microsoft Word for Windows | Word Star |
| • Spreadsheet<br>  Used to prepare analysis, summaries, etc., of numerical data | Lotus 1-2-3<br>Microsoft Excel | CA-Supercalc |
| III. Other Business Functions | | |
| • Project Management<br>  Used to collect and report information by project | Project Scheduler 5<br>Microsoft Project<br>ABT Project Workbench | |
| • Time Management<br>  Used to manage calendar, collect time spent by client, etc. | Instant Recall<br>Calendar Creator Plus<br>Timeslips | |
| • Tax<br>  Used to assemble tax returns | Tax Partner<br>Tax Cut<br>Turbo Tax | |
| • Data Utilities<br>  Used to access data files residing outside the company (see section 5-10, "On-Line Data Bases") | Prodigy<br>Dow Jones<br>Knowledge Index<br>Compuserve | |

This outline is not intended to be a comprehensive listing of all applications and/or all the software packages available to handle these applications. It is merely an attempt to give a (noncomputer expert) controller a start at developing in-house computer capability for the financial function. The software industry is a volatile one with many new products being introduced and many others being discontinued. Only a thorough review of alternatives available at the time of acquisition will ensure that the best product is being obtained. The controller might want to solicit the suggestions of the independent accountants used by his/her company, if there is no computer specialist on the company's staff.

For those interested in computer software, commentary on popular software packages as compared with software developed in house is contained in Chapter 46.

Given the importance of computers in the management reporting system, a detailed discussion of certain aspects with which the controller should be knowledgeable is contained in the new Part VII, Computer Systems and Related Technology, of this supplement.

## 5-17  SUMMARY

**p. 95.** *Delete* **PC World** *from the listed periodicals in the last line of the section.*

# CHAPTER 8

# Financial and Operating Ratios, Trends, and Relationships

* p. 139. *Add after last item:*

## 8-4A CASH FLOW RATIOS (NEW)

Another category of ratios gaining popularity is cash flow ratios. Increasing use of this group began after the Financial Accounting Standards Board required the preparation of a statement of cash flows—the successor statement to the statement of sources and uses of cash.

Cash flow ratios may be classified in two groupings: (a) sufficiency ratios and (b) efficiency ratios. The sufficiency ratio describes the adequacy of the cash flows in meeting the needs of the entity. The efficiency ratio indicates how well a company generates cash relative to selected measures. These ratios can be compared to those of other companies and to successive years in the same entity.

The *sufficiency* ratios are outlined as follows:

| Ratio | | Derivation |
|---|---|---|
| Cash flow adequacy | = | $\dfrac{\text{Cash from operations}}{\text{Long-term debt paid + Funds for assets purchased + Dividends paid}}$ |
| Long-term debt repayment | = | $\dfrac{\text{Long-term debt payments}}{\text{Cash from operations}}$ |
| Dividend payout | = | $\dfrac{\text{Dividends}}{\text{Cash from operations}}$ |
| Reinvestment | = | $\dfrac{\text{Purchase of assets}}{\text{Cash from operations}}$ |
| Debt coverage | = | $\dfrac{\text{Total debt}}{\text{Cash from operations}}$ |
| Depreciation − Amortization relationship | = | $\dfrac{\text{Depreciation + Amortization}}{\text{Cash from operations}}$ |

The *cash flow adequacy ratio* measures the ability of the entity to generate sufficient cash to pay its debts, reinvest in its operations, and pay dividends to the owners. A value in excess of 1 over a period of years reflects an ability to satisfactorily cover these principal cash requirements.

The next three ratios—*long-term debt repayment, dividend payout,* and *reinvestment*—indicate the sufficiency of cash to meet each of these purposes. When added, and expressed as a ratio, the resulting number shows the share of cash required for these three purposes combined, without the need to borrow or use other sources of funds.

The *debt coverage ratio* reflects how many years, at the current level of cash generation, is needed to retire all existing debt.

The *depreciation–amortization relationship* reflects how much of the cash flow from operations is due to the impact of the depreciation and amortization charges, and the ability of the entity to maintain its asset base.

The three efficiency ratios growing in use are:

$$\text{Cash flow to sales} \qquad \frac{\text{Cash flow from operations}}{\text{Sales}}$$

$$\text{Operations index} \qquad \frac{\text{Cash flow from operations}}{\text{Income from continuing operations}}$$

$$\text{Cash flow return on assets} \qquad \frac{\text{Cash flow from operations}}{\text{Total assets (or total assets employed)}}$$

The cash efficiency ratios reflect the effectiveness or efficiency by which cash is generated from either operations or assets. Specifically:

1. The cash flow to sales ratio reflects the percentage of each sales dollar realized as cash.

2. The operations index reflects the ratio of cash generated to the income from continuing operations.

3. The cash flow from assets reflects the relative amount of cash which the assets (or assets employed) are able to generate.

These cash flow ratios are just more measurements which the company management can use to compare its performance with specific competition, or the industry results.

# 8-16  SELECTED REFERENCES

* **p. 165.**   *Add these references:*

Berton, Lee, "Investors Have a New Tool for Judging Issues' Health: 'Cash Flow Adequacy,'" *The Wall Street Journal,* Jan. 10, 1994, pp. C1, C1 1.

Giacomino, Don E., and David E. Mielke, "Cash Flows: Another Approach to Ratio Analysis," *Journal of Accountancy,* March 1993, pp. 55–58.

# CHAPTER 9

# Internal Control—A Change in Emphasis: Prevention of Significant Errors and Fraud

## 9-2 BASIC ELEMENTS OF AN INTERNAL CONTROL STRUCTURE

**p. 169.** *Add before "The Accounting System":*

### MANAGEMENT PHILOSOPHY AND OPERATING STYLE

The main volume, as well as much of the current literature, discusses the control system as made up of these three segments:

- The control environment
- The accounting system
- Control procedures.

As experience is gained in the operation of control systems, and especially with the increased attention to business ethics, (see Chapter 1), changes in organization structure, downsizing, and changes in manufacturing and information technologies, it is to be expected that new facets will be emphasized in developing and maintaining an effective control system. One such change is in the management philosophy and operating style of many companies—an important element of the control environment.

As the internal control structure became more widely discussed among management members, the authors noticed that many operating managers regarded the matter as primarily a financial or accounting concern—not theirs. In part this may have been due to the fact that evaluations were made as a result of audits by either the internal auditors or the independent accountants. There was no direct tie-in to corporate governance and the achievement of the corporate objectives—profitability, growth, adherence to ethical standards, and so on. What was needed, and what is occurring in many companies, is the education of operating management about their role as it involves the control system.

One company, in an effort to educate all of departmental management, held a series of one-day seminars for the professional and management staff of the organization. In these meetings, the business objectives for each department were stated by the departmental vice president and supplemented by group discussion. Basically the "control mechanisms" or actions required to accomplish each department's objectives were reviewed for their effectiveness. The relationship of the elements of internal control to attaining the departmental objectives were appraised.

While the elements may differ by entity, these were the control segments covered by this company as meaningful to its operating management.[0.1]

- Organization controls: Personnel standards, a plan of organization, and the corporate culture
- System development and change controls
- Authorization and reporting controls; planning and budgeting; accountability
- Accounting system controls
- Safeguarding controls: Protection of assets and avoidance of unintentional risks
- Management supervisory controls: Supervision and management information
- Documentation controls: Formal policies and procedures; systems documentation

The objective of the approach was to involve all of management in the educational process and make use of the informal mechanisms of the company.

## INFLUENCE OF EXTERNAL FACTORS

The other aspect of the control environment now receiving greater recognition is the influence of external factors. These outside influences, as previously stated, are largely beyond the control of the entity; but how management deals with them may be relevant to how it attains its objectives. Until recently, external factors received scant attention in evaluating control systems. The Auditing Standards Board (ASB) in an internal control risk assessment pronouncement stated merely that there are various "external influences that affect an entity's operations and practices, such as examinations by bank regulatory agencies."[0.2]

When external factors are mentioned, often it is legislatures and regulatory bodies and their laws or pronouncements that first come to mind. In a report prepared for the Treadway Commission relating to fraudulent financial reporting, its authors stated that "The scope of internal auditing responsibilities for examining and evaluating control should extend to every point affected by the organization—even to certain external entities."[0.3]

---

[0.1] Paul G. Makosz and Bruce W. McCuaig, Gulf Canada Resources, "Is everything under control? A new approach to corporate governance," *Financial Executive,* Jan./Feb. 1990, p. 26.

[0.2] Auditing Standards Board, "Consideration of the Internal Control Structure in a Financial Statement Audit," SAS No. 55 (AICPA, April 1988), paragraph 9.

[0.3] Michael J. Barrett and R. N. Carolus, "Control and Internal Auditing," *The Institute of Internal Auditors Report on Fraud,* Institute of Internal Auditors, Sept. 1986, p. 65.

The report grouped the external entities into these three general classes: regulators, customers, and suppliers. Our concern in this segment is with significant suppliers and customers.

Consider, first, the recent trend to just-in-time (JIT) manufacturing, purchasing delivery and inventories. A successful JIT system depends on a close buyer-vendor relationship, with a limited number of dependable suppliers who will deliver on time the required materials or part. Moreover, the supplier will deliver in smaller lot sizes, using statistical quality control to maintain a high quality, defect-free product, and thus reduce or avoid the cost of inspecting the incoming units. In effect, the input inspection is transferred to the supplier organization, and an important control point is moved to an external location. When such a transfer happens, the internal auditors of the manufacturer, in conjunction with the purchasing and manufacturing staff, must at least consider the need to review (audit) the adequacy and effectiveness of the external inspection system. Or, is it enough to note the number of defective finished units by reason of faulty supplier input? Some companies have decided that changes in manufacturing technologies require periodic audits of these inspection and similar external control points.

In like fashion, with the expansion of electronic data interchange between large suppliers, as well as large customers, the concept of external control becomes relevant. If, for example, certain predetermined conditions automatically trigger large buy or sell orders, some of the traditional control mechanisms disappear, and new concerns must be addressed. Thus, as between a manufacturer and a large retailer, who has the right or authority to structure a transaction, place it in the electronic envelope, send it, and to receive the message? Under such circumstances transaction control becomes the responsibility of the seller-buyer partnership and not that of a single party.

To summarize, there are now many circumstances where new technologies are making it desirable to examine external control points. Sometimes this examination may be part of a JIT agreement. In other instances, no legal agreement might exist, but the buying and selling parties established close working relationships that facilitate internal auditor access to selected external control points.

## 9-9   RESPONSIBILITY FOR PROPER INTERNAL CONTROLS

**p. 180.**   *Change title in second line from* **Report of the National Committee . . .** *to* **Report of the National Commission. . . .**

**p. 195.**   *Add at the end of section 9-12:*

## 9-12A   REPORT OF THE COMMITTEE OF SPONSORING ORGANIZATIONS (COSO) (NEW)

Perhaps the most significant recent event regarding internal control was the issuance, in September 1992, of the COSO report. By way of background, the Report of the National Commission on Fraudulent Financial Reporting (NCFFR), issued in October 1987 (see section 9-11), made certain recommendations about internal control to be considered by the management and boards of directors of public companies, by independent accountants, by the SEC and other regulatory or law enforcement bodies, and by academia. In addition to its specific comments for each of the enumerated groups, the NCFFR suggested that the sponsoring organizations of the Treadway Commission work together in an effort to integrate the various internal control concepts and definitions, and that they develop a common reference point. (Different groups emphasized somewhat differing aspects of internal control, depending on their particular interests.) The resulting task force issued its report—the COSO report—to provide practical and broadly accepted criteria for establishing internal control and for evaluating its effectiveness.

The COSO report, entitled *Internal Control—Integrated Framework,* consists of four volumes:

1. *Executive Summary,* a top-level overview directed to the CEO, other senior executives, and the board of directors, as well as to legislators, regulators, professional organizations, and academics.

2. *Framework,* which defines internal control together with its components and provides criteria against which managements, boards of directors, and others can assess a relevant control system.

3. *Reporting to External Parties,* which provides guidance to entities that report publicly on internal control (or intend to do so) regarding the preparation of relevant published financial statements.

4. *Evaluation Tools,* which provides rather extensive illustrations of material that could be useful in conducting an evaluation of an internal control system.

In addition to presenting a framework for internal control, which may assist business management, the report can enable parties at interest—members of boards of directors, business management, shareholders, auditors, regulators, legislators, and academicians—to secure a common understanding about controls generally and how they may be integrated into business operations.

To learn firsthand what the COSO report says concerning internal control, it is suggested that the controller, and those other financial executives who have an interest in the subject, read the report. Many of the topics, such as the importance of the control environment, are discussed at length earlier in this chapter, and little purpose is served in repeating the information. It may be helpful, however, to make the following brief comments about how the COSO report has expanded the concept of internal control from that reflected in earlier writings, and to review *some* of the subject matter stressed in this recent report.

## EVOLUTION OF INTERNAL CONTROL CONCEPT

As judged by the COSO report, the concept of internal control has been expanded from that contained in earlier accounting literature. In the 1930s and 1940s, internal control seemed to concentrate on accounting controls and administrative controls so as to safeguard the assets of the corporation by reducing theft as well as internal fraud. Later, attention became focused on compliance with laws and regulations because certain managements became engaged in illegal payments to foreign representatives, bribery, or similar practices. Finally, in the 1980s, attention was further expanded to encompass fraudulent financial reporting. Now, according to the COSO report, a review of internal control should extend to the entire range of business activities that have to do with achieving various business objectives (such as meeting the annual business plan, penetrating a given product market, and so on) and to the related risks inherent in the process. To many, it has seemed that the review of internal controls does not sufficiently distinguish between such processes and the other aspects of the business management function. In fairness, however, it should be stated that the COSO report attempts to make clear that such management activities as establishing objectives, reaching business decisions, and carrying out management plans are activities that should be integrated with, but not made a part of, the internal control system. In today's competitive world, the existence of effective and efficient operations is germane to the survival of the business and the enhancement of shareholder value.

A highly condensed interpretation of some segments of the COSO report, which deserve emphasis, is given below. Commentaries on relevant phases of internal control that are discussed at length in earlier sections of this chapter are excluded.

## REVISED AND ENLARGED DEFINITION OF INTERNAL CONTROL

According to the COSO report, internal control is broadly defined as a process or group of processes, effected by an entity's board of directors, management, and other personnel, designed to provide reasonable assurance regarding the achievement of objectives in each of the following three categories:

1. Effectiveness and efficiency of operations.
2. Reliability of financial reporting.
3. Compliance with applicable laws and regulations.

Several concepts are inherent in this definition.

First, internal control is not just a single event or circumstance, but rather a series of actions that permeate an entity's activities. They are innate or intrinsic to the way a management runs the business. Internal control is intertwined with a business's operating activities and exists for fundamental reasons.

Second, the system provides only reasonable, not absolute, assurance to management and the board of directors that the specified objectives are being achieved. It cannot provide absolute assurance because systems do break down, and controls can be circumvented by the collusion of two or more individuals. Moreover, management has the ability to override the internal control system. (See section 9-10.)

Third, internal control is accomplished or effected by people—whether the board of directors, or management, or other personnel in the entity. People establish the objectives and put the controls into operation. By the same token, internal controls affect the actions of the people involved, and these people may fail to understand, to communicate properly, or to perform consistently.

Fourth, internal controls are objective-oriented and relate to many categories. The three categories mentioned in the above definition concern (1) the effective and efficient use of resources, including safeguarding assets or meeting the business plan; (2) the preparation of reliable published financial statements; and (3) the tracking and enforcement of compliance with applicable laws and regulations.

It will be observed that the definition of internal controls is broad. This phrasing facilitates the use of subsets of internal control definitions and activities so that those concerned with special aspects (such as accounting control or budgetary control) can focus on those concerns and establish consistent subdefinitions. The system of controls in particular business units or activities of the entity can be accommodated. The definition is broad, also, because this is the manner in which top management often views the subject of controls.

## THE COMPONENTS OF INTERNAL CONTROL

The COSO report identified a fivefold segregation of the components of internal control, all of which are interrelated and all of which must exist to a sufficient degree if the internal control system is to function properly and if the business objectives are to be achieved. These components are described here, with related brief commentary.

**Control Environment.**   The control environment sets the "tone" of the entity and influences the control consciousness of all members of the organization. Because it provides both structure and discipline, it is the very foundation of the other four components of internal control. The factors in the control environment include:

1.  The integrity, ethical values, and competence of the people.
2.  The philosophy and operating style of the management.
3.  The manner in which management assigns authority, responsibility, and accountability.
4.  The ways in which management organizes and develops its people.
5.  The direction provided by the board of directors and its various committees.

This topic is discussed further in section 9-2 of the main volume.

**Risk Assessment.**   Risk assessment is the identification and analysis of relevant risks to achieving certain stated objectives. It forms the basis for determining how risk should be managed. Thus, objective setting—which is not an internal control function—is a precondition to risk assessment, which *is* an internal control function.

Given the definition of internal control, it can be seen that three broad categories of objectives can be established:

1.  Operations objectives, which pertain to the effectiveness and efficiency of the entity's operations. Operations objectives may range from profitability goals or objectives down to division objectives, department objectives, and even activity objectives such as processing sales orders or handling customer invoices. (See section 9-5.)
2.  Financial reporting objectives, which relate to the preparation of reliable published financial statements and the prevention of fraudulent public financial reporting.
3.  Compliance objectives, which relate to the adherence to laws and regulations with which the entity must comply.

When the objectives are set, procedures must be established to track performance in meeting the objectives and keeping the identified risk within acceptable bounds.

As to risk assessment, when internal controls were more restricted to safeguarding assets and similar concerns, the relevant objectives seem to have had a narrower nature (such as seeing that all sales invoices were recorded in the accounts receivable), rather than the present broad management objectives, such as profit goals.

**Control Activities.** Control activities are the policies and procedures (the latter being the actions of personnel to implement the policies) that help to ensure that the necessary actions are taken to address the risks involved in achieving the objectives of the entity. Control activities occur throughout the entire organization—at all levels and for all activities and conditions. In addition to a top-management review of entity performance, they include a vast range of actions: reviewing unit and departmental performance, requiring certain authorizations or approvals, performing reconciliations, verifying certain conditions, segregating duties, restricting access to certain areas or assets, and so on.

This subject is discussed in some detail in sections 9-3 through 9-8.

**Information and Communication.** For management to be effective, it is essential that all relevant and pertinent information be identified, secured or captured, and communicated in a proper format and within a suitable time period so that the people may carry out their responsibilities. This information is of the type discussed throughout this volume. (See especially Chapters 6 through 8, and Chapters 35 through 37.) In summary, it should be relevant, timely, and accurate, and should be prepared in a format that is usable, comparable, and accessible. It may be financial or nonfinancial, and it may relate to some standard or objective, to internal or external operations, or to specific conditions. In short, the information to be made available should be that which facilitates decision making and related reporting.

Not only must the information itself be available, but it must also be communicated in a manner that secures attention and gets it used. It may be necessary to communicate the data to more than one individual—to higher and lower echelons; to those in charge of related functions; and to creditors, customers, suppliers, regulatory agencies, owners, and other outside parties.

**Monitoring.** The final component of an effective control system consists of monitoring. This process of watching, observing, or checking the internal control system permits an assessment of the quality of the system's performance. Monitoring may be performed in an ongoing fashion by observing the findings or results of each regular, periodic review of each element—for example, each day, each month, or each quarter. Or, it may be accomplished as a separate evaluation. Whether a special evaluation is necessary (a management judgment) will depend on the extent and nature of occurring changes, the extent of risks, the competence of the people who implement the controls, and what developments are disclosed by the ongoing monitoring. Perhaps both types of monitoring will be necessary.

Monitoring should extend, as circumstances demand, to every element of the internal control system (control environment, risk assessment, control activities, information and communication, and so on). Important deficiencies or violations should be reported to either senior management or the board of directors.

## EFFECTIVENESS OF INTERNAL CONTROL

The controller, and indeed the management of a public company or any other entity, often must ask: "How can we judge that the internal control system of our organization is effective?" Because the internal control system is defined as a threefold objective-oriented process, the COSO report and other writings, perhaps influenced by the COSO report, have provided the following standard:

> Internal control can be judged effective in each of the three categories, respectively, if the board of directors and management have reasonable assurance that:
>
> 1. They understand the extent to which the entity's operations objectives are being achieved.
> 2. Published financial statements are being prepared reliably.
> 3. Applicable laws and regulations are being complied with.

Conclusions regarding the effectiveness of the control system can be reached for each of the three objectives only when the five components (control environment, risk assessment, control activities, information and communication, and monitoring) are present and are functioning properly. In each entity, each component may function somewhat differently. Further, components may complement each other in differing degrees, or may differ in how they address a particular risk. Determining whether a particular internal control system is effective is, therefore, a subjective judgment and must include a review of the components as well as the objectives. A member of management may know that risks have been evaluated, but may not realize that an important risk has been overlooked. Continuing periodic monitoring and evaluation are necessary.

In the fourth volume, *Evaluation Tools,* the COSO report contains a good discussion of the effectiveness of the internal control system and includes an excellent guide to assist the cognizant executive and others in appraising the internal control system and its various components. The coverage is specifically stated to be illustrative only, and not indicative of all matters that need to be considered in a particular situation. The listings of points of focus, objectives, and risks should prove useful.

Other topics that the COSO report addresses, which are not commented on here, include: responsibility for internal control by the various members of management, by external auditors, and by other interested groups reporting to external parties; and limitations on internal control. These subjects and others are reviewed earlier in this chapter.

For a more thorough review of the subject, it is suggested the reader secure a copy of *Internal Control—Integrated Framework.* (Orders are processed by the AICPA.)

Any report on a subject as important and complex as internal control is bound to raise controversy. A 1993 article in the *Journal of Accountancy* raised some interesting points. (See Selected References.)

\* **p. 195.**   *Add at the end of section 9-12:*

## 9-12B   REVISION IN GOVERNMENT AUDITING STANDARDS (NEW)

Just as the Report of the Committee of Sponsoring Organizations (COSO), as discussed in section 9-12A, has influenced the enlarged concept of internal control as applied to public companies, so also it appears to be having an impact on government auditing standards. The U.S. General Accounting Office (GAO) is now seeking comments on an exposure draft of *Government Auditing Standards,* also known as the yellow book.

The current yellow book reflects the views of Statement on Auditing Standards No. 55, *Consideration of the Internal Control Structure in a Financial Statement Audit.* But research performance by the GAO staff, and the experience of the members of the Government Auditing Standards Advisory Council, concluded that the SAS No. 55 minimum requirements were no longer adequate.

Among other things, the exposure draft proposes to expand the auditors' responsibilities in two areas: the control environment and the safeguarding of assets. Under current requirements, auditors need not specifically assess the control environment. The exposure draft requires that auditors specifically assess whether or not the control environment enhances or undermines the effectiveness of control procedures. Additionally, auditors will be given responsibility for considering how management safeguards assets. They must identify potentially vulnerable assets and search for a link between such assets and possible material misstatements of financial statement assertions. If a link could exist, the auditors must determine what controls management has in place to safeguard the assets.

## 9-13  SELECTED REFERENCES

**p. 195.**  *Add these references:*

Kelley, Thomas P., "The COSO Report: Challenge and Counterchallenge," *Journal of Accountancy,* Feb. 1993, pp. 10–18.

\* McNamce, Patrick, "The New Yellow Book: Focus on Internal Controls," *Journal of Accountancy,* Oct, 1993, pp. 83–86.

# CHAPTER 10

# The Internal Audit Function

## 10-4   THE BASIC ACTIVITIES

**p. 202.**   *After the last item under "Financial Audits," add:*

### EXTERNAL FACTORS

The audit program necessary to achieve the financial audit objective—ascertaining the sufficiency of the internal control system—may require modification as the method of conducting business changes. While a review of internal control long has related to matters *within* the company and rather completely under the control of the management, now the control environment must recognize the impact of external factors—especially the newer and closer relationship between the company and its important customers and/or suppliers.

Two examples will illustrate the new conditions. With the development of extensive electronic transmission, a large retail customer may by-pass the sales department of the manufacturer, avoid the extensive paperwork and control points of its own order department, and send the purchase request directly to the factory. Therefore, the internal audit department may need to review the control procedures for the buyers department of the retailer. Or, with the widely used just-in-time (JIT) manufacturing system, inspection of the raw materials or purchased parts may in fact be performed by the supplier instead of the receiving department of the manufacturer. Again, the internal auditors may have reason to review the (external) quality control system and control over defective units.

Adequacy of the internal control system, and other required procedures, may extend to an examination or consideration of external influences, including regulatory agency required procedures. (See also Chapter 9.)

## 10-5   SOME ORGANIZATIONAL MATTERS

**p. 212.**   *Add at the end of section 10-5:*

### INTERNAL AUDITORS/EXTERNAL AUDITORS; REDUCING THE TENSION

As indicated in the section on the relationship of the internal auditors to the independent accountants, there are several points of shared interest between the two organizations. Yet the cooperation between the two groups, especially at year-end, often is accomplished with some strain on both sides, and might be viewed as an uneasy alliance. It is the controller who is the principal interface of company management with those partners or managers conducting the independent audit and who, at the same time, must rely on the chief internal auditor's reviews to help maintain a strong system of internal controls, proper financial reporting, and a high ethical level of business conduct. Given the controller's interface role with both groups, he may be in a position to improve the working relationship between the two functions.

The extent and cause of the uneasy relationship differs from organization to organization, but these generalizations probably are valid: The outward strains between the two audit groups probably are more evident at the staff level rather than at the partner/chief internal auditor level. In some situations, the internal auditors are well-qualified CPAs, with prior public experience; but in others they do not have the advantage of the professional education and training, with the natural result that the public accountants sometimes regard the internal auditors as second-class citizens—mere accounting clerks, if you will. Moreover, the two audit groups have differing audit objectives; and the year-end audit by the independent accountants is more financially oriented than are the reviews by the internal auditor with his greater concern about efficiency and effectiveness of operations, compliance with policies and procedures, and internal controls. Further, there may exist a difference in emphasis, with the independent auditor concerned with the materiality threshold, but the internal auditor concentrating on correcting the procedure. Moreover, requirements as to working paper documentation, or methods of reviewing working papers, or clearing of review notes may differ. On the one hand, the external audit staff may have only a limited understanding of the function of the internal auditor and the business environment in a particular entity. On the other hand, the internal auditor may not appreciate the need for some of the independent auditor procedures. Then, too, the independent audit staff tends to be quite young, while the internal auditors tend to be older, and often with long business experience. So each side shares in the cause of the problem.

What can the controller do to improve the relationship? It might be argued that the principals in each of the two audit groups should enlighten their staffs on the role of the other organization, and about the objectives, problems, and environments, and so on. But perhaps it is worthwhile for the controller to chair a joint one-day meeting with each group (or combined groups in some cases) to describe the functions and viewpoint of the other organization—from the perspective of the chief accounting officer of the entity. Each of the groups can benefit from a better understanding of the audit assignments of the other.

* **p. 241.** *Add new chapter:*

# CHAPTER 11A

# Globalization: Complexities and Opportunities (New)

## 11A-1   INTRODUCTION: PERVASIVE NATURE OF GLOBALIZATION

Those active in business know that change is constant. It seems some subjects are emphasized, then de-emphasized and later emphasized again, for example, benchmarking, re-engineering, empowered workteams, leveraged buyouts, mergers and acquisitions, explosion of new technologies, the changing nature of capital markets. And now we have globalization.

Chapter 11 in the main volume discusses many of the technical aspects of financial planning and control related to international trade when it was in a less expansive or encompassing mode than at present. The points made therein are still valid. But the recent changes in international trade practices and investment possibilities complicate the tasks. This chapter discusses how the new globalization is impacting U.S. economy and U.S. business.

In the 1970s and 1980s, international trade, in the eyes of many, focused on North America, Europe, and Japan—the most developed markets. Now vast new markets are opening for Western-type goods in Asia, South America, and Eastern Europe. It is these developing areas, which include the Pacific Rim, India, and Latin America, and to which China and Africa will soon be added, that attention needs to be given. This is where the largest growth probably will be.

As a matter of fact, the U.S. Department of Commerce has identified the emerging markets for U.S. companies for the share of U.S. export growth in 1992, as illustrated in Figure 11A-1.

With the greatly expanded global horizon, the financial executive should be aware of these aspects:

1. The expanded markets for U.S. goods and services, and the related impact on specific industries, required changes in packaging and product design, and distributions to meet local tastes.

2. Potential changes in sources for raw materials and supplies.

3. Widened financial investment opportunities, with differing rates of return and diversification possibilities in foreign stocks (including ADRs—American Depositary Receipts), bonds, and global mutual funds specific to a particular county or region.

4. Possible impact on organization structure, including top management structure and related local management chain of command and financial management structure.

**Figure 11A-1**   Emerging Markets for U.S. Companies—Share of U.S. Export Growth in 1992. Even now in the mid-1990s these same countries offer significant markets.

|  |  |
|---|---|
| Eastern Europe | 42.0% |
| Central America | 26.0% |
| South America | 20.0% |
| China | 18.0% |
| Other Asia | 13.0% |
| Africa | 11.0% |
| Middle East | 10.0% |
| East Asian NICs | 6.5% |
| Former Soviet Union | 6.0% |

5. Possible changes in corporate or entity relationships, including the virtual corporation.

6. Changes in policies and procedures relating to planning and control responsibilities or other activities required by U.S., or foreign national, or local, laws and regulations—as well as transfer pricing guidelines.

Some of the subjects are discussed in this chapter; some other topics are reviewed in Chapter 11. Additionally, the Selected References provide further information.

## 11A-2   THE CHANGING NATURE OF INTERNATIONAL TRADE

U.S. companies have engaged in international trade for many years by (a) exporting U.S. produced goods or services, (b) importing selected foreign products, and (c) utilizing factories in foreign countries to assemble products for sale in the United States. With the emergence of huge trading blocs in North America (including the implementation of the North American Free Trade Agreement (NAFTA), Europe (the European Union), and East Asia (the Pacific Rim)) and the growth in other areas, major changes are taking place as to the manner in which global or multinational organizations are doing business. Cross-border trade and investments are both rising dramatically.

These specific developments illustrate the trend:

- Many U.S. companies are increasing their foreign capital investments in plant and equipment.

- U.S. investors are putting record funds into foreign investment—ADRs, some stocks, bonds, and mutual funds.

- Some U.S. corporations are engaging in sophisticated or advanced research and development (R&D) in foreign laboratories instead of the United States.

- U.S. owned companies are beginning to employ large numbers of foreign workers relative to the number of U.S. employees.

- Many U.S. owned corporations are exporting foreign produced goods to the United States. Conversely, some foreign-owned companies are establishing manufacturing plants and distribution facilities in the United States for the sale of their U.S. produced goods.

- Many non-U.S. companies with facilities in the United States are exporting a significant value of U.S. produced goods to foreign markets.

For many years U.S. global companies regarded foreign plants as appendages for the manufacture and sale of products designed or engineered in the United States. But, given competitive pressures, the superior knowledge that foreign nationals have about local practices or customs in their country, and perhaps a less dominant position of some U.S. products and services, there is now more of a cross flow of technology, capital, and talents in many directions. In reality, the nationality of a company is not as clear as it once was; and the chain of command may include many U.S. citizens as well as foreign nationals.

All these developments add to the complexities of doing business on a global basis.

## 11A-3   THE IMPACT OF GLOBAL TRADE ON SEGMENTS OF THE U.S. ECONOMY

It should be of general interest to know how global trade affects different segments of the U.S. economy. How does it impact a particular industry or company? Because U.S. government statistics do not provide much assistance, *Business Week* made its own review after dividing the U.S. economy into three segments: (1) exporting trade, (2) import-competing trade, and (3) domestic trade.[1] The make-up of the sectors and the general conclusions are as follows:

1. *Exporting trade.* The exporting sector consists of industries that are competing effectively in markets at home and abroad. To be included, the industry group must export at least 10 percent of its output. The exporting sector includes industries such as:

    | | |
    |---|---|
    | Aircraft | Financial services |
    | Business services (e.g., consulting and accounting) | Higher education |
    | | Instruments |
    | Chemicals | International communications |
    | Computers | and transportation |
    | Drugs | Lumber and paper products |
    | Electronic equipment and | Moviemaking and other |
    | components | entertainment |

    The *Business Week* report indicates that workers in the exporting sector are winners in the trend toward a global economy. Exporters have expanded output and sales, and they also have boosted productivity by reducing jobs and substituting capital for labor. Although employment was flat, average real wages increased by 5.2 percent since 1980. As one economist stated, "Export success means rising wages."

2. *Import-competing trade.* Industries in the import-competing category import no more than 10 percent of foreign goods into the U.S. market. This sector includes the following categories of industry:

    | | |
    |---|---|
    | Automobiles and motorcycles | Screws, nuts, and other small |
    | Cement | hardware |
    | Clothing | Shoes and luggage |
    | Consumer electronics | Steel, aluminum, and other |
    | Furniture | metals |
    | Machine tools | Tires |
    | Mining | Toys |
    | Most industrial machinery | |

    Employees in this segment have been hurt by the direct and indirect effects of foreign competition. Jobs have become scarce, and wages, once good, have fallen.

3. *Domestic.* This category includes industries that do little importing or exporting. Most are service industries, although some manufacturing is included (e.g., concrete

---

[1] Michael J. Mandel and Aaron Bernstein, "Dispelling the Myths That Are Holding Us Back," *Business Week,* Dec. 17, 1990, p. 67.

blocks) when local tastes, standards, or economics limit international trade. The domestic sector includes these industries:

Business services
Commercial printing
Concrete products
Construction
Domestic transportation and
 communications
Education (primary and secondary)
Financial services, real estate,
 and insurance

Food processing
Health services
Personal services (e.g., hair
 dressing and automobile
 repair)
Publishing
Rubber and plastic products
Wholesale and retail trade

Global competition has pushed down wages in the domestic sector. While it may be relatively easy to find work, pay has decreased and is getting lower. Moreover, as imports or increasing productivity reduce the number of jobs in other categories, many employees have migrated to the service sector, making competition a more important factor.

Global trade can affect just about everyone in every sector of the economy.

## 11A-4   SOME STEPS TO HELP U.S. MANUFACTURERS COMPETE GLOBALLY

From 1945 to the late 1960s, the United States had an unusual advantage in the global business competition: It possessed a very large home market that had not been damaged by the war; and the country benefited from the surge in technology that grew out of the war. But the position of dominance was not a normal one. The United States has lost such a preferred status and is now in a global market where it is merely one of several competitors. The reasons for this change in position are as follows:

- U.S. merchandise imports grew more rapidly than exports.
- Growth in productivity has lagged behind that of both Germany and Japan.
- During the 1980s, the United States lost technical leadership in some important areas, such as computer chips and machine tools.
- Civilian investment in R&D is a lower percentage of GNP in the United States than it is in Germany and Japan.
- The national savings rate is below that of many industrialized countries.

Given the circumstances, what changes must take place so that U.S. companies can secure an increased share of the global market? H. A. Hammerly, Executive Vice President of 3M Company, discussed this subject at some length in one of his articles.[2] Summarized below are his recommendations on what must be done:

---

[2] See H. A. Hammerly, "Can American Manufacturers Compete Outside the U.S.?" *Financial Executive,* Sept.–Oct. 1990, pp. 27–31.

*Actions required on the part of U.S. companies*

- Make the acquisition of global markets a higher national priority.
- Establish a commitment to quality of manufacturing.
- Focus on customer satisfaction in the local market, and not on what the customer should want as determined from a nationwide perspective—as 3M says, "Think global and act local."
- Make the required investments in individual foreign markets.
- Emphasize innovation in products as well as services.
- Stress to both the U.S. government and the public the need to improve the nation's position among global competitors.

*Actions required on the part of the U.S. government*

- Put the U.S. financial house in order by reducing the national deficit and encouraging investment rather than consumption (e.g., through consumption taxes and discontinuation of entitlement increases).
- Ensure access to foreign markets by means of tough U.S. government demands (such as renewing executive order Super 301).
- Correct the tax structure by eliminating (1) the tax on foreign profits that are earned overseas, taxed by foreign government, and never brought back to the United States; (2) the double taxation of dividends; and (3) the advantage of debt financing over equity financing.
- Use the Export Control Act realistically, and not so as to restrict trade (as in the case of grain embargoes), thus risking loss of the market.
- Adopt realistic environmental regulations. Some regulations may be so unreasonable as to restrict trade.
- Attain realistic currency values.
- Adopt a stronger national technology policy to support the U.S. position in manufacturing.
- Encourage industrial research by committing government funds to this purpose.
- Remove antitrust barriers to joint manufacturing efforts.
- Provide stronger support to education.

It is Hammerly's belief that U.S. manufacturers can compete in global markets. However, industry and government must work together more effectively, and U.S. society must be committed to competitiveness in the global marketplace.

Other actions also may be taken, such as the use of the *virtual corporation,* to assemble the needed core competencies—as discussed in section 11A-7, or acquiring significant minority interests in foreign corporations.

## 11A-5  DETERMINING AND IMPLEMENTING SUCCESSFUL GLOBAL STRATEGIES

A great many factors influence whether a particular entity will be successful in the global marketplace. Perhaps no factor is more important than the selection of the proper strategies; and this includes determining the strategy decided upon in the proper manner. It is a reflection of the "NIH" syndrome—not invented here.

A key player in carrying out global strategies is the subsidiary top manager. Some research into the viewpoints of these managers revealed these conclusions as to the process by which strategies should be determined:[3]

1. *It is important that the head office executives become familiar with local conditions.* Only where the subsidiary managers believe the head office executives understand how the local market operates do they respect the decisions reached, and make a greater effort to follow them.

2. *Two-way communication is essential.* Subsidiary top managers value the ability to voice their opinions and exchange ideas with the home office in reaching a strategic decision.

3. *Subsidiary managers must regard the decision-making practices as consistent.* In other words, strategic decision making is a *political* process as well as any *economic* and *competitive* process. Subsidiary managers must not conclude that those on the "inside track" will be heard, but that all others will be overlooked.

4. *Subsidiary managers must believe they have the ability to reflect or openly challenge the head office decision.* In such an environment, the subsidiary managers think the head office may better recognize that strategic decisions will be of a higher quality, and will be made in the overall economic interest—not primarily a political interest.

5. *Subsidiary top managers think it is only fair that the head office explain the reasons for the final global strategic decisions.* When such a procedure is followed, many subsidiary managers tend to believe that the head office at least considered the subsidiary position, and that they thereby acted in a fair and impartial manner.

The existence of a fair *process* of establishing global strategies is key to making the strategy successful. It tends to cause subsidiary managers to pursue *voluntary* execution—doing more than is required—rather than *compulsory* execution—meeting minimum requirements. The traditional mechanism for strategy enforcement—incentive compensation, auditing or monitoring systems, heavy-handed disciplining by the head office, and other rewards or punishments—are of some worth. But these mechanisms are of declining value by reason of such trends or factors as these, among others:

- Increasing size of subsidiary units.
- A growth in unique or distinctive skills in the subsidiaries.
- Growing and extensive communication between the subsidiaries in comparing ideas (and excluding the home office).
- Growing importance of subcultures.
- Increasing difficulty in monitoring efforts in enforcing the prescribed strategy—due to an inability to distinguish the cause of failure—whether the result of

---

[3] W. Chan Kim and Renee A. Mauborgne, "Making Global Strategies Work," *Sloan Management Review,* Spring 1993, pp. 11–26.

factors beyond the control of the manager, or poor implementation that he or she *can* control.

- Growing loss of control by the central office.

The growing complexities in the global marketplace make a participative management approach, perceived as fair and equitable, increasingly important. Aside from the psychological environment, the most important factor is the actual strategy adopted. The predominant philosophy or type of strategy will depend, among other things, upon the product, the industry, the specific market, and the nature of the competition. A study of styles of competition in the semi-conductor business made by a Fordham University Graduate School of Business professor concluded that, in this instance, U.S. firms tended to develop a unique strategy while the effective Japanese competitors tended to win by implementing in a superior manner a not-so-unique strategy.[4] A comparative summary of different competitive actions in this specific market are shown in Figure 11A-2.

As might be expected, the dominant competitive style influences any industry structure, which in turn influences the industry's member firms, their suppliers, and their customers. Figure 11A-3 compares the impact of the two competitive styles on some important industry factors and characteristics. Note that the impact could be either an advantage or a disadvantage for any given particular firm.

## 11A-6   ORGANIZATION STRUCTURE IN A GLOBAL ENTERPRISE

The removal of trade barriers and the trend toward a global economy is changing the manner in which companies do business and, as a consequence, often also causes a change in some organizational arrangements. As entities become global, new threats appear in the home market as well as the foreign market. New products enter the marketplace, and competition increases for existing as well as new customers. These competitive forces are causing these changes:

- *Increased Customer Demands.* Customers tend to require faster deliveries, improved quality, and more numerous other related services.

- *Quicker Responses.* It becomes increasingly necessary to react quickly to competitive actions, as well as changing market conditions, and to shorten the time for development of new products and services.

- *Improved Outsourcing or Subcontracting.* Another frequent requirement is the developing of closer relations with key suppliers so as to facilitate just-in-time delivery of materials or parts or other fast response needs.

- *Strengthening Core Competencies.* With the need to assemble and strengthen core competencies, some entities are forming flexible partnerships—as discussed in section 11A-7. These business adaptations, coupled with the changes in information technology and the inflexibility of traditional, cumbersome, and bureaucratic

---

[4] See William G. Egelhoff, "Great Strategy or Great Strategy Implementation—Two Ways of Competing in Global Markets," *Sloan Management Review,* Winter 1993, pp. 37–50.

**Figure 11A-2**   Comparative Competitive Styles.

| | Dominant Competitive Style | |
|---|---|---|
| Action | U.S. Company | Japanese Company |
| Securing unique product-market advantage. | Attempts to develop unique advantage for each product line. | Does not seek unique product-market advantage; relies on low cost and high quality. |
| Role of process technology (which transfers a product design into marketable products). | Great variance from company to company. Large firms may attempt to stay in the forefront of process technology, whereas firms that rely most heavily on product-market differentiation may consider process technology less important. | Emphasizes staying at the forefront of technology—both for product development and for capital improvement. |
| Sources of process technology know-how. | Often depends on external sources—e.g., by engaging in collaborative research, by outright purchase, or by seeking assistance from equipment manufacturers. | Tending to favor internal development. |
| Withdrawal from the market. | Tends to withdraw from product-market segment when clear advantage cannot be gained, often after competitive pressures make segment unprofitable. | Seldom withdraws from market; tends to remain in product segment and to strive for profitability through efficiency. |
| Status of vertical integration. | Generally values such integration only when related products contribute uniqueness. | Highly values vertical integration as part of drive to self-sufficiency. |

structures, excessive management layers, and onerous procedures, are resulting in some new organization structures. Some may be recognized in a realigned organization, and others are reflected in "new organizations" that are not usually a part of the typical organization chart. A few of these new relationships are reflected in the phenomena listed next.

- *High Performance Teams.* This is a group of individuals with differing skills brought together to function as a team and to completely re-engineer a process—such as filling customer orders or a manufacturing sequence. The team works as a group using shared information and groupware—especially designed software to support collaborative effort.

- *Integrated Organization.* In reality this is a change in the access and flow of information. Instead of, for example, three separate resource areas (a) financial, (b) physical assets, and (c) human resources, a new integrated information system lets executives directly access the required data. This new information system removes layers of management and modifying influences.

**Figure 11A-3**   "Superior Strategy" vs. More Effective Implementation of a Non-Unique Strategy.

| Distinguishing Characteristics | Competing Style | |
| --- | --- | --- |
| | "Superior" Strategy | More Effective Implementation |
| *Impact on Factor* | | |
| Strategic variety. | Greater variety of strategies results in greater range of products as well as greater segmentation of markets. | Fewer strategies, resulting in more direct competition between products and product substitutes, with emphasis on quality and cost. |
| Industry concentration. | Many successful competitors and low industry concentration. | Only a few successful competitors and high industry concentration. |
| Industry survival pattern. | Innovative competitors survive and dominate industry, with high turnover among leaders. | Efficient competitors survive and dominate industry, with lower turnover among leaders. |
| *Industry Characteristics* | | |
| Product life cycle. | Strategy is most effective in early stage of product life cycle, when technological and/or environmental change is rapid and a variety of feasible product designs exist. | Strategy works best in later stages of product life cycle, when technological and/or environmental change is slow and the basic designs have evolved. |
| Risk of Technological or environmental change. | Entity risks losing competitive advantage when there are fewer such changes and when imitators enter market. | Entity risks losing competitive advantage when technological and/or environmental change dominates market. |
| Profit margins. | Less direct competition, resulting in higher profit margins. | More direct competition, resulting in lower profit margins. |

- *The Extended Business.* With the help of industry standards, computer systems are extending outward and linking with both customers and suppliers. In a sense, a change is taking place from a vertical organization to a horizontal entity. Again, some of this change is seen in the virtual corporation.

We see the impetus of international competition forcing the elimination of layers of management, and effective working groups built around key processes instead of single functions or departments. Moreover, knowledge of local markets and important customers argues for a great deal of decentralization.

In the context of organization structure, two other changes are occurring:

1. *Unit Headquarters.* In this increasingly global economy, many U.S. companies are transferring abroad the world headquarters of important business units.

Astute managements are recognizing that they must operate near key customers and closer to competitors—not in a far away location. Many large businesses are finding that a company cannot be run from a single location; several different headquarters may be required for different product lines or competitive postures. With such changes, some loss of control may result. Hence, the controller must be sensitive to these developments.

**2.** *The Finance Organization.* Just as the principle of decentralization applies to the marketing function, it could be advantageous in the finance organization. The chief financial planning and control office of the subsidiary unit should report *administratively* to the local unit manager. This structure tends to make the financial executive a member of the local management, and not be perceived as the eyes and ears of the corporate office. Also, it should make the local financial manager more responsive to the needs of local management. The corporate controller could then provide *functional* guidance, such as the financial procedures to be used, internal control procedures, and report requirements for the home office.

The staff relationship of the unit controllers to the corporate controller is illustrated in Figure 11A-4. See Chapter 11 for additional discussion of this relationship.

**Figure 11A-4**   Global Organization Structure (with Emphasis on the Financial Organization).

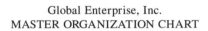

Global Enterprise, Inc.
MASTER ORGANIZATION CHART

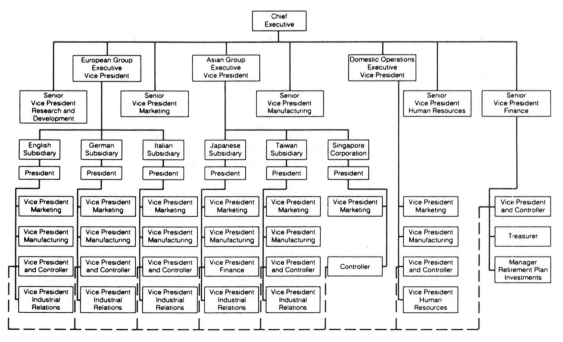

## 11A-7    THE VIRTUAL CORPORATION

In the context of meeting global competition, a new form of organization—the virtual corporation—is emerging to more quickly take advantage of new economic opportunities. This development in organization structure warrants discussion in a separate section. While often used in connection with outsourcing, the concept may spread to other functions.

*Webster's Ninth New Collegiate Dictionary* defines "virtual" as "being such in essence or effect though not formally recognized or admitted." By this definition, a virtual corporation is an entity that, although not formally recognized or admitted as a corporation, is such in effect. As typically described, it is a temporary, flexible network of independent organizations linked by information technology for the purpose of sharing skills, costs, and access to one another's markets. It is a means of quickly meeting competitive pressures. The principal characteristics of this form of organization are these:

1. *Excellence.* Each participant in the organization commits its "core competence" to the joint effort—with the result that each function or process can be world class in a faster time than other methods. A single corporation only rarely can achieve world class status in most of its functions.

2. *Opportunistic and Temporary.* The association is less likely to be either permanent or formal than other arrangements. The entities band together to meet a particular need or to take advantage of a particular opportunity. When the need no longer exists, or the benefits have been realized, then the organizations disband. But benefits have accrued for each member.

3. *Existence of Indeterminate Borders.* With the many contacts among suppliers, customers, and perhaps competitors, the corporate boundaries often become blurred.

4. *Technology Dependent.* The new information technology enables the widely dispersed entities to communicate and work cooperatively. The electronics interchange reduces greatly the time required for legal decisions, or link-ups, or making changes.

5. *Co-Dependence.* The nature of the new relationship makes each participant quite dependent on the other members of the group.

6. *Loss of Control.* The various characteristics listed above results in some loss of control over some operations, with possible related difficulties.

This form of organization should be considered by some global entities.

## 11A-8    FINANCIAL REPORTS TO MEASURE PERFORMANCE OF GLOBAL UNIT MANAGERS

From the viewpoint of the controller, the financial planning and control reports for a foreign operation have these three objectives:

1. To reflect the financial plan for the activities under the control or responsibility of the local manager.

2. To measure actual results against plan for those matters under the control of the local manager and excluding those facets he cannot control.

3. To reflect planned results translated into the parent company currency; and to identify planned vs. actual results segregated between (a) those resulting from the entity manager's performance and (b) those which are due to the impact of currency fluctuations.

Comments on these objectives are discussed in Chapter 11. Additionally, as also discussed in Chapter 11, the controller must assure that worldwide uniformity in financial data definitions and procedures accomplishes these results:

- It simplifies consolidation of financial statements and reports.
- It allows for reasonable comparability of results.
- It permits timely release of financial reports to all interested parties.

Other financial aspects of foreign operations, including transfer pricing, are reviewed in Chapter 11.

## 11A-9  FINANCIAL EVALUATION IN A GLOBAL ENTERPRISE

Aside from the measurement of performance of global unit managers, financial evaluations are needed to reach a judgment on the wisdom of expending funds on any number of transactions where the activity or action will be primarily foreign. Some examples include:

- Evaluating capital expenditures.
- Evaluating the desirability of an acquisition or merger.
- Evaluating specific programs such as a particular R&D project.

Additional discussion of these subjects is contained in Chapters 18, 24, and 32. Where foreign investments or operations are under consideration, the impediments to cash flow *to the parent* must be weighed. Factors to be considered include:

- Currency restrictions
- Foreign exchange rate fluctuations
- Withholding taxes
- Inflation
- Political risk.

## 11A-10  THE GLOBAL INVESTOR

The bulk of this chapter relates to global trade and the impact of such growth on business management or operations including organization, especially the financial organization, and financial procedures. We would be remiss, however, if we did not comment on global financial investments, especially since the chief financial officer and the controller may have an interest in this subject.

Many portfolio managers recommend some investment, whether for diversification or otherwise, in foreign funds or stocks or other investment vehicles. This is an area where recent growth in value has been greater than in U.S. financial investments. The opportunities and vehicles are much greater than a decade ago. The United States now accounts for less than 40% of the world equity market.

To be sure, there are great risks in some foreign investments, and there is a lack of adequate information on many. Accounting methods differ sharply from country to country so that comparisons of price/earning ratios and book value can be frustrating. Choice of vehicles for foreign investment have been growing, and include:

- Global U.S. mutual funds
- Area or country-specific mutual funds
- Specific stocks or ADRs registered on the New York stock exchange
- Listings on foreign bourses

As a further example, investors in London can even buy into a developing markets index fund, called Emerging Markets Index Tracer Funds with stocks from Greece to Brazil to Thailand. In any event, when discussing the global economy, the possibility of investment in foreign instruments sometimes could prove to be worthwhile. The financial executive can seek guidance from those knowledgeable in this field.

# 11A-11   SELECTED REFERENCES

Abdullah, Wagdy M., and Donald E. Keller. "Measuring the Multinational's Performance," *Management Accounting,* Oct. 1985, pp. 26–30.

Allio, Robert J. "Formulating Global Strategy." *Planning Review,* Mar.–Apr. 1989, pp. 22–28.

Byrne, John A., Richard Brandt, and Otis Port. "The Virtual Corporation." *Business Week,* Feb. 8, 1993, pp. 98–102.

Egelhoff, William G. "Great Strategy or Great Strategy Implementation—Two Ways of Competing in Global Markets." *Sloan Management Review,* Winter 1993, pp. 37–50.

Garsombke, Diane J. "International Competitor Analysis." *Planning Review,* May–June 1989, pp. 42–47.

Glasgall, William et al. "The Global Investor." *Business Week,* Oct. 11, 1993, pp. 120–126.

Hale, David D. "Global Finance and the Retreat to Managed Trade." *Harvard Business Review,* Jan.–Feb. 1990, pp. 150–162.

Hammerly, H. A. "Can American Manufacturers Compete Outside the U.S.?" *Financial Executive,* Sept.–Oct. 1990, pp. 24–31.

Keefe, Gary L. "Helping Clients Prepare for Global Markets." *Journal of Accountancy,* July 1989, pp. 54–65.

Kim, Chan W., and Renee A. Mauborgne. "Making Global Strategies Work." *Sloan Management Review,* Spring 1993, pp. 11–26.

Kupfer, Andrew. "How to Be a Global Manager." *Fortune,* Mar. 14, 1988, pp. 52–58.

Menssen, Merle D. "A Contract Price Policy for Multinationals." *Management Accounting,* Oct. 1988, pp. 27–31.

Porter, Michael E. "The Competitive Advantage of Nations." *Harvard Business Review,* Mar.–Apr. 1990, pp. 73–93.

Prahalad, C. K., and Gary Hamel. "The Core Competence of the Corporation." *Harvard Business Review,* May–June 1990, pp. 79–91.

Reich, Robert B. "Who Is Us?" *Harvard Business Review,* Jan.–Feb. 1990, pp. 53–64.

Sookdeo, Ricardo. "The New Global Consumer." *Fortune,* Autumn/Winter 1993, pp. 68–77.

# CHAPTER 13

# The Controller's Role in Investor Relations

**p. 268.** *Add new section:*

## 13-10A  CHANGES IN THE CAPITAL MARKETS (NEW)

The basic volume sets forth in a succinct manner the general objectives of the investor relations function, the evolving nature of the function, the basic players in the game and their informational needs, together with a discussion of the role of the CFO, the controller, and other company officials. Among other objectives, a purpose of the function is to enable the company to raise funds to meet its needs, on an acceptable economic basis, so as to enhance the long-term interests of the shareholders.

But the financial environment changes, among other things, as the business cycle changes, or the perceived relative status of the company or industry changes, or, indeed, as the moods of the investor vacillates. Some recent developments in the early 1990s include: Demands by some pension funds that they have a greater voice in certain company policy decisions; increased agitation by unhappy shareholders about exorbitant levels of executive compensation or perquisites; pressures by some institutional investors to make the board of directors more independent of the CEO; proposals by company management for the "protection of shareholders" in the event of an unsolicited bid for the corporation; and vastly increased volatility in the stock market. While circumstances will differ company by company, there will be instances wherein the CFO, probably assisted by the controller, will find it necessary to become more aggressive in cultivating the financial market, and take these actions: (1) Establish *specific* financial market related objectives, which will be in the shareholders' interest, and (2) Develop some methods of helping to reach these (new) objectives. All of this is to say that the investor relations function is not merely a passive communication caper.

### SOME SUGGESTED FINANCIAL MARKET OBJECTIVES

The objectives of the company, with respect to financial markets will depend on what condition appears to need improvement or change. In the experience of the authors, here are some typical objectives, one or more of which might apply to a particular entity:

- Increase the P/E ratio to X, or to the S&P 500 level, or to the best in the industry.
- Lengthen the average stock holding period by attracting more long-term investors.
- Reacquire 25% of the present outstanding shares through stock repurchase programs.
- Increase the average daily share sales volume—to, say, 100,000 (so that institutions can buy or sell in a given day without significantly moving the stock price).
- Reduce volatility by expanding the shareholder base.
- Build shareholder demand (by diversifying the shareholder base).
- Create a greater demand for company bonds or other debt securities.
- Reduce the proportion of shares held by institutional investors.

While consistent earnings growth, based on good products and capable marketing, and a sound financial position, are fundamental in attaining and maintaining many of these objectives, another aid is to target particular markets and properly communicate relevant financial information. Which targets need to be reached will require an analysis of the present shareholder types, etc. A few comments on this phase follow.

## SOME SUGGESTED METHODS

A successful investor relations program involves providing reliable, consistent, timely, and truthful information about the company on such matters as depth of management, developments as to products and markets, probable trend of sales and earnings, and some guidance on company financial objectives—not only to the usual array of stock brokers, security analysts, and individuals, but more especially to carefully selected institutions that probably would be a desirable type of shareholder—who could aid in meeting the objectives set out in the investor relations agenda. Some suggestions include these actions:

1. *Maintain a current, well-documented background book which is available to all key executives, and for all key contacts with the investing groups.*

   Such an information source would provide these benefits:

   (a) The reader will have a better idea of what subjects are matters of concern to an investor or potential investor.

   (b) The executives will have a consistent and uniform response to the queries.

   (c) The reader will be up-dated on the current developments in his company which should be communicated to the investing public.

   In terms of content, aside from the financially relevant information on the company itself, the data book might contain information about potential investor contacts: location, position, investment patterns, availability for conference calls, and so on.

2. *Be certain that all key internal officers are current on new and important developments and that the investor significance is understood.*

With such a background, the likelihood is reduced of making offhand comments which can be misinterpreted.

3. *Establish close one-on-one relationships with selected institutional investors where particular investor relations objectives can be furthered.*

It already has been mentioned that increasing the investor base by the addition of long-term investors will lengthen the average holding period. Creating closer relations with institutional investors also may reduce volatility. Volatility occurs or increases because large segments of the shareholder population decide to take the same action at the same time, for example, sell the shares. If large shareholders are kept informed about the company, this may decrease the tendency to follow the actions of other investors. These long-term investors may buy more shares while the short-horizon investors may be selling—thus creating a balance in the marketplace, and maintaining the price.

The program for contacting large institutional investors or potential investors can include periodically scheduled visits (once or twice a year) to the financial centers (New York, Boston, Chicago, San Francisco, etc.) to meet particular institutional investors and security analysts.

4. *Consider the possibility of conference calls to selected investors or security analysts.*

This has the advantages of (a) making one call instead of numerous ones, (b) releasing the data to many sources at the same time, and (c) tends to keep the message more consistent. A disadvantage arises of making it more difficult to answer all the questions of every analyst, and so on.

5. *In some circumstances, increase the contacts with non-institutional investors.*

Some corporate financial executives have felt their company might be vulnerable to extend pressures when too large a portion—say 75 to 80%—of the shares were in the hands of institutional investors. For example, the entity might become a target for a hostile take-over. Hence, there could be merit in expanding the ownership base through appropriate and frequent contacts with buy-side security analysts, brokers, and so on.

So there is much to be said for considering certain *specific* investor relations objectives and developing a specific program to meet them.

# CHAPTER 14

## Business Plans and Planning: The Interrelationship of Plans, Strategic Planning

### 14-20 ENVIRONMENTAL ANALYSIS

**p. 288.** *Add at end of first paragraph:*

#### THE CRITICAL SUCCESS FACTORS (CSFs)

The "success" factors mentioned on p. 287 of the main volume are also called key success factors, or perhaps more popular now, in planning jargon, the *critical* success factors (CSFs). These normally would be identified in the environmental analysis. They are so essential to a company's success and to sound strategic planning, that some elaboration about them is desirable.

The characteristics that surround or identify the CSFs are:

- Vital or essential to achievement of the overall corporate objectives
- Expressed as actions that must be taken, either continuously or when threats appear, or as conditions develop that must be overcome
- Somewhat limited in number, that is, not everything that can be done is critical
- Controllable by the entity to which they apply, or capable of being offset by other actions of the entity
- Hierarchical by nature, that is, they may apply to the business as a whole, or for each division, or for each major function, such as marketing, manufacturing, finance, or research and development
- Applicable to each entity that has the same objective in the industry.

While the CEO and other long-time major executives probably will have in mind some or all of the critical success factors, some logical spots to search or examine in the environmental analysis are these:

- Product or service areas where the greatest growth is expected
- Product areas that are generating, or are expected to generate, a major portion of the sales and/or operating income
- Functional or product/service areas where the greatest technological advances are expected.

Critical success factors may be deduced from the strategies selected by particular companies or by the major problems the management thinks it must solve. Here are some examples:

*For a food products manufacturer:*

- Need to improve quality control
- Necessity of making packaging more attractive
- Need to introduce competitive product within three months of the leader.

*For a retail food chain:*

- Need to increase gross margins on meats, and fruits and vegetables
- Necessity of expanding in more affluent suburbs
- Desirability of adding a delicatessen.

*For an aircraft manufacturer:*

- Desirability of adding a manufacturing and repair facility in country X to better service customers in that growing market
- Need to introduce just-in-time (JIT) inventory controls
- Need to penetrate foreign markets of Asia to offset declining U.S. business.

# 14-23  DEVELOPING STRATEGIES

**p. 299.**  *Add after item 4 of strategy development:*

### APPRAISING ALTERNATIVE STRATEGIES

As the strategic planning cycle illustration in Figure 14-5 of the main volume reflects, the last step before preparing the long-range plan is to develop the principal strategies by which the company objectives and basic purposes will be achieved. But as also stated, the process of selecting the proper strategies involves a great deal of art as well as science.

Presumably, after much discussion between the principal functional officers and the CEO, the most appropriate strategies will be tentatively selected. If the process is done properly, the chosen means will be evaluated both qualitatively and quantitatively. It is in the realm of quantitative analysis that the controller can bring to bear his expertise in marshalling the financial facts in order to present the financial effect on the company of the strategy. Depending on the subject matter, the strategy may impact on:

- Net revenues
- Manufacturing costs
- Selling expense, and distribution costs
- Research and development
- General and administrative expense
- Assets or investment required
- Liabilities assumed
- Return on assets and equity
- Earnings per share.

But in the experience of the authors, evaluating the one strategy may not be enough. Business decisions usually involve the selection of alternatives. Therefore, a good financial job would include evaluating one or two *practical* alternatives. And the most favorable, after full review by the management, would be that included in the formal strategic plan.

In presenting the formal strategic plan to top management, or the board of directors, it may be desirable to advise the audience of the impact of the other feasible, practical, or considered likely, scenarios. The impact on earnings per share of the alternative strategies is shown in Figure 15-11 of the main volume.

Should some of those more drastic, but *unlikely,* events be appraised, even if not formally incorporated in the plan presentation? For example, should the impact of war, or a major earthquake, or loss of a major customer (if the strategy fails) be evaluated? We believe that the answer is "yes," *within reason.* By such appraisals, management will gain insight as to the effect (both cost and duration) of major unlikely events. This type of information would be restricted to the top management of the entity.

**p. 302.**   *Add after section 14-25:*

## 14-25A   IMPROVING THE STRATEGIC PLANNING PROCESS (NEW)

We have attempted to explain the desired procedures to make strategic planning a success, but weaknesses do creep into procedures. Here is a summary of comments which express the thoughts of many experienced strategic planners:

- In too many companies, strategic planning has become overly bureaucratic, absurdly quantitative, and largely irrelevant (because of the changing environment).
- Companies must think and act strategically every day—not just in the annual planning (once a year) cycle.
- Key words for the 1990s are "focus" and "flexibility." Focus refers to the need to figure out what the company does best, and build on it. It means developing the "core competence" to meet customer needs. Flexibility means sketching rough scenarios of the future—the "bands of possibilities" —and being ready to use them when the opportunities arise.

- The basic function of the "corporate planner" is to coordinate and advise the line managers. It is the latter who have prime responsibility for formulating and implementing the planning.
- Because many companies reward short-term results, such as increasing sales or reducing costs, it is difficult to encourage truly long-term, far-sighted planning.
- Strategic planning still largely involves unquantifiable factors such as experience, instinct, guesswork, and just pure luck.

## 14-27 SELECTED REFERENCES

**p. 303.** *Add these references:*

Fisher, Anne B., "Is Long-Range Planning Worth It?" *Fortune,* April 23, 1990, pp. 281–284.

Henkoff, Ronald, "How to Plan for 1995," *Fortune,* Dec. 31, 1990, pp. 70–79.

# CHAPTER 18

# Financial Planning and Analysis for Acquisitions, Mergers, and Divestments

**p. 425.** *Add after section 18-15:*

## 18-15A  LEVERAGED BUYOUTS (LBOs) (NEW)

The basic viewpoint of this chapter has been that of evaluating a particular acquisition candidate. Other than briefly discussing the economic effect of differing cash/securities packages, we have not attempted to explain the mechanics of *how* an acquisition should be accomplished. Thus, such matters as hostile tender offers or leveraged buyouts have been avoided. But the number of LBOs and their dollar value in the late 1980s and early 1990s have been so high—reaching $60 billion in 1988 alone—and the later heavy defaults and discounts on junk bonds have been so disastrous in some cases—that some general comments on this popular acquisition procedure are warranted. As the LBO method is also a study in managing liabilities (or not properly managing them) some facets of the subject are discussed in Chapter 33.

But first, let us review what the procedure is, and why it is so popular. The basic steps in a leveraged buyout are these:

1. A company with the desired characteristics (discussed later) is purchased (often by the management).
2. Most of the funds needed for the purchase are borrowed.
3. Unwanted assets are sold. The funds from such sales, plus the cash flow, are used to service the large debt and to pay down the indebtedness to reasonable levels as quickly as possible.

In a typical LBO, the transaction is financed with these securities:

| Security | Share of Capitalization (%) |
|---|---|
| Secured senior debt | 50–60 |
| "Junk" bonds—unsecured, less-than-investment grade junior bonds—carrying a very high interest rate | 30–40 |
| Preferred stock and common stock | 10 |

Why have LBOs been so popular? Among other reasons, if the candidate is well selected, properly managed, and successful, the return on the investment is very high. Additionally, the incentives paid to the investment bankers for corralling the funds is lucrative. And the rewards to a successful management are bountiful.

On the other hand, the risks to the equity holders (and junk bondholders) are great when the venture is ill-planned and/or ill-managed. In the event of an economic downturn, the results can be disastrous—restructuring or insolvency.

What are some of the desirable characteristics for a leveraged buyout? They include many of these attributes:

- A heavy and stable cash flow
- Segments or businesses that can be sold without negatively impacting the remaining operations
- A relatively low debt-to-equity ratio
- Stable working capital requirements
- Stable capital expenditure needs
- Preferably, management continuity
- A noncyclical business pattern
- Sizeable cash dividends.

In summary, the essence of an LBO is the payment for the entity from its future earnings and from proceeds arising through the sale of assets.

A highly leveraged LBO forces the management to focus on effectively and efficiently running the business—or the management won't have a business to run. Some of the techniques or methods of achieving a successful operation include:

- *Emphasizing cash flow.* The need to reduce debt (and interest expense) causes a focus on increasing cash flow and cash availability. How can the investment in receivables be reduced? Through JIT techniques, can we lower inventories?

- *Relating compensation to cash flow and/or profitability of operation.*

- *Motivating the officers and managers through stock ownership.* Heavy stock ownership can stimulate an entrepreneurship attitude—and more aggressive action.

- *Involving the board of directors.* The outside directors, frequently investors also, often have good ideas—which are listened to.

- *Communicating effectively and frequently with employees.* The fact that they are "wired in" and kept informed motivates them. They feel they are "part of the team."

- *Focusing on the "critical success factors"—the essentials.* These elements, and the reasons for their importance are communicated to the managers. They thus know where their attention should be directed. Proper emphasis is given to matters such as:

  (a) Customer satisfaction

  (b) Improved quality

  (c) The sales organization

(d)  Renegotiating contracts

(e)  Reducing nonvalue adding activities

(f)  Keeping research and development effective

(g)  Expanding product uses, etc.

- *Involving all of management in the annual planning process.* When the managers have a say in the annual plan, then it becomes "their" plan—not that of the CFO.

But high rewards can carry high risks. Comments on some unpleasant LBO results are contained in Chapter 33.

**p. 426.   *Add at end of section 18-16:***

# 18-16A   MULTINATIONAL BUSINESS VALUATION (NEW)

The discussion in the main volume relative to the analysis and evaluation of a potential acquisition implicitly relates to valuing a domestic U.S. company or units thereof. With the trend to globalization, there is a need to understand some of the complications of considering a *foreign* acquisition. While the same basic principles and procedures used in evaluating a domestic entity are employed in appraising a foreign operation, there are these several additional factors to be considered:

- Translation of the foreign currency or currencies
- Restrictions on currency transfers
- Differences in foreign tax and accounting regulations or purchases
- Impact of transfer pricing on earnings and taxes
- Lack of adequate and relevant data about markets, competitive activity, and so on
- Need to evaluate political risk
- Impact of foreign exchange (FX) hedging on value
- Determining the appropriate cost of capital.

Some of these subjects are discussed in the following sections. It is assumed that the valuation basis is the discounted cash flow (DCF) method.

Representative cash flows of a U.S. domiciled parent, with a wholly owned subsidiary domiciled in England, is shown in Figure 18-12A.[4] In this example, the English subsidiary receives revenues from both France and England, buys raw materials supplied from Denmark, incurs costs for labor and materials in England, and borrows funds from Switzerland as well as England. Further, it receives capital and raw materials from its U.S. parent, and provides cash flow to its parent in the form of both dividends and license fees. These many sources and uses of cash must be properly accounted for.

---

[4] From Tom Copeland, Tim Koller and Jack Murrin, *Valuation: Measuring and Managing the Value of Companies* (New York: John Wiley, 1990) p. 282. Used by permission.

**Figure 18-12A**   Cash Flow for a U.S. Company's Foreign Subsidiary.

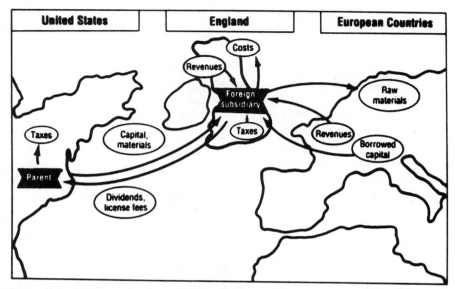

*Source: Valuation: Measuring and Managing the Value of Companies,* Thomas Copeland, Tim Koller, and Jack Murrin, © 1990, John Wiley & Sons, Inc. Reprinted by permission of John Wiley & Sons, Inc.

The steps in valuing a foreign subsidiary are reflected in Figure 18-12B.[5] The starting point is to estimate or forecast the free cash flow in each foreign currency. English revenues are estimated in pound sterling and French revenues are estimated in French francs. Next the nonsterling cash flow is converted into pound sterling by using forward FX rates. When the estimated cash flows are converted to pounds, they are discounted at the English cost of capital. This sterling value is then converted to U.S. dollars, the home currency, using the spot FX rate. In forecasting free cash flow, the political risks, convertibility restrictions, withholding taxes, proper transfer prices, and the estimated inflation rate must be considered. A key point in foreign acquisition analysis is to focus on the cash available to the *parent.* Impediments to cash flow from the subsidiary to the parent might be:

- Currency restrictions
- Exchange rate fluctuations
- Withholding taxes.

The reader may wish to review Chapter 10 of the reference in footnote 4 as well as section 11-8 of the main volume. Further, because of the changing tax regulations and political risks, it might be appropriate to seek the assistance of knowledgeable counsel when evaluating a specific foreign acquisition prospect.

---

[5] *Ibid.,* p. 283. Used by permission.

**Figure 18-12B**   Steps in Valuing a Foreign Subsidiary.

**1. Forecast free cash flow in the foreign currency**

- Use nominal foreign currency cash flow
- Make accounting adjustments for FX translation, foreign accounting standards, and for "hidden assets"
- Use foreign inflation predictions
- Estimate the effective tax rate
- Use appropriate transfer prices

**2. Use forward FX rates to convert cash flow to subsidiary's domestic currency**

- Predict forward FX rates
- Translate foreign-denominated cash flow to subsidiary's domestic currency

**3. Estimate the subsidiary's cost of capital**

- Estimate subsidiary's capital structure
- Estimate cost of equity
- Estimate after-tax cost of debt
- Use the after-tax weighted average cost of capital to discount cash flows

**4. Estimate the subsidiary value in your domestic currency**

- Discount the translated foreign currency free cash flow at the subsidiary's cost of capital
- Translate the subsidiary value to your currency using the spot FX rate

*Source: Valuation: Measuring and Managing the Value of Companies,* Thomas Copeland, Tim Koller, and Jack Murrin, © 1990, John Wiley & Sons, Inc. Reprinted by permission of John Wiley & Sons, Inc.

**p. 435.**   *Add at end of section 18-18:*

# 18-18A   MISTAKES BY MANAGEMENT (NEW)

In the past decade, there has been a high number of successful acquisitions. Yet, there also have been a significant share that have not achieved the results anticipated. While expectations may have been too high in some instances, in other cases some seemingly minor oversights led to disappointment by the new owners. A summarization of some causes of failure may be useful:

- *Failure to respond to customer needs, or to emphasize quality.* Perhaps the emphasis was on costs or selling prices, while neglecting customer complaints.

- *Failure to properly integrate the acquisition.* This aspect is discussed in the preceding section 18-18 of the main volume.

- *Undue emphasis on labor costs.* Some acquirors have focused attention on labor costs, even though, with automation, such costs aggregate less than 15% of total costs. Perhaps more is to be gained by motivating the labor force instead of downsizing.

- *Focusing attention on the high margin products while neglecting low margin items.* In some endeavors, such as the commodity business, attention to small but vital upgrades in the high volume products can produce significant profit improvement.

- *Failure to recognize the weaknesses of portfolio management.* Some acquiring managements treat each acquisition as a separate investment, emphasizing growth market share and growth rate. It hopes to move each investment into a more favorable cash generator sector.

  If the management of an acquired business regards itself as a stand-alone or salable business, barriers arise between the two managements, and the exchange of technology or management ideas becomes inhibited. Moreover it may become necessary to match the investment of less diversified competitors of each such separate businesses—reducing the anticipated rate of return.

- *Failure to commercialize innovation.* Often it is said the Americans invent the product but the Japanese successfully sell or commercialize it. Such mismatching can be reduced in many cases by closely linking R&D, and manufacturing and marketing. U.S. companies perhaps should consider the setting of goals for commercializing of innovation, measuring the development time, and making every effort to shorten it.

- *Failure to take a long-term view of discounted cash flow analysis.* The DCF process gives great weight to the immediate years; but it may be necessary to consider the entire product life cycle. The near-term development years may reflect a low DCF rate of return which is more than offset by a very high rate of return in the later years. As someone allegedly has said, "If IBM had demanded as high a rate of return on its early computers as it earned on other products, it might still be making adding machines."

- *Acquiring a business the new management did not really understand.* This is discussed in the next section.

## DIVERSIFICATION AWAY FROM THE CORE BUSINESS

As mentioned in section 18-2 of the main volume, among the reasons for acquiring another business may be diversification for growth as well as diversification by customer or market to offset seasonal factors or a declining product market. These, indeed, may be legitimate reasons for diversification.

However, in connection with the environmental analysis desirable in strategic planning, a company management should be aware of the "success" factors, also called "critical success factors" that are responsible for a company's progress. (See p. 287 of the main volume.) It is equally true that in making an acquisition the acquiring company management should really understand the business of the acquiree. Many company managements assume that if they can successfully run one business, then they can run any other business. An implicit assumption in this thinking is that it can learn sufficient about the new business in a timely manner. But the numerous failed acquisitions attest to the fact that the acquiring management simply did not understand the critical success factors. So the generalization can be made that diversification into new, unrelated lines carries with it increased risk; and some provision should be made to at least partially compensate for these risks. But how? One well-known authority, in a thought-provoking article has these suggestions for improving the success rate of nonspecialized diversification.[6]

- *Choose the right people.* Quite often, the people at the top corporate level are those who built the company. They may have strong ideas about changing the method of doing business. Therefore, if a present manager is unable or unwilling to accommodate rapid change, a reassignment of duties may be desirable before attempting to diversify.

- *Change the environment.* Any major change in how business is done usually carries with it a major change in the corporate culture. It may be prudent, therefore, to relocate the company headquarters in an attempt to eliminate the old cultural trappings.

- *Choose the proper organization structure.* In many old companies there exists strong central control—perhaps too strong. Yet, many successfully diversified companies are decentralized so as to allow the local business managers to make competitive decisions as to product prices and customers. But, top corporate management continues to plan the *general* course of the company and to *monitor* the subsidiary or division businesses it controls. Therefore, two levels of management, physically separated, may be necessary.

- *Choose the right strategies when diversifying.* Quite often, when companies decide to diversify they select the wrong acquisition before considering these courses of action:

  1. Diversify gradually—since assimilation takes time. Don't attempt to digest too much too soon.

  2. Identify the acquiring company's distinctive capabilities to see if they can be used. These might include special manufacturing know-how, research and development expertise, a marketing organization, or organization strength.

  3. Eliminate the (old) industry-imposed restrictions that impede business decisions.

  4. Explicitly plan for change as distinct from business operational planning. This will include a two-tier planning organization as previously mentioned.

- *Choose the right timing.* As in many actions, the proper timing is important. For example, a growing company in a growing industry would seem to lack a compelling reason to diversify. If the potential acquiree is in decline, the best time to make the purchase may have passed.

---

[6] Adapted from Milton Leontiades, "The Case for Nonspecialized Diversification," *Planning Review,* Jan.–Feb. 1990, pp. 28–32.

## 18-21 SELECTED REFERENCES

**p. 440.** *Add these references:*

Kitching, John, "Early Return on LBOs," *Harvard Business Review,* Nov.–Dec. 1989, pp. 74–81.

Leontiades, Milton, "The Case for Nonspecialized Diversification," *Planning Review,* Jan./Feb. 1990, pp. 26–32.

Loomis, Carol J., "The Biggest Looniest Deal Ever," *Fortune,* June 18, 1990, pp. 48–72.

# CHAPTER 19

# General Problems of Accounting Control—Standards

**p. 448.** *Add at end of section 19-5:*

## 19-5A  RELATIONSHIP OF ENTITY GOALS TO OTHER PERFORMANCE STANDARDS (NEW)

Some of the overall *financial* goals for a business, as outlined in Chapter 7, include (1) measures of *profitability,* such as return on shareholder equity, return on assets, return on sales, (2) measures of *growth,* such as increase in sales, increase in net income, and increase in earnings per share, and (3) *cash flow* measures, including aggregate operating cash flow or free cash flow. But is there, or should there be, any relationship between such overall goals, which are a type of standard, and more specific performance measures, such as the direct labor hour standard in cost center 21 for manufacturing product A? A business usually has goals or objectives as well as strategies for reaching them. It is only logical, therefore, that the goals or standards of a cost center, or factory, or function or division, support the entity goals. The hierarchy of goals, or performance measures or standards, may be pictured as a pyramid. (See Figure 19-1.)

In examining performance measures, beginning at the top of the pyramid (company goals) and moving down the structure, these characteristics exist (although not all are identified):

- Performance measures usually become narrower and more specific.
- The planning horizon becomes shorter.
- In the lower levels, cost factors tend to dominate more; and the measurement or activity period shortens considerably from years to months, days, or even hours.

Performance measures at the lower levels should be expressed in terms of what an individual employee can do. For example, an accounts payable clerk might have as a standard the number of invoices processed per day, or the number of cash discounts

**Figure 19-1**   The Hierarchy of Performance Measures.

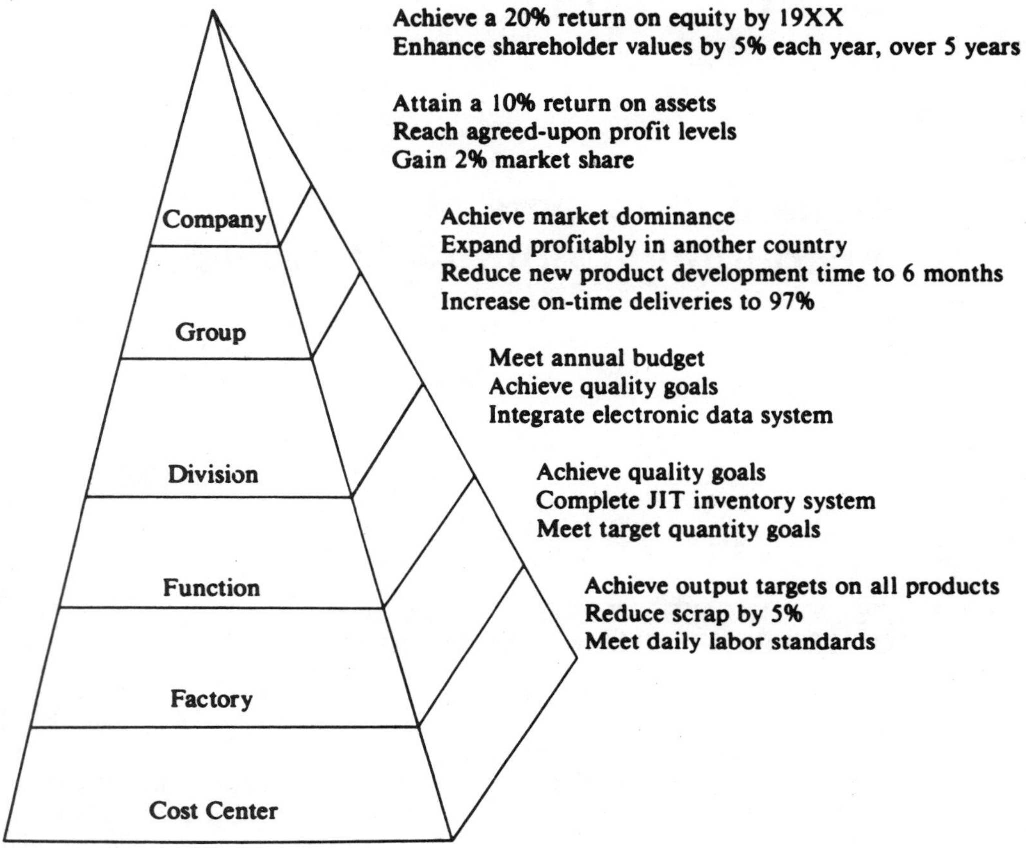

Achieve a 20% return on equity by 19XX
Enhance shareholder values by 5% each year, over 5 years

Attain a 10% return on assets
Reach agreed-upon profit levels
Gain 2% market share

Company

Achieve market dominance
Expand profitably in another country
Reduce new product development time to 6 months
Increase on-time deliveries to 97%

Group

Meet annual budget
Achieve quality goals
Integrate electronic data system

Division

Achieve quality goals
Complete JIT inventory system
Meet target quantity goals

Function

Achieve output targets on all products
Reduce scrap by 5%
Meet daily labor standards

Factory

Cost Center

taken (or lost). This activity level performance cannot be directly measured against a percent return on assets goal.

As the standards are expressed in terms of smaller, specific tasks, the time span between assigning the task, accomplishing the task and rewarding the employee should grow shorter.

Care should be taken that objectives at the lower levels are not contradictory. For example, encouraging higher throughput should not be at the expense of causing excess inventories in another department. A given individual, cost center, or department should not be overpowered by having to meet too many different standards. Standards should be current, that is, they should relate to the processes or methods in use—not obsolete ones. They should be updated minimally each year, ideally, each quarter.

Formulating consistent standards that move the company objective forward takes a great deal of thought and time and is a management task of great importance.

**p. 453.**  *Add at end of section 19-6:*

# 19-6A  TREND TO MORE COMPREHENSIVE PERFORMANCE MEASURES (NEW)

The vast majority of the standards illustrated or described in the prior segment relate to very specific activities and are largely *cost* standards (labor cost per unit). Additionally, some relate to number or size of functions performed (number of sales calls made), or financial relationships. It is common practice in U.S. companies to compare hourly, daily, weekly, or monthly actual performance with such a standard, or a budget, or prior experience. Such comparisons with the relevant internal activity of a prior period or calculated proper measure are useful.

But managements are discovering that other types of measures may be helpful for a number of reasons:

- Some *noncost-related* measures can highlight functional areas that need improvement, for example, number of new customers, number of customer complaints, product development time.

- For some activities, comparisons with an *external* standard, such as industry average, or performance of a principal competitor may provide useful guidelines. Examples include inventory turnover, research and development expenditures.

- Quantified standards may cause supervisors to focus attention on the wrong objective. For instance, attention to the average size of sales orders may take attention away from the need for a profitable product mix.

- On occasion, emphasis on output can create problems in, or transfer problems to, other departments (defects, excessive inventory, or wrong mix of parts).

- Some standards may conflict with other management efforts, such as attempting to reduce indirect manufacturing expense as related to direct labor, when the overall trend is to automation.

In this search for a possible broader base—broader than accounting or financial standards—to check or measure company performance, the controller or his representatives, perhaps in collaboration with other functional executives, could take these actions:

- Discuss with management members the critical success factors of the company, suspected areas of weaker performance, and what changes might be examined.

- Review existing performance measures and try to ascertain if they are relevant to the newer techniques or processes (JIT purchasing, delivery and manufacturing).

- Seek to determine if the measures relate to the true cost drivers of the function under review. (See Chapter 4A.)

- Update practices, using the current literature or periodicals for possible leads to examine.

- Talk with controllers, line managers, or workers, in other companies about the performance measures and other guides they use.

- Consider hiring outside consultants to review areas of suspected weaknesses and to make recommendations. Such a review might lead to a starting list of (1) cost measures and (2) noncost performance measures for important internal activity checking (based on trends and relative *internal* importance, and relative cost and noncost measures when examined or compared to *external* factors).

From a review of the *internal* activities or functions, the impact of these factors, and the importance of trends, could be weighed:

**(A)    Internal Factors**

*Cost Measures*

Direct labor costs

Direct material costs

Manufacturing expense

Marketing expense

Research and development costs

Delivery costs

Inventory carrying costs

Accounts receivable carrying costs

*Noncost Measures*

Length of design cycle

Number of engineering changes

Number of new products

Manufacturing cycle time

Number of parts/raw material deliveries

Number of on-time customer deliveries

Number of suppliers

Number of parts

**(B)    External Factors (Relative Measurement)**

*Cost Measures*

Relative R&D expense

Relative material content cost

Relative labor cost content

Relative delivery expense

Relative selling expenses

## TIME-BASED STANDARDS

One group of standards now receiving more attention than formerly are time-based measures. Those managements which use these diagnostic tools believe that time analysis is more useful than simply cost analysis because activity review identifies exactly what occurs every hour of the working day. It seems to encourage such time oriented questions as: Why are the two tasks done serially and not in parallel? Why is the process speeded up in some departments only to then let the product lie idle? When points of time are identified, then related cost reduction possibilities can be examined.

Examples of time-based standards that have been found useful in some key functions include:

1. *Decision-making process:* Time lost in waiting for a decision
   —product development
   —manufacturing
   —marketing
   —finance—accounting

2. *New product development*
   • Total time required from inception of idea to marketing of product
   • Number of times (or percent) company has beat a competitor to market
   • Number of new products marketed in a given time period

3. *Manufacturing or processing*
   • Cycle time from commencement of manufacture through billing process
   • Inventory turnover
   • Total elapsed time from product development to first time acceptable output
   • Value added per factory hour
   • Credit approval time
   • Billing cycle time—from receipt of shipping notice to completion of invoice preparation
   • Collection time—from mailing of invoice to receipt of payment

4. *Customer service*
   • Number (or percent) of on-time deliveries
   • Response time to customer questions
   • Quoted lead time for
     —shipment of spare parts
     —repairs
     —product delivery
   • Delivery response time.

The Selected References include the name of a useful volume on time-based management.

## BENCHMARKING

The second paragraph in section 19-6A mentions comparisons with an external measure as another type of standard. The practice by a company of measuring products, services and business practices against the toughest competitor or those companies best in its class, or against other measures, has been named "benchmarking." Technically, those who consult about the process differentiate between three kinds, depending on the consultant. Distinctions are made about these three types:

- Competitive benchmarking
- Noncompetitive benchmarking
- Internal benchmarking

Competitive benchmarking studies compare a company's performance with respect to customer-determined notions of quality against direct competitors.

Noncompetitive benchmarking refers to studying the "best-in-class" in a specific business function. For example, it might encompass the billing practices of a company in a completely different industry.

Internal benchmarking can refer to comparisons between plants, or departments, or product lines within the same organization.

In any event, the benchmarking studies involve some steps such as the following:

- Determine which functions within the company to benchmark.
- Select or identify the key performance variables which should be measured.
- Determine which companies are the best-in-class for the function under review.
- Measure the performance of the best-in-class companies.
- Measure the performance of your company as to the function under study.
- Determine those actions necessary to meet and surpass the best-in-class company.
- Implement and monitor the improvement program.

Numerous well-known companies have successfully implemented a program for benchmarking. This includes Xerox, Hughes Aircraft Company, Consolidated Rail Corp., Douglas Aircraft Company, Hewlett-Packard, and Digital Equipment Corporation, among others. One group active in this effort is International Quality & Productivity Center of Upper Montclair, New Jersey. Guidance from some consultants experienced in the benchmarking process may be helpful.

Although benchmarking has produced some legendary corporate successes, it often has not produced an improvement on the net income line. In part, this reflects the fact that it is a complicated process and does not consist merely of some random observations of different methods used by some businesses, or some short field trips. A successful benchmarking effort must be undertaken in a clearly defined and systematic manner. A benchmarking study wherein the only product or result is a report to management, with no modification of a substandard activity, could be regarded as a failure.

To put the topic of benchmarking in the proper perspective, it should be recognized that successful benchmarking efforts have addressed a wide variety of issues, including:

- Increased market share
- Improved corporate strategy

- Increased profitability
- Streamlined processes
- Reduced costs
- More effective research and development activities
- Improved quality
- Higher levels of customer satisfaction.

In those instances when benchmarking activity has not met expectations, some of the reasons include:

1. Top management did not comprehend the full potential of the proposed changes and consequently did not push aggressively for their adoption.
2. The functions or activities selected for improvement may in fact have been improved, but the greater efficiency was too small to have a meaningful impact on overall business performance.
3. The study team made observations but failed to develop an actionable plan.
4. In some instances, the analysis was incomplete: the study team learned *what* the best-in-class companies were doing, but it did not learn *how* the actions were implemented.

One other facet of benchmarking should be noted: the makeup of the study team is rather important. It should, of course, include persons in the company who have been performing the function, but those selected should be highly knowledgeable about the function, should be good communicators, and should be curious and highly analytical. It probably is preferable to have consultants, and not company employees, make contacts with competitors. In some circumstances, the presence of a member of the board of directors might be the means of better communicating to the board the complexities and potential impact of the study.

In summary, benchmarking is a complicated process, and full preparation should be made. The subject cannot be adequately discussed in this volume; but some of the Selected References may be useful.

## A BALANCED SYSTEM OF PERFORMANCE MEASURES

A perusal of the main volume, and this supplement, on the subject of performance measures will reveal, as shown in Figure 19-1, that they range from broad company standards to *detailed* functional standards applied to a daily departmental manufacturing activity. Moreover, many of these standards are used for both planning and control purposes. Then, too, some are cost-related and others are noncost measures; some address the important subject of customer satisfaction, and others simple efficiency; and finally, some deal with innovation while others emphasize routine operations.

To be sure, many years ago the use of standards for control purposes was the point of emphasis—and they generally were of a cost type. But management long has recognized that it cannot rely on one set of measures to the exclusion of all others. Rather, a combination of measures are necessary; moreover they must properly relate to each other, and must take into account the critical success factors of the enterprise. This is to say that management needs a balanced set of performance measures.

The article by Kaplan and Norton, which is included in the Selected References, mentions a company that grouped its performance measures into four types, each with separate measures of performance, and each critical to the future success of the entity.

The four measurement groups discussed, together with some added goals and measures of individual performance which are mentioned earlier in this chapter follow.

| Financial Perspective | | Customer Perspective | |
|---|---|---|---|
| Goals | Measures | Goals | Measures |
| Survive | Cash flow | New products | % of sales from new products |
| Succeed | Sales & income growth | Customer supply | Number of on-time deliveries |
| Prosper | Return on equity | Preferred supplier | Share of key account purchases |

| Internal Business Perspective | | Innovation Perspective | |
|---|---|---|---|
| Goals | Measures | Goals | Measures |
| Manufacturing excellence | Unit cost cycle time | Time to market | Vs. competition |
| New product introduction | Actual vs. planned introduction schedule | Technology leadership | Time to develop new process |

The emphasis on the need for a balanced scorecard represents a mature viewpoint.

# 19-13    SELECTED REFERENCES

**p. 462.**    *Add these references:*

Kaplan, Robert S., and David P. Norton, "The Balanced Scorecard—Measures That Drive Performance," *Harvard Business Review,* Jan.–Feb. 1992, pp. 71–79.

Maturi, Richard J., "Benchmarking: The Search for Quality," *The Financial Manager,* Mar./April, 1990, pp. 26–31.

Stalk, George, Jr., and Thomas M. Hout, *Competing Against Time: How Time-based Competition Is Reshaping Global Markets* (New York: The Free Press, 1990).

# CHAPTER 20

# Planning and Control of Sales

## 20-1  INTRODUCTION

**p. 464.** *Add to the end of section:*

The sales plan is the very heart of the annual business plan, as well as the strategic or long-range plan. Primary responsibility for developing, implementing, and achieving the sales plan is that of the principal marketing or sales executive. The chief financial executive, and a close associate, the controller, need evidence that the marketing/sales plans are attainable because much of the financial planning, to say nothing about the operational plans of all other executives, depends in large part on the success of sales planning.

## 20-10  METHODS OF DETERMINING THE SALES LEVEL

**p. 480.** *Add at end of paragraph under MATHEMATICAL/STATISTICAL METHODS:*

An excellent summary of the various methods of sales forecasting is contained in "Manager's Guide to Forecasting," by David M. Georgoff and Robert G. Murdick, included in the Selected References of the basic volume. The article includes a matrix of the various listed methods and the strengths and weaknesses of each.

### OTHER METHODS

#### Share of Market

**p. 483.** *Add at end of first paragraph:*

To the sales manager inexperienced in estimating future sales, it might seem a relatively easy task to plan company sales if industry demand forecasts are available. Yet, there are at least two hazards: (1) Industry-wide forecasts can be grossly inaccurate; and (2) many times an individual company may not be selling in the entire industry market, but only in a single segment—for which special information is required. Here are two illustrations of both cases. In 1974, U.S. electric utilities made plans to double generating capacity by the mid-1980s, based on an annual growth demand of 7% per year. In fact, during the 1975–1985 decade, load grew at only 2% per year. So the excess capacity has hurt the industry for years. As to market segments, if a gas water heater manufacturer services only the replacement market, and not the new construction market, then total industry estimates of demand would be of little value.

William Barrett[0.1] has suggested that there are four necessary steps in developing a useful total market forecast:

1. Define the market.
2. Divide total industry demand into its main components or markets.
3. Forecast the drivers of demand in each of the segments and project how each is likely to change.
4. Conduct sensitivity analyses in an effort to understand the most critical assumptions and to judge risks to the baseline forecast.

In defining the market, it probably is prudent to describe it so broadly as to include *all* potential users, and thus identify the demand drivers as well as any potential surprise product substitutes. The factors that drive the total market may not be those that determine a particular market share or product category share (as in the gas water heater example). By careful study of customer usage patterns, the probability of future product switching can often be detected; and the review of relevant technologies possibly can uncover potential product threats.

The second step of dividing total demand into its principal components is for the purpose of making the necessary analysis. Those responsible for the study must decide whether existing data on segment size appears adequate and reliable. Some large industries may have adequate data, whether from industry associations, or the federal government, or private sources. For others, an independent study by a knowledgeable group may be desirable. It should be mentioned, also, that the segment size should be small enough that the demand drivers will apply to most of the segment constituency, but large enough to make the analysis worthwhile. Further, a "tree" approach may be useful in identifying the various end-use categories, and then dividing each limb (end use category) into branches, each of which represents a cost driver. The objective is to accurately identify the demand drivers for each end use category, and then to develop forecasts of demand. Both facets, identifying the real demand drivers, and predicting demand can be difficult. As each driver, and the rate of growth/nongrowth is determined, the analysis must consider what could make the estimated future level go wrong, and how much each driver would influence the market. Good analysis should identify the potential risks, including competing technologies, the industry competitive status, and supplier changes. Use of sensitivity analysis should reveal which assumptions or factors are most critical.

---

[0.1] F. William Barrett, "Four Steps to Forecast Total Market Demand," *Harvard Business Review,* July–Aug. 1988, p. 3 (HBR reprint No. 88401).

**p. 483.**   *Add at the end of section 20-10:*

## 20-10A   IMPACT OF GLOBALIZATION (NEW)

A few words are in order about globalization and its impact on sales planning. Current business literature is replete with the successes of globalization, but the failures are seldom mentioned. Undoubtedly, many sales executives are fully aware of the complexities and risks, and reflect these in the sales plans for the company. The controller must also be sensitive to the possible greater exposure as the entity increases its efforts in the global marketplace. Some of the reasons for less than sensational sales results include these factors:

- *Inadequate or insufficient market research.* Some marketing executives sometimes think that the experience in one market is automatically transferable to others.
- *Tendency to overstandardization.* Instead of encouraging some local innovation, some salespersons think the same product or same packaging applies to all markets. "Be reasonable; accept the U.S. product." This logic often does not apply.
- *Inflexibility in the entire marketing program.* The same programs are forced on every unit. Yet experience has shown that some facets are unacceptable in local markets. While some central guidance is desirable, forced adoption, without listening to local arguments, destroys local enthusiasm.
- *Lack of adequate follow-up.* While there may be impressive kickoff programs, momentum is lost because local progress is not monitored.

If a company is alert to the advantages of globalization and is desirous of taking advantage of the economics of scale in marketing, manufacturing, R&D, distribution and purchasing, then it needs to avoid the deficiencies mentioned above. And the controller should be aware that progress is being made by monitoring results, and seeing that the weaknesses are not developing.

As stated at the beginning of this section, these comments relate to the impact of globalization on sales planning and control. Business management obviously must be aware of, and plan for, the exposures on foreign operations—currency risks, taxation, transfer prices and cash flow from—and capital expenditures, as discussed in Chapter 11 of the main volume, and Chapters 11A, 18, and 32 of this supplement.

## 20-11   USEFUL SOURCES OF FORECASTING INFORMATION

**p. 489.**   *Delete last sentence regarding* **Business Conditions Digest,** *and add:*

The makeup of the components of each index, as well as its weighting, occasionally are changed by the Bureau of Economic Analyses. Data on the changes and the current composition now is published in the *Survey of Current Business.*

## 20-14   PRODUCT PRICING— POLICY AND PROCEDURE

**p. 516.**   *Add at end of section:*

### TRANSFER PRICING

The prior discussion on product pricing has to do principally with establishing prices for unrelated customers under competitive conditions. A special aspect of product pricing relates to international transfer prices—the value assigned to goods or services produced in one country for the use or benefit of a *related* company in another country. This topic is of particular interest in that the IRS regulations are now being changed, and such prices are under special scrutiny with the objective of increasing U.S. tax revenues.

Transfer prices, which should be reflected in the sales plans and planned net income of both the producing and receiving companies, probably should be established through the joint efforts of the sales executive and a member of the controller's department. Why? Simply because precise and complicated IRS regulations, which must be followed carefully, relate to actual or expected costs, capital employed, functions performed by each party, and the risks involved. Proper cost accounting is essential.

## 20-15   SELECTED REFERENCES

**p. 516.**   *Add these references:*

Allio, Robert J., "Formulating Global Strategy," *Planning Review,* March/April, 1989, pp. 22–27, 26–28.

Davis, Stanley M., "From 'Future Perfect' Mass Customizing," *Planning Review,* March/April, 1989, pp. 16–21.

Kashani, Kamran, "Beware the Pitfalls of Global Marketing," *Harvard Business Review,* Sept.–Oct. 1989, pp. 91–98.

Olsen, Richard J., "Niche Shock: And How to Survive It," *Planning Review,* July/Aug. 1988, pp. 6–13.

Weiner, Edith, "Six Principles for Revitalizing Your Planning," *Planning Review,* July/Aug. 1990, pp. 16–22, 27.

# CHAPTER 24

# Planning and Control of Research and Development (R&D) Expenses

## 24-9 DETERMINING THE TOTAL R&D BUDGET

**p. 650.** *Delete Figure 24-3.*

\* **p. 651.** *Delete the two sentences following "R&D Scoreboard" in line 8 and substitute:*
This data, usually published in June or July of each year provides statistically helpful information for the R&D executive as well as the controller. Among the information presented annually is:

- The amount spent on company sponsored research each year, as reported by each entity to the SEC on Form 10K, and grouped by industry. An illustrative segment is shown in Figure 24-3A for the paper and forest products industry for a recent year.
- R&D expenditures by industry in the manner of Figure 24-3B, also for a recent year.
- Commentary or opinions on significant developments in the United States.

Some qualitative comments in a recent year included these:

1. Too much attention is focused on the "development" side of R&D, to the detriment of basic research.
2. The United States still spends far more than any other country on R&D.
3. The U.S. government needs to get its technology investments more in line with the technology investments of private industry.
4. Attempts to make R&D more effective should be emphasized. (See section 24-13 of this Cumulative Supplement.)

Because the information published in the *Business Week* "R&D Scoreboard" is readily available annually, much earlier than in this volume, the *cumulative supplement* will no longer provide such data. It will, however, continue to publish commentary on

**Figure 24-3A**  R&D Scoreboard—Paper and Forest Products.

R&D SCOREBOARD

| Company | Stock Symbol | R&D Expenses | | | | | | Sales | | | | Profits | | |
|---|---|---|---|---|---|---|---|---|---|---|---|---|---|---|
| | | 1991 $ Mil. | Change from 1990 % | Per Employee 1991 $ | 1991 Rank | Avg. 1987–91 $ | Avg. 1987–91 Rank | 1991 $ Mil. | Change from 1990 % | Per Employee $ Thous. | R&D as % of Sales | 1991 $ Mil. | Change from 1990 % | R&D as % of Profits |
| **16  PAPER & FOREST PRODUCTS** | | | | | | | | | | | | | | |
| *Industry Composite* | | 536.2 | 5 | 1789.8 | | 1704.0 | | 52458.8 | −4 | 175.1 | 1.0 | 1847.7 | −49 | 29.0 |
| Badger Paper Mills | BPMI | 0.7 | 2 | 1539.3 | 6 | 1474.6 | 6 | 69.1 | −9 | 150.8 | 1.0 | 6.3 | 13 | 11.3 |
| Boise Cascade | BCC | 11.0 | −4 | 559.8 | 11 | 504.6 | 11 | 3950.5 | −6 | 201.4 | 0.3 | −128.1 | NM | NEG |
| Consolidated Papers | CPER | 7.0 | 21 | 1460.8 | 7 | 1154.7 | 7 | 871.9 | −8 | 181.9 | 0.8 | 145.7 | −36 | 4.8 |
| International Paper | IP | 82.7 | −4 | 1173.0 | 10 | 1148.6 | 10 | 12703.0 | −2 | 180.2 | 0.7 | 638.0 | −33 | 13.0 |
| James River Corp. of Virginia | JR | 45.9 | 51 | 1176.9 | 9 | 1176.9 | 9 | 4561.7 | −16 | 117.0 | 1.0 | 132.8 | NA | 34.6 |
| Kimberly-Clark | KMB | 148.8 | 10 | 3604.1 | 1 | 3161.4 | 1 | 6776.9 | 6 | 164.1 | 2.2 | 757.1 | 5 | 19.7 |
| Mead | MEA | 38.5 | 15 | 1782.4 | 5 | 1963.5 | 5 | 4579.3 | −4 | 212.0 | 0.8 | 129.9 | −18 | 29.6 |
| Scott Paper | SPP | 64.4 | −3 | 2213.1 | 3 | 2227.5 | 3 | 4976.5 | −7 | 171.0 | 1.3 | −81.7 | NM | NEG |
| Union Camp | UCC | 50.5 | −3 | 2512.2 | 2 | 2417.2 | 2 | 2967.1 | 4 | 147.6 | 1.7 | 199.8 | −45 | 25.3 |
| Westvaco (10) | W | 30.4 | −3 | 2107.2 | 4 | 2021.4 | 4 | 2301.2 | −5 | 159.4 | 1.3 | 225.9 | −31 | 13.5 |
| Weyerhaeuser | WY | 56.3 | −2 | 1454.8 | 8 | 1338.9 | 8 | 8701.6 | −4 | 225.0 | 0.6 | −177.8 | NM | NEG |

**Figure 24-3B**   Industry Categories—Selected R&D Expenditures, 1991.

| Industry | Total 1991 R&D Expenditures (millions) | Per Employee R&D Expenditures | R&D as a % of Sales | R&D as a % of Profits |
|---|---|---|---|---|
| Aerospace | $ 4,111.9 | $ 5,295.1 | 3.8% | 105.4% |
| Automotive | 11,477.4 | 7,540.1 | 4.2 | neg |
| Chemicals | 5,144.0 | 9,812.4 | 4.1 | 59.6 |
| Conglomerates | 3,550.4 | 4,275.7 | 2.6 | 39.8 |
| Consumer Products | 2,022.0 | 2,201.4 | 1.4 | 13.2 |
| Container Packaging | 112.3 | 1,061.1 | 0.8 | 16.3 |
| Electrical & Electronics | 7,374.9 | 6,421.4 | 5.8 | 135.4 |
| Food | 557.9 | 1,198.8 | 0.7 | 8.6 |
| Fuel | 2,928.3 | 4,094.8 | 0.8 | 12.5 |
| Health Care | 10,006.7 | 14,188.2 | 9.0 | 48.9 |
| Housing | 484.5 | 2,741.6 | 1.8 | neg |
| Leisure Time Products | 1,957.3 | 8,203.6 | 5.7 | 145.7 |
| Manufacturing | 3,379.3 | 3,827.0 | 2.9 | 71.2 |
| Metals & Mining | 428.5 | 2,134.3 | 1.3 | 315.2 |
| Office Equipment & Supplies | 16,188.4 | 13,012.2 | 8.3 | 358.4 |
| Paper & Forest Products | 536.2 | 1,789.8 | 1.0 | 29.0 |
| Service Industries | 144.3 | 630.3 | 0.9 | 26.1 |
| Telecommunications | 3,786.8 | 5,507.2 | 4.0 | 59.9 |

significant R&D trends that may be of value to business executives in establishing the annual company R&D budget.

Two significant developments in late 1993 and early 1994 are worthy of special comment.

In November 1993, President Clinton created the National Science Technology Council, a cabinet-level body on a par with the National Security Council and the National Economic Council to review R&D matters related to reinvigorating the economy. Among other things to be considered is the fate of the nation's three nuclear weapons-building facilities (Livermore, Los Alamos and Sandia) in light of the need to cut the defense budget. Are there "dual-use" research projects which have both military and industrial applications?

As might be expected, there is a diversity of opinion about the probable outcome. Some are pleased about the prospect for solid, results-oriented goal driving research— not just research for research's sake. Others believe the science bureaucracy will get larger, and that many wasteful or irrelevant programs will continue.

Another major development relates to research efforts in Japan. For many years Japan has relied on advances made elsewhere on basic research and fundamental technology. Now, just as the West seems to be restricting such basic effort, Japan is pursuing long-term projects. That country's research strategy, in a dramatic about-face, seems to include these actions:

1. Budgets for university and government laboratory research are being increased.

2. The government is now directing funds towards such long-term projects as environmental research, disease, physics, and space.

**3.** There is increased internationalism in that

- More research is headquartered overseas
- Research efforts are now open to foreign participation
- New technology is being shared with developing countries and
- Patent rights are being shared among participants.

Japan is not forgetting its product-focused efforts.

## 24-13   THE EFFECTIVENESS OF R&D EFFORT

**p. 666.**   *Add at end of section:*

The effectiveness of R&D effort is principally the responsibility of the executive in charge of such activity. With the high level of foreign competition, in those instances where research and development is a critical success factor for the business, the process of benchmarking may be a means of increasing R&D productivity. Although this method has been used extensively with regard to manufacturing and marketing functions, it can be applied also to R&D activity. As discussed in Chapter 19, benchmarking is the measuring of a company's functions against those of companies considered to be the best in their class, and the initiation of actions to improve the activity under review.

In the event the controller is asked for advice regarding the application of benchmarking in R&D activities, he/she should be aware that the process has been a factor in creating (for the R&D function) the following benefits in some companies:

- Significant acceleration of the time-to-market for new products and new processes.
- Assistance in transferring technology from the R&D organization to the business unit involved (an operating division or subsidiary).
- Identification and definition of the core R&D technologies needed to support the companies' planned long-term growth.
- Help with the companies' efforts to tap global technical resources.
- Assistance in evaluating research project selection.
- Improvement in cross-functional participation in many R&D projects.

A review of the relevant articles in the Selected References may provide some useful ideas for the R&D executive as well as the controller.

## 24-14   SELECTED REFERENCES

\* **p. 666.**   *Add these references:*

Elmer-Dewitt, Philip, "Don't Tread on My Lab," *Time,* Jan. 24, 1994. pp. 44–45.

Faltermayer, Edmund, "Invest or Die," *Fortune,* Feb. 22, 1993, pp. 42–52.

Gross, Neil, John Carey, and Joseph Weber, "Who Says Science Has to Pay Off Fast?," *Business Week,* March 21, 1994, pp. 110–111.

Krause, Irv, and John Liu, "Benchmarking R&D Productivity," *Planning Review,* Jan./Feb. 1993, pp. 16–21, 52–53.

# CHAPTER 25

# Financial Planning and Control in a Service Company

## 25-1  INTRODUCTION

**p. 667.**  *Insert after first paragraph:*

For the last 40 years or so, successful service companies have adopted, up to a point, the mass production techniques of the manufacturing companies. But there is a fundamental difference in the underlying philosophy of a service vs. a manufacturing activity: the methods of achieving efficiency must not be at the expense of customer satisfaction. Servicing and satisfying the customer must be foremost in the minds of the front-line employees. Their attitude is reflected, consciously or unconsciously, in the quality of the front-line service. Therefore, the planning and control techniques which are the most successful in a service company recognize these elements:

- Investments in people may be just as important, and sometimes more important, than expenditures for new equipment.

- Advanced technology should support the efforts of the front-line men and women, and not be just a means of monitoring their activities.

- Sound recruitment and training of salespersons and other front-line employees is just as important as for the executives.

- Incentive compensation for the front-line employees, linked, of course, to performance, may be highly desirable.

Useful background on the need for properly motivating front-line service workers, as the basis for securing customer satisfaction, when developing the planning and control system, will be found in the *Harvard Business Review* article by Schlessinger and Heskett, as listed in the Selected References, along with the succeeding debate in the Nov.–Dec. 1991 issue. With this background on a fundamental viewpoint necessary in a service company, we can now turn to the technical discussion of financial planning and control.

## 25-9   SELECTED REFERENCES

p. 682.   *Add these references:*

Schlesinger, Leonard A., and James L. Heskett, "The Service-Driven Service Company," *Harvard Business Review,* Sept.–Oct. 1991, pp. 71–81.

(Numerous authors), Debate—"How Does Service Drive the Service Company?" *Harvard Business Review,* Nov.–Dec. 1991, pp. 146–158.

p. 708. *Add new chapter*

# CHAPTER 26A

# Productivity Improvement (New)

## 26A-1   INTRODUCTION

Whether judged by the number of articles in business books, periodicals or newspapers, or the broad scope of the subjects reviewed, productivity improvement has been an important and popular subject for the past several decades. In this short chapter, we address some of the concerns, causes, and possible solutions to the problem. Moreover, we will review the role of the controller, as well as other members of management, in productivity improvement.

But, first, what is "productivity"? The Bureau of Labor Statistics defines productivity as the value of goods manufactured divided by the amount of labor input. In this chapter, the term is used in the same sense, although we will also discuss services as well as manufacturing.

## 26A-2   THE PRODUCTIVITY CYCLE IN THE UNITED STATES

In the 15-year period ending in 1973, the output per labor hour increased annually about 2.7%, which was significantly higher than the 2% growth rate in the preceding century.[1] But since 1973, the output has increased an average of only 1%.[2] Government estimates published in late 1990 indicate that output per hour in manufacturing for 1989 grew just 2%. This is the second consecutive year that U.S. manufacturers have been at the low end of achievers.[3] (See Figure 26A-1.)

It was reported in early 1993 that productivity increased an estimated 2.2% in 1992, which is the best showing in many years. Moreover, in the current recovery, which was three years old in March of 1994, productivity growth has accounted for a larger share of economic growth, by a wide margin, then in any of the upturns since 1960.[3.1]

When U.S. factory output per hour in the early post-World War II period grew more slowly than most other industrial nations, few seemed to be alarmed. It was recognized that the war-ravaged countries would report a major improvement in productivity as they

**Figure 26A-1**   U.S. Manufacturers Lag in Productivity Gains.

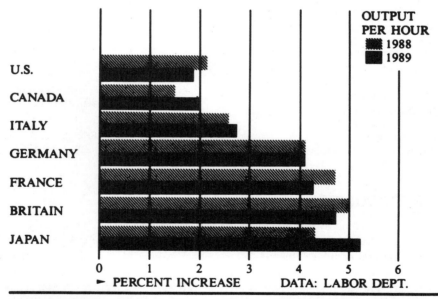

*Source:* Reprinted from October 8, 1990 issue of *Business Week* by special permission, copyright © 1990 by McGraw-Hill, Inc.

---

[1] Laura D'Andrea Tyson, "On Participation and Productivity," *The Los Angeles Times,* May 28, 1989, Part IV, p. 2.

[2] *Ibid.*

[3] Gene Koretz, "The Surge in Factory Productivity Looks Like History Now—," *Business Week,* Oct. 8, 1990, p. 24.

[3.1] James C. Cooper and Kathleen Madigan, "More Jobs + Productivity = a Free Lunch," *Business Week,* Mar. 21, 1994, p. 31.

rebuilt their shattered industries. However, in the early 1970s when the U.S. plant productivity growth slowed more than other industrial nations, concern grew about American weaknesses, and a special effort to improve productivity began—and it succeeded following the 1982 recession. More recently, as the chart shows, Japanese and German productivity gains of about 4% to 5%, far exceed those of the United States. Americans are coming to realize that to meet global competition they must improve operations.

Aside from output per hour what other clues exist as to our possible inability to compete in the world marketplace? Some statistics in the early to mid-1980 period, comparing the United States and Japan show this:

**Table 26A-1**  Comparative Statistics.

| Item | Japan | United States |
| --- | --- | --- |
| Time from order to shipment (machine tool industry) | 1–2 months | 5–6 months |
| Working stock and inventory | Under 2 months | Up to 9 months |
| Quality defects and rework (electronics industry) | 1% or less | 8%–10% |
| Average age of equipment | 10 years | 17 years |
| Annual investment per worker (1975) | $6,500 | $2,600 |

*Source:* Karen Penner, "The Productivity Paradox," *Business Week,* June 6, 1988, p. 102.

Statistics, such as these limited samples, should cause U.S. business management to take a broad and comprehensive viewpoint, not a narrow one, in examining ways to increase productivity, and profitability, and ability to compete. They are all related.

There are some statistics that reflect a recent lag in productivity gains among U.S. manufacturers compared to other leading industrial nations. Other statistics also reflect unfavorably on certain aspects of American business. And top Japanese politicians sneer about U.S. workers being lazy and illiterate. It is certainly true that U.S. business faces serious competition in foreign markets and that the gain in productivity has occasionally slowed. But some of the statistics reflect numbers not adjusted for inflation, and others improperly treat the fluctuating exchange rates. Moreover, the slowdown in productivity may be an aberration due to the millions of babyboomers flooding the job market. Yet the fact remains that "the American worker is unequivocally No. 1 among the industrial powers—and his overall productivity [is] 30% higher than his Japanese counterpart's and his manufacturing productivity 28% higher."[4]

## THE KNOWLEDGE AND SERVICE WORKERS

While some statistics may reflect a drop in the rate of gain in *average* productivity, it is not because productivity in manufacturing and moving goods has declined. These activities in the United States were still displaying a rising productivity level in the 1980s—at 3.9% a year and larger in absolute terms than in Japan and Germany. The difficulty is that too few people are employed in making and moving goods for their increase in productivity to greatly influence the average rate of improvement for *all* workers. In most of the developed countries workers in manufacturing constitute no more than 20% of the workforce, with about 80% of the workers being in other fields. As Peter F. Drucker says,

---

[4] Myron Magnet, "The Truth About the American Worker," *Fortune,* May 4, 1992, p. 50.

"The single greatest challenge facing managers in the developed countries of the world is to raise the productivity of knowledge and service workers."[5] This category ranges from research scientists and cardiac surgeons to the workers in fast-food restaurants.[6] Another source has indicated that service productivity is no better than it was about a dozen years ago, but that the two-year drop in output per hour has halted.[7]

Moreover, in the service area, greater productivity probably does not require heavy capital expenditures. Better operational practices could lead to a great improvement, and some of these are outlined in the next section. The primary purpose of this brief statement is to alert the controller to the basic problem area of low productivity—the knowledge and service segment of business, and not manufacturing per se. Those manufacturing companies faced with international competition may have to more closely examine the service segments of their businesses—where there are difficulties in measuring productivity.

## 26A-2A    SOME BASIC ACTIONS TO INCREASE PRODUCTIVITY

Before discussing productivity improvement programs, it may be helpful to summarize how many American companies in recent years have sought to increase productivity. Beginning with the severe 1980–1982 recession, a period when U.S. business was in a weak competitive position as compared to some foreign entities, management commenced (and in 1993 is still engaged in) a massive restructuring that has involved assets, management procedures, and, to a lesser degree, finances.

As to restructuring that involves assets, the first category might be classified as *strategic* asset restructuring—a decision is made to dispose of the product line. It could result from a conclusion that the potential return on investment will be insufficient because of the relative cost of capital. Or, it might be concluded that the rate of return on the product line could never be as profitable as available alternatives. Other reasons for management's disposing of the line can result from a conclusion that the entity could never become the lowest-cost producer—a key requirement for survival—or that the company could never achieve a market leadership position, i.e., the number one or two marketeer—also regarded as a strategic requirement for growth and/or profitability. Examples of such strategic decisions include the sale by Pfizer of its Coty perfume business and the sale by General Electric of its small electrical appliances business to Black & Decker.

An example of a *tactical* sale of assets could be the disposition of outmoded manufacturing plants or warehouses and relocation to a modern and more suitable site.

An illustration of a restructuring that involves management practices and procedures would be a reorganization as a flatter type organization, eliminating layers of management in an environment that has become too slow and inefficient in reacting to negative conditions or in simply reaching business decisions. It may be decided that a new management could employ the principle of worker participation or cross-functional teams that motivate employees, reduce costs, improve quality, and respond more quickly to customer needs. Incidentally, such an environment could lead to reduced inventories through just-in-time manufacturing practices, or perhaps to a lessened need for new equipment.

---

[5] Peter F. Drucker, "The New Productivity Challenge," *Harvard Business Review,* Nov.–Dec. 1991, p. 69.
[6] *Ibid,* p. 71.
[7] Joseph Spiers, "Productivity Looks Promising," *Fortune,* Mar. 9, 1992, p. 21.

The third type of restructuring that has taken place is of a financial nature and involves the balance sheet. In some cases, high-cost debt has been eliminated and replaced with equity; or, the debt has been refinanced at a much lower interest cost, which has reduced the interest burden.

In some instances, these restructurings may have involved heavy one-time income charges related to personnel reduction. However, the final results often were a more competitive company, improved long-term profitability, improved productivity, and a financially stronger entity.

## 26A-2B   INCREASING PRODUCTIVITY—OR MEETING COMPETITION—IN THE GLOBAL ARENA

With the intense competition in the global marketplace, a new type of operation is emerging and becoming more prevalent—the virtual corporation. The virtual corporation is a temporary network of independent companies, linked by information technology, to share skills, costs, and access to each other's markets. It may be so named because of the dictionary definition of "virtual": "being such in essence or effect though not formally recognized or admitted," as in a virtual promise to do something.

This type of organization seems to have these six characteristics:

1. *Excellence*—Each partner commits its "core competence" to the effort. It follows that every process or function could be world-class—a condition that most entities would find hard to achieve.

2. *Opportunism and temporary status*—The associations are less permanent and less formal. They band together to meet a particular need and disband when the need no longer exists. Presumably, there is a benefit for each member.

3. *Technology dependence*—The widely dispersed companies link up, communicate, and work together through information networks. The use of electronics speeds up exchange of ideas and information, and reduces the amount of legal work.

4. *Indeterminate borders*—With the numerous contacts among customers, suppliers, and others, it is more difficult to define corporate boundaries.

5. *Co-reliance*—The nature of the new relationships is such that each member of the group may become highly dependent on the other participants.

6. *Loss of control*—Within this more flexible organization, one problem can be the possible loss of control over some operations.

The controller should be alert to this emerging form of organization. It gathers together competencies and offers the possibility of increased productivity and effectiveness.

## 26A-3   FACTORS BEARING ON LOW PRODUCTIVITY

In undertaking studies of low productivity, sometimes the emphasis wrongly is on factory direct labor—even though direct labor now is often only 15% or less of total costs—

or on the factory, even though other functions many times constitute a larger element of the total cost. Then, too, some study team members emphasize capital equipment and tend to downplay the need to properly motivate and train the employees despite a possible deterioration in the quality of future workers. Worker involvement is a key factor in productivity levels.

Before reviewing a productivity improvement program (PIP), we suggest these areas of possible study:

- *Capital assets*

  Extent of investment in modern equipment

  Proper maintenance of plant and equipment

  Proper training of employees in use of equipment (new and used)

  Use of proper criteria in reviewing economics of new equipment (DCF, etc.)

  Effective utilization of equipment

- *Inventories*

  Use of "just-in-time" (JIT) techniques

  Use of consignment accounts

  Changes in lot sizes

  Fewer stocking points (hence, less handling)

  Improved vendor selection and/or scheduling

  Possibly increased standardization or simplification

- *Operational changes*

  Use of "just-in-time" (JIT) production techniques

  Increased subcontracting or out sourcing

  Improved quality control methods

  Changes in material types used

  Improved training and motivation of all employees

  Elimination of nonvalue-adding functions

  Improved attention as to the real "cost drivers"—those factors which increase costs—engineering changes, schedule changes, product design methods

- *Organizational changes*

  Elimination, or better grouping, of functions

  Reduced levels of organization

  Reducing service departments employees through transfer to direct departments

  Increased responsibility, or scope of operations, of individual workers

- *Changes in information technology and cost control techniques*

  Improved use of computers in providing real-time cost control information

  Use of local area networks (LANs) in tracking production and inventory status at various sites

  Expanded use of computers and LANs for scheduling vendor deliveries and customer orders

From the above listing, it can be deduced that the emphasis on productivity improvement is in eliminating or reducing nonvalue-adding functions, not on simply working faster.

## 26A-4 THE NATURE AND ROLE OF A PRODUCTIVITY IMPROVEMENT PROGRAM (PIP)

A productivity improvement program may be described as an organized effort for reviewing internal operations with a view to securing increased efficiency and economy. The emphasis is on the internal operations—those which the entity can control—as distinguished from those external conditions which the company cannot control. This type of undertaking is sometimes called a *cost reduction effort*—although in fact the program can extend to price increases and margin improvement or a profit improvement program (PIP).

But if a company has a good product and an ostensibly sound planning and control system, why should another organized effort be required to improve productivity? There are at least two answers to this question. First, if a management is even just reasonably successful, over a period of time it tends to become somewhat lax and often simply ceases to look for more efficient methods. Second, the outside world keeps changing, and competition usually grows more intense. So an entity is forced to improve, or it may cease to exist. Some signs of a need for internal change include: severe reductions in sales volume, substantially reduced margins, major competitive product changes, new products for the same market, and growth of world class competitors. Consequently, in most companies there is a need for a continuing formal program to increase productivity.

## 26A-5 STEPS IN A PRODUCTIVITY IMPROVEMENT PROGRAM

The exact nature of a productivity improvement effort in a particular company will depend on the local circumstances. Some of the factors that will influence both the vehicle or organization structure used and the intensity and duration of the activity include:

- Perceived extent of the problem
- Company organization structure and style of management
- General status of planning and control techniques
- Availability of qualified internal personnel to participate in the study
- Financial constraints
- Complexity of the different functions or activities to be reviewed.

Under the usual circumstances, as discussed later, representatives of the controller's department, because of their knowledge of costs and the expense structure, participate in the studies. For like reasons, including his understanding of the cost-volume-profit relationships, cost trends, and a need for his appraisal of the financial impact of proposed actions, the controller himself is likely to be involved in certain phases. In some instances, although this is not necessarily recommended, he may be the leader or coordinator of the effort.

In any event, here are some suggested steps in formulating and implementing a profit improvement program (to be conducted largely by in-house personnel and not by consultants):

1. Designate an executive of sufficient stature who will be held responsible for directing the program (at least initially) either overall, or in each major department.

2. Develop some productivity improvement objectives for the company, division, or profit center, taking into account some tentative objectives for each function or activity.

3. Identify those study areas that should have priority, based on the potential improvement thought possible, or the opportunity to show early results.

4. Tentatively schedule the reviews.

5. Select the study participants, using a team or task force approach.

6. Plan the audit or review in reasonable detail.

7. Conduct the study or audit.

8. Review with the appropriate level of management the tentative recommendations.

9. As necessary, conduct an in-depth analysis to ascertain the need for a further study by outside consultants or to verify the extent of cost savings, the practicality of the recommendations, the impact on the company, and the difficulties of implementing the suggested changes.

10. Implement the changes.

11. Monitor the progress towards the productivity improvement objectives.

An elaboration on some of these suggestions follows.

## ORGANIZATION STRUCTURE AND LEADERSHIP FOR THE PIP

The organization structure and leadership assignments for productivity improvement programs (PIPs) will depend largely on the management attitude about such studies and its style of management as well as the size of the company. In some situations, especially larger entities, PIPs will be included in strategic planning and the required organization would be more or less permanent. In other circumstances, perhaps the core manager and an assistant might be the only "permanent" staff, with a temporary staff for the periodic bursts of activity—perhaps every two or three years or more. In even smaller companies the PIP staff would be entirely temporary with other duties being the principal activity of the participants.

In any event, the corporate leader of the PIP, and the leader for each large functional department should have specific duties. A position description for the coordinators (of the entire operation or a large department) is illustrated in Figure 26A-2 for a large petroleum company. As can be seen, a team or task force approach (discussed later) is employed.

## SETTING PIP OBJECTIVES

In most companies, an analysis of historical data will reveal (1) the areas of highest costs; (2) those spots where cost growth has been the greatest in the past several years; (3) the nature of the costs, segregated as between fixed and variable; (4) comparisons of cost levels or productivity of the entity vs. competitors; and (5) relative profitability information, where applicable. Quite often such data can be provided and interpreted by the controller or his staff. In any event, the company and departmental PIP leader and coordinators should have such information available in setting the departmental and/or company PIP objectives.

**Figure 26A-2** Position Description—PIP Coordinator.

BASIC FUNCTION:
The PIP coordinator is primarily responsible for planning and supervising profit improvement studies within his department. In addition, he is responsible for guiding the implementation of study recommendations to ensure that identified savings opportunities are realized.

SPECIFIC DUTIES AND WORKING RELATIONSHIPS:
Within approved limits of authority and company policy, the PIP coordinator is responsible to the department manager for carrying out the duties and relationships set forth below:

1. Recommends studies to be undertaken based on an evaluation of savings potential, overall value to Chemicon and the ease with which savings can be achieved. Assigns priorities to studies using the stated criteria.

2. Works with the department manager to set ambitious savings goals for each study.

3. Selects and trains study team members, with particular emphasis on those who can contribute materially to the study effort, can help to implement the team's recommendations, and can benefit from the experience.
    a. Indoctrinates team members in the purpose and objectives of the PIP program and the specific study.
    b. Provides specific training in fact-finding, analysis, and other study techniques.

4. Assists the team in writing the preliminary study plan, ensuring that the plan is sound and that all relevant tasks are included.
    a. Ensures that the plan is targeted toward the study objectives and that a reasonable timetable has been established for conducting the study.
    b. Reviews the plan with appropriate supervisory personnel to ensure its completeness and feasibility.

5. Monitors the fact-finding phase of all PIP studies to ensure that the team develops adequate, useful, and accurate information. Reviews sources of information to ensure that supervisors and other appropriate personnel are contacted.

6. Reviews the team's work planning and scheduling summary sheet to ensure that all ideas are being considered and that all savings opportunities have been identified. Helps the team to develop a sound analytical approach.

7. Reviews an outline of the team's report to ensure that it is accurate and complete.
    a. Analyzes recommendations to ensure that they are practical and that they will meet the savings objectives.
    b. Ensures that the report contains an action plan which includes specific responsibility assignments and time schedules.
    c. Ensures that recommendations are supported by adequate controls.

8. Assists the team in preparing a study abstract and an edited summary sheet to serve as an index for the working papers.

9. Reviews a final draft of the report with department management to secure concurrence with recommendations and action plan. Negotiates modifications as required.

*(Continued)*

10. Assists line supervisors in the implementation of recommendations.
    a. Checks periodically with responsible supervisors at all levels to be sure that implementation schedules are being met.
    b. Reviews implementation problems with appropriate managers to seek satisfactory solutions.
    c. Maintains a current file of working papers to assist in solving implementation problems.

11. Publishes periodic progress reports on all PIP study activities for appropriate management personnel.
    a. Issues a monthly savings summary to the department manager, comparing savings achieved against savings identified.
    b. Issues a program progress summary at the completion of each study.
    c. Releases a biannual report of the studies scheduled during the next 12 months.

12. Maintains close working relationships with team leaders and coordinates activities of various study teams within the department.

13. Provides liaison between department management and study teams. Participates in all observer sessions.

14. Maintains contact with his counterparts in other departments by exchanging project abstracts and other pertinent data.

## SELECTING PRIORITY STUDY AREAS

Probably most human efforts will be further spurred or encouraged when progress can be shown. For this reason, while most areas may be expected to provide some productivity improvement, and while not all functions necessarily can be studied at the same time, it is desirable to give priority for review to those departments that are expected to provide the maximum improvement in a minimum of time. Those knowledgeable about the operations and the cost levels normally will have some rather definite ideas about the best targets of opportunity. Consideration should be given to:

- Relative ease of accomplishment
- Importance of the function
- Magnitude of expected improvement
- Transferability of the productivity improvement techniques to other functions or departments.

## THE PIP TASK FORCE

Most PIP efforts, whether as part of a long-term program, or a short-term "burst of activity," which are directed and handled mostly by an in-house staff, are structured as part of a team or task force effort. Aside from the executive leadership, the composition of this task force probably is the primary determinant of the success of the project.

The task force should include these elements:

- The *team leader* must train the team members and direct the review.
- The *program coordinators* (see Figure 26A-2) often from both the corporate office and the division or subsidiary headquarters can provide ideas, secure some of the needed background data, summarize results, and monitor implementation.
- The *individual team members* in the proper mix or composition, including one from the department being studied; a skilled functional specialist; one from the financial department who has knowledge of the costs, their behavior, and significance of financial or accounting procedures; and one or more from other departments who are scheduled for review (to train them) or from functions that are in some way affected by the department under review.

The key to a successful study often is how effectively this diverse group or team can operate together in ferreting out an appropriate solution.

### OTHER STEPS IN THE PROGRAM

Only the basics of productivity improvement are commented upon in this chapter. Suffice it to say that the other steps in a PIP program mentioned earlier in this chapter should be pursued in a careful, analytical way. Many companies have manuals that discuss the steps from planning the reviews through monitoring progress. The American Productivity Center in Houston, Texas, may have relevant guides, or may otherwise be of assistance. The functions of planning the reviews, conducting the study, implementing the recommendations, and monitoring progress normally would be conducted just as any other analytical review of costs or operations would be.

It is desirable to monitor progress, either by each departmental project, or as to the cumulative total accomplishment. A simple line graph comparing actual savings with the original target and a tougher, revised target is illustrated in Figure 26A-3.

## 26A-6 MANAGEMENT RESPONSIBILITIES

As with any important function, the success of a productivity improvement program is aided by the support of top management. And in these days of intense global competition, a fruitful productivity improvement activity may be the difference between growth and stagnation, as well as the key to survival. That being the case, what are the responsibilities of senior management as regards a PIP? These basic steps are suggested:

1. Advise the entire organization of the commitment by senior management and departmental leaders to productivity improvements.
2. Assign sufficient resources to the program.
3. Review the major planned objectives to assure that they are consistent with the organization's goals and strategies.
4. Determine that the PIP is properly integrated into the management process. This might include such actions as: (a) making productivity improvement an element of the evaluation (and compensation) process; (b) assuring that productivity

**Figure 26A-3**   Graph—Progress in Productivity Improvement Program.

**Millions of dollars**

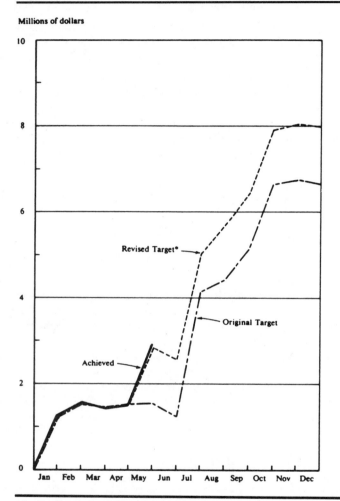

*In April more ambitious improvement goals were agreed upon. These goals are represented by the Revised Target.

improvement activity is one element of the job description; (c) possibly incorporating some productivity improvement factors in the planning and budgeting process for each department.

5. Periodically monitor progress of the program by comparing actual results with the goals set.

The controller may be one of the prime movers in encouraging a productivity improvement program. For many reasons, some psychological, it is probably desirable that a line executive head up the PIP activity. However, the controller as the chief accounting executive, and a skilled financial analyst, should accomplish these functions:

- Assure that the PIP executive and the coordinators receive in a practical and useful form the financial data they request (or that the controller can suggest tactfully would be helpful).
- Based on his or her knowledge of cost trends and behavior within the company, and on observations and talks with financial executives in other entities, suggest areas or functions for possible review.
- Review for business and financial impact or exposure (such as insurance and taxes) the major recommendations and convey his or her thoughts to the appropriate executive.
- Ascertain that productivity is measured in an acceptable manner.
- Assure that the results of any productivity improvement are reflected in the planning and control procedures, if appropriate.
- Assure that his or her staff makes a full effort on improvements in the accounting/financial departments.

## 26A-7  WORKER PARTICIPATION

The primary focus in this chapter has been on a brief and intensive organized effort, largely or entirely by inhouse personnel, to secure increased efficiency. Some alternative studies may be longer in duration and involve the assistance of outside consultants.

In an effort to increase productivity, and thus be competitive in a global economy, as most controllers would recognize, some of the emphasis in such studies has been on the need for capital expenditures or extended use of high technology. Yet such solutions take time and may require high investment. Studies in the early 1990s are showing that increased productivity can result from workers participation in the decision-making process—and often at lower cost. Employee participation, when accompanied by appropriate forms of worker compensation (such as profit sharing), can be a quicker route to improved productivity. So the message is: "Listen to the workers."

### WHITE-COLLAR OVERHEAD

Encouraging worker participation is one means increasingly used in the 90s. Another area being screened is white-collar overhead. Excessive overheads are a second reason why, in 1992, there is so much cutting of white-collar forces and the delayering of management.[8]

A 1990 survey conducted by Boston University found that overhead equaled 26% of sales for U.S. manufacturers, vs. 21% for Western Europe and 18% for Japan.[9] This is one of the types of organizational change mentioned on p. 104.

---

[8] Thane Peterson, "Can Corporate America Get Out From Under Its Overhead?," *Business Week,* May 18, 1992, p. 102.

[9] *Ibid.*

## 26A-8   SELECTED REFERENCES

Byrne, John A., Richard Brandt, and Otis Port, "The Virtual Corporation," *Business Week,* Feb. 8, 1993, pp. 98–102.

Chew, W. Bruce, "No-Nonsense Guide to Measuring Productivity," *Harvard Business Review,* Jan.–Feb. 1988, pp. 110–118.

Drucker, Peter F., "The New Productivity Challenge," *Harvard Business Review,* Nov.–Dec. 1991, pp. 69–79.

Dumaine, Brian, "Who Needs a Boss?" *Fortune,* May 7, 1990, pp. 52–60.

Frost, Halsey R., "Office Technology: Streamlining the Controller's Job," *Management Accounting,* Nov. 1989, pp. 46–49.

Hayes, Robert H., and Kim B. Clark, "Why some factories are more productive than others," *Harvard Business Review,* Sept.–Oct. 1986, pp. 66–73.

Klein, Lawrence, and Randy M. Jacques, "'Pillow Talk' for Productivity," *Management Accounting,* Feb. 1991, pp. 47–49.

Magnet, Myron, "The Truth About the American Worker," *Fortune,* May 4, 1992, pp. 48–65.

# CHAPTER 27

# Planning and Control of Cash and Short-Term Investments

**p. 735.** *Add at end of section 27-4:*

## 27-4A  USING THE COMPUTER (NEW)

The proper planning and control of cash is essential to the well-being of the company. In many circumstances, this may involve making alternative assumptions about matters such as the impact on cash receipts of special promotional sales, extension of special terms to selected major customers, or perhaps deferring payments on notes payable, and so on. Such shifts in timing of cash receipts or cash disbursements require that the planned weekly or monthly cash balance be checked for availability or that interest expense, or interest income from temporary investments, be recalculated.

These changes in cash plans can be calculated manually. But figuring the changing cash balances, the amount of temporary investments, the interest expense, or the interest income for each day, week, or month (and the changes are cumulative) is time consuming and tedious. Fortunately, there are computer software programs that can speed up the process and make the necessary computations quite easily. The output of such programs can indicate cash balances, amounts of excess cash, amounts and timing of required borrowings, as well as the impact on the income statement.

One useful cash forecasting package is the Lotus 1-2-3 spreadsheet template. It can be easily modified to reflect various time frames and changed assumptions about cash receipts and disbursements. The article by Gary J. Saunders and Ruth E. Saunders (see Selected References) provides a detailed explanation of programming and using the template. As other software packages are developed, a knowledgeable salesperson can advise you about their features, advantages, and disadvantages.

## 27-10  SELECTED REFERENCES

**p. 757.** *Add this reference:*

Saunders, Gary J., and Ruth E. Saunders, "Cash Forecast Template," *The Financial Manager,* Sept./Oct. 1989, pp. 40–45.

# CHAPTER 32

# Planning and Control of Plant and Equipment or Capital Assets

## 32-16  FOREIGN INVESTMENTS

**p. 866.**  *Add at end of section 32-16:*

When a discounted cash flow method is used to evaluate investments in another country, it is to be emphasized that the significant test is the cash flow to the *parent—* not to the foreign subsidiary or entity. Among the impediments to cash flow to the parent, which must be considered (for each year) and factored into the decision, are such items as:

- Currency restrictions
- Fluctuations in the foreign exchange rate
- Political risk
- Withholding taxes
- Inflation (as mentioned).

Limited discussion of these topics is contained in Chapter 11, Section 11-8 of the main volume.

## 32-16A  IMPACT OF THE NEW MANUFACTURING ENVIRONMENT (NEW)

Investments are made in capital assets with the expectation that the return will be sufficiently high not only to recoup the cost but also to pass the hurdle rate for such an expenditure. But the nature of the investment is changing, as are the attendant risks, in the new manufacturing environment.

The nature of this net setting is reflected in these characteristics:

- While automation is viewed as a primary source of additional income, this often is preceded by redesigning and simplifying the manufacturing process, before automation is considered. Many companies have achieved significant savings simply by rearranging the plant floor, establishing more streamlined procedures, and eliminating the nonvalue-adding functions such as material storage and handling. After this rearrangement is accomplished, then automation might be considered.

- Investments are becoming more significant in themselves. While a stand-alone grinder may cost $1 million, an automated factory can cost $50 million or $100 million. Moreover, much of the cost may be in engineering, software development, and implementation.

- The equipment involved often is more complex than formerly, and the benefits can be more indirect and perhaps more intangible. If there are basic improvements in quality, in delivery schedules, and in customer satisfaction (which seems to be the emphasis today), then methods can be found to measure these benefits. (These gains may lie in improvements or lower costs in the support functions (such as purchasing, inventory control) and greater sales volume.)

- Because of the high investment cost, the period required to earn the desired return on investment is longer. This longer-term horizon, together with the intangibles to be considered and the greater uncertainty, require the controller, budget officer, or management accountant to be more discerning in his evaluation. Usually the indirect savings and intangible benefits need to be recognized and included in the investment analysis. (The *direct* benefits may be insufficient to justify the investment.)

Some of the Selected References detail the complexities of the investment decision in the light of the new technologies.

## 32-16B   ACTIVITY-BASED COSTING (NEW)

Chapter 4A in this supplement discusses some of the changes required in the typical cost system as the result of activity-based costing. However, it should be mentioned here that one output of the cost system may be used to determine the real net cash flow from the capital investment—and that is the sales revenues less the variable costs or direct cash costs of the specific products to be manufactured. Often, the allocation methods and the depreciation system do not reflect the realities of the manufacturing process. Hence, the relevant cost of sales may be substantially incorrect, leading to an improper cash flow calculation. Alternatively, the technology costs related to the product may be in error and, the larger the technology costs, the greater the impact of misallocation of product costs. Accordingly, the controller as well as the financial analyst developing, or reviewing, the capital investment justification should ascertain that the costing system accurately mirrors the resources needed in the relevant decision.

## 32-18   BOARD OF DIRECTORS' APPROVAL

p. 870.   *Add before Section 32-19:*

### IMPACT OF GENERALLY ACCEPTED ACCOUNTING PRINCIPLES (GAAP)

Just as the discussion of activity-based costing has stimulated management accountants to recheck the cost drivers and allocation methods of the cost systems used in their companies, so also recent articles about the tendency of GAAP applications to discourage needed investment in new equipment such as computer integrated technology, is causing some thought about the accounting methodology in use in certain circumstances. Some of the alleged difficulty arises because of the practice of expensing, and not capitalizing, the start-up costs of the new project, or perhaps the tendency to focus on short-term earnings, or the failure to recognize life-cycle accounting (see pp. 287 and 299 of the basic volume). The impact of a capital expenditure on earnings may cause the small company to reflect a loss in the initial years after the investment, even though the ultimate rate of return is excellent. But, allegedly a prospective loss might deter some banks from making a loan. (A diligent bank will carefully examine the cause of any expected loss.) This brings us to a consideration of what information should be provided to the board of directors and top management about the impact of new product development or major capital expenditures on the *earnings* of the company. It has nothing to do directly with the rate of return or project justification; these are separate considerations. It does relate to making the decision-makers aware of the profit impact of capital investments and the related costs.

Perhaps these three supplemental forecast earnings statements may be useful to an informed management when considering any *major* expenditure (as well as for the purpose of obtaining necessary financing):

1. A statement of estimated income and expense without the new investment—for a number of years in the future.

2. A statement of estimated income and expense, with the new investment, using GAAP (with emphasis on start-up expenses and depreciation)—if that is a point to emphasize.

3. A statement of estimated income and expense, with the new investment, with a modified or alternative capitalization and depreciation practice.

These are illustrated in Figures 32-8A through 32-8C.

Figure 32-8A shows the anticipated decline in the operating profit of the Electronics Division without the investment under consideration (new manufacturing equipment also having additional capacity).

Figure 32-8B reflects the tremendous increase in operating profit, after the first two years, by making the investment in Project X. It also shows the effect of the write-off, in the years of incurrence of the start-up costs, and the depreciation of the capital asset cost of $1,500,000 over a five year life (straight line depreciation, with a one-half year of depreciation in 19XX). The use of a generally accepted accounting practice involving immediate write-off of start-up costs in the years of occurrence, and

**Figure 32-8A** Statement of Estimated Income and Expense Without Project X Investment.

**The Johnson Company**
**Electronics Division**
STATEMENT OF ESTIMATED INCOME AND EXPENSES
WITHOUT PROJECT X INVESTMENT
19XX THROUGH 19X6
($ IN THOUSANDS)

| Item | Year 19XX | 19X1 | 19X2 | 19X3 | 19X4 | 19X5 | 19X6 |
|---|---|---|---|---|---|---|---|
| Net sales | $2,500 | $2,400 | $2,100 | $1,900 | $1,700 | $1,500 | $1,200 |
| Cost of sales | 1,500 | 1,440 | 1,300 | 1,200 | 1,100 | 1,050 | 1,000 |
| Gross profit | 1,000 | 960 | 800 | 700 | 600 | 450 | 200 |
| Selling expense | 200 | 200 | 200 | 200 | 200 | 200 | 200 |
| General and adm. expense | 100 | 100 | 90 | 90 | 90 | 90 | 80 |
| Operating profit or (loss) | $ 700 | $ 660 | $ 510 | $ 410 | $ 310 | $ 160 | $ (80) |

**Figure 32-8B** Statement of Estimated Income and Expense with Project X Investment Using Current Accounting Practices (GAAP).

**The Johnson Company**
**Electronics Division**
STATEMENT OF ESTIMATED INCOME AND EXPENSE
WITH PROJECT X INVESTMENT
USING CURRENT ACCOUNTING PRACTICES (GAAP)
19XX THROUGH 19X6
($ IN THOUSANDS)

| Item | Year 19XX | 19X1 | 19X2 | 19X3 | 19X4 | 19X5 | 19X6 |
|---|---|---|---|---|---|---|---|
| Net sales | $2,500 | $2,700 | $3,200 | $4,000 | $5,000 | $6,000 | $7,000 |
| "Cost of sales" | 1,500 | 1,620 | 1,920 | 2,400 | 2,500 | 3,000 | 3,500 |
| "Gross profit" | 1,000 | 1,080 | 1,280 | 1,600 | 2,500 | 3,000 | 3,500 |
| Selling expense | 200 | 200 | 200 | 200 | 200 | 200 | 250 |
| General and administrative expense | 100 | 100 | 100 | 100 | 100 | 100 | 100 |
| Operating profit before start-up expenses and additional depreciation | 700 | 780 | 980 | 1,300 | 2,200 | 2,700 | 3,150 |
| Start-up expenses | 500 | 100 | — | — | — | — | — |
| Additional depreciation | 150 | 300 | 300 | 300 | 300 | 150 | — |
| Operating profit | $ (50) | $ 380 | $ 680 | $1,000 | $1,900 | $2,550 | $3,150 |

commencement as early as possible of depreciation charges on a straight line 5 year basis, (not on a per unit of output), causes an operating loss in 19XX and a severe reduction in operating profit in 19X1.

Figure 32-8C shows the impact of a less conservative accounting practice—the immediate capitalization of the start-up costs, with the subsequent amortization of the charge over a two-year period of operation, and the deferment of immediate depreciation of the capital assets, also for a two-year period, and a subsequent write-off over a five-year period. Such a practice avoids an operating loss in the first year of operations and avoids a large reduction in the operating profit of the second year of operation—with the heavier additional costs being deferred until there is a significant pick-up in sales and operating profit (before such additional charges).

Providing such data to the Board of Directors advises them of the impact on expected operating profit of the proposed investment on two different accounting bases. This information would be in addition to that listed on p. 868. It rounds out the financial picture and perhaps avoids later questions. The annual plan and strategic plan should incorporate the effect of the expenditures on the statement of income and expense, the statement of financial position, and the statement of cash flows. This same data should be made available to the commercial banks, or other financial

**Figure 32-8C**   Statement of Estimated Income and Expense with Project X Investment and with Modified Accounting Practices.

**The Johnson Company**
**Electronics Division**
STATEMENT OF INCOME AND EXPENSE
WITH PROJECT X INVESTMENT AND WITH
MODIFIED CAPITALIZATION AND DEPRECIATION PRACTICE
19XX THROUGH 19X6
($ IN THOUSANDS)

| Item | 19XX | 19X1 | 19X2 | 19X3 | 19X4 | 19X5 | 19X6 |
|---|---|---|---|---|---|---|---|
| Net sales | $2,500 | $2,700 | $3,200 | $4,000 | $5,000 | $6,000 | $7,000 |
| "Cost of sales" | 1,500 | 1,620 | 1,920 | 2,400 | 2,500 | 3,000 | 3,500 |
| "Gross profit" | 1,000 | 1,080 | 1,280 | 1,600 | 2,500 | 3,000 | 3,500 |
| Selling expense | 200 | 200 | 200 | 200 | 200 | 200 | 250 |
| General and administrative expense | 100 | 100 | 100 | 100 | 100 | 100 | 100 |
| Operating profit before start-up expenses and additional depreciation | 700 | 780 | 980 | 1,300 | 2,200 | 2,700 | 3,150 |
| Start-up cost capitalized | 500* | 100* | | | | | |
| Additional depreciation capitalized | 150* | 300* | | | | | |
| Amortization of start-up costs (1) | | | 300 | 300 | | | |
| Amortization of capitalized depreciation (2) | | | 225 | 225 | | | |
| Additional depreciation | — | — | 300 | 300 | 300 | 150 | — |
| Operating profit | $ 700 | $ 780 | $ 155 | $ 475 | $1,900 | $2,550 | $3,150 |

*See related write-offs (1) and (2).

sources, who are asked to provide the financing. The authors suggest full disclosure of the financial statements of the annual plan and long-range plan to the financing institution, including the schedule for complete payment of the obligation.

## 32-23   SELECTED REFERENCES

**p. 884.**   *Add these references:*

Brimson, James A., "Technology Accounting," *Management Accounting*, March 1989, pp. 47–53.

Brimson, James A., *Activity Accounting: An Activity-Based Costing Approach*, New York: John Wiley, 1991.

Copeland, Tom, Tim Koller, and Jack Murrin, *Valuation: Measuring and Managing the Value of Companies*, New York: John Wiley, 1990, Chapter 10.

Hendricks, James A., "Applying Cost Accounting to Factory Automation," *Management Accounting*, Dec. 1988, pp. 24–30.

Howell, Robert A., and Stephen R. Soucy, "Capital Investment in the New Manufacturing Environment," *Management Accounting*, Nov. 1987, pp. 26–37.

Kaplan, Robert S., "Must CIM be justified by faith alone?" *Harvard Business Review*, March–April 1986, pp. 87–95.

King, Alfred M., "Let's Make America Competitive," *Management Accounting*, May 1992, pp. 24–27.

Parker, Thornton, and Theodore Lettes, "Is Accounting Standing in the Way of Flexible Computer-Integrated Manufacturing?," *Management Accounting*, Jan. 1991, pp. 34–38.

# CHAPTER 33

# Management of Liabilities

**p. 903.**  *Add after section 33-12:*

## 33-12A  LBOs; STATUS OF THE DEBT MARKET IN 1991–1992 (NEW)

In the 1980s, such factors as easy access to debt financing, undervaluation of corporate assets, a long economic expansion, and a greater recognition of the advantages of debt caused the boom in leveraged buy-outs or simply highly leveraged financing. (The benefits of LBOs, and some of the conditions that favor a successful operation are discussed in Chapter 18.) Corporate America has learned that we need debt, but as someone has said, "It's like salt in our diet: Too much is harmful, but so is too little."

Given the heavy publicity of some defaulted junk bonds, it should not be assumed that highly leveraged debt was rather uniformly incurred by much of industry. Stephen S. Roach, senior economist at Morgan Stanley & Co., made a study of leveraged debt.[6.1] In this undertaking, he divided the debt holders into two categories: (1) stable industries (which includes utilities, manufacturing, and services) that are hurt relatively less in a recession because demand for their products remains quite steady, and (2) the cyclical sectors that tend to be impacted quite hard during an economic contraction such as the United States experienced in 1991.

Stephen Roach found that 70% of the debt incurred in the 1980s was assumed by the stable sector and only 30% by the cyclical industries. Consequently, in 1989 the stable companies, on average, found it necessary to use only 25% of their cash flow to pay interest costs—up from the 16% in 1980. Moreover, the more prudent borrowers in cyclical companies needed to spend only 16.3% of cash flow to pay interest costs, not much different from the debt burden ratio in 1980. The trend of interest expense as a percent of cash flow for the two industry categories is shown in Figure 33-1A.

Roach is of the opinion that the borrowing patterns are quite different because (a) cyclical companies are well aware of the vulnerability of cash flow, and consequently are modest when it comes to incurring debt; and (b) stable industries take advantage of

---

[6.1] Kathleen Madigan, "O.K., So the Debt Spree Wasn't All That Risky," *Business Week,* Nov. 26, 1990, p. 22.

**Figure 33-1A**   Interest Expense as a Percent of Cash Flow.

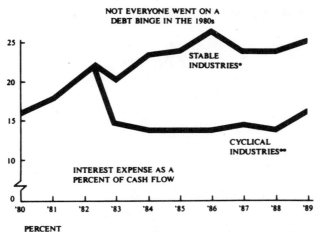

NOT EVERYONE WENT ON A
DEBT BINGE IN THE 1980s

STABLE
INDUSTRIES*

CYCLICAL
INDUSTRIES**

INTEREST EXPENSE AS A
PERCENT OF CASH FLOW

PERCENT
* INCLUDES NONDURABLE MANUFACTURING, UTILITIES, AND SERVICES
** INCLUDES MINING, CONSTRUCTION, DURABLE MANUFACTURING,
TRANSPORTATION, COMMUNICATIONS, AND TRADE
DATA: MORGAN STANLEY & CO.

*Source* Reprinted from November, 26, 1990 issue of *Business Week* by special permission, copyright © 1990 by McGraw-Hill, Inc.

the U.S. tax code that favors debt over equity. While he thinks there can be difficulties in some cyclical segments (such as retail trade, where the debt burden is 21.1% of cash flow)[6.2] the fear of debt may not be warranted.

Different executives will appraise the national economic impact of debt quite differently. That is one reason why the prudent financial executive, including the controller, should rather constantly keep informed about the status of the debt market and how it could influence the financial plans of his company and industry. Thus, in the beginning of 1991, here are some indicia about the condition of the U.S. credit markets from several viewpoints:

- *Credit quality has deteriorated.* In the judgment of one eminent source, Henry Kaufman, the credit quality of American corporations, even throughout the recent expansion, now ended, has deteriorated.[6.3] As an example, interest payments require 28% of the corporate cash flow of nonfinancial corporations as compared to 20% early in the expansion cycle. Moreover, publicly offered corporate bonds with credit ratings below A now account for 47% of such total outstanding debt as contrasted with 30% in the depth of the 1982 recession. Also, as reflected in Figure 33-1B, interest payments as a % of cash flow for all U.S. corporations has increased to 42% in the 1989–1990 time period, in sharp contrast to the approximate 5% in 1946.[6.4]

---

[6.2] *Ibid.*

[6.3] Henry Kaufman, "The Great Debt Overload Will Keep the Recovery Feeble," *Fortune,* Dec. 31, 1990, p. 23.

[6.4] "1989: A Year to Cherish," *The Babson Staff Letter,* Dec. 29, 1989, p. 2. Used with permission.

**Figure 33-1B**    Interest Payments as a Percent of Cash Flow.

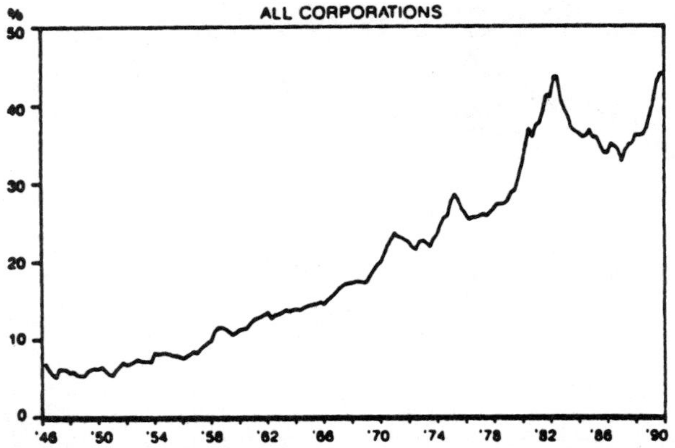

*Source: The Babson Staff Letter,* December 29, 1989, p. 2. Used by permission.

- *Junk bond yields have soared.* The yield of junk bonds can mirror the expected default or restructuring rate among this lower class of borrowings. The average yield on 20 widely held noninvestment grade bonds tracked by Donaldson, Lufkin, Jenrette Securities Corp. has risen to 20.5%. Such a yield, and the related wide gap over the rate on seven-year treasury notes, indicates that investors will buy junk bonds only if the yields offered are expected to offset the risks of defaults or restructuring. Such defaults are occurring at a 7% rate of all junk bonds outstanding as compared to the 3.6% experienced in the past two decades.[6.5] The spread in late 1990 seems to be allowing for an extraordinary high default rate of 15%.

     The yields on junk bonds are quite volatile as the speculators appraise the impact of a recession or a recovery on junk bonds. Thus, on March 1, 1991, the First Boston Corp. index of 350 junk bonds posted a total return of 8.6% for the month of February, following a return of 2.6% in January—bringing the year-to-date gain to 11.6%.[6.6]

- *Many lenders feel restricted in their granting of loans.* Because of write-downs of real estate loans, LBO loans, and loans to third world countries, many banks, insurance companies, and thrift institutions are under severe capital constraints. With the tremendous drop in the value of their equity and bond investments, they are having difficulty in attracting new equity funds and are limited in their capacity to lend.

As a result, some reasonably conservatively financed companies are finding it difficult to borrow funds at reasonable rates.

The debt binge of the 1980s is being followed by a much more conservative cycle. Perhaps this will give rise to increased savings, lower financing costs, and finally a

---

[6.5] George Anders and Constance Mitchell, "Junk Bond Yields Go Through the Roof," *The Wall Street Journal,* Oct. 10, 1990, p. C1.
     [6.6] Tom Petruno, "Junk Bonds Are Hot, But So Is Money Fueling the Rally," *Los Angeles Times,* p. D1.

more balanced debt picture. The financial executive should be aware of the cycle as he plans the financial strategy for his company.

Indeed, already in 1992, the evidence is clear. With the dual advantage of low interest rates and a bull stock market, many companies are taking advantage of the favorable markets. A great number of companies deep in debt are refinancing with a resulting substantial interest savings. And others are easing the debt load through new stock offerings.

Most fortunate among the debt-heavy companies are those whose interest rate is pegged to the U.S. prime rate, or the London interbank offered rate (LIBOR), used by banks dealing in U.S. currency held in Europe. Thus, RJR Nabisco, with rates pegged to LIBOR in 1992 is paying only 5% on its $3.5 billion in bank loans compared with the 12.3% RJR paid in 1989.[6.7]

Some managements think the best way of reducing debt is by selling new shares of stock. It is estimated that a raft of new stock offerings by many companies, large and small, will help reduce corporate debt to about 46% of capital by the end of 1992.[6.8] Even General Motors in late April 1992 announced that it is seeking clearance from federal securities regulators to issue as much as $2.9 billion of new stock for the purpose of "repairing its battered balance sheet and bolster its under-funded pension trust." This is the company's first issue of basic common shares since 1955.[6.9]

However, the accumulated debt of the 1980s may require more than a year or two to work it down to acceptable levels. Now that the excessive debt is being reduced, a great many CEO's are of the opinion that LBO's really didn't pay, and that management squandered its attention on short-term financial concerns.

**p. 913.** *Add after section 33-21.*

## 33-21A MANAGING LIABILITIES— SOME PRACTICAL STEPS (NEW)

The main volume discusses the objectives of liability management and, among other things, provides some of the standards to measure the amount of current debt as well as long-term debt. While the concerns of the controller and other financial executives have been addressed, perhaps it will be helpful to summarize some of the desirable steps in properly managing liabilities. Because of the differing nature of the various types of liabilities, it is practical in the accounting, planning, and control activities to treat each group separately. Here, then, are some suggestions as to what the controller might do to assist, in properly managing the liabilities:

*Current Liabilities*

1. *Plan* the liabilities by month or quarter or year as may be applicable (as in the annual business plan or longer term strategic plan). This can be accomplished after the various assets levels (cash, receivables, inventories, plant, and equipment)

---

[6.7] Larry Light, et al., "A Stampede for Cheaper Money," *Business Week,* Jan. 20, 1992, p. 27.

[6.8] *Ibid.*

[6.9] Joseph B. White, "GM is Planning $2.9 Billion Issue of New Stock," *The Wall Street Journal,* April 27, 1992, pp. A3–A4.

are planned and when the operational plans (sales, manufacturing expenses, direct labor, direct material, selling expense, G&A) are completed.

It is practical to group the current liabilities according to the categories to be identified in the Statement of Estimated Financial Position, such as accounts payable, accrued salaries and wages, accrued expenses, accrued income taxes, notes payable.

The accounts payable plan or budget, when finalized, for the annual plan might appear as in Figure 33-11. The budget or plan for all current liabilities, by quarter, for the annual plan could be somewhat as in Figure 33-12. Note that certain pertinent ratios are shown.

2. *Test* the plan for compliance with credit agreements or other internally developed standards such as current ratio, inventory turns, net working capital, and industry average or competitor performance. If necessary, modify the plan.

3. *Analyze* each line item for ways to reduce the obligation, for example, use of JIT inventories to reduce accounts payable or notes payable. "What if" analyses of actions on other assets (terms of sale, etc.) or liabilities can be made to improve the status, if warranted. Take any appropriate action.

4. *Monitor* the monthly or quarterly balances for any unfavorable developing trends, and take appropriate action.

5. *Issue* the appropriate control or informational reports, such as to the supervisor of accounts payable, board of directors, or creditors. This might include updating the projected debt status to the year end.

6. When appropriate, as in major developments, *revise* the financial plan.

### Long-Term Liabilities

1. *Plan* the long-term debt, by appropriate category, as in Figure 33-10 of the main volume, for the annual plan, or strategic plan, based on the commentary or factors reviewed in the chapter.

2. *Test* the plan, before finalizing, against credit agreement requirements, or standards for debt capacity, including that which might exist under the least favorable business conditions which are likely to prevail in the planning period. Adjust the plan, if required.

3. *Monitor* actual performance or condition periodically during the plan term for unfavorable developments, and take appropriate action.

4. *Report* on the financial condition and outlook to the appropriate interests (bankers, bondholders, board of directors, etc.).

### As to All Indebtedness Items

1. Review the accounting to ascertain that GAAPs are followed, to the extent practical.

2. Periodically have the internal controls checked to assure the system is functioning properly. (See also Chapter 9 in the main volume on this subject.)

3. Keep reasonably informed on the status and probable trend of the debt market, and the new debt instruments, both short- and long-term. If appropriate, this includes foreign markets. Such information may be gained from informal

Figure 33-11  Accounts Payable Budget.

**The New York Company**
ACCOUNTS PAYABLE BUDGET
FOR THE YEAR ENDING 12/31/XX
(DOLLARS IN MILLIONS)

| Item | 1st Quarter | | | | Year |
| --- | --- | --- | --- | --- | --- |
| | Jan. | Feb. | March | Total | 19XX |
| Balance, beginning of month | $21,600 | 29,800 | 19,500 | 21,600 | $ 21,600 |
| Add: | | | | | |
| Purchases—Raw Materials and Parts | 14,300 | 12,400 | 13,600 | 40,300 | 149,800 |
| Purchases—Capital Items | 9,500 | 1,500 | 1,000 | 12,000 | 20,000 |
| Subtotal | 23,800 | 13,900 | 14,600 | 52,300 | 169,800 |
| Expenses— | | | | | |
| Manufacturing | 4,800 | 4,300 | 4,500 | 13,600 | 52,400 |
| Selling | 2,100 | 2,000 | 2,300 | 6,400 | 25,900 |
| R&D | 1,200 | 1,400 | 1,500 | 4,100 | 15,000 |
| General and Administration | 1,900 | 1,900 | 1,900 | 5,700 | 22,800 |
| All Others | 100 | 200 | 100 | 400 | 1,400 |
| Total Additions | 33,900 | 23,700 | 24,900 | 82,500 | 287,300 |
| Deduct: | | | | | |
| Payments—Raw Materials and Purchased Parts | 13,600 | 14,400 | 12,900 | 40,900 | 161,700 |
| —Capital Items | 1,500 | 9,500 | 1,500 | 12,500 | 20,000 |
| —Operating Expenses | 10,600 | 10,100 | 11,200 | 31,900 | 124,200 |
| Total Deductions | 25,700 | 34,000 | 25,600 | 85,300 | 305,900 |
| Balance, End of Month | $29,800 | 19,500 | 18,800 | 18,800 | $ 3,000 |

Figure 33-12   Summary—Current Liability Plan.

## The New York Company
### SUMMARY—CURRENT LIABILITY BUDGET
### FOR THE PLAN YEAR ENDING 12/31/XX
(DOLLARS IN MILLIONS)

| Item | Estimated Balance 12/31/XX−1 | Plan Year Ending 12/31/XX Quarter | | | |
|---|---|---|---|---|---|
| | | 1 | 2 | 3 | 4 |
| Notes Payable—Banks | $ 4,700 | 4,100 | 3,600 | 3,000 | $ 2,000 |
| Current Maturities—Long-Term Debt | 1,500 | 1,400 | 1,300 | 1,200 | 1,200 |
| Accounts Payable | 21,600 | 18,800 | 17,400 | 10,600 | 3,000 |
| Accrual Salaries and Wages | 5,800 | 5,200 | 6,400 | 6,900 | 7,400 |
| Accrual Income Taxes | 1,400 | 2,300 | 2,500 | 2,500 | 1,500 |
| Other Accrued Items | 800 | 700 | 600 | 600 | 500 |
| Total | $35,800 | 32,500 | 31,800 | 24,800 | 15,600 |
| **Selected Ratios/Balances** | | | | | |
| Current Ratio | 1.9 to 1 | 2.2 to 1 | 2.4 to 1 | 2.4 to 1 | 2.5 to 1 |
| Quick Ratio | .50 to 1 | .70 to 1 | .70 to 1 | .80 to 1 | 1.1 to 1 |
| Net Working Capital | $68,020 | 71,500 | 76,320 | 59,520 | $39,000 |

discussions with commercial bankers as well as investment bankers. Perusal of financial and business literature or periodicals also may be helpful.

Additionally, the controller and other financial executives should be sensitive as to the impact of new debt issues on the holders of existing debt.

By following these few common-sense practices, there should be no unpleasant surprises regarding the management of liabilities.

## 33-22 SELECTED REFERENCES

**p. 913.** *Add these references:*

Light, Larry, Leah Nathans Spiro, and Wendy Zellner, "A Stampede for Cheaper Money," *Business Week,* Jan. 20, 1992, pp. 26–27.

Teitelbaum, Richard S., "LBO's Really Didn't Pay, Say the Chiefs," *Fortune,* Aug. 26, 1992, pp. 73–76.

# CHAPTER 34

# Management of Shareholders' Equity

**p. 930.** *Add at end of section 34-12:*

## 34-12A  MANAGING THE CAPITAL STRUCTURE (NEW)

Section 34-12 provides guidance in allocating required funds annually between debt and equity. The disposition depends on the urgency of attaining a given preferred capital structure, or meeting debt indenture constraints, or other limitations. But managing the capital structure involves more than allocating the new capital needs between debt and equity. It also includes watching for signals that funding problems are slowly (or faster) developing, as well as providing safeguards against unwarranted action by the suppliers of funds.

A few of the steps that might be taken by financial management to avoid being caught off guard could include these:

- *Be sensitive to those product lines which provide the highest return on capital as compared to those that consume or require relatively heavy amounts of capital, and produce a low rate of return.*

   Thus, if a small share of the products requires, say, 70% of the new capital needs, and provides at least 70% of the return on capital, then the situation seems satisfactory. If, however, the products consuming 70% of the capital supply but a small return, then the matter requires careful monitoring. Perhaps a hurdle rate is needed by product line, or geographical area, or other factor. Then, careful estimates of requirements, by year, and expected return, by year, are made. Finally, actual performance then should be monitored to see if the expected increasing yields are forthcoming. Of course, conservatism is required in predicting the capital requirements as well as the yield.

- *Continuously monitor the equity markets in an effort to judge when new equity should be acquired.*

   There are several stock market indicators to be followed which provide clues on the strength of the market, whether the market is overvalued, and whether new capital stock may be sold without diluting earnings. Included are these:

136

— The S&P 500 price earnings ratio, as well as the p/e of the company stock.

— The S&P 500 dividend yield and the yield of the company security.

— Price-to-book ratio. Typically the price of a stock is considerably higher than its book value. One major reason is inflation, since book value understates the replacement cost of the underlying assets. Since about 1950, the S&P Industrials index has moved in a wide band defined in market bottoms as one times book value, and 2.5 times book value near market tops.

So this ratio may be a signal as to whether the market is overvalued. This price-to-book measure sometimes is less significant than others due to the influence of large stock buy-back programs, corporate restructuring, or merger frenzy.

The market breadth—changes in the Dow Jones average vs. the S&P 500 or the Nasdaq index.

The relative trading volume. A high volume of, say, more than 200 million shares traded is said to be the sign of a strong market. Such factors, as well as the advice of investment bankers, may aid management in deciding on the approximate timing of a new stock issue.

- *Be careful in the search for the lowest cost sources of capital.*

  Not only must the cost be competitive, but the method and terms should be acceptable. Thus, in a private placement, perhaps the provisions should include a buy-back option to avoid the creation of a major voting block. Or maybe the acquisition of a cash-heavy source (existing cash balances and high cash flow) may be feasible.

- *Periodically check the cost of carrying current assets vs. the return.*

  Must a switch be made from asset intensive activities to low-cost service type business?

- *Analyze existing investment in assets for sales candidates or improved utilization possibilities.*

  Strategic planning implies more than calculating the changes in each asset category each year, based on expected operations and existing turnover rates. It requires an analysis of turnover to see where improvements can be made (e.g., use of JIT inventory methods) or idle assets, such as land which may be sold.

- *Relate predictable seasonal asset investment patterns, or cyclical ones, to incentives so as to reduce capital requirements.*

  Customers can be given special terms for early orders or early payment. Or, if an economic upturn is anticipated, this knowledge can be used to advantage in inducing earlier-than-usual orders.

Proper strategic planning should look beyond operational expectations to wise asset usage (and prudent use of supplier credits).

* **p. 995.** *Add new chapter:*

# CHAPTER 35A

# Improving Financial Accounting and Reporting (New)

## 35A-1  SOME RELEVANT BACKGROUND

The field of accounting may be grouped or classified in these categories: management accounting, tax accounting, financial accounting (and reporting), not-for-profit accounting, international accounting, national income accounting, and certain specialized areas of accounting. A brief review of these areas follows.

- *Management Accounting.*  Management accounting is internal accounting specifically designed to meet the informational needs of managers. It consists of data used in making business decisions, and in the planning and control of operations at various administrative levels of a business enterprise or a not-for-profit organization. This is the type of information emphasized in this volume of *Controllership,* encompassing as it does, the activities of the management accountant. Such data is much more detailed than is considered appropriate or necessary for much external financial reporting—even though the same system often accumulates and processes the same accounting information for both management and external purposes.

- *Tax Accounting.*  Tax accounting relates to the accumulation and analysis of appropriate data needed by individuals, corporations or other entities for preparing the tax returns and reports needed to comply with tax laws and regulations, especially the U.S. Internal Revenue Code, and various state, local and international taxing authority laws.

- *Financial Accounting (and Reporting).*  A more precise but cumbersome title for this category would be *general purpose external financial accounting and reporting.* This branch of accounting is concerned with general purpose financial statements of both business enterprises and not-for-profit organizations. The data are identified as general purpose external financial statements because several groups have common interests and common informational needs. These entities include investors, creditors, and other resource providers. It should be noted that these groups generally lack the power to compel the entity to supply the accounting data they think they need. They must rely on information made available by the entity.

- *Not-for-Profit Accounting.*  This category includes educational, charitable, eleemosynary, and governmental organizations whose goals are different than business, and whose informational needs also may be quite different.

- *International Accounting.*  This group includes global or multinational or transnational companies where differing accounting practices or standards for various countries must be used and often harmonized.

- *National Income Accounting.*  This system relates to the *nation's* economic system and such segments as production, consumption, and capital formation. Gross domestic product (GDP) is related to net sales abroad, and to public and private consumption. Information is developed to guide fiscal and monetary policy, and to relate the impact of relationships among households, government, and foreign trade. It is statistically oriented and is used in activities and studies of the U.S. Department of Commerce.

- *Specialized Areas of Accounting.*  Finally, the last category of accounting relates to those industries and activities that have special accounting or reporting problems, and accordingly must supplement the general purpose accounting phases with specialized supplemental practices.

It is to be noted that the controller, as the chief accounting official, often is concerned with all of these types of accounting. And while his or her involvement may be the least in accumulating data for incorporation in the national income accounting, it is especially concentrated in both management accounting and general purpose financial accounting. The controller has a large responsibility in seeing that (a) management has the accounting data for its needs in business decisions, especially planning and control; and (b) for the timely issuance of proper financial data to the general public.

## 35A-2  EVOLUTION OF ACCOUNTING PRINCIPLES AND PRACTICES

In the management accounting area, the controller and other accounting executives operate in an environment where sufficient leeway or flexibility exists so that financial data can be analyzed, classified, and presented to meet the needs of the management. For example, in evaluating capital expenditures, the impact on net income might be reflected as in Figure 32-8B, using "generally accepted accounting principles." Yet, if such a presentation did not make clear the complete story deemed essential, the controller might have prepared an income statement, similar to Figure 32-8C, using other modified accounting. Communicating certain opinions usually is quite easy.

But communicating to the general public or others who need general purpose financial statements often presents problems of comparability and standards. Most such statements refer to being prepared "in accordance with generally accepted accounting principles."

Yet the term "accounting principles" for a long period was somewhat elusive. Accordingly, different organizations or individuals—all accounting oriented—developed their version of what was variously called principles, standards, postulates, conventions, or concepts. During an extensive period, beginning in the 1937–1942 era, much public discussion took place as to the nature of accounting principles.

But even as late as the 1970s, none of the statements had come to be accepted or relied upon as the definitive statement of accounting's basic principles. There were essentially two schools: One group believed that accounting principles were generalized or drawn from practice without reference to a systematic or theoretical foundation. Another school was of the opinion that accounting principles are based on a few fundamental premises that, together with the principles, provide a framework for solving the accounting problems encountered in practice. It has been largely through the efforts of the Financial Accounting Standards Board (FASB) that a conceptual framework for financial accounting and reporting was developed. Since this initial effort in 1976, there has been continued improvement and development of other FASB statements.[1]

In the late 1980s and early 1990s, there have been renewed calls for improvement in financial statements and reporting.

## 35A-3   RECENT EFFORTS TO IMPROVE FINANCIAL ACCOUNTING AND REPORTING

The Concepts Statement No. 1 "Objectives of Financial Reporting by Business Enterprises" issued by the FASB in November 1978 states:

> Financial accounting and reporting is not an end in itself but is intended to provide information that is useful to present and potential investors, creditors, other resource providers, and other users outside an entity in making rational investment, credit, and similar decisions about it.

A good reporting system makes possible the efficient allocation of capital that in turn fuels economic growth under the private enterprise system. Capital markets depend on reliable financial information to operate properly. Moreover, to carry the process a step further, the financial decision makers depend upon the independent auditor for assistance that information is indeed reliable. For the above-stated objective of financial accounting and reporting to be effective, the user must believe the process is sound. Highly publicized business failures raised questions not only about financial statements themselves but also about the effectiveness of the independent audit function, as well as the integrity, objectivity, and competence of independent auditors and the self-regulatory system under which the system exists. Hence, the American Institute of CAPs was wise, in its undertaking in 1993 an effort to review

---

[1] See *Accountant's Handbook, Seventh Edition,* D. R. Carmichael, Steven B. Lilien, and Martin Mellman (eds.), Chapter 1, (New York: John Wiley & Sons, 1991) for a comprehensive discussion of the evolution.

and improve financial reporting, to take a broad viewpoint and consider these five aspects of the process:[2]

- Improving the prevention and detection of fraud.
- Enhancing the utility of financial reporting to those who rely on it.
- Assuring the independence and objectivity of the independent auditor.
- Discouraging unwarranted litigation that inhibits innovation and undermines the profession's ability to meet evolving financial reporting needs, and
- Strengthening the accounting profession's disciplinary system.

From the standpoint of the controllership function, the remainder of this chapter relates to the more narrow topic of improving the usefulness of financial reporting.

## 35A-4    THE JENKINS COMMITTEE—THE SPECIAL COMMITTEE ON FINANCIAL REPORTING

In 1991 the board of directors of the AICPA appointed a Special Committee on Financial Reporting, also known as the Jenkins Committee, to take a fresh look at financial reporting. The Board charged the Committee as follows:[3]

> The special Committee should recommend (1) the nature and extent of information that should be made available to others by management and (2) the extent to which auditors should report on the various elements of that information. In developing its recommendations, the Special Committee should (1) determine the understanding of the information currently provided by financial statements and the perception of assurances provided by auditors and (2) evaluate the full range of information and assurances that should be made available.

The Jenkins Committee consists of 11 senior representatives from various accounting firms, 2 senior representatives from industry, and a well-known academic. To assist the effort, the FASB, the AICPA, and some of the large accounting firms have provided staff support. Moreover, representatives of the FASB and the SEC attend many of the Committee meetings.

That there is general support for the objectives of the Jenkins Committee is reflected in many widespread comments from various committees, study groups and individuals concerning financial statement deficiencies. Perhaps these piecemeal short statements are indicative:

- In their present form, financial statements are seriously incomplete.
- It is time to commit to enhancing the relevancy, usefulness, and credibility of corporate reporting.

---

[2] Board of Directors of the American Institute of CPAs, "Meeting the Financial Reporting Needs of the Future: A Public Commitment from the Public Accounting Profession." *Journal of Accountancy,* August 1993, p. 17.

[3] Gaylen N. Larson, "A Crisis of Confidence in Financial Reporting," *Management Accounting,* Feb. 1994, p. 52.

- There is a growing irrelevance of conventional financial reporting in this new information age.
- Historically, financial statements have focused on how management has used the resources provided to it, but for the most part, financial statements do not disclose plans or forecasts—or risks and uncertainties facing the business.

In developing its recommendations, the Committee is following a practice of seeking out the view of various users, including equity investors and their advisors, creditors and their advisors, and groups representing these interests. Documents written by investors and creditors have been studied and analyzed.

The issues being considered by the Jenkins Committee vary greatly in nature. Some relate to nonfinancial information, forward-looking information, possible new accounting bases, segmented data, graphic displays, comparison of actual versus planned performance, and disclosures in footnote form.

Some of the areas being examined regarding adequate disclosure include these:[4]

- *Nonfinancial Information*

  Mission of the company

  Company objectives and strategies

  Key nonfinancial statistics used by management to run the business, e.g., average compensation per employee, prices of products or services

  Description of industry structure

- *Segment Information*

  Financial and nonfinancial information for each business segment

  Ditto for each material geographic region that presents significantly different uncertainties, risks, etc.

- *Leading indicators*

  Identity and future effect on key trends

  Factors or conditions management considers critical to achieving the broad company objectives

- *Accounting Issues*

  Should material noncancellable leases currently classified as operating leases by lessees be recognized as assets?

  Should nonoperating assets and liabilities be measured at current market value?

- *Issues of Display*

  Should the three categories of earnings—core earnings, net income and comprehensive income—be displayed in the income statement?

  If income statement should display core earnings, should the statement of cash flows display data such as cash flows?

---

[4] For a more extensive listing of issues under consideration, *see Ibid* pp. 53–54.

- *Issues of Interim Reporting*

  Should segment information be presented quarterly?

  Should quarterly statements be a part of regular financial reporting?

  Should interim financial statements consist of a complete set of statements, including condensed notes?

## 35A-5  AS AN EX-CONTROLLER SEES IT

To reiterate a statement made earlier regarding the controllership function, the chief accounting officer is involved with most of the types of accounting which are outlined. However, a great deal of time typically is directed to (a) management accounting and (b) general purpose external financial accounting and reporting. The growing professionalism of most controllers, coupled with the demands on them from management for relevant and timely financial data is reflected in sophisticated financial analyses and vastly improved presentations for internal purposes.

In the area of general purpose financial statements, the roadway is not as clear. Most of us have experienced situations in which financial statements "prepared in conformity with generally accepted accounting principles" didn't reflect what the user wanted to know. Or didn't disclose the extent of non-operating facilities or their impaired value. And we have recognized that in some situations the cost basis accounting was simply inadequate. Many controllers of public companies recognize the need for improvement in public reporting.

There is continuing progress in the nature of financial data being disclosed and in the quality of its presentation. A perusal of some 1993 annual reports to shareholders indicates further steps in making known data concerning some of the subjects under review by the Jenkins Committee. For example, the Hewlett-Packard 1993 Annual Report, in addition to many of the usual topics reviewed, has excellent commentary on: Factors that may affect future results; risk of off-balance sheet financing; concentrations of credit risks; and estimated fair value vs. carrying value of certain financial instruments.

It is understood that some of the initial findings of the special committee have been formulated.[5] If this report or an early draft of the report of the Jenkins Committee is made available, it is hoped some of the more aggressive controllers as well as other members of the accounting profession will let their views be heard before the recommendations of the Committee are submitted to the AICPA board of directors late this spring. Continued improvement in the financial reporting process is in the best interest of all concerned—the users and the preparers.

We recognize that any additional disclosure must carefully consider:

- Competitive harm to the company
- Litigation exposure (because the entity did not achieve plan, etc.)
- The need for clearly defined safe harbors, as well as possible tort reform
- The cost vs. benefit trade-off of providing more data.

---

[5] Paul H. Rosenfield, "Progress Report—AICPA Issues Report on Information Needs of Investors and Creditors," *Journal of Accountancy,* Jan. 1994, p. 21.

## 35A-6    SELECTED REFERENCES

King, Alfred M., "Asset impairment. Is current value accounting sneaking in the back door?," *Management Accounting,* March 1994, pp. 36–39.

Larson, Gaylen N., "A Crisis of Confidence in Financial Reporting," *Management Accounting,* Feb. 1994, pp. 52–54.

Miller, Stephen H., "AICPA Announces Major Initiative to Strengthen Financial Reporting and Further Tort Reform Prospects," *Journal of Accountancy,* Aug. 1993, pp. 15–19.

# CHAPTER 36

# Reports to Shareholders

## 36-6 REPORT OF MANAGEMENT'S RESPONSIBILITIES

**p. 1016.** *Add after "Other Disclosures":*

### ONGOING CRITICISMS OF FINANCIAL DISCLOSURE

Notwithstanding the continuing increase in financial disclosures, criticism of corporate financial reporting continues, especially by regulators and security analysts. There are two areas that are usually singled out as inadequate; they are:

- The Management Discussion and Analysis (MD&A)
- Information on Business Segments.

The MD&A has become an absolutely vital part of financial reporting and many companies do an excellent job in preparing it. However, there is still a long way to go for some. The SEC has, again in 1991, commented that MD&As are, in their opinion, generally inadequate. The controller, as the key preparer of financial reports must take the lead in producing a comprehensive MD&A that gives the user a clear understanding of the condition of the business along with a comprehensive explanation of its operation. This can be done without giving away company secrets or commenting on future strategic and operating plans (although planning information would clearly be welcome). Controllers must develop and maintain a willingness to reveal all the hard information an investor needs to make an informed decision.

More information on business segments is regularly requested at analysts' meetings with top management. Most companies provide only the information mandated by Financial Accounting Standards No. 14, Financial Reporting for Segments of A Business Enterprise and No. 30, Disclosure of Information About Major Customers. Until companies disclose, and explain the condition and operating results of its major segments, in substantially more detail than is currently the practice, dissatisfaction with this aspect of the annual report will continue to be heard.

\*

In a 1993 review of the MD&A section of annual reports to shareholders, two accounting academicians reported on the improvement or lack of improvement in such a document.[1] Comments made in the executive summary include:

- The SEC still is not satisfied with the management's discussion and analysis (MD&A) sections in the annual reports of public companies. The sections are supposed to provide investors with information about predictable future events and trends that may affect the future operations of the business.

- While most companies did a good job of describing historical events, very few provided forecasts or projections that were useful and accurate.

- When prospective data were disclosed, a strong bias was found in favor of correctly projecting positive trends; but negative trends tended to be either ignored or not fully reported.

- Many companies made almost no predictions.

**p. 1017.**   *Add at the end of section 36-6:*

An example of a Summary Annual Report is the 1989 Annual Report of McKesson Corporation. This company allocated just five pages to the presentation of financial information, excluding a Highlights page on the inside front cover. There is no MD&A nor are any notes to financial statements shown. The format used in the financial section of this annual report is:

First page:

- Statement of Management's Responsibility
  (for the financial statements)
- Independent Auditors Report
- Quarterly Highlights of Revenue and Earnings
  (current and prior year)

Second page:

- Six Year Highlights by Operating Segments

Third page:

- Six Year Highlights—Consolidated Operations
                         —Consolidated Financial Position

Fourth page:

- Condensed Statements—Consolidated Income
                          —Consolidated Balance Sheet
  (for current and prior years)

---

[1] Moses L. Daua and Marc J. Epstein, "How Good Is MD&A as an Investment Tool? *Journal of Accountancy,* March 1993, pp. 51–53.

Fifth page:

- Condensed Statements of Consolidated Cash Flows
  (for current and prior years)

A reference is later made on the inside back cover as to where the corporation's Proxy Statements and Form 10K can be obtained upon request.

\* **p. 1027.** *Add before "Selected References":*

## 36-10A   IMPACT OF JENKINS COMMITTEE REPORT (NEW)

Some extensive comments about the efforts of the Jenkins Committee of the AICPA are made in Chapter 35A. While it will be some time before the final recommendations are made public, some of the probable conclusions are leaking into the press,[2] including:

- Eliminate the standard auditor's statement in the annual report (which is mainly boilerplate unless a company has a major financial problem) and instead recount in some detail any problems or potential for problems at the company.
- Require companies to report "core" and comprehensive earnings instead of merely stating companywide profit.
- Require financial statements to include so-called "soft" information such as estimates of potential competitors able to enter the industry.
- Require larger companies to issue much more financial data than smaller entities.
- Demand that companies break down financial data into more segments than at present so that investors and financial analysts could know more about the individual business segments.

And, as reported in the *Journal of Accountancy:*[3]

1. Management should not report information that would harm the company's business.
2. Management should not report information about other companies.
3. Management should not be required to provide projected financial or nonfinancial measures, but should provide information that help users made projections for themselves.
4. Management should be under no obligation to search for nonfinancial information it does not have or need to manage the business.

---

[2] Lee Beton, "Accounting Group Is Expected to Call for Increase in Data in Annual Reports," *The Wall Street Journal,* Aug. 26, 1993, p. A3.

[3] "Special committee on financial reporting," *Journal of Accountancy,* Dec. 1993, pp. 76–77.

5. Management should not be expected to disclose forward-looking information carrying a high risk of subsequent litigation.

It is also reported that the committee plans to develop a prototype financial reporting model to illustrate the application of its ideas. However, final recommendations will be made only after a survey of users is completed as to the responsiveness of the model to their needs.

# CHAPTER 38

# Reports to Governmental Agencies and Stock Exchanges

* **p. 1061.** *Add just before Section 38-5:*

## 38-4 NATURE OF DEFICIENCIES REPORTED BY THE SEC

Slowly, sometimes very slowly, the SEC is causing changes and improvements in the type and extent of information made available to shareholders. For example, based on the furor that arose over exorbitant executive pay packages, the SEC issued new regulations affecting proxy statements issued after January 1993. Improvements in both prose and charts make executive compensation information more easy to comprehend. Many shareholders, for example, are interested in knowing what total compensation is for the major executives, whether company executive pay is based on performance, among other things. The new proxy statement now usually contains these elements:

1. *A Summary Compensation Table.* It describes pay for the five highest paid executives for the past three years including salaries, bonuses, long-term compensation, and the value of company-aid perquisites such as use of automobiles, boats, planes and vacation homes.

2. *A Summary Statement on Pay Plans.* This statement from the board of directors indicates what the company is attempting to accomplish with its various pay plans.

3. *Stock Price Performance Graph.* This segment compares the price performance of the company stock with other market indexes. It is presumed that the price of the stock would move generally in the same direction as executive pay.

4. *An Option Grant Chart.* This chart or tabulation indicates how many stock options were given to executives during the current fiscal year, and the approximate value.

The SEC does not have uncontested authority as to proxy content; and 1994 may be one of the more litigious years. For example, usually the SEC provides advice to companies about what resolutions proposed by shareholders they may exclude from their proxy statements under the so-called ordinary business exemption. This exemption permits companies to limit matters that the management thinks can be best handled in the board room. It protects the company from excessive court action.

However, recently (in late 1993) the SEC has had its authority undermined by several unfavorable court rulings. For example:

- A federal district court in October ruled that the SEC couldn't ban employment-related shareholder proposals from proxy statements.

The SEC has appealed the decision.

- In a suit by the clothing and textile union, a federal district court ordered Wal-Mart Stores to include in the proxy statement a proposal seeking a report on an affirmative action and equal employment record.

So, until the courts resolve the issues, the Commission now refuses to give companies any advice until the relevant matter is resolved.

Another subject that the new SEC chairman, Arthur Levitt, is exploring is the lack of adequate information in the secondary market for municipal bonds. It is stated by many market participants that investors often do not have material and relevant facts on the value of bonds outstanding in the secondary market. So updated disclosures are under consideration.

The financial press, including *The Wall Street Journal, Business Week, Forbes,* and others, regularly publish current information on the SEC efforts.

# 38-5  REPORTING FORMS TO THE SEC

**p. 1064.**  *Add at the end of section 38-5:*

### NEW PLANS FOR EDGAR

Mandated electronic filings on EDGAR are now expected to begin in the summer of 1993, a slippage of about a year from the plan announced in December 1990. The operational phase-in will still be done by groups with the 2500 large companies going first along with the pilot group. After these initial filings are received and the system is certified operational all remaining filers will be phased into EDGAR in groups of about 1500 every six months. This general transition will probably begin in mid-1994 and be completed by the end of 1996. All filers will be required to submit paper copies to the SEC along with electronic filing for their first year on EDGAR.

Temporary EDGAR rules and forms were adopted in April 1992 to permit pilot group filers to transit from the pilot to the operational mode. These rules will be effective July 15, 1992, when the SEC begins to accept operational filings from pilot participants. These temporary rules will be in effect until the mandated filing period begins. Prior to the beginning of the mandated filing period in the summer of 1993, permanent rules and forms will be adopted governing the operational EDGAR system.

EDGARLINK software supplied free by the commission does the following:

- Submits electronically all communications including correspondence with the SEC. (EDGARLINK can be used for this purpose.)
- Converts files into ASCII format before submission to the SEC.
- Assists in building electronic files with help screens, validates the file before submission, and highlights error conditions through edit features.
- Includes data compression capability for rapid transmission of files.
- Interfaces with the SEC to change passwords and connects with the commissions E-mail system provided by CompuServe.

## GETTING ORGANIZED

The present schedule of the SEC calls for a volunteer filer phase-in schedule beginning in April 1993, with three waves through December 1993, to the end that 2,500 corporations and 800 investment management companies will be in the system by January 1994. Congress ordered this "significant test group" to file successfully for six months before the next groups are phased in, in batches of 1,500 to 2,250 each quarter, until the process is completed in 1996.

Until it is operating smoothly, the Electronic Data Gathering, Analysis, and Retrieval (EDGAR) system will require additional effort by controllers. The EDGAR rules proposal and phase-in schedules are available in the SEC's public reference room, from service bureaus that provide copies of SEC-related data, and from sources that provide companies with legal and accounting services.

Because a great deal of effort is required to prepare for electronic filing, it is suggested that the controller consider forming an EDGAR working group to evaluate resources available, secure timetables, and develop a proposed response. The group must have the technical expertise to electronically convert each document into the filing format, complete an effective review of the electronic document, execute the transmission, and confirm the receipt and acceptance at the SEC. The MIS department should have a leading role, but the legal and finance departments, the corporate secretary, and perhaps outside counsel and the independent accountants should also be involved. Because it is possible now to secure assistance from a competent SEC filer support group, the controller might consider gathering data now and securing help from the SEC before the rush starts. Each company must decide whether to "EDGARize" and file in-house or to use a filing agent.

## 38-12  SELECTED REFERENCES

* **p. 1095.**  *Add these references:*

Himelstein, Linda, and Michael Schroeder, "The SEC Resolves to Bow Out," *Business Week,* Nov. 29, 1993, p. 124.

Kristof, Kathy M., "New Proxies Spotlight Exec's Pay," *Los Angeles Times,* April 12, 1993, p. D1, D5.

O'Neil, James P., "At Long Last, Meet EDGAR," *Financial Executive,* Jan./Feb. 1993, pp. 44–48.

# CHAPTER 45

# Insurance Records and Procedures

## 45-3 SELECTING THE INSURABLE HAZARDS TO BE COVERED

**p. 1193.** *Add at end of section 45-3:*

### CHANGING NATURE OF HAZARDS

Over the last several decades several new liability exposures have come into being that must be considered for insurance protection. The most significant of these are environmental and discrimination violations.

With over 700 different elements and compounds designated as hazardous substances by the EPA, the potential liability for damage to natural resources as well as people is huge. Both civil and criminal liability could be incurred in connection with incorrect waste disposal or faulty emission control. This area deserves special consideration in assessing the liability insurance coverage the company needs to acquire.

Instances of discrimination against a protected group (or individuals within the group), or failure to comply with affirmative action, can leave a company exposed to financial liability for such violations. This exposure must be reviewed as part of the regular insurance analysis.

## 45-5 TYPES OF INSURANCE

**p. 1195.** *Add to the item listed as "Group Life, Health and Accident" the word "Pensions."*

\* **p. 1195.** *Add to the listing:*
Directors' and Officers' liability insurance.

# CHAPTER 46

# Selecting and Implementing a Financial Information System (New)

## 46-1  INTRODUCTION

The controller is primarily responsible for seeing that the financial information system meets the needs of those who receive and use its output—management, shareholders, creditors, suppliers, customers, government agencies, and stock exchanges as well as the general public.

This chapter contains a proven approach to selecting and implementing an automated financial information system (FIS). It includes an overview of reasons why financial system software should be purchased instead of developed in-house, how to thoroughly define systems requirements, an approach to preparing a Request for Proposal (RFP), ways to evaluate software, hardware, and the associated vendors, and a brief discussion of how to implement the selected system. Selection and implementation of an FIS are extremely important to an organization's financial operation. As a result, the organization must be willing to devote a substantial amount of time and effort to these activities, or hire outside consultants to assist in the process.

For the purposes of this chapter, it is assumed that the selection process includes both computer hardware and software. Many selecting organizations already have computer hardware in place. However, where possible, it is recommended that an organization select software that best meets its needs without being constrained by the hardware currently in place.

## 46-2    REASONS TO PURCHASE SOFTWARE

In general, it is recommended that software packages be purchased, instead of developed in-house, to meet the needs of an organization's financial operations. The reasons include:

- *Implementation Speed.* Packaged software generally can be implemented much quicker than software developed in-house because the software is readily available and the process of designing and coding the systems is not necessary.
- *Fewer Software Problems.* Packaged software normally has already been thoroughly tested and "debugged" before it is sold.
- *Lower Overall Cost.* The total cost of packaged software tends to be significantly less than the cost of software developed in-house. Software developed in-house normally requires a very significant investment of time and human resources.
- *Software Vendor Assistance.* Most software vendors, especially those in the mid-range (i.e., minicomputer) and mainframe market, provide ongoing support and maintenance for their software. This means that the support required from in-house information systems (IS) staff can be minimized.
- *Package Enhancements.* To maintain market position and sales, software vendors generally provide enhanced functionality and new modules.
- *Documentation.* Most software packages come with a variety of manuals including user, technical, and operations. Therefore, the acquiring organization does not have to invest in developing this type of documentation.
- *Training.* The vast majority of software vendors provide a variety of training classes for user and technical personnel.
- *Research and Development.* Software vendors are in the business of selling system solutions. To maintain (and improve) a competitive market position, they must invest a substantial amount of money in research and development. (Most organizations can't afford to invest substantial sums in improving existing in-house-developed financial systems.)
- *Information Systems Support.* In general, it is much easier to locate personnel who are familiar with packaged software and can support it than with in-house systems. Also, with in-house developed software, employee turnover presents greater problems.
- *Prevalence of Software Problems.* Software vendors normally thoroughly test their products before allowing them to be sold. In addition, packaged software is

generally used by numerous users in a wide variety of ways. Therefore, software problems (i.e., "bugs") are likely to appear relatively early in a package's life cycle. To survive in the long run, the software vendor must correct these bugs as rapidly as possible. This is not necessarily so for systems developed in-house, which are generally used only by the developing organizations. As a result, it may take years before a bug is uncovered. Also, once the bug is found, considerable time may pass before it is corrected.

- *The User Group.* Packaged software vendors tend to support and encourage user groups. Participation in these groups can be an effective means of identifying ways in which to more efficiently use the system. Also, it tends to be an effective way of encouraging the vendor to improve its software.

## 46-3   WAYS TO DEFINE SYSTEMS REQUIREMENTS

Before software is selected, the specific requirements need to be precisely defined. The application areas typically included in an FIS are:

- Budgeting
- Purchasing
- Accounts payable and check reconciliation
- General ledger
- Accounts receivable and revenue accounting
- Fixed assets
- Cost accounting
- Inventory
- Order entry and billing
- Cost accounting

If application requirements are not thoroughly defined and documented, the software selected probably will not meet the organization's needs. It will be useful to a Systems Requirements Definition (SRD) document that:

- Serves as the basis for the Request for Proposal (RFP).
- Communicates the organization's requirements to the vendors.
- Helps the selected software meet the organization's current and future needs
- Enhances the organization's understanding of each application area (e.g., accounts payable and accounts receivable) and how automation can assist in improving access to information in that area.
- Prioritizes the application areas to be automated.
- Matches requirements against the software's capabilities to determine where it is deficient, and where modifications must be developed.

There are a number of approaches that may be used to develop FIS requirements. These approaches include questionnaires, executive interviews, document reviews, and outside sources.

## QUESTIONNAIRES

Questionnaires may be used to develop a general understanding of an organization, its objectives, and the environment in which it operates. They may also be used to define major financially-oriented tasks, analyze transactions, determine major systems interfaces, and assist with the development of FIS requirements.

Prior to developing a questionnaire, the individuals preparing it (normally an FIS steering committee or some other such group) need to make sure that they have top management's support for the selection project. Without this support, it is doubtful that the questionnaire will be returned in a timely manner with complete and accurate responses.

The questionnaire should not be so long that it discourages completion. Alternatively, it should not be so brief that it does not identify specific requirements. Figure 46-1 illustrates the types of questions that can appear in the questionnaire. Note that a cover letter should be attached to the questionnaire, clearly defining its purpose, the date it is to be returned, and the importance of complete and accurate responses. Also, the cover letter should be signed by someone with authority, such as the Chief Financial Officer, Controller, or the Director of Information Systems.

## EXECUTIVE INTERVIEWS

The purposes of conducting executive interviews include:

- Developing an overall understanding of the organization—its environment and objectives.
- Defining executives information needs.
- Determining the executives opinions on the current system
- Identifying the organization's goals, objectives, and critical success factors.
- Identifying executives system expectations.
- Predicting growth areas or new needs that must be planned for by IS
- Improving executives "buy in" to the selection process.

Executive interviews should not be designed to elicit detailed information on systems specifications. Rather, they should help elicit general information needs and strategic goals and objectives of the organization.

It is important that the information and reporting needs of executives be emphasized and identified early in the selection process. Too frequently, only the needs of staff and middle management are incorporated. The resulting FIS frequently does not provide executives with the necessary reports for effectively managing the application areas.

## DOCUMENT REVIEWS

Another way to develop systems requirements is to review input forms and reports. Doing so provides the organization with a listing of its current data elements and helps to define the minimum reporting requirements of the proposed FIS.

Audit work papers often contain information that may be useful for developing system requirements. The flow charts contained in the work papers frequently provide

**Figure 46-1** Sample Questionnaire for Defining Application Requirements.

QUESTIONNAIRE TO DEFINE FIS APPLICATION REQUIREMENTS

1. For what functions are you responsible?

   _____

   _____

2. What are the primary goals of your job?

   _____

   _____

3. With what other departments do you interface?

   _____

   _____

4. What major tasks do you perform?

   _____

   _____

5. What reports do you prepare? (Please attached a sample of each report.)

   _____

   _____

6. What forms do you use? (Please attach a sample of each form.)

   _____

   _____

7. Where do these forms originate?

   _____

   _____

8. Where do these forms go when you complete them?

   _____

   _____

9. What financial information do you receive from other departments?

   _____

   _____

10. What changes do you predict will occur in your job over the next one to three years?

    _____

    _____

11. What additional information could you use?

    _____

    _____

12. What automated system do you currently utilize?

    _____

    _____

an overview of how an accounting "system" operates. Also, the work papers often contain volume estimates, such as the number of A/P checks issued and the number of customers in the accounts receivable file.

## OUTSIDE SOURCES

A final source of requirements that should be included in an SRD is the environment in which the financial organization exists. Economic trends, changes in laws and practices, and revisions to governmental regulations may all affect the reporting requirements of an FIS and, therefore, should be reviewed.

There is a cost involved in collecting systems requirements. As a result, an organization should not spend an excessive amount of time documenting them, because it may never get to the point of selecting software.

## 46-4   EXISTING SYSTEM DOCUMENTATION

After the questionnaires and executive interviews have been completed and the other sources of information reviewed, it is critical the existing manual and/or automated financial systems be documented. Included in this documentation should be the following factors:

- The key objectives of the system (e.g., maintain the general ledger and produce financial reports)
- Who supports the system
- The major system inputs, edits, controls, and outputs (i.e., reports)
- All system interfaces and special features
- The volume of transactions processed by the system
- The approximate costs of operating the system.

In addition, if the system is automated, it is important to note the hardware platform on which it operates, the language in which it is written, its age, and the approximate amount invested in the system.

The main objectives of documenting existing manual and automated systems include:

- Ensure the SRD contains, at a minimum, the features currently available, if desired
- Identify specific weaknesses in the current system
- Determine what is currently available and what is missing from the existing systems
- Document required and unnecessary reports
- Highlight procedures that are poorly defined.

## 46-5   JOINT SESSIONS

An effective and efficient means of ensuring a thorough system requirements survey is by conducting "joint sessions" with the employees who will be utilizing and supporting the system. The benefits of conducting joint sessions include development of a more complete SRD and an improved user "buy in." The steps required to conduct a joint session include:

- Prepare "straw man" requirements for each application (e.g., accounts payable). These requirements generally are based on research previously conducted by the organization, information obtained from software vendors or computer-related literature, or IS consultants.

- Distribute the requirements document to the employees interested in or affected by the specific application. (For example, the accounts payable (A/P) requirements should be distributed to the A/P supervisor and clerks and other interested accounting personnel.)

- Conduct a joint session for each application area. During these sessions, which generally are facilitated by a selection team member or a consultant, the participants are asked to:

  — Prioritize each requirement (i.e., state whether the requirement is required, desired optional, or not applicable).

  — Identify additional requirements.

After the current financial systems are documented and the joint sessions conducted, it is then time to finalize the SRD. The purpose of the SRD, which will become part of the RFP, is to communicate to software vendors the organization's systems requirements and allow the vendors to identify software products that can meet those requirements.

The SRD should be divided by application area (e.g., general ledger and accounts payable). The application area should be further divided into the following topics:

- General systems narrative
- Processing requirements
- Inquiry requirements
- Reporting requirements
- Data requirements.

The requirements should be stated as a single sentence. Figure 46-2 gives a very abbreviated example of these factors for an accounts receivable system. System requirements

**Figure 46-2**  Accounts Receivable System Requirements.

## ACCOUNTS RECEIVABLE SYSTEM NARRATIVE

The accounts receivable system should be designed to handle all of the organization's receivable and collection requirements. The system must interface with both the order entry system, to obtain billing information, and the general ledger system, to post billings, cash receipts, and bad-debt journal entries.

**Processing Requirements**

The accounts receivable system should be able to perform the following functions:

☐ Post to different revenue accounts depending on the type of service performed.

☐ Enter non-accounting data to the master file on-line.

☐ Disallow the deletion of data with an account balance greater than zero.

☐ Interface with the order entry/billing system.

*(Continued)*

**Figure 46-2**   *(Continued)*

**Inquiry Requirements**

The accounts receivable system should include the following inquiry features and capabilities:

☐ On-line review of billing and payment history

☐ Inquiry as to the status of a bill using a variety of data elements including:

- Customer name

- Customer number

- Invoice number

**Reporting Requirements**

The accounts receivable system should produce the following reports:

☐ *Accounts receivable aging report*—a report indicating the amount of time an accounts receivable balance has been outstanding.
Frequency: weekly and on demand

☐ *Cash receipts register*—a register containing information on:

- Date of receipt

- Check number

- Customer name and number

- Dollar amount

- Invoice number applied to

- General ledger account posted to

Frequency: daily and on demand

**Data Requirements**

The Customer Master File should contain the following data elements:

- Customer Name—60 alpha/numeric characters

- Customer Number—20 alpha/numeric characters

- Customer Address 1

  —Street—60 alpha/numeric characters
  —City—20 alpha characters
  —State—2 alpha characters

- Customer Address 2

  —Street—60 alpha/numeric characters
  —City—20 alpha/numeric characters
  —State—2 alpha characters

- Customer Contact 1

  —Name—40 alpha/numeric characters
  —Phone number—9 numeric characters
  —Street—60 alpha/numeric characters
  —City—20 alpha characters
  —State—2 alpha characters

documents may be from 5 to well over 100 pages per application, depending on the number and the level of detail desired. Be careful not to overdefine the requirements or make the SRD so general that it allows all software packages to meet its needs.

After completing the SRD, the prioritization of the applications should be performed. It is vital for an organization to clearly define each application in the order of importance, to help it evaluate the completed RFP and identify the factors upon which the software selection will be decided. Factors to consider when assigning priorities to applications to be automated include:

- *The impact of the system on the organization and its customers.* How many employees will come into contact with the system? Will the system affect relations with customers (as would a billing system)? How will the system benefit the selecting organization?

- *The costs and benefits of the system.* Will the system affect the organization's financial position? Can the system influence the organization's productivity? What are the total direct and indirect costs of the system?

- *The demand for the system.* Are accounting employees requesting a new system? Does senior management support the system? How long will it take to get the system implemented?

- *The dependence of the system on other systems.* Will the implementation of the accounts receivable system, for example, have to be delayed until the billing system is on-line?

## 46-6   PREPARING THE REQUEST FOR PROPOSAL (RFP)

An RFP is used to effectively communicate the FIS's requirements to software and/or hardware vendors. It is prepared after the SRD and serves the following purposes:

- Communicates the organization's systems requirements to vendors and facilitates a uniform response to those requirements.

- Requests specific commitments from vendors, such as the system's functionality, the level of support and documentation provided, the costs, and contractual arrangements.

- Serves as a tool for effectively comparing vendors. The RFP should be designed in a way that allows the selecting government organization to easily compare the proposals of various vendors.

Depending on the organization's situation, RFPs may be prepared for software, hardware, or both. However, no matter what the organization selects, the RFP must be well-structured and precise in order to elicit a clear and concise response from vendors. A vague and poorly organized RFP is likely to result in proposals that are too general and difficult to compare and are lacking details in many areas. Figure 46-3 shows a typical Contents page for an RFP.

### COVER LETTER

The cover letter notifies the hardware and/or software vendor that the organization is requesting a proposal for specific applications and/or hardware. In addition, the cover

**Figure 46-3** RFP Table of Contents.

REQUEST FOR PROPOSAL
TABLE OF CONTENTS

I. Cover Letter
II. General Information/Proposal Guidelines
III. Background Material
IV. Vendor Questionnaire
V. Vendor Cost Summary
VI. System Requirements

letter should contain the following information: important deadlines (such as the date of the bidders conference and when the proposal is due) and the projected installation and implementation dates; the overall objective of the RFP; the individual within the organization to contact with questions; and the format and content of the RFP.

## GENERAL INFORMATION/PROPOSAL GUIDELINES

The general information/proposal guidelines section contains information on how the proposal is to be completed, how the selection process will be conducted, and the importance of a concise and timely response. Also included in this section is whether site visits will be made by the organization, a statement that the cost of preparing the proposal is entirely the vendor's responsibility, that the organization reserves the right to reject any and all proposals, and that the confidentiality of the material contained in the RFP.

## BACKGROUND MATERIAL

The background material includes information about the organization that is of interest to the vendor. Generally included in this section is a description of the organization's different business functions currently being performed and by which departments; volume statistics (e.g., the number of payroll and accounts payable checks issued per month and the number of general ledger transactions); the current hardware, financial system software and modules, and operating system, if any; and the hours of operation. This information is very useful for vendors when preparing their proposals.

## VENDOR QUESTIONNAIRE

The vendor questionnaire asks a variety of questions on the vendor's background, clients, training, and growth; systems reliability, security, and performance; how modifications are handled; how reports are produced; acceptance testing and implementation schedule; data control; staffing; R&D expenditures; documentation; and hardware proposed, if any. The answers to these questions will assist the organization with determining the final vendor. This section must be extremely well-constructed and the questions concisely formulated. (See Appendix 1 for examples of vendor evaluation criteria.)

## VENDOR COST SUMMARY

In the vendor cost summary, the vendor is requested to complete a cost schedule specifying the costs of the proposed FIS. Each vendor generally is asked to provide information on recurring and nonrecurring costs over a five-year period and supplemental schedules to explain the derivation of all costs and what is included in such items as installation and maintenance fees. An example of a vendor cost summary schedule is shown in Figure 46-4.

## SYSTEM REQUIREMENTS

The system requirements section sets forth the processing, inquiry, reporting, and data requirements developed during the systems requirement definition process. Each vendor is asked to complete a matrix that contains all application requirements.

The vendor is asked to respond to the following categories for *each* requirement:

- Whether the current system can satisfy the requirement. The only acceptable responses are yes or no.
- Cross Reference (X-REF)—Where in the vendor's documentation is the requirement described.
- Comments—Any comments the vendor may have regarding the specific requirement.

Figure 46-5 reproduces a page from an accounts payable information requirements section, together with a possible vendor response.

# 46-7   DISTRIBUTION OF THE RFP

Once the RFP is completed, the organization must determine the vendors to whom it will be sent. With over 50,000 software packages available, narrowing the field can be a difficult task. However, there are some basic factors to consider.

- *Geographic location.*  The ability to receive timely support is extremely critical. Since many software vendors may not have offices located near the organization, this factor can be used to eliminate many vendors.
- *Hardware considerations.*  Many software programs run only on certain hardware configurations (e.g., IBM or Hewlett Packard hardware only). Therefore, if the organization owns hardware or has a preference for a certain manufacturer, the software options are significantly reduced.
- *Organization size.*  The size of the organization influences the size of the computer system that must be acquired. Software is generally designed to run on either microcomputers, midrange systems, or mainframes. As a result, the software vendors to which the organization may send the RFP are limited.
- *Organizational preference.*  Some organizations prefer to deal with firms that only develop software. Other organizations prefer to deal with turnkey vendors that supply both a hardware and software solution. The organization's decision in this area will influence the number of vendors to which the RFP can be sent.

**Figure 46-4**  Vendor Cost Summary.

## VENDOR COST SUMMARY

| | Year 1 | 2 | 3 | 4 | 5 | Total |
|---|---|---|---|---|---|---|
| *Recurring costs* | | | | | | |
| Hardware | | | | | | |
| CPU lease | $___ | $___ | $___ | $___ | $___ | $___ |
| Terminal lease | ___ | ___ | ___ | ___ | ___ | ___ |
| Printer lease | ___ | ___ | ___ | ___ | ___ | ___ |
| Other lease | ___ | ___ | ___ | ___ | ___ | ___ |
| CPU maintenance | ___ | ___ | ___ | ___ | ___ | ___ |
| Terminal maintenance | ___ | ___ | ___ | ___ | ___ | ___ |
| Printer maintenance | ___ | ___ | ___ | ___ | ___ | ___ |
| Other maintenance | ___ | ___ | ___ | ___ | ___ | ___ |
| Software | | | | | | |
| Software license | ___ | ___ | ___ | ___ | ___ | ___ |
| Software support | ___ | ___ | ___ | ___ | ___ | ___ |
| Other fees | ___ | ___ | ___ | ___ | ___ | ___ |
| Supplies | | | | | | |
| Disks, tapes | ___ | ___ | ___ | ___ | ___ | ___ |
| Ribbons, paper | ___ | ___ | ___ | ___ | ___ | ___ |
| Other | ___ | ___ | ___ | ___ | ___ | ___ |
| Total | $___ | $___ | $___ | $___ | $___ | $___ |
| | | | | | | |
| *Nonrecurring costs* | | | | | | |
| Hardware | | | | | | |
| CPU purchase | $___ | $___ | $___ | $___ | $___ | $___ |
| Terminal purchase | ___ | ___ | ___ | ___ | ___ | ___ |
| Printer purchase | ___ | ___ | ___ | ___ | ___ | ___ |
| Other purchase | ___ | ___ | ___ | ___ | ___ | ___ |
| Software | | | | | | |
| Software purchase | ___ | ___ | ___ | ___ | ___ | ___ |
| Installation | | | | | | |
| Freight | ___ | ___ | ___ | ___ | ___ | ___ |
| Cabling | ___ | ___ | ___ | ___ | ___ | ___ |
| Site preparation | ___ | ___ | ___ | ___ | ___ | ___ |
| Training | ___ | ___ | ___ | ___ | ___ | ___ |
| Customization | ___ | ___ | ___ | ___ | ___ | ___ |
| System initializing | ___ | ___ | ___ | ___ | ___ | ___ |
| Installation | ___ | ___ | ___ | ___ | ___ | ___ |
| Other | ___ | ___ | ___ | ___ | ___ | ___ |
| Total | $___ | $___ | $___ | $___ | $___ | $___ |
| | | | | | | |
| TOTAL | $___ | $___ | $___ | $___ | $___ | $___ |

**Figure 46-5**   Completed Accounts Payable System Requirements.

| Requirement | Response Yes | Response No | X-REF | Comments |
|---|---|---|---|---|
| 1. Enter invoices on-line. | X | | User Manual Pg.5-22 | |
| 2. Enter vendor credit memoranda future payments. | X | | User Manual Pg. 6-21 | $5,000 additional fee |
| 3. Write checks automatically based on invoice date and a predefined pay period (e.g., 30 days from invoice date). | X | | User Manual Pg.3-22 | |
| 4. Automatically process recurring payments. | | X | User Manual Pg.2-10 | |
| 5. Process and post manual checks to correct vendor and general ledger account. | X | | User Manual Pg.3-12 | |
| 6. Automatically interface with general ledger system. | X | | User Manual Pg.7-12 | |
| 7. Edit for duplicate invoice numbers to the same vendor. | X | | User Manual Pg.6-10 | $3,000 additional fee |
| 8. Allow for standard discount terms (e.g., 1/10 net 30). | X | | User Manual Pg.3-20 | |

- *Vendor characteristics.*  It is frequently possible to prescreen vendors to determine if it is appropriate to send them an RFP. This can be accomplished by calling a vendor representative, reviewing vendor literature, looking at one of the many software reference manuals such as *Datapro* or *Data Decisions,* or discussing vendors with organizations similar to yours. When prescreening a vendor, look at factors such as the vendor's stability and related experience, list prices, and flexibility.

Other means of identifying vendors that should receive the RFP include engaging a consultant experienced in hardware and software selections, reviewing computer-oriented magazines, contacting hardware vendors for lists of potential software suppliers, and networking with other organizations.

In general, the RFP should be sent to between five and ten vendors; any more than that, and the process becomes cumbersome; any fewer, and the choices become too limited. The vendor should be given sufficient time—3 to 6 weeks—to complete the RFP accurately and thoroughly.

## 46-8   REVIEW OF THE VENDOR'S COMPLETED PROPOSAL

When the proposals are returned, they should be given an initial brief review. This brief review will most likely eliminate the proposals that do not meet the organization's minimum critical needs.

In general, systems decisions should be more heavily influenced by the software, not the hardware. Therefore, the organization should first review the software proposed by the vendors. The goal of this review is to determine the two or three finalists. (The field should be narrowed to two or three, because any more makes the final selection cumbersome; any fewer leaves the organization in a risky situation. For example, if only one finalist vendor is selected and it goes out of business, the organization will have to begin the selection process again.)

There are two types of software the organization needs to evaluate: application and systems. Application software is the software that performs the functions needed by the end-user, such as generating paying invoices, preparing financial statements, and recording cash receipts. It is used to perform specific processing or computational tasks. Examples of application software include accounts payable, accounts receivable, and general ledger systems. Systems software makes it possible to utilize the application software. Included in this broad category are operating systems, database management systems, report writers, database compilers, and debugging aids.

The system requirements section of the RFP is used to review the vendor's application software. As previously mentioned, each vendor is asked to respond to each requirement. The selecting organization should tabulate these responses to determine how well the vendor's software meets the organization's needs. Use the following guidelines:

1. Prepare a spreadsheet listing all of the requirements. The spreadsheet should look exactly like the information systems requirement section displayed in Figure 46-5.
2. Determine the number of points a response is worth. For example, a "Yes" response to a "Required" requirement may be worth 10 points, but only 6 points on a desired feature. (A sample scoring scheme follows.)
3. Tally the vendor's responses.
4. Total the score by application area.
5. Determine the vendor's total score.

| Response | Required | Desired | Optional |
|---|---|---|---|
| Yes | 10 | 6 | 4 |
| No | 0 | 0 | 0 |

The spreadsheet should look exactly like the information systems requirement displayed in Figure 46-5.

The rating sheet in Figure 46-6 can be effective in evaluating the vendor responses. In addition, the organization should review the following characteristics of each vendor's application software:

- *Flexibility.* Is the software easy to modify? Will it handle the organization's needs five years from installation? Is it easy to debug? Flexibility is also an important factor to consider when reviewing systems software and hardware.

- *Documentation.* Is it easy to use? Is it accurate and thorough? Is it regularly updated? Does it describe all error messages? Are all screen formats presented? Does it clearly describe recovery procedures? Are terms defined? Who maintains it?

**Figure 46-6** Application Software Rating Sheet.

| Requirement | Required or Desired | Response Yes | No | Comments |
|---|---|---|---|---|
| 1. Enter invoices on-line. | R | | | |
| 2. Enter vendor credit memoranda on-line and apply credits to future payments. | R | | | |
| 3. Write checks automatically based on invoice date and a predefined pay period (e.g., 30 days from invoice date). | R | | | |
| 4. Automatically process recurring payments. | D | | | |
| 5. Process and post manual checks to correct vendor and general ledger account. | R | | | |
| 6. Automatically interface with general ledger system. | R | | | |
| 7. Edit for duplicate invoice numbers. | R | | | |
| 8. Allow for standard discount terms (e.g., 2/10 net 30). | D | | | |

- *Controls.* Is a clear audit trail of all transactions available? Are data validated before files are updated? Does password security exist? Are all errors flagged? Is a listing of log-on attempts provided? Are different authorization levels available? Can check digits be used? Are batch totals available?

Analyzing systems software can be more difficult than analyzing application software, because it is harder to quantify. However, the following guidelines can be useful:

1. *Determine the systems software factors to be evaluated.* For example, it is likely that the selecting organization will want to review the following:
   - The operating and database management system.
   - Multiuser capabilities.
   - Programming language utilized.
   - Compilation speeds.
   - Systems utilities such as file maintenance programs, backup and restore programs, and sorting and text editors.
   - Systems support software such as file management processors, password protection, screen formatters, report writers, and print spoolers.
   - Compatibility of the system with other software products.
   - Interactive and communications capabilities.
   - Ease of operation.

2. *Once the factors have been determined, prioritize and assign numeric values to them.* For example, the selecting organization may need a certain type of operating system. Therefore, this would receive a high priority.

3. *Review the vendor's proposal and assign a score to each factor.* Assigning scores is a somewhat subjective process. However, it is important that it be performed.

4. *Total the vendor's score in this section.* Figure 46-7 provides an example of how systems software can be prioritized and scored.

As previously mentioned, the software decision usually takes precedence over the hardware decision. However, a thorough review of the proposed hardware is extremely important to ensure that the FIS will meet the organization's needs.

The size of the proposed hardware system depends on a number of factors:

1. The volume statistics listed in the background section of the RFP.
2. The organization's projected growth rates.
3. The vendor's experience with similar clients.

Acquiring a system that meets the organization's current and future needs is extremely important. Either an in-house IS specialist or an experienced IS consultant must review the capabilities and flexibility of the proposed hardware configuration. Other hardware factors to review include:

- Central processing unit.
- Peripheral devices (such as disk and tape drives).
- Remote devices (such as communications support equipment).
- Environmental considerations.
- Flexibility and expandability.
- Systems reliability.

**Figure 46-7**   Scoring for Systems Software.

### SYSTEMS SOFTWARE

| Factor | Points Assigned | Vendor A Score |
|---|---|---|
| 1. Operating system | 18 | 16 |
| 2. DBMS | 12 | 12 |
| 3. Multiuser capabilities | 10 | 6 |
| 4. Programming language | 6 | 6 |
| 5. Compilation speed | 6 | 2 |
| 6. Systems utilities | 8 | 6 |
| 7. Systems support software | 10 | 7 |
| 8. Compatibility | 8 | 8 |
| 9. Interactive and communications capabilities | 10 | 9 |
| 10. Ease of operations | 12 | 8 |
| Total Points | 100 | 80 |

Once the hardware evaluation factors have been identified, they should be prioritized and assigned a numeric value. (This is similar to the method recommended for reviewing systems software.) Then, each vendor's proposal should be reviewed and assigned a score on each factor. The total score on hardware is then determined.

After the hardware and software have been evaluated, the next step is to evaluate the vendor(s). Depending on the system desired, this may involve reviewing a software vendor and a hardware vendor. The primary factors to consider when evaluating a vendor are:

- Product support.
- Reputation and financial stability.
- Experience.
- Product availability and enhancements.
- Documentation.
- Training.

Once the software, hardware, and vendor have been thoroughly evaluated, the selection of the finalist vendors can occur. The finalists are then analyzed further by means of reference calls, attendance at vendor demonstrations, and site visits. Because substantial amounts of time and money are invested in reviewing the finalist vendors, it is vital that the selecting organization choose vendors who can actually provide it with an FIS that meets its needs.

## 46-9   REFERENCE CALLS

One of the most important aspects of the systems selection process is making reference calls to existing systems users. Reference calls are a means by which an organization can find out what a vendor may not want them to know. For example, the organization may discover that a vendor's documentation and support are not as good as its sales literature claims.

Reference calls should be made for all finalist vendors. The calls should be directed to users with similar hardware and software configurations to get the most relevant information. Software does not run equally effectively on all hardware platforms.

The questions asked during a reference call should be both fact- and opinion-oriented. The users should be asked to list the software implemented and their overall opinion of the software. Topics to cover when making a reference call include:

| | |
|---|---|
| • Type of Organization | • Approach to System Selection |
| • Volume Statistics | • Why Vendor(s) Were Chosen |
| • Software Packages Purchased | • Ease of Operation |
| • Software Packages Implemented | • Quality of Training |
| • Ease of Installation | • Quality of Documentation |
| • Operating System | • Modifications Made |
| • Data Base Management System | • Quality of Support |
| • Hardware Installed | • Vendor Dependability |

- Hardware Dependability
- Systems Security
- Response Time
- Quality of Reports

- Unforeseen Costs
- User Group Membership/Satisfaction
- Overall Satisfaction
- Names of Other Users

The names of other systems users are important because vendors frequently provide only the names of satisfied users. Asking a user for names of other users may lead to one who is not pleased with the system.

## 46-10   DEMONSTRATION

After the reference calls have been completed, the organization should consider attending vendor demonstrations to:

- Obtain additional information on the software and vendor.
- See how the software operates.
- Review the "look and feel" of the system, its ease of use, and the level of complexity.

Prior to attending the vendor demonstration, the organization should:

- Prepare an agenda for the vendor to follow.
- Develop a feedback form for the attendees to rate various aspects of the software and the vendor (e.g., screen layout and ease of use).
- Prepare a list of questions and sample transactions for the vendor to enter into the system (e.g., matching a purchase order and invoice).

It is important to remember that the vendors obviously will be presenting their software in its "best light." You must be in a position to evaluate this information.

## 46-11   SITE VISITS

After the reference calls have been made and demonstrations attended, the organization should arrange to see the system at a working installation, not at the vendor's headquarters. The purpose of the site visits includes:

- Viewing the system in a "real-life" environment.
- Answering questions that may have arisen during the selection process.
- Assisting the organization in deciding whether the system will meet its current and future needs.

The site visit should take place at a user's place of business and should be on a "live," not "demo," system so that the vendor has no opportunity to manipulate the demonstration to its advantage. Although the majority of vendors are ethical, manipulation of potential customers is not unheard of.

The individuals present at the demonstration should include in-house IS personnel; potential system users, such as the accounts payable supervisor; and the IS consultant, if one is being used. The visit should take no more than a day to complete. The selecting team representatives should come prepared with a set of questions to ask the other organization and a feedback form on which to record ratings of the vendor.

If possible, the organization should arrange to make site visits within a two-week period to more easily compare the systems.

## 46-12 COST OF THE SYSTEM

The costs of purchasing hardware, software, and implementation support can be a very critical factor in a selection process and should be carefully analyzed.

The vendor cost summary portion of the RFP may be used to compare the costs of proposed systems. However, other cost factors need to be clarified before comparing the total costs of the proposed systems, consider:

- What will the proposed enhancements cost?
- How will the cost of future enhancements be determined?
- Is there an additional fee for installation?
- Is there an additional fee for training?
- How much does maintenance cost?
- Is there an additional fee for twenty-four-hour support?
- Is there a charge for system updates?
- Will the organization receive a discount if it purchases other applications?
- Does the software license allow for the use of the software at multiple sites? If not, what is the charge for the other sites?
- How much does the warranty cost and how long is it in effect?
- When does the warranty go into effect? (Ideally, the warranty should go into effect on the date the system is accepted, not on the date the system is installed.)
- Does the vendor guarantee in writing a full refund if the software does not perform as promised?
- Is the price of documentation included in the total price?
- Can the organization duplicate the documentation, or must it pay for additional copies? If so, what is the cost for additional copies?
- Is the source code (i.e., copy of the programs) included in the system's price? If not, what is the charge for the source code?

## 46-13 FINAL SELECTION

Once the software, hardware, and vendor have been thoroughly reviewed and the reference calls, demonstrations, and site visits completed, the organization is in a position to select the system. If the organization has completed the steps outlined in this chapter, it should find itself with an FIS that meets current and future needs. Once the final selection has been made, the organization is in a position to begin contract negotiations.

## 46-14  CONTRACT NEGOTIATIONS

After the software and hardware have been selected, preparation for contract negotiations between the organization and the vendor(s) should ensue. The objectives of contract negotiations are:

- Define the organization's expectations clearly to avoid misunderstandings.
- Define precisely what remedies are available if the vendor fails to perform as promised.
- Protect the organization against unexpected occurrences, such as the bankruptcy of the vendor.
- Ensure the best terms possible for the organization.

Negotiating a contract can be a long and costly process. When negotiating, there are several points to remember:

1. *Do not accept the vendor's standard contract.* These contracts tend to be one-sided in favor of the vendor and to disclaim all responsibility for performance and support.
2. *Negotiate with someone with the authority to bind the vendor.* Negotiating with a vendor representative who has no power is useless, because the promises they make may be overturned by their superiors.
3. *Never accept oral promises.*
4. *Do not make unreasonable demands.*
5. *Obtain advice from a professional experienced in contract negotiations.* The organization should not assume it can negotiate a mutually beneficial contract without the help of a professional (e.g., a lawyer specializing in contract law).

Four specific steps are essential for effectively negotiating a mutually beneficial contract:

1. Select a negotiating team to represent the selecting organization, including an IS specialist, an individual who will be using the system, an attorney or consultant with significant computer-related contract experience, and a purchasing department representative.
2. Determine the specific objectives of the negotiations and prepare a plan of action to take if the negotiations fail.
3. Review the standard contract terms offered by the vendor and identify problem areas and points that are missing.
4. Meet with the vendor to negotiate the contract.

The contract should clearly specify the costs for hardware, software, maintenance, installation support, modifications testing, and upgrades. The organization should attempt to ensure it is protected from any price increases without its written consent. The contract should also clearly identify the terms of payment. The organization should hold back a substantial portion of the purchase price (e.g., 10 to 30 percent) until the system is fully operational for a specified period of time and has passed all acceptance tests.

## 46-15  IMPLEMENTATION STEPS

After the hardware and software have been selected and the sales contract negotiated, the organization is ready to begin implementing the system. Implementation requires the commitment of a substantial amount of human and monetary resources. Therefore, the organization must make sure that it properly plans for the implementation to avoid many of the typical problems that arise. Fewer than 10 percent of FISs are implemented on time and between 15 and 20 percent of financially oriented minicomputer systems are currently not operational. For these reasons, the organization must carefully plan and manage the implementation process. (See Chapters 47A and 53 for additional implementation-related materials.)

Generally, the first step in the implementation process is selecting the implementation team. The team is responsible for managing all aspects of the implementation and ensuring they take place in a timely and cost-effective manner. The team should be composed of IS professionals, systems users, representatives from senior management, and the hardware and software vendors. In addition, a project manager should be assigned who is responsible for ensuring the ultimate success of the implementation. Each team member should be given specific areas for which he or she is responsible.

After the implementation team has been selected and assigned application areas and responsibilities, the team needs to determine the sequence in which the applications will be implemented. Many organizations make the mistake of trying to implement all of the FIS applications at once, which often leads to significant problems. To avoid this, the applications must be assigned preferential ratings based on the organization's needs, the resources available, and the relative ease of implementation.

Once the applications have been prioritized, the implementation team must develop a schedule containing a detailed work plan with clearly specified responsibilities and target dates. Many software and hardware vendors and IS consultants have developed "prototype" implementation plans. Therefore, the organization may not need to develop its own plan from scratch. The implementation plan should take into account the following factors:

- The human, IS, and monetary resources the organization will dedicate to the implementation.
- What, if any, outside resources (such as consultants) will be utilized.
- Potential projected bottlenecks (e.g., year-end closing).
- The frequency of status meetings.
- Contingency plans.
- An approach for managing issues.
- How communication lines should be established.

One of the most important factors in a successful implementation is management support; without it, the implementation is far less likely to succeed. Therefore, the implementation team should enlist the support of top management early in the implementation process.

The team members responsible for a particular application area must thoroughly understand the needs of that area. For example, they should review the requirements detailed in the RFP and ensure that they have not changed in the interim. After this, the team members must work with the end users to design the input forms and output reports to be generated by the system. (Software vendors frequently have standardized input forms and reports that the team needs to review to determine whether they meet the organization's needs. If they do not, modifications must be made.)

A schedule for the completion of software modifications, along with the responsibility for the modifications, must be determined. If the software vendor will be used to make the modifications, it should be contractually obligated to meet the schedule.

A particular team member should be given the responsibility for interfacing with the hardware vendor on site preparations. A computer room with specialized air conditioning and power supply may need to be constructed before the hardware can be installed. A schedule delineating specific responsibilities should be established and communicated.

One of the most important aspects of the implementation process is training end-users. Unless the training is done in a timely and thorough manner, the system may never be completely and appropriately utilized. Many software and hardware vendors provide user and technical training. The implementation team should review the content of this training and make modifications where necessary. Then it should schedule the appropriate personnel for the classes (i.e., end-users and IS professionals).

The implementation team then needs to prepare test data to use to check the accuracy and functionality of the system. The test data must be as close to "live" material as possible. The implementation team should then compile the expected results from the test, which will be used to test the accuracy and functionality of the system.

It is normally the responsibility of the hardware and software vendors to actually install the systems. However, the implementation team must monitor the installation.

As soon as the system has been installed, the relevant databases and files, such as the chart of accounts and vendor and customer master files, should be loaded into the system. In some cases, that can be done automatically (e.g., by loading a tape). In other cases, the data must be manually entered by the organization.

After the FIS is installed, the implementation team must perform an acceptance test of the system. Using the test data previously prepared, the team should compare the expected results with the actual results. Where differences arise, they should be resolved and the test rerun. The team should also ensure that the system meets all of the requirements stated in the RFP. In addition to the acceptance test, the organization should consider performing additional system tests (e.g., volume/stress, integration, interface, documentation, multi-site, security, recovery, and production pilot).

After the system has been thoroughly tested, the organization is ready to begin full operations on the new system. At this time, the old system should be totally phased out of existence. The time required to successfully implement an FIS greatly varies and depends on a variety of factors including resources committed and the applications to be installed.

As mentioned elsewhere in this chapter, many implementations do not succeed. The reasons for the lack of success include:

- Poor planning.
- Lack of management involvement.
- Lack of user involvement.

- Poor communication between implementation team members.
- Unrealistic or hidden expectations.
- Poorly defined priorities.
- Limited commitment of resources.
- Unrealistic time schedules.

## 46-16   POST-IMPLEMENTATION REVIEW

After a system has been implemented, a post-implementation review (PIR) should be completed, with the following objectives:

- Determining if the anticipated results of the selection and implementation process have been attained.
- Comparing the original cost estimate to the actual costs.
- Identifying weaknesses in support, documentation, training, and functionality.
- Reviewing the adequacy of reports, security, and ease of use.
- Identifying additional systems enhancements that may be required.
- Reviewing the timeliness of report preparation and distribution.

The best time to perform a post-implementation review is approximately 6 to 18 months after the system is installed. During this period, users have become familiar with the new system. This timing also allows significant system problems or issues to surface. Conducting the review prior to six months will not allow time for people to relinquish old habits.

The areas to be reviewed during the PIR include:

- How successfully the system has been implemented.
- The efficiency and effectiveness of the system.
- How well the system is being utilized.
- If system features exist that have not been implemented or used.
- If users needs are being met.
- If the system is sufficiently secure.

The steps to be taken to perform a PIR include:

1. Reviewing the statement of requirements, RFP, and the selected vendor's proposal.
2. Interviewing key individuals from the selection committee, implementation team, IS staff, user group, and internal audit.
3. Reviewing the system's implementation, training, documentation, support, security, operations, input forms, and reports.
4. Evaluating the implementation process.
5. Formulating the findings, conclusions, and recommendation in a report.

The benefits of performing a PIR include:

- Detecting issues related to the system.
- Evaluating the effectiveness of training and determining whether additional training is required.
- Determining whether additional documentation is necessary.
- Determining whether the expected benefits have been realized.
- Preparing recommendations for improvements to the system to maximize its use.
- Providing guidance and insight for future systems implementations.

## 46-17    SELECTED REFERENCES

### PERIODICALS

*Computerworld*

*Computers in Accounting*

*Information World*

### PRODUCT REVIEW/INFORMATION

*Datapro*

*Data Sources*

*Gartner Group*

*ICP Software Directory*

### BOOKS

Willson, James D., and Jack F. Duston, *Financial Information Systems*, 2nd ed., New York: Warren, Gorham & Lamont, 1986.

Eliason, Alan L., and Kent D. Kitts, *Business Computer Systems and Applications,* Chicago: SRA 1979.

# APPENDIX 1: VENDOR EVALUATION CRITERIA

Key factors to consider when evaluating vendors:

## PRODUCT SUPPORT

- Location of nearest sales and support office.
- Size of the support staff at nearest service office and their qualifications.
- Availability of remote diagnostics.
- Availability of twenty-four hour support and associated cost.
- Guaranteed response time for system problems.
- Preventive maintenance approach and policies.
- Problem resolution procedures.
- Availability of installation and implementation support.
- Existence of and level of support of a user group.
- Existence of complete user and technical documentation.
- Frequency of documentation and system updates.

## REPUTATION AND STABILITY

- Number of years in the computer industry.
- Number of similar installations of the particular system still operating.
- Sales growth rate of applications being reviewed.
- Financial condition of the vendor and/or its parent company.
- Research and development budget and number of staff.

# CHAPTER 47

# Computer Hardware Trends (New)

## 47-1  INTRODUCTION

Business managers must perform many jobs in order to effectively manage their organizations. Unfortunately, the manager cannot be a specialist in all functional areas of the organization. Accounting personnel cannot and should not be expected to be information technology specialists; however, some knowledge of the current trends in computer hardware technology is recommended. This chapter provides a summary overview of the current computer hardware trends and capabilities relevant to finance and accounting professionals.

## 47-2  PC-BASED SYSTEMS

### MICROPROCESSORS

The core of any computer system is its central processing unit or CPU. It is the capability of the CPU that ultimately determines the overall usefulness of the total computer system. The CPU is the "engine" of the system. The development of the microprocessor can be illustrated through the IBM compatible personal computers. The microprocessors used in IBM-compatible personal computers are predominately supplied by Intel

---

The author of this chapter is David M. Bassett, Consultant, Ernst & Young, Denver.

and a handful of other manufacturers supporting the Intel standards. When referring to processor types, it is common to use an Intel-based numerical reference (e.g., 286, 386, 486) which refers to the model number of the microprocessor. Intel's newest processor has broken this trend by using a tradename for its 586 (Pentium).

A CPU runs at a *clock speed* that greatly affects the operating speed of the unit; clock speeds are referred to in Megahertz (Mhz), millions of machine cycles per second. An alternative measure of a processor's speed is millions of instructions executed per second or MIPS. The original IBM personal computer introduced in 1982 used an Intel 8088 running at 4.77 Mhz, the IBM AT personal computer used an Intel 80286 running at 8 Mhz—both the 8088 and 80286 are now technologically obsolete. Today processor speeds of greater than 33 Mhz are common.

## 80386 SERIES MICROPROCESSORS

Not only have the speeds of CPUs increased; the organization (or architecture) of the chips has also changed. Internal "roadways of information" have been widened from 8 to 16 and finally to 32 lanes in Intel's current 80386 processor. The "386 series" of microprocessors has the capability to run multiple applications (i.e., "virtual mode") at the same time. The 80386 differs from its cousin, the 80386SX, in that the SX's external "roadways" are limited to 16 lanes while the 80386 has a full 32 lanes available for input and output from the CPU. The 80386 processor is now considered to be obsolete.

## INTEL 486 AND PENTIUM

Intel introduced the 80486 microprocessor in 1991. The 80486 has a small but effective memory cache built into the microprocessor. It is currently available in two versions. The DX version has a built in math coprocessor that can greatly reduce processing time in certain numeric-intensive applications, the SX version does not have the math coprocessor. While running at compatible speeds to the 80386 series, the 80486 realizes more processing throughput for a given speed in Mhz. Another very important feature built into the 80486 processor is the option of installing a "clock-doubling" processor chip. Tests have shown the resulting improvement from this option in system performance is around 70 percent. A fully configured 486-based system can be purchased for about $1,000. Single-user systems using the 486 processor with a speed of 33 Mhz should be considered the absolute minimum requirement for new business system applications. Intel released the next generation of the $80 \times 86$ microprocessor in the Spring of 1993. The processor, called Pentium, is capable of running over 100 million instructions per second (MIPS) or roughly twice as many as the fastest 80486 66-Mhz computer. By the end of 1994, it is anticipated that pentium-based systems will replace the 486 as the minimus business workstation.

## INTERNAL CACHES

Many systems offer the option of an internal memory cache. A cache is a special type of short-term memory that holds information frequently used by the microprocessor. Since the cache memory is faster than standard and extended memory, processing throughput speed is increased. Internal caches are a relatively inexpensive way to significantly improve system performance.

## STORAGE DEVICES

Nearly every system has at least one removable media storage device. Frequently, these are floppy disk drives. There has been an increasing standardization on the 3.5-inch disk system that holds roughly 1.44 million characters of information. The 5.25-inch drive is losing popularity partially due to the growth of laptop PCs. Non-PC-based microcomputers such as the Macintosh also utilize the 3.5-inch format. Fixed or hard disk drives are increasing in speed and storage capacity while decreasing in physical size. In years past, there were several interface options available; however, there is a movement to the integrated drive controller (IDE) on the hard disk that provides greater speed and standardization. Although the reliability of today's fixed disks, measured by the mean time between failures (MTBF) is very good, it is still necessary to make backup copies of important data. One way this can be accomplished easily is with a magnetic tape drive. Tape storage is good for reading and writing large amounts of sequential data and therefore optimally suited as a backup media.

## PORTABLES

One of the segments of the PC market that is experiencing significant growth is the portable or laptop PC market. A new benchmark system for laptop PCs would include a 486 microprocessor and a hard disk with a capacity of about 80 million characters (megabytes), and a fax/modem for communications over telephone lines. As of mid-1994, such systems cost about $1,500. Many manufacturers have introduced portables based on the "clockdoubled" 486 microprocessor, which carry a premium of $500–$1,000 over similar non-"clockdoubled" 486 models. Such systems cost less than $1,500. Upcoming trends recently introduced and likely to gain popularity include the proliferation of color displays, integrated modem and Local Area Network (LAN) connections on the system board of the unit and cellular modems for communications from virtually any location. Some units also have built in pointing devices analogous to a desktop "mouse." These devices, also called "ballpoint" mice are a necessity for users of graphical users interface programs such as Microsoft's Windows. There will also be growth in special purpose or nontraditional portables such as the Pen(Stylus) or notebook PC. These units are designed to read handwriting with a special pen on a flat screen display. While applications are still developing, many units have been introduced. Eventual applications will likely be oriented to gathering data such as insurance claims, inventory control, rental car returns, and so on.

## 47-3   PERIPHERALS

The term *peripherals* refers to the accessory devices connected to a CPU for a specific task. Peripherals generally fall into the categories of input devices and output devices; however, some are both input and output devices. Many new types of peripherals are nearing commercialization. In addition, technological improvements have been made in existing peripherals.

## PRINTERS

The laser printer has become the standard for the majority of businesses. While impact printing is still necessary in some business applications, laser printers are the choice because of their output quality, flexibility, and quietness. Resolutions of 300 dots per inch (dpi) is standard with some manufactures reaching beyond 600 dpi. Greater resolution in dots per inch requires more printer memory; to print 300 dpi full-page graphics requires 1.5 million characters of printer memory.

One major printer manufacturer has developed technology that changes the sizes of the individual dots to give the illusion of higher effective resolution. Many laser printers now support an industry standard method of communicating typefaces and sizes called Post Script. Post Script-compatible output is available across different computer systems including the Apple Macintosh. While output quality is generally superior, Post Script compatible lasers carry a $500 to $1,000 premium over basic models. Post Script is highly desirable in graphically intensive applications such as desktop publishing.

Color printing similar to laser output has existed for several years. Recently, prices for color capable lasers has dropped below $5,000. While the laser printer has gained tremendous acceptance, impact printing is still necessary for certain applications such as multiple part form printing. Technology also has improved impact printers; one recent enhancement was the introduction of software scalable typefaces for dot matrix impact printers.

## VIDEO DISPLAY MONITORS

Video display technology is also rapidly advancing. The recent Enhanced Graphics Array (EGA) standard of the late 1980s has given way to the newer Video Graphics Array (VGA) technology. The primary difference between the EGA displays and VGA is that EGA used digital signals to achieve a maximum of 16 onscreen colors at one time. Displays using VGA technology operate using analog signals similar to a standard television; therefore, each of the primary colors can be blended in an almost infinite combination to achieve up to 256 simultaneous onscreen colors. Since the systems are intrinsically different, displays and interfaces cannot generally be intermixed. An analog VGA monitor will not work with a digital EGA display interface. Standard VGA resolution is 480 screen pixels (points) by 800 pixels. Most VGA video display interfaces and many software applications also support a Super-VGA mode of 800 × 600 pixels that enables more data to be seen onscreen at one time. Similar to laser printers, increased display resolution requires more memory. To support basic (640 × 480) resolution with 16 colors usually requires 256 million characters of video memory; the same resolution with 256 colors requires 512 million characters of video memory. Systems using 1024 × 768 resolution have begun to gain market acceptance and are likely to be the new standard in the early 90s as applications which use Graphical Users Interfaces (GUIs) such as Microsoft's Windows and IBM's Operating System/2 proliferate. Newer technology includes putting the video system on the same processing system as the microprocessor. Called Local Bus Video (LBV), improves display speeds for new graphics-intensive applications such as teleconferencing, multimedia, and so on. Some of the speed benefits of LBV can be achieved by add-in video accelerator boards available from a variety of manufacturers. On certain applications, such as Microsoft's Windows, video can be improved over tenfold with a graphics accelerator.

## CD ROM

Compact Disc Read-Only Memory (CD ROM) is a technology that has existed since the mid-1980s but has now gained mainstream acceptance. Prices have fallen from the thousands of dollars at introduction to below $200 and sales of the units are increasing at 30 to 40 percent per year as of mid-1993. A CD ROM operates on the same principles as an audio compact disc. Tiny pits in an encoded disc are read and translated into the digital language of computers, streams of 0s and 1s or bits. Also similar to an audio compact disc, the information is read-only and therefore cannot be rerecorded. Whereas a floppy disk can hold the equivalent of approximately 1,000 pages of information, one CD ROM can hold 350,000 pages. CD ROM technology is promoting the development of multimedia hardware that utilizes the integration of interactive video, sound, and language. Some companies in the travel industry are utilizing CD ROM to give their customers an interactive preview of their destinations including pictures and data on disk. Many more companies are using CD ROM in more traditional applications such as reducing the costs of distributing and receiving large volumes of data and increasing the timeliness of data access. Applications such as parts catalogs, marketing statistics, and on-line references for professionals are particularly well-suited to CD ROM. The next trend in CD ROM technology is write-once-read-many storage, or WORM, technology. WORMs are similar to CD ROMs in that information is digitally stored in a compact disc similar to audio compact disks; however, a WORM disk can be written once by the user. After it is written, it operates in the same read-only manner as a CD ROM. WORMs are still quite expensive with prices currently in the multiple thousands of dollars.

## MODEMS

The growing need for connectivity and networking frequently requires computers at different locations to be connected. A modem is a device that takes digital computer signals and translates them into analog signals for transmission over telephone lines. Modems are rated by the speed at which they communicate data in bits per second (bps). Most currently installed modems provide a speed of at least 2,400 bps. Some manufacturers have introduced various data compression techniques into their hardware that can effectively double a modem's speed if communication conditions are favorable. More and more businesses are switching to the newer 9,600 and 14,400 bps modems. With new error correction technology and data compression schemes, effective data communication of over 20,000 bps can be realized. Businesses should consider upgrading to faster modems which can quickly pay for themselves with reduced long distance bills. In the long term, all modems will become obsolete as analog telephone connections are replaced by the Integrated Services Digital Network (ISDN), a digital telephone and communications network. Users will eventually be able to plug their systems directly into a high-speed network outlet, thus bypassing the need for a modem altogether.

## CONNECTIVITY AND INTEROPERABILITY

One recent trend is the movement toward connecting systems via a network. There are two classifications of networks. Local area networks (LANs) tie systems together within small geographic regions such as a work group, department, or building. Wide area networks (WANs) link systems or individual LANs over greater geographic areas. There are many types of networks in common use but most make use of a common "server" machine that provides storage, communication, and printing services for the various "client" computers connected to it via telephone, coaxial, or fiber optic cable. Each unit connected to a network requires a specific adapter. The most prevalent networking cabling and signaling scheme for small systems today is the Ethernet system which is supported by the leading industry networking system provider, Novell, and many others. Ethernet systems utilize a shared one-way "electronic roadway" with "collision avoidance" software to access the server. Another common signaling scheme found in many business networks is the IBM Token-Ring system. Token-Ring networks look to the machine ahead of them for a "token" or authorization to access the network. The "token" is continuously passed around the "ring" of machines. The more expensive Token-Ring system is commonly found where connection to a mainframe or minicomputer is required because it treats mainframes and PCs as peers on the same network. Through the use of devices called bridges, routers, and gateways, networks have dissimilar signaling schemes can be linked. For example, an Macintosh AppleTalk network can be routed to an Ethernet PC network which is bridged to a mainframe in a Token-Ring network. The linking of dissimilar systems is referred to as *interoperability* or systems integration.

## DOWNSIZING AND CLIENT-SERVER COMPUTING

The advent of widespread networking has generated significant interest in mainframe downsizing. Downsizing refers to taking an application, such as a database or general ledger system, from a mainframe and running it on smaller systems. Many full-featured accounting software packages capable of running a medium-size organization run very well in a LAN environment. Another upcoming trend is toward "client-server" computing. With client-server technology, the data remains on the client host system. The server becomes a "mini-mainframe" serving many clients. Once heralded as distributed processing systems where processing would be shared between the client and server, in reality, much of the processing work is still taking place on either the client or server individually. True client-server applications involve two applications running on two computers as shown in Figure 47-1.

Currently, client-server systems are primarily limited to database queries and decision support systems. Fully implemented client-server applications such as accounting and personnel management are available; however, businesses's attitudes to client-server technology are mixed.

**Figure 47-1**   Client Server Architecture: *A Client/Server Application Is Actually Two Applications Executing on Two Computers.*

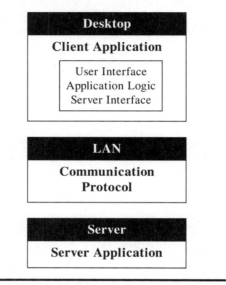

*Source: The Socrates Group, Inc. and Computerworld.*

## 47-4   ALTERNATIVE SYSTEMS

### SINGLE-USER SYSTEMS

While the IBM compatible PC has gained the most support of business users, it is estimated that 25 percent of all businesses have Macintosh systems as well. Sales of Macintosh systems accounted for 13 percent of all single-user computers sold in 1991 or one for every six IBM compatibles sold. A single-user system refers to a small computer system where the CPU is typically utilized by one user.

The Macintosh was designed with a Graphical User Interface (GUI) in mind. In a GUI interface, applications and data files are represented on screen as icons which are graphic depictions of their functions; applications run within visual windows which can be re-sized. Users manipulate icons and windows through the use of a pointing device such as a mouse. Since the MacIntosh was designed with a GUI in mind it is particularly well suited to graphical applications. The latest Macintosh models can read and write PC files directly thus eliminating file-sharing problems for businesses that support both standards.

Another system available is the workstation. A workstation is based on a different type of microprocessor called a RISC (Reduced Instruction Set Chip). More powerful than even the fastest PC or Macintosh, these systems are most suitable for engineering design and scientific use where speed and superior graphics are a necessity. Workstations usually operate on the UNIX operating system; therefore, business application software availability for workstations is significantly less than for the PC or Macintosh.

## MINIS AND MAINFRAMES

Single user systems continue to attract a significant amount of attention in business circles. Single user systems have put sizable computing power on the desks of the end users at a fraction of the cost of larger systems. Users have seized the opportunity to circumvent long lead times associated with requests from information technology departments. While the trend is to downsizing, minicomputers and mainframes will continue to fill a niche in business computing. Mainframes and minicomputers remain the best systems for wide-scale online access, heavy file processing, or large numbers of end users as shown in Figure 47-2. How the various pieces of hardware fit together is shown in Figure 47-3.

## 47-5 CONCLUSION

It is axiomatic to state that Information Technology is continually advancing. While finance and accounting professionals do not need to be information technologists aware of every development, a top-level overview of current computer trends and capabilities is strongly recommended. Such knowledge can enhance the quality of a professional's planning, control, and decision-making process by enabling recognition of new opportunities and effectively evaluating technology alternatives.

**Figure 47-2** Applications Running on Mainframes and Midrange Systems in 1991.

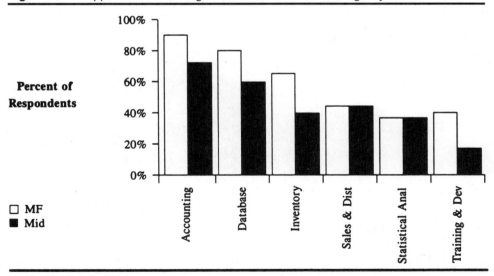

*Source: Datapro Reports.*

**Figure 47-3**    Schematic Showing How Hardware Fits into a System.

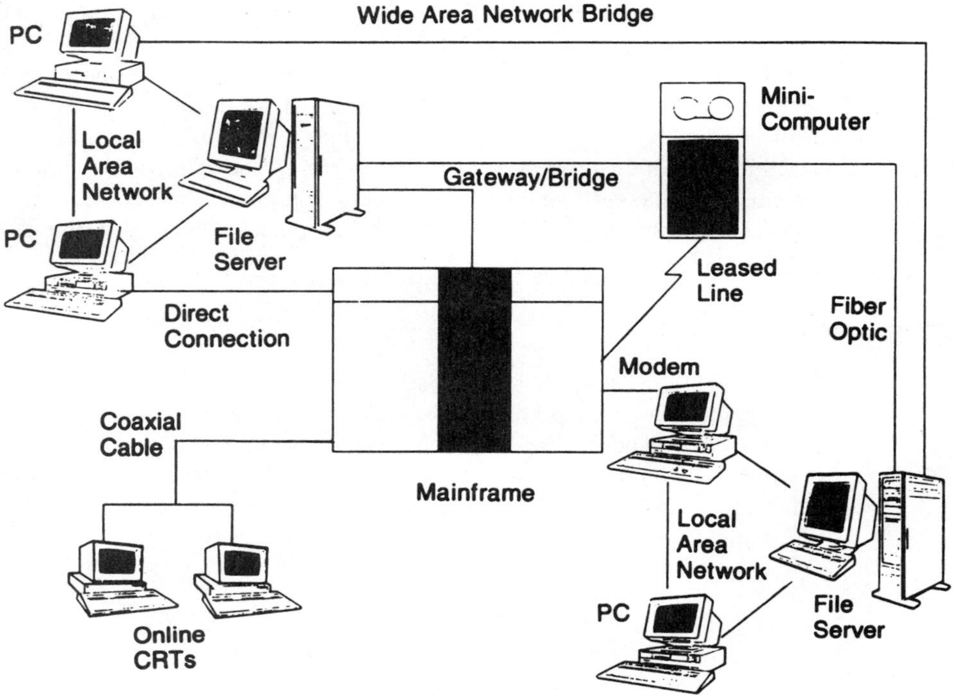

## 47-6    SELECTED REFERENCES

### MAGAZINES

*Computerworld*

*Datamation*

*Datapro Reports: Computer Systems Series*

*Information Systems Management*

*Information Week*

*Journal of Systems Management*

*LAN Magazine*

*LAN Technology*

*Network Computing*

*PC Week*

*PC Magazine*

# CHAPTER 47A

# Management Techniques for Software Package Integration (New)

## 47A-1  OVERVIEW

Software package integration projects (e.g., the implementation of an accounting or human resources system) differ from custom-built projects in that the application to be integrated is already coded, operational, and, in most cases, marketplace-tested. Once the software package is selected, only the steps to integrate it into the organization remain. The execution of these steps can result in a successful project or in a project that fails miserably. Because of this, certain management strategies have been identified and used on software package integration projects, to better ensure their success.

In this chapter, four specific management strategies are discussed: project management, risk management, change management, and quality management. These strategies, used in tandem, will increase the chance of success of the project by overcoming common project stumbling blocks (see Figure 47A-1). System implementation projects typically do not fail because of technical problems; rather, they fail because of a lack of management. Controllers and chief financial officers (CFOs) frequently are responsible for the successful implementation of a variety of systems; therefore, it is particularly important for them to ensure that project, risk, change, and quality management issues are addressed.

---

The author of this chapter is Sandra Borchardt, Senior Manager, Ernst & Young, Boston.

**Figure 47A-1**    Management Techniques for Software Integration.

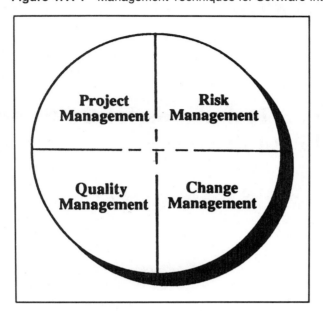

## 47A-2    PROJECT MANAGEMENT

Project management is the process by which a project is planned, executed, and completed. The objective of project management is to conduct the project in a systematic and organized fashion in order to reduce uncertainty and encourage productivity.

Project management is made difficult by the very nature of projects. The communication process is at best inexact, causing potential misunderstandings of the project scope, requirements, and expectations. Changes in the regulatory environment or in the business itself may change the goals of the project or even render the project unnecessary. A project estimate is just that—a best guess at how long it will take to complete the project; how many resources, when, and with what skill set, will be needed; and what costs will be incurred. Quality deliverables may take more time than expected to complete. To obtain high productivity, project team members must be led, motivated, counseled, and apprised of their performance. To combat these difficulties, however, certain project management techniques can be used. Project planning, although an estimate at best, can provide the initial focus and step-by-step guide for the project. Project tracking can then be used to monitor actual progress against plan, identifying exceptions early and allowing for replanning based on these experiences.

### MANAGING PROJECTS

Project management begins at the start of a project and continues throughout the project until its completion. Project management techniques are project-tested and have been used successfully to integrate software packages into organizations. Some common project management techniques include the following:

- *Planning.* The planning process begins by identifying and confirming the business problem to be solved. How to overcome the problem becomes the initial definition of the project. The project scope is then defined, deliverables are identified, and high-level estimates of time frames, required effort, and costs are developed.

- *Estimating.* The estimating process builds on the information developed during the planning process. Plans are detailed to achieve the project objectives within the terms defined in the project scope; for example, a detailed work plan would clearly define what work needs to be done, how long it will take, who will do it, and when it will be completed. Risk, change, and quality management plans are incorporated in the detailed work plan.

- *Defining Deliverables.* After the planning process has outlined the types of deliverables required by the project, this process customizes these deliverables for the project situation. Deliverable definitions clearly identify exactly what work will and will not be done during the project. These definitions serve as a communication tool to help ensure that project members have the same expectations for the project.

- *Monitoring.* The monitoring process is an ongoing process that measures actual progress against planned progress and identifies those areas requiring corrective action or adjustments to the plan. Results of this process feed subsequent estimating processes.

- *Managing Risk.* The risk management process consists of early identification and control of project risks through the use of tools and techniques for identifying project risks, assessing their criticality, and developing and implementing strategies to manage these project risks. (Risk management will be discussed in more detail later in this chapter.)

- *Managing Change.* In the context of project management, change management has two important meanings:

  1. *A technique that targets the human factor affected by the project*—This type of change management identifies resistance to the changes brought on by the project, works to understand the nature of the resistance, and implements change management strategies to overcome the resistance. (The change management concept will be discussed later in this chapter.)

  2. *A mechanism through which project changes can be requested, tracked, investigated, and rejected or approved*—A change of this nature is an addition to, deletion from, or modification of a system during its design, development, or implementation. Although these types of changes are normal occurrences during a project, they can have a serious impact on a project's scope, cost, or schedule. The change management process for this type of change works to identify changes that are good for the project and those that, in the overall analysis, may not benefit the project or may cost more than the benefits to be gained.

- *Managing Quality.* The quality management process consists of the use of tools and techniques to build quality into a project. Through the use of quality management techniques that focus on preventative-based strategies, projects should better meet expectations, requirements, budget estimates, and planned time frames. (Quality management will be discussed in more detail later in this chapter.)

Project management tools support project management techniques throughout the life of the project. Some of the more common project management tools include:

- *Scope Document.* The project scope document identifies what will be accomplished by the project and what will not. It contains the definition of the project, its boundaries, and its completion criteria. Other information about the project, such as the budget, time frames, and resource requirements, may be included in the scope document.

- *Work Plan.* The project work plan is a detailed, step-by-step plan that clearly defines what work needs to be done, how long it will take, who will do it, and when it will be completed. The project work plan provides a tool against which actual progress can be measured. Figure 47A-2 provides a sample work plan in a Gantt chart presentation. Figure 47A-3 summarizes the plan in Figure 47A-2, using a PERT chart format.

- *Status Reports.* Status reports identify accomplishments, work-in-progress, issues, and tasks that, when compared to the project plan, are overdue. Status reports should be frequently and regularly produced by project team members. These reports communicate progress against plan and outstanding issues.

- *Issue Log.* Issues identified during the project (e.g., on status reports) are captured, reported, and tracked using an issue log. Issues are matters that require decisions to be made by project team members or other organizational representatives. Issues may impact project progress and must be analyzed in a timely manner.

- *Project Meetings.* Frequent and regular project meetings with project team members, and separate meetings with project sponsors, provide a forum for discussing progress to date, outstanding issues, and follow-up items. Responsibilities and deadlines can be assigned to issues and follow-up items during these meetings; in subsequent meetings, reports of progress on these assignments can be discussed. Presentations of status reports and issue logs can be used to guide these meetings. Project meetings are an excellent communication tool and also serve to evaluate progress against plan.

- *Change Requests.* Change requests are the formal documentation of an addition to, deletion from, or modification of a system during its design, development, or implementation. Change requests allow for the proper tracking of changes and their resulting rejection or approval.

- *Project Documentation.* Project documentation organizes the project management information used to manage the project. Project documentation contains the project scope, project organization, detailed project plans, standards and procedures, project deliverables, and all project authorizations and related correspondence.

## 47A-3  RISK MANAGEMENT

Risk in a software integration project is the probability that the project will not finish on time or within budget, or, upon completion, that the system will not function as expected. Other risks include the possibility that the application will not integrate with the hardware or other applications systems, or will not meet technical performance expectations, or will fail to provide the expected benefits. Risk management is the early

Figure 47A-2   A Project Work Plan in a Gantt Chart Format.

GANTT CHART                PAGE    1

Materials Management System

Materials Management System

1       Project Management
1.1     Prepare for Resource Coordinator's Meeting
1.2     Attend Resource Coordinator's Meeting
1.3     Prepare for Project Management
1.4     Attend Project Management Meeting

6       Interfaces
6.1     Complete Vendor Specification (OVERDUE)
6.2     Complete User Specification
6.3     Coordinate Interfaces
6.4     Construct and Bench Test User Interface

7       File Construction
7.1     Prepare for File Construction
7.2     Build Files-For Test
7.3     Complete File Construction

8       Policy & Procedures
8.1     Complete Design Documents (OVERDUE)
8.2     Identify the List of Procedures
8.3     Identify Procedure Steps
8.4     Document Procedure
8.5     Review/Revise Procedure
8.6     Re-Document
8.7     Identify and Document Additional Procedures
8.8     Design and Input Application Security

9       Test Design
9.1     Design Testing Strategy
9.2     Identify Test Objectives
9.3     Identify Test Conditions
9.4     Document Test Cases
9.5     Group Tests into Cycles
9.6     Generate Test Schedule

        Test Execution
9.7     Execute Unit Test
9.8     Execute System Test

10      Training
10.1    Prepare For Training
10.2    Conduct User Training

11      Cutover
11.1    Initial Planning for Cutover
11.2    Final Cutover Planning
11.3    Cutover

1993  1993  1993  1993  1993  1994
Jan  Feb  Mar  Apr  May  Jun  Jul  Aug  Sep  Oct  Nov  Dec  Jan  Feb  Mar

**Figure 47A-3** A PERT Chart Representation of the Project Work Plan Shown in Figure 47A-2.

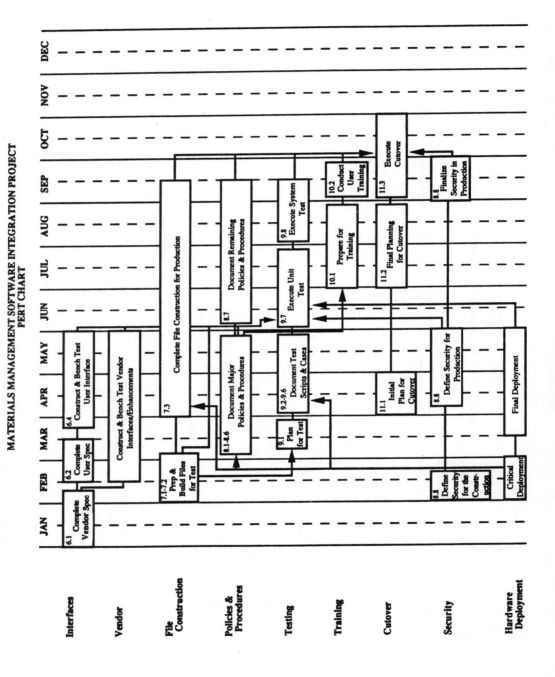

MATERIALS MANAGEMENT SOFTWARE INTEGRATION PROJECT
PERT CHART

identification and control of these and other project risks through the use of tools and techniques for identifying project risks, assessing their criticality, and developing and implementing strategies to manage these project risks (see Figure 47A-4).

## IDENTIFYING RISKS

The risk identification process should begin early in an implementation project and be reviewed and adjusted throughout the project. Early identification allows for a broader choice of options to deal with the risk. Detailed questionnaires of typical project risks are often used to perform the initial and follow-up risk identification. These questionnaires cover topics ranging from project size to project structure and technology.

Examples of risks related to the size of the project include: the number of hours estimated to complete the project, the project time frame (estimated over calendar months or years), the size of the project team, the number of interfacing systems, and the number of entities within the organization involved in the project. The greater the magnitude of any of these project size indicators, the greater the risk of the project.

Risks related to project structure include:

- How well defined are the scope, deliverables, benefits, and requirements of the project?
- Does the project team include knowledgeable application, technology, and business area specialists?
- Does the project have an organizational sponsor and the support of management and users?
- How extensively will the system change current work flows, policies, procedures, and organizational structure?

A well-defined project, when staffed with a knowledgeable project team, supported by the organization, and expected to have little impact on current operations, is a much less risky project than any of the alternatives.

**Figure 47A-4**   The Risk Management Process.

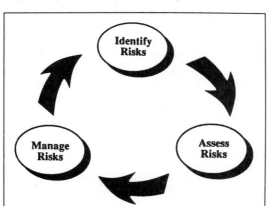

Technology risks include those risks related to the need for new hardware or systems software, the number of technologies required by the new system, and the project team's knowledge of the package to be installed. A project that requires no new hardware or software and only minimal additional technologies and that is supported by a knowledgeable project team will be less risky than a project that requires new hardware and systems software, supports multiple technologies, and lacks a knowledgeable project team.

## ASSESSING RISKS

Once potential project risks have been identified, these risks must be assessed as to their criticality. Different projects may identify similar risks; however, the magnitude of these risks is project-specific. For example, the risks identified for the following two projects were:

Project I    Implementation of an automated system to replace manual processes.

Project II    Implementation of additional automated features to enhance already automated processes.

The types of risks these two projects may encounter include:

- *Timing.* Can the new automated processes accomplish the tasks as fast as or faster than the current processes without additional staffing? Will the new automated processes cause bottlenecks? How will the new processes work if the system experiences downtime?
- *User Acceptance.* Can the user community be trained adequately to understand the new system's functionality, the changes in work flow, and the changes in their job descriptions, in order to successfully operate the new system once it is in place?

In this example, Project I is much riskier than Project II. Timing is less of an issue in Project II, because changes to processes would be less drastic than in Project I. Further, contingency plans would more likely be in place and experienced in Project II as a result of the current automation, whereas these would need to be developed as part of the integration of the new system in Project I.

User acceptance would also be less of a risk in Project II because the users are experienced and comfortable with automation; thus, changes in their current processes, work flows, and job descriptions would most likely be less severe.

Risk identification and assessment should involve all levels of the project team, including the project sponsor, project management, and user and technical representatives. Reconciling these different perceptions of risk will enable all parties to come to the same understanding of the risks of the project. With this basis, these project representatives can then reduce risk by revising the assumptions on which the project is based, or accept risk by agreeing that the result is in line with the organization's goals.

## MANAGING RISKS

Although most of the recommended approaches to risk management focus on specific aspects of the project (e.g., size, structure, or technology), there are some general strategies to manage a project's overall risk, as follows:

- Understand and document expectations and what will be done during the project.
- Assign appropriately trained staffed to the project, including industry, application, and technology specialists.
- Partition the work into manageable segments.
- Reduce the dependency of the project on other development efforts.
- Involve users in the project.
- Prepare the organization for changes that will occur as the result of the system's implementation.

Specific risk management strategies relate to the specific risks identified. For example, risks associated with a lengthy implementation time frame include the following:

- Team members may leave the project and other personnel inexperienced in the specifics of the project may be assigned to replace them.
- Team members' motivation and sense of urgency are hard to maintain on a long project, and a potential result may be lower levels of productivity.
- A change in the organization's business could cause a change in user requirements.
- A change in the organization's executive levels could lead to revised priorities.

Strategies for managing these risks include:

- Partition work into subprojects that build on one another and show results frequently.
- Identify clear milestones and deliverables throughout the project.
- Recognize individual needs of team members and provide work variety accordingly.
- Use application development tools (e.g., Computer-Aided Software Engineering (CASE) tools) to enhance productivity, thereby reducing the time needed to complete specific tasks. Note that this strategy may mean introducing new technology, which may increase risk in that area.
- Reduce project scope to reduce the amount of work to be done, which in turn will reduce the overall project time frame.

When developing strategies to manage risk, examine the relationships and dependencies among risk factors. In some cases, a strategy to reduce risk in one area actually increases risk in another. For example, a decision to reduce the risk of a lengthy project by increasing team size may increase the risk of ineffective team coordination and communication.

## 47A-4   CHANGE MANAGEMENT

Change management in a software integration project is a technique that targets the human factor affected by the project. A software application project may be successfully integrated, but if the new system and surrounding changes to work flows, policies, and procedures are not accepted by the users, the entire project could fail.

In one example, patient billing software was successfully integrated into a multi-physician clinic. Less than three months later, piles of patient charges had yet to be entered and several hundred thousand dollars' worth of insurance claims remained unbilled. Upon closer investigation, it was discovered that the office manager was threatened by the new system and prevented the billing department from completing its work by prioritizing other tasks over system tasks.

The human factor is one of the most powerful determinants of the success or failure of any new system. An application system that exceeds all user expectations might sit idly on a desk if the users do not want to use it, do not know how to use it, are frightened of changing their ways, or are worried that their jobs might be threatened. Before bringing in a new application, the organization must try to determine the attitudes and responses of the people who will actually use the application. If the organization suspects these attitudes are negative, then the organization must determine how to change them.

## IDENTIFYING RESISTANCE

A person's tendency to resist change is the result of many factors. Some personalities are more apt to accept and even look forward to change; others prefer stability and constancy. Certain personalities are sure change will mean a loss of status, power, or even their jobs; others expect to move ahead with the change. It is often difficult to determine people's true feelings, because these feelings are securely masked or even unknown.

Organizational culture may breed innovation or encourage routine. An organization that is tradition-bound and committed to time-tested systems and procedures will probably be less likely to accept new systems and new procedures than an organization with a more flexible attitude.

Resistance to change is inevitable. Thus, the success of a project hinges on the ability of management to understand change from the perspective of the user. Once the true reason for resistance is identified, management can begin to implement strategies to reduce the cause. Most importantly, once the users can feel secure that the project will have a positive effect on their role in the organization, then and only then will they begin to accept the change.

## MANAGING CHANGE

Managing change begins with an understanding of the concerns of the organization, as illustrated in Figure 47A-5. Once these concerns are identified, the following basic strategies can be employed to reduce resistance:

- *User Involvement.* Involving the people who will actually use the application in the project will provide them with a better understanding of the change and, thus, will help in "demystifying" the change. Making these users responsible for aspects of the project, such as planning and design, will encourage acceptance of the change because they will be accepting their own decisions. Further, involved users will serve as role models, encouraging other peer users to understand and accept the change.

  Many projects that are less than successful have been conducted with minimal user involvement. When turned over to the users, these projects have been saddled with problems such as: a poor understanding of the system design; a system design that did not meet user requirements or expectations; an inability of the users to quickly take over ownership of the system, resulting in a dependence on the system designers; or an inability of the users to understand the system and use it properly.

- *Communication.* Often, the fear of change is the fear of the unknown, and, too frequently, the unknown becomes false information or rumors. Disseminating true information as soon as possible to all employees affected by the change will demystify the change and reduce rumors. One technique to communicate change is holding regular forums to provide information to and elicit feedback from employees. Other techniques include circulating newsletters or posters to communicate information, and using contests or social and information events to encourage employee learning and participation.
- *Training.* For users to be able to use the new application, they must be trained. Training includes not only classroom training, but also training events, occurring throughout the project, that provide information about the overall project, and training assistance during the initial days or months of using the new system.

**Figure 47A-5** The Change Management Process.

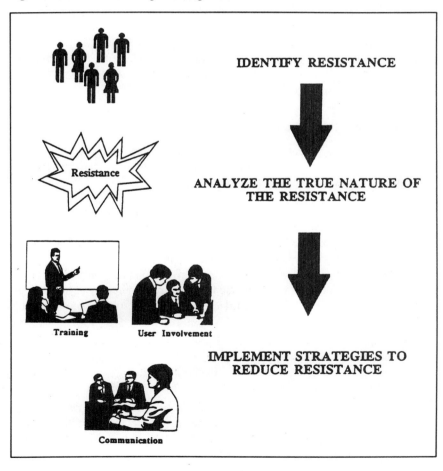

Follow-up classroom training, once the system is operational, will enforce current understanding while providing retraining on functionality not absorbed in the initial session. Training content should include not only application functionality but also policies, procedures, and work flows.

- *Timing.* Resistance to change cannot be conquered overnight. Change that occurs over time will have a better chance of overcoming resistance than immediate change. Involving users early, maintaining effective communication throughout the project, and continuously "training" users on the change will allow users to slowly but more comfortably overcome their resistance.

## 47A-5   QUALITY MANAGEMENT

Quality management is the use of tools and techniques to build quality into a project. Through the use of quality management techniques, projects should better meet expectations, requirements, budget estimates, and planned time frames.

Quality assurance is the set of actions performed to bring about quality in a project. Quality control checks for, and corrects, exceptions in completed work products or projects. The difference between the two is that quality assurance techniques are preventative measures whereas quality control techniques are after-the-fact quality measures.

It has been proven that preventative measures are much more cost-effective than inspection-based measures. However, it is important to note that quality control can be used to monitor the quality assurance program, indicating how closely the project is meeting expectations and requirements, and in what areas improvements are needed to provide a better quality product.

### MANAGING QUALITY

The quality management process is based on building quality strategies into the project, beginning at the start of the project. Each of the quality management strategies illustrated in Figure 47A-6 is discussed below:

- *Exceed Expectations.* Every project team member—in fact, the project as a whole—should strive to exceed the expectations of the organization, project management, and users. Expectations can be exceeded through advanced delivery of quality deliverables and by completing tasks under budget.
- *Do It Right the First Time.* Careful project planning and monitoring, along with knowledgeable and experienced project management, will help ensure that the correct tasks have been identified and that the project team is executing the tasks properly.
- *Follow an Implementation Methodology.* A quality project will, more likely than not, result from following a proven implementation methodology. Project management should be experienced with the methodology, and the methodology should be project-tested and should include steps for building quality into the project.
- *Use Project Planning and Tracking Techniques.* A detailed plan constructed by knowledgeable and experienced project management will clearly define what work needs to be done, how long it will take, who will do it, and when it will be completed. Tracking actual results to the detailed plan will allow for revision of

**Figure 47A-6**   Quality Management Strategies.

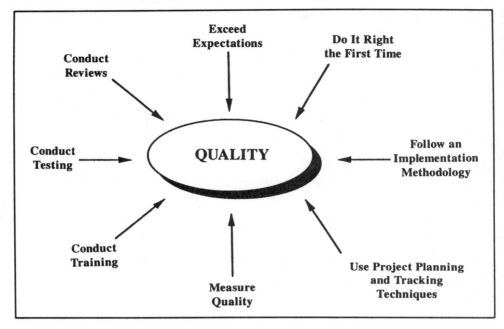

estimates, early identification of bottlenecks and potential problems, and actual experience that can be used in the next planning effort.

- *Measure Quality.* Although many quality indicators are not easily measured, certain indicators, such as project costs, time frames, and results, can be measured against initial cost and time-frame estimates and user requirements, respectively. Quality measurements can also point out weaknesses in the software integration process so that improvements can be made to the implementation methodology prior to initiating the next project.

- *Conduct Training.* Training project team members is essential for a quality project, especially if team members have never before been involved in a software integration project. The types of training needed by project team members include understanding of the project scope; user requirements; implementation methodology; project technology; project plan, including work steps, budgets, and time frames; project tracking and documentation tools; and key deliverables.

- *Conduct Testing.* A formal, rigorous test of the system prior to placing the system into production is essential to the quality of the project for several reasons. Testing new custom programs ensures that the code executes without error and meets all requirements documented in the technical specifications. Unit testing the software modules ensures that each module executes as expected, without error. Integration testing of the entire system ensures that all modules interact with each other as expected and without error. Acceptance testing ensures that the system accomplishes the user requirements in a manner acceptable by the user community.

    All tests should be documented and expected results identified prior to executing the test, thus providing for an objective and formal test. Once the tests are executed, actual results should be documented and compared to expected results, and all inconsistencies should be noted, researched, and resolved. Representatives throughout the organization—including programming, operations, users, and even the software vendor—must be involved with testing. Not only will these representatives assist in the execution and documentation of the tests, but they will be responsible for the research and resolution of any inconsistencies.

- *Conduct Reviews.* The earlier an exception from expected results is identified, the broader the options for handling the exception. Quality review points throughout the project will assist in the identification of any exception. Among the several types of reviews recommended for integration projects are:

  1. *Project Team Review.* Project management reviews work products to ensure consistency across the project, to ensure completeness of individual pieces of the project, and to provide the final, comprehensive review of a deliverable before it goes to the organization for approval.

  2. *Organizational Review.* Organization management and users review the work products to ensure that expectations and requirements are met, to allow for feedback of concerns or suggestions, to communicate project information and status, and to involve responsible executives in the major organizational and operational decisions related to the project.

  Reviews can be executed by reading the deliverable and meeting with appropriate project team members to question points and provide feedback. Reviews can also be executed through the use of formal presentations, where the project team member(s) responsible for the deliverable presents the ideas and conclusions to an audience of reviewers. This type of structured presentation provides immediate feedback and a forum for working through revisions to the deliverable.

  In all cases, reviews should be strategically placed throughout the project to ensure a quality project through early identification of inconsistencies. The need and placement of review points will vary from project to project. For example, identification of a high-risk situation in a project may call for additional reviews to monitor and control the risk. Review points also communicate project information and status to the organization, which aids the change management process.

## 47A-6  SUMMARY

Project, risk, change, and quality management techniques work together to help ensure the success of any software integration project. The key to their success is their early and constant deployment throughout the life of the project. However, do not be fooled into thinking the same strategies in the same combination on similar projects will reap similar benefits. Each project is different and thus calls for an individual evaluation and subsequent identification of the management strategies best suited to handle the unique characteristics and issues of the project. If done, however, the project will have a greater probability of absorbing surprises during the integration and concluding in a manner that results in a cost-effective system that meets the goals and requirements that justified the project in the first place.

# CHAPTER 47AA

# Software Package Integration (New)

## 47AA-1  INTRODUCTION

Software package integration is the process of preparing for and establishing operations a new application (i.e., a new piece of software—often referred to as an application). Many organizations find it difficult to structure, plan, and budget for an integration project and then meet these estimates with a successfully executed integration effort (i.e., one that results in an application system that meets user and organizational requirements). Many factors can contribute to the success or failure of an integration project. However, the success of any project depends on a few fundamental factors that must be present:

- An Understanding of the Project.  This includes clearly defining and understanding the expectations for the project, the project risks, and the methodology (i.e., structured approach) being used to integrate the application.

- Executive Commitment.  The executive sponsors of the project play an important role in the success of the project. Specifically, at the outset of the project, the executive sponsors should at the very least establish reasonable, specific goals;

---

This chapter was written by Sandra Borchardt, Senior Manager, Ernst & Young, Boston, Massachusetts.

provide the necessary resources; actively show support for the project; take action on requests and issues; and facilitate the project team's interface with support departments.

- Effective Leadership. A successful project must have an effective leader. The role of an effective project leader includes: managing expectations and relationships, providing recommendations and not just alternatives, involving team members in the decisionmaking process, minimizing outside pressure on the project team, and facilitating the achievement of team members' personal goals during the project.

- Organizational Adaptability.  A new application will probably necessitate changes in the organization or its culture. Several strategies can be deployed to assist in the change process: sensitivity to the organization and the cultural changes required by the new application; identification of the factors that will most likely facilitate or hinder the project; and planning ahead to overcome resistance and anxiety.

- Planning and Control.  One aspect of effective project management is to ensure that the right work gets done the right way, the first time. Planning and controlling the project is one way to accomplish this. Specifically, developing realistic budgets, schedules, and goals; identifying as soon as feasible potential problems and contingencies to mitigate these problems; managing and controlling change; and effectively communicating project issues and progress are critical to successfully planning and controlling the project.

No matter how complex the new application or the organizational boundaries it crosses, the steps to integrate remain approximately the same. The focus of this chapter is to zero in on the specific steps of an integration project and alternative scenarios to accomplish each step. Note that no one scenario is "correct" for every project, because each integration project is unique. This uniqueness comes from several sources which in combination create a new and different integration environment for each project. Factors that affect the integration environment include but are not limited to: corporate culture; the personality of the organizations affected; priority within the overall business strategy; and the extent, power, and authority of sponsorship.

## ROLES AND RESPONSIBILITIES

Project organization is a critical aspect of the project planning process. Before the project can get underway, it is necessary to identify the major project roles and the responsibilities that accompany those roles. Individuals must then be selected to fill the roles, based on their skills and experience in solving similar problems.

The organization for a specific project depends on the nature of the project: the software package being installed, the particular project responsibilities of the organization, the vendor, and other project characteristics. However, certain roles are common to every project. The following paragraphs discuss these roles and Figure 47AA-1 shows how they fit into a sample project organization.

- *Project Sponsors.*  Project sponsors have the ultimate authority over and responsibility for the project. The sponsors are executives who have a vested interest in the

**Figure 47AA-1**   Sample Project Organization

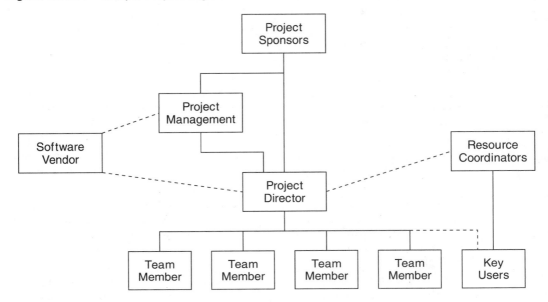

results of the project, fund the project, resolve conflict over policy or objectives, and provide high-level direction. Project sponsors are also responsible for approving changes to the software package during the integration process, for providing the additional funding required to implement those changes, and for accepting the new system at the end of the project. The project sponsors do not need to have systems development experience or knowledge of information systems, since their role is primarily that of a business decisionmaker for the project.

- *Resource Coordinators.* Hold management level roles in the organization and are in some way, shape, or form affected by the project. Resource coordinators provide support to the project by providing staffing for project tasks and subject matter expertise for the organizational functions for which they are responsible. Resource coordinators themselves may not be members of the project team; their staff may. The resource coordinators must commit resources and take responsibility for their commitment. Resource coordinators in turn should be kept up to date on project status and informed well in advance of the resources needed from their area.

- *Project Managers.* Executives within the organization who have a direct responsibility or stake in the results of the project. Project management is not only responsible for approving the work of the project team throughout the entire project but also ensuring that the information system that results from the project will meet the requirements and be properly integrated into the organization. Other responsibilities include inspecting project deliverables and making the decision regarding final acceptance of the system.

- *Project Director.* Has primary management responsibility for the entire project, including administration, planning and scheduling, issue resolution, and technical leadership. This person works closely with Project Management in addressing the needs of the organization and in coordinating joint implementation efforts within the organization. The Project Director's role is further defined in the *Project Management* step below.

- *Project Team.* Is made up of various individuals with various skill sets which in combination provides the overall talent necessary to successfully integrate the application into the organization. System analysts, designers, programmers, documentation specialists, and trainers all comprise the types of roles of the project team. Project Team members may represent all areas of the organization affected by the integration effort, including user and technical organizations. Although a core project team will support the integration effort from start to finish, other project team members may be brought in (e.g., for system acceptance testing) as specialized talent is needed.

- *Key Users.* May not support the project directly as project team members but are important to involve in the integration project for two reasons. User involvement is essential to ensure that the new application is designed and integrated in a manner that satisfies user requirements and that the transition to the new system is straightforward (because the users have been involved and have a stake in the effort). Key users can supplement the project team on an as-needed basis to assist with the design of the application as well as any decisionmaking regarding functionality. Key users should be kept informed throughout the project as to project status and key decisions and be involved in the project as much as their schedules permit.

- *Software Package Vendor.* The software vendor is primarily responsible for the delivery and installation of the base software package. In addition, the software vendor or an independent consultant may participate in validation and system testing, provide user and operations training, and assist in conversion activities. Software vendors are frequently responsible for customizing the software packages. The exact nature of the vendor's and consultant's responsibilities on an engagement should be clearly defined in a contract. A more comprehensive list of services most often provided by vendors or independent consultants can be found in Figure 47AA-2.

## 47AA-2    INTEGRATION STEPS

This section deals with the specific steps necessary to integrate software. In some cases, certain steps may not apply. For example, one integration step pertains to hardware/software installation. If in fact the software to be integrated will operate on hardware already installed and operational in the organization, the step of hardware installation is not applicable to this particular integration project. Thus, when beginning an integration project, all integration steps should be reviewed and elaborated as to their specific role in the project under consideration.

### PROJECT MANAGEMENT

The objective of project management is to plan and control the integration project from initiation to conclusion with high levels of productivity and quality and low levels of

**Figure 47AA-2**   A List of Vendor/Consultant Integration Services.

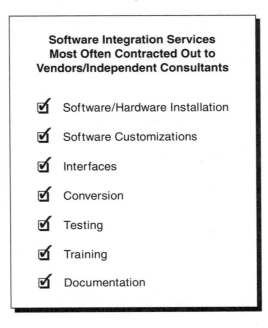

**Software Integration Services
Most Often Contracted Out to
Vendors/Independent Consultants**

- ☑ Software/Hardware Installation
- ☑ Software Customizations
- ☑ Interfaces
- ☑ Conversion
- ☑ Testing
- ☑ Training
- ☑ Documentation

uncertainty. Thus project management begins at the start of a project and continues throughout the project until its completion.

The role of a Project Director is one of a leader and a process manager. As a leader, the Project Director is responsible for managing and communicating a clear vision of the project objectives, and motivating the project team to achieve them. As a process manager, the Project Director must ensure that the right timing, resources, and sequencing of work efforts are applied to create the project deliverables within a given timeframe and budget.

Characteristics of a good Project Director generally include previous system integration and/or company experience, flexibility, sound interpersonal skills, and the ability to say "no"! Project sponsors as well as project team members will be more apt to follow direction from an experienced Project Director; simply put, an experienced Project Director is more credible. Projects, even with carefully and completely documented scopes, are rarely static; thus, a Project Director must be flexible. For example, discovery of additional tasks not originally documented in the scope, identification of required functionality thought not necessary at the start of the project, and the loss of seasoned project team members or the addition of new team members all require the Project Director to incorporate these new tasks and resources into the project plan. A Project Director must have the interpersonal skills necessary to lead and motivate the project team, manage the project sponsorship relationship, create a highly productive and synergistic project environment, and be able to say "no" to additions not originally planned for if the cost of these additions outweigh their expected benefits.

Project management activities can be grouped into six major processes as depicted in Figure 47AA-3.

**Figure 47AA-3** Project Management Processes.

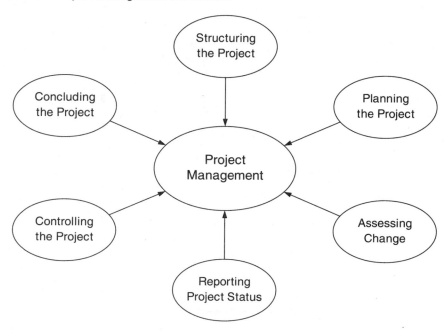

- *Structuring the Project.* The focus of this project management process is to document the objectives of the project, secure project sponsorship, define the project approach, and estimate the project in terms of effort, duration, and cost. These tasks are conducted initially at the start of the project but are also revisited throughout the project as the project evolves and changes.

- *Planning the Project.* Tasks in the planning process include developing a detailed work plan including a budget and resource assignments; defining a plan to manage risk, quality, issues, and scope; and gaining approval from project sponsors and executive management on the project plans. Again, these tasks are conducted initially at the start of the project but are also revisited throughout the project as the project evolves and changes.

- *Assessing Change.* In the context of project management, change management has two important meanings:

  1. A technique that targets the human factors affected by the project, and
  2. A mechanism through which project changes can be requested, tracked, investigated, and rejected or approved.

It is the second meaning that is the focus of this project management process. A change of this nature is an addition to, deletion from, or modification of the system during its design, development, or implementation. Although these types of changes are normal occurrences during a project, they can have a material impact on a project's scope, cost, or schedule. The change management process for this type of change works to identify changes that are good for the project and those that, in the overall analysis, may not benefit the project or may cost more than the benefits to be gained. This project management process occurs throughout the project.

- *Reporting Project Status.* Status reports identify accomplishments, work in progress, issues, and tasks that, when compared to the project plan, are overdue. Status reports should be frequently (e.g., weekly) communicated to project management, project sponsors, the user community, and other interested parties. This project management process occurs on a regular basis throughout the project.

- *Controlling the Project.* During the execution of the project, it is the responsibility of the Project Director to compare actual progress to planned progress, evaluate the results of this comparison to determine project status, and recommend or take appropriate actions based on the results of the evaluation. This process occurs on a regular basis throughout the project.

- *Concluding the Project.* This process normally occurs in the final stage of a project. It takes place once project management and sponsorship have agreed that the project has satisfied its completion criteria as defined at the start of the project. However, this process may be invoked for a project which has yet to satisfy its completion criteria (i.e., a project that the organization has decided to stop midway through the project, for whatever reason). In either case, concluding the project is the process by which the project is formally ended and the project history and its resources evaluated.

## PROJECT PLANNING

Project planning is one of the first steps of any integration project. Tasks included in project planning are: documenting the scope of the effort, assessing project risks, evaluating change management challenges, identifying a quality management program, and constructing a detailed work plan. Each of the deliverables of this step in the integration project is discussed in more detail below.

- *Scope Document.* The project scope document identifies what will be accomplished by the project and what will not. It contains the definition of the project, its boundaries, and its completion criteria. Other information about the project, such as the budget, timeframes, and resource requirements, may be included in the scope document. The project scope document therefore becomes a tool with which to manage the "boundaries" of the project as well as expectations.

- *Risk Assessment.* Early in a project, potential risks should be identified, assessed as to their criticality, and strategies and programs developed to manage the risks. Examples of risks in a software integration project are the probability that the project will not finish on time or within budget, or, upon completion, that the system will not function as expected. Note that risks differ from project to project either in type or criticality; thus, each project must be looked at individually as to the associated risks. Risk assessment should not only take place early in the project but throughout the project to identify new or previously unidentified risks or to eliminate risks that have been successfully mitigated.

- *Change Evaluation.* Before bringing in a new application, the organization must try to determine the attitudes and responses of the people who will actually use the application. If the organization suspects these attitudes are negative, then the organization must determine how to change them. The resulting change management program must be incorporated into and implemented along with the integration project.

- *Quality Checkpoints.* The concept of quality, as applied to integration projects, is quite complex. Quality not only refers to a final deliverable which meets or exceeds user expectations and satisfaction, but also refers to the process of developing the deliverable. Quality should be measurable and continually measured throughout the integration project; a quality process should be accepted and used consistently by the organization; and the integration process should be as close to fault free as possible in order to deliver a consistently high quality deliverable. Quality defined in these terms suggests that at the start of the project, quality management strategies should be agreed upon and built into the project; that the project should be executed using a formalized and proven-successful process; and that to ensure user satisfaction at the end of the project, they, the user, must be involved in defining the quality program at the start of the project as well as be involved in the execution of the project.

- *Work Plan.* The project work plan is a detailed, step-by-step plan that clearly defines what work needs to be done, the level of effort (i.e., number of hours) required, who will do it, and when it will be started and completed. Incorporated into the work plan are tasks and time estimates which take into consideration the results of the risk assessment, change evaluation, and quality strategy documented as part of the planning effort. Once the project is underway, the project work plan provides a tool against which actual progress can be measured. Figure 47AA-4 presents a high level project plan in a PERT Chart format while Figure 47AA-5 provides a sample page of a detailed project plan. Generally, the work plan should be entered into and maintained in an automated project management software tool (e.g., ABT's Project Workbench or Microsoft's Project).

## PROJECT START-UP

Tasks in the project start-up step include: identifying the project team members who will satisfy the resource requirements identified in the plan; establishing the project environment (e.g., desks, telephones, supplies, computer equipment, system access); briefing the project team, user community, and other interested parties on the project goals, approach, and schedule; and establishing the project control system (e.g., documentation standards, issue capture and control mechanisms, time reporting, filing). Often, application and technical training are considered parts of this task. Initial application and technical training are conducted (usually by the vendor or independent consultant) for all project team members, to establish an initial basis of understanding regarding the design and functionality of the application to be integrated.

## PROJECT MEETINGS

Although at first glance, this step would appear to be more logically associated as a task of another step in the integration project instead of its own step, it is broken out due to

**Figure 47AA-4** A Pert Chart Representation of a Project Workplan.

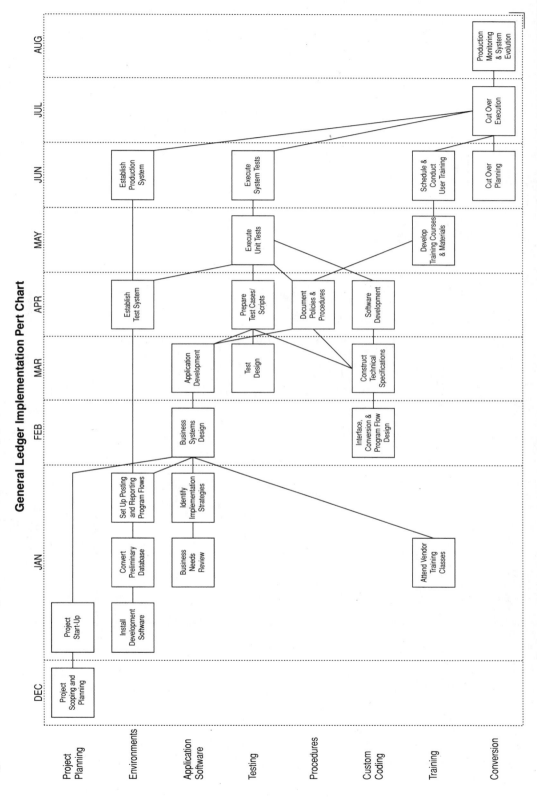

**General Ledger Implementation Pert Chart**

**Figure 47AA-5** A Page of a Detailed Work Plan.

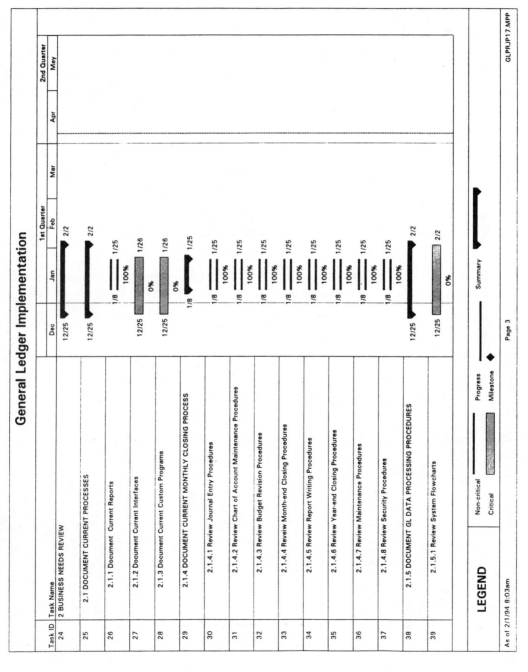

210

the number of hours associated with preparing for, attending, and documenting project meetings. The project meetings covered under this step include:

- *Project Team Meetings.* Conducted by the Project Director on a frequent basis (usually weekly), these meetings facilitate communication regarding progress to date on assigned tasks, outstanding issues, and follow-up items. Assignments and deadlines are often distributed during these meetings as well as responsibility for follow-up on issues and other items. In subsequent meetings, reports of progress on the assignments can be discussed. Project meetings are an excellent communication tool and also serve to evaluate progress against plan.

- *Project Management Meetings.* Conducted by the Project Director, these meetings can occur less frequently than team meetings. They serve to keep project management up to date on the project status and major project issues. As project management is comprised of executives with a stake in the project, these meetings serve as a communication tool for project activities and as a forum to outline strategies and action steps to resolve major project issues like resource shortfalls, critical design issues, and application/technical direction. At these meetings, project management in turn serves in a support role to the Project Director while addressing project approach and execution issues.

- *Senior Executive Meetings.* Conducted on a more infrequent basis or on an as-needed basis, these meetings serve as a communication tool for appropriate senior executives in the organization. The first Senior Executive Meeting is usually conducted once the project scope and plan are finalized to communicate and gain agreement on the overall project objectives, scope, approach, schedule, and budget. Subsequent meetings focus on project status or on recommendations resulting in major changes to the original project objectives, scope, approach, schedule, or budget. These meetings are conducted by the Project Director or a member of the project management team.

- *Resource Coordinator Meetings.* As noted previously, resource coordinators are organizational representatives affected by the integration project but do not participate directly on the project team. Resource coordinators usually support the project team in one of two ways: by providing additional resources to assist in accomplishing project tasks, and/or by supplementing project team knowledge with their expertise of their organizational function. Usually the Project Director works closely with resource coordinators, confirming resource availability and commitment and securing resource coordinator review and approval of project deliverables.

- *User Meetings.* Users who are not part of the project team must be kept up to date regarding the project. This communication begins at the start of the project often via a formal meeting at which the project objectives, approach, and schedule are presented. Throughout the project, user involvement is critical not only in designing and integrating an application that meets their needs, but also in facilitating the change process so that once the application is available for everyday use, the users feel comfortable and confident with the new application. Involving the users can take many forms: design interviews, deliverable reviews, update meetings, and even special programs such as newsletters, poster campaigns, and informal social outings.

- *Organizational Meetings.* Any major integration project will be of interest to the organization as a whole. Communication via a formal meeting to organizational representatives (or the entire organization) will provide the organization with real information regarding the project rather than allowing informal communication, which could misstate elements of the project, to satisfy curiosity. At the very least, an organizational meeting at the start of the project will present project objectives, approach, schedule, and team members, and a second meeting prior to going live on the application will confirm the objectives, expected results, and final timetables of the integration project. These sessions should encourage questions from the audience so that, to the extent possible, all unanswered questions and concerns regarding the project are satisfied.

## BUSINESS NEEDS REVIEW

The results of the Business Needs Review step form the foundation for the new application. It is critical to the success of the integration project to review the business requirements to confirm or redefine the application needs. To accomplish this, key members of the project team gather and finalize data about the information requirements of the business areas with appropriate business managers and staff. As the result of these interviews, project team members document, at a high level, current business inputs and outputs, processes, manual workflows, and controls. These interviews will also provide the project team with the necessary information to develop high-level information models. Additionally, high-level specifications for key interfaces as well as data, operational, and technical requirements will be reviewed. Lastly, a current systems reports and forms binder is constructed as part of this step.

The deliverables of this step include a requirements document and documentation of the current processes. Figure 47AA-6 provides an example of documentation for one of the current system processes: a high-level interface chart.

## HARDWARE/SOFTWARE INSTALLATION

At the very least, a software integration project requires that the software to be integrated must be installed on the organization's information systems. It is often the case, however, that new hardware and/or system software (i.e., software necessary to operate the hardware and application software together) is required and must be installed as well. This step of the project represents these installations as well as testing of the installation to ensure that the new software and hardware are operational. Information systems representatives usually participate in the hardware and software installation, but information systems and user representatives both should participate in the execution of the installation test scripts. Testing the installation not only helps ensure a proper and complete installation of the software and hardware but also provides additional training for information systems personnel and the users regarding application functionality as well as system construction and operation.

Hardware and software vendors usually provide additional assistance during this step of the integration project. Vendors may provide on-site assistance with the installation as well as supply and help execute test scripts to ensure a complete installation. Alternatively, instead of providing on-site assistance, software vendors may provide a tape with instructions for loading the software and executing test scripts. Installation

**Figure 47AA-6**   Interface Chart.

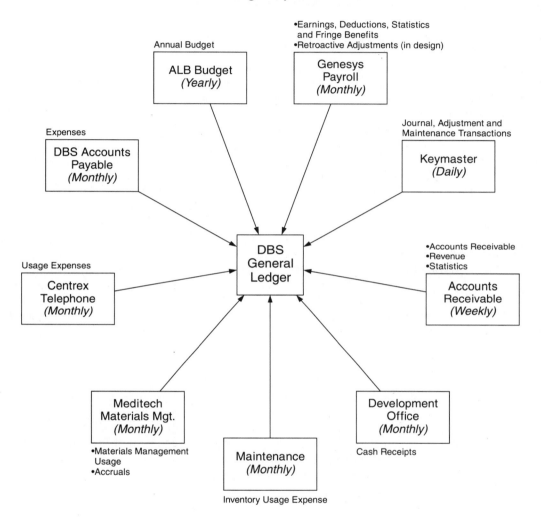

## General Ledger Input Interfaces

support is also available via a "1-800" phone number which accesses the vendor's help desks. It is important to understand exactly what type of installation assistance will be provided by the vendor's contract terms prior to signing the contract for the purchase/lease of hardware and software. Prior to executing the contract, compare the installation services offered with the capabilities and comfort of your own information systems staff and construct an installation support agreement that is satisfactory to all parties.

Additional software and hardware may need to be installed in order to allow user access from their desks. This is often referred to as remote hardware installation and includes the installation of the wiring, hubs, emulation and/or network software, desktop terminals/personal computers, printers, and so on that are needed for users to access the new software and operate the application from their desks in the business unit.

## BUSINESS SYSTEMS DESIGN

In this step, the application is designed from the end user's perspective. Project team analysts design application parameters, tables, and files as well as the policies and procedures necessary to support the business. Reports and forms for each module of the application are also designed.

At this point in the project, project team members should have a fairly good understanding of system functionality based on the vendor training provided in the *Project Start-Up* step. Matching the application's functionality to the requirements identified in the *Business Needs Review* step will often highlight deficiencies in functionality that must be addressed. Decisions as to how to handle these gaps must be made. Several alternatives for handling these gaps are available and are discussed below.

- *Customize the Application.* This alternative requires design, implementation, and testing of application customizations that will overcome gaps in required application functionality. In many cases, the vendor will code these customizations based on a design (or functional specification) provided by the organization. Further, if known at the start of the project, customizations can be included in the vendor contract. However, it should be noted that customizations increase the complexity and length of the project, usually significantly. Additionally, it can invalidate the software warranty and make the application of upgrades extremely difficult. Therefore, any customizations should be carefully reviewed and every attempt made to avoid customizations for this very reason.

- *Create a Work-Around.* Instead of specifying a customization to the application, this alternative suggests the development of a process in or around the application that will handle the requirement. In many cases, the cost of customizing the application to meet the requirement far outweighs the benefit of the functionality. In this situation, other application functionality or manual processes should be considered for handling the requirement.

- *Reject the Requirement.* In many cases the requirement driving the gap in functionality is a desire but not critical to the application's success in solving the business need. In these cases, it is recommended to integrate the application as is, operate the application at least six months, and then determine if the functionality is required. If the functionality is determined necessary, then the organization can begin the process of specifying the functionality design and contracting with the vendor to customize the application to include the functionality.

No matter which alternative is determined to be the most optimal for handling each gap in functionality, the results of this task must be incorporated into the project work plan.

Another task included in this step is process assessment and redesign. In the past, organizations have integrated new applications to solve their business needs with little or no attention paid to the processes existing before and after the integration of the new application. This particular task suggests that the current business processes should be reviewed and non-value or redundant processes eliminated. Then, based on the functionality of the new application, the current processes should be redesigned to take advantage of the new application. The deliverable for this particular step is a design of new workflows which maximizes the benefits of the new application.

Last, strategies for future steps in the integration project are defined at a high level. Strategy statements for data conversion, testing, training, and operations are developed as part of this step. For example, a strategy statement for data conversion would include a high-level discussion of the following aspects of conversion: the scope and pace of the effort; data conversion techniques; the approach for data reconciliation, maintenance, and synchronization; the plan for data security; and a contingency strategy for production cut-over.

Deliverables for this step include:

- A brief description of what data will be loaded in the parameters, tables, and files of the new application; where the data will come from; resource requirements; and timeframe necessary to complete the data loading.
- An outline of the procedure manuals proposed for the project, a design of the structure of these manuals, identification of the resource requirements, and the timeframe necessary to complete the documentation effort.
- A design of new reports and forms required by the new application.
- A gap analysis report with recommendations of how functionality gaps will be handled by the project.
- A design of the processes surrounding the new application.
- High level strategy statements for key steps of the integration project: data conversion, testing, training, operations, etc. Figure 47AA-7 provides an example of one such strategy statement.

## INTERFACE AND PROGRAM FLOW DESIGN

This step defines a specific approach for developing automated interfaces to and/or from the new application. Also, as part of this step, technical design of program flows and the nightly batch processing are completed, if necessary. Each will be discussed separately.

When investigating which interfaces might be appropriate for the new application, apply the following tests:

- If the new application replaces a previously automated system, any established automated interfaces to/from the to-be-replaced application are prime candidates for replacement (and probably should be replaced).
- If data needed for input into the new application is available from a report generated by an automated system, an interface is quite feasible from the source system.
- If data needed for input into the new application is available on another automated system, an automated interface should be evaluated.
- If data which is expected to be in the new system is needed in a downstream system, an automated interface from the new application to the downstream system should be investigated.

**Figure 47AA-7**   Sample Training Strategy.

Two types of general ledger training efforts will be undertaken during this project: 1) training the implementation team and 2) training end users.

The implementation team consists of those users who will assist in the definition of how the upgraded software will be implemented for the organization and in the execution of this design. Depending on their role in the implementation, implementation team members will attend vendor training courses on the general ledger and/or both report writers. We will also provide internal training to project team members who did not attend the vendor sessions. We envision that this internal training will occur at various times during the implementation on an as needed basis.

End user training will be scheduled for late June/early July as we hope to time the training of users with their actual use of the system for the July close. At this point in the project we think that an off-site training session would be beneficial for end users for several reasons:

- Motivation—Getting away from the office for a day and spending the day in a nice training facility will have a motivational impact to learn the new features and functionality and focus on how to apply these features to their own environment.

- Positive PR for the upgrade—A day away from the office in a nice facility with professional trainers will definitely boost the goodwill towards the system.

- Focus—A day away from the office will allow the end users to focus entirely on the subject matter at hand: learning the new general ledger.

- Training Expertise—Professional trainers will set scripts and exercises that will not only cover the necessary material completely but will reinforce how to use the general ledger through exercises and question and answer periods.

Since we have developed internal training classes, we will need to evaluate whether or not the off-site training will be handled by the organization at its training center or by the vendor at their training location.

In either case, we envision end user training to consist of a one day session which will cover the following topics: basic journal processing, special journal processing, maintenance and error correction. We plan to include organization specific information into the training session, like how to number journal batches, how to use source code, how to code intercompany journals, etc.

We also plan to develop reporting and budget training courses for use initially to train implementation team members. These courses would be offered to a subset of end users; those users who will be actively involved with report writing and/or budgeting for the department.

Once live on the upgraded general ledger, each operating area will be responsible for training new employees or retraining current employees on the use of the general ledger.

Many system integration projects limit the number of interfaces to be implemented to only those that replace a previously automated interface. This is done for several reasons, but primarily to limit the scope of the project and by doing so, better ensure project success (by meeting aggressive deadlines and conservative budget estimates). Interfaces, because they usually result in custom coding, add significant time and resource needs to the integration project for design, coding, testing, and so on. Further, interfaces identified but not implemented during the initial integration of the application can always be implemented once the application is up and running.

Software vendors can assist with coding the side of the interface that will directly interact with their application, usually for a price. Thus, custom interface needs should be identified prior to contracting with the software vendor and included in the contract at an agreeable price. On the other hand, the organization is usually responsible for coding the side of the interface that directly interacts with a source or destination system (again the vendors of these systems can assist in designing, coding, and testing the interface for a price). Note that interface requirements include the reports necessary to balance and reconcile the interfaces. These reports contain information such as records read and records written and dollar (or other totals) balancing. Interface reports are reconciled with source and destination system reports. These source and destination system reports should be identified prior to determining the design and format of the interface reports so that similar levels of detail can be generated on the interface reports to allow for easier balancing/reconciling.

As part of designing the interfaces, their relationship to how the application operates must also be determined. For example, if a daily interface from an accounts receivable package to a new general ledger application is proposed, and if the accounts receivable transactions are posted in the general ledge application once received, a potential program flow scenario might be to execute the interface (which loads the transactions into the general ledger) then execute the general ledger posting program. Each interface must be reviewed individually as to where it fits in relation to the new application's program flows, resulting in a new flow design.

Further, applications may provide for many different program scenarios which also must be designed in this step. For example, suppose that the expectations for the new general ledger application include nightly posting (five days per week), weekly reporting, and on the last working day of the month, posting of all allocations of overhead and monthly interfaces and the generation of the monthly reports. Thus, the program flow on Monday through Thursday (except at the end of the month) would include posting but would not include reporting, allocations, or interfaces. The program flow on Fridays (except at the end of the month) would include posting and weekly reporting but not allocations, interfaces, or monthly reporting. Saturday and Sunday cycles would not include posting, reporting, allocations, or interfaces. On the last day of the month, all monthly cycles would be executed (including posting of the allocations and interfaces). A monthly schedule for this example is illustrated in Figure 47AA-8. It is easy to see that determining daily, weekly, monthly, etc., program flows is not straightforward and must be carefully planned. Also allow for a process to insert ad hoc programs into an established program flow as needed (for example, if the weekly reporting programs need to be executed midweek).

The deliverables for this step of the integration project include functional specifications for all automated interfaces, interface reports, and program flows.

## DATA CONVERSION DESIGN

This step defines a specific approach for converting necessary data from each to-be-replaced source system to the appropriate destination database. Two types of approaches are most often used in data conversions:

- Automated—This approach transfers data automatically from the source system to the new application's database(s) while providing an audit trail of the process.

**Figure 47AA-8**   A Sample Monthly Processing Schedule.

| June | | | | | | |
|---|---|---|---|---|---|---|
| **SUNDAY** | **MONDAY** | **TUESDAY** | **WEDNESDAY** | **THURSDAY** | **FRIDAY** | **SATURDAY** |
|  |  |  | 1 | 2 | 3 | 4 |
|  |  |  | Posting | Posting | Posting, Weekly Reporting |  |
| 5 | 6 | 7 | 8 | 9 | 10 | 11 |
|  | Posting | Posting | Posting | Posting | Posting, Weekly Reporting |  |
| 12 | 13 | 14 | 15 | 16 | 17 | 18 |
|  | Posting | Posting | Posting | Posting | Posting, Weekly Reporting |  |
| 19 | 20 | 21 | 22 | 23 | 24 | 25 |
|  | Posting | Posting | Posting | Posting | Posting, Weekly Reporting |  |
| 26 | 27 | 28 | 29 | 30 |  |  |
|  | Posting | Posting | Posting | Allocations Overhead Posting Monthly Reports |  |  |

- Manual—This approach is used when an automated approach is not practical and consists of manual procedures for loading the application database(s).

Most data conversions consist of both of these approaches. An automated approach is ideal for converting a source database that is very similar to a destination database. For example, most general ledgers store account balances. If a general ledger is being replaced and the chart of accounts for the most part remains the same, an automated program to convert the chart of accounts and account balances to the new application may be beneficial. When deciding on a data conversion approach, factors such as the amount of time it would take to manually convert a database versus the amount of time it would take to design, code, and test an automated conversion program must be weighed. Factors that can complicate automated conversions include combining data from multiple sources where data records are not a one-to-one match, where the data cannot be sorted in the same manner, or where data elements were used inconsistently between and within each system.

Manual conversions are usually recommended for converting data off of a manual system; for converting data from a source database that differs significantly from the destination database; for source databases that require a maximum of scouring to produce data that is accurate, complete, and timely; or for new applications where automated conversions are not recommended. One way to convert manually is to develop an input sheet that closely resembles the input screen of the new application. Each input sheet is then completed with the data to be input and then reviewed for completeness and accuracy. Data conversion, then, is accomplished by manually inputting the data off of the input sheet directly into the new system. (Data input can be accomplished by temporary help if available resources are limited.) Often, the manual conversion will be partially automated by creating the data input sheets automatically from the source system, including information available from the source system. The data automatically loaded on these sheets from the source system can then be reviewed and updated and new data items, not available on the source system, can be added.

Prior to conversion, using either approach, it is recommended that the organization make a concentrated effort to review, correct, or delete the information to be converted so that the database which is ultimately converted is accurate, complete, and timely. A software integration project is a perfect opportunity to clean up current information and establish an accurate, complete, and timely database on the new system.

A third conversion option exists: not to convert. Some situations warrant the completion of open transactions on the current system while executing all new transactions on the new system. For example, it might be more cost beneficial to complete the open purchase orders on the current accounts payable system rather than converting these to the new system. Reasons for doing this include the complexity of converting one system's transaction records to another system's format. Many times this conversion is not straightforward. Also, the new system numbering scheme usually differs from that of the old system, yet all vendor correspondence regarding the old system's purchase order will include the old system's purchase order number. This approach, however, has its costs, including maintaining the old system and staff to operate it, sorting invoices and check requests between old system transactions and new system transactions, and responding to inquiries, some regarding old system transactions and some regarding new system transactions. At some point, it becomes more cost beneficial to convert the remaining transactions off of the old system and phase out the old system. Usually this conversion can be accomplished manually due to the small number of transactions remaining on the old system.

The deliverables of this step of the integration project include:

- An overall design document which discusses the approaches, strategies, resource requirements, timing, and contingency plans to be used to establish the databases in the new application system.
- A functional specification for each automated data conversion being considered, including the approach, strategy, and overall discussion of the particular data conversion; mapping of the source system file layout to the new application system file layout; timing considerations; resource requirements; security needs; reconciliation processes; contingency plans; and documentation strategy to satisfy internal/external audit requirements. This functional specification will be used by programmers to develop the conversion programs.
- A functional specification for each automated download being considered. Again, these automated downloads would consist of source system data formatted onto an input document representing the input screen of the new application. Included

in this specification are the approach, strategy, and overall discussion of the file download; mapping of source system data records to positions on the input document; plans for reviewing, confirming, and completing the input documents; resource requirements; prioritization schemes; documentation control processes; contingency plans; and documentation strategy to satisfy internal/external audit requirements. This function specification will be used by programmers to develop the programs to create the input sheets.

## TEST DESIGN

During this step, high-level plans for unit, integration, and acceptance testing of the application software components are developed. Test plans defined the approach, control system, objectives, conditions, and test scripts for conducting software testing. The three primary objectives of testing are:

- Prove that the application system addresses the business problem and satisfies the user's requirements.
- Uncover application system defects.
- Help ensure quality throughout the project.

Several types of tests are planned for in this step and include:

- *Unit Tests.*  The most basic level of testing to verify that the software code works according to its specifications and to validate program logic. Unit tests are independent tests of application functionality and include tests of the baseline software, interfaces, conversion programs, and any other customizations. The objective of these tests is to ensure that each function of the application independently operates as expected. Typically, the test team is responsible for executing unit tests.

- *Integration Tests.*  The testing of combinations of individually unit-tested pieces of code as they are united into a complete unit, i.e., testing of the application as a whole. Whereas unit testing ensures that each application function can operate independently, integration testing ensures that all functions, interacting together in a simulated live environment, operate as expected. Often the information systems staff that will be responsible for the application once it is in production, will participate to simulate the true live environment. The test team, in this test, usually functions as the user would in the live environment.

- *System Tests.*  Many types of tests can be conducted as part of system tests including: usability tests, final requirements tests, volume and stress tests, performance tests, security and control tests, recovery tests, documentation and procedures tests, and multi-site tests. Although all of these tests are important, a focus on volume, stress, and performance tests is critical to ensure that the application will function as expected under typical operating conditions.

- *Acceptance Tests.*  Demonstrates that the application meets the original business objectives and satisfies user and information systems requirements. If the user is not involved in the execution of unit and/or integration tests, acceptance testing is a must. Acceptance tests are executed by the user so that the user can confirm (and feel comfortable) that the application will function as expected under normal operating conditions. Usually a subset of the integrated tests are used in the acceptance test with the focus on simulating a typical day, month-end, and year-end situation. At the end of these tests, users often sign-off on the results of the tests and their acceptance of the application. It is important to note that some training of the user must take place prior to their involvement in acceptance testing so that they know how to conduct the tests. Even with training, users participating in the acceptance test may need assistance executing the tests. It is also recommended that user application training occur prior to acceptance testing so that the user, with a minimum amount of training on how to conduct acceptance tests, is able to independently execute the tests.

- *Bench Tests.* Another type of test conducted as part of an integration project and is related to custom code development. Bench testing is the first of all tests conducted and is performed by the programmer to ensure that the custom code developed meets the requirements identified in the functional and technical specifications. Custom code is developed for interfaces and conversion programs, for example, and thus bench testing is an integral part of the development of that code. Bench testing will be discussed in more detail in the *Software Development* section of this chapter.

A test plan or design consists of several components: an overall test strategy; the test control system; and test objectives, conditions, and scripts. Each are discussed below:

- *Test Strategy.* Discusses the overall plan for accomplishing testing during the integration project. A test strategy identifies which tests will be conducted, by whom, and in what time frames. The strategy also defines the scope and approach for each of the tests to be executed. Other elements of the test strategy include specifications for the test environment (i.e., a controlled copy of the application that is only used for testing); requirements for security; the design of the initial database (some data may need to be loaded prior to conducting the first tests); backup and recovery considerations; documentation needs (including requirements necessary to satisfy internal/external auditors); and resource and responsibility assignments.

- *Test Control System.* The system developed to document and control when tests will be executed and by whom, what tests are complete, what tests have yet to be executed, and what tests did not complete as expected and require follow-up. Typical output of a test control system is a schedule of tests by day and responsibility, a log of all tests and their status, and a log of all tests needing follow-up (usually called an issues log). The issues log indicates the specific test that did not execute as expected, who was responsible for executing the test, who is responsible for following up and resolving the issue, priority of the issue, current status of the issue, resolution of the issue, and date resolved. The issue log is used to manage incomplete tests and their timely resolution.

- *Test Objectives, Conditions, and Scripts.* Once the test strategy is understood, the detailed tests can be documented. Detailed tests consist of three major elements: objectives, conditions, and scripts as presented in Figure 47AA-9. Test objectives

**Figure 47AA-9** Sample Test Objective, Conditions, and Script.

**Unit Test Script**
**Accounts Payable—Invoice Entry**                                     **Case Number:** AP01

| | |
|---|---|
| **Test Objective:** | To unit test the invoice function using all invoice types of the organization. |
| **Test Cycle:** | 1 |
| **Test Schedule Date:** | 6/4/94 |

| | |
|---|---|
| **Forms/Reports Used:** | Vendor Invoice |
| **Report(s) Produced:** | Transaction Schedule, Transaction Log |

| Condition # | Condition Description | Activities | Expected Results | Verified By | Date | Issue # |
|---|---|---|---|---|---|---|
| 1. AP01.01 | Complete Match: Invoice total matches P.O. and Receiver. | Process the invoices, using the Invoice Entry Procedure and the invoice(s) marked to be used for this condition. | Invoice is able to be entered in summary due to complete match. | B. Scott | 6/4/94 | None |
| 1. AP01.03 | Incomplete Match: Invoice total does not match P.O. and Receiver but within tolerance. | Process the invoices, using the Invoice Entry Procedure and the invoice(s) marked to be used for this condition. | Invoice is within tolerance and is able to be input in detail. | B. Scott | 6/4/94 | 9 |
| 1. AP01.06 | Enter an invoice a second time. | Process the invoices, using the Invoice Entry Procedure and the invoice(s) marked to be used for this condition. | System replies "already on file" for duplicate invoice. | B. Scott | 6/4/94 | None |
| 1. AP01.57 | Process a standing order invoice. | Process the invoices, using the Invoice Entry Procedure and the invoice(s) marked to be used for this condition. | Standing order invoice is able to be processed. Adjusted standing order balance correct. | B. Scott | 6/4/94 | 11 |

are the overall statement as to the goal of the test. Test conditions break the objective into testable components. Test scripts document the input, predicted results, and execution conditions of a given test item. Test scripts in total provide tests for each objective and condition. For each test script, specific data is collected and anticipated results are predicted. In other words, test scripts provide the information for the tester of exactly how to test the condition(s) and includes an expected outcome for each of the tests. The expected outcome, during test execution, is compared to the actual outcome to verify that the test executed as expected. If the expected outcome does not match the actual outcome, the test is then logged on the issues log and investigated as to why it performed as such. Note that there is not necessarily a one-for-one relationship between a test script and condition. For example, multiple conditions may be tested by a single script, a single condition may be tested by a single script, or even a single condition may be tested several times in several scripts, scripts which also test other conditions, etc.

## TRAINING DESIGN

During this step, detailed training programs for users and information systems support staff are developed. Included in the training material are participant training manuals, training presentation materials, and "hands-on" exercises. Prior to developing the training materials, the types of training classes necessary and their content must be identified. To do this, the training audience and their skill set must be evaluated. Often the vendor provides training and materials; however, vendor training is usually generic and not customized for the organization's needs. Customized training that reflects the system use expected on a day-to-day basis is much more beneficial and easier to understand by the user. It is more difficult to learn a system whose examples reflect a car dealership and translate that use into a manufacturing organization than it is to learn a new system using everyday examples of the transactions currently processed in the manufacturing organization. However, vendor training materials are a great basis for building training programs customized for the organization.

Identifying who will conduct the training is another task covered by this step in the integration project. Again, the vendor usually is able to supply a trainer for a cost (vendor training can be contracted for when the software is purchased/leased). However, it is important to develop trainers internally not only to provide ongoing training to new users or update classes for current users but also to eliminate the dependency and cost of resorting to vendor training once the system is operational.

A train-the-trainer program can be used to train a number of employees to become trainers on the software functionality. A train-the-trainer program is one where a knowledgeable project team member or vendor representative trains a group of users, identified as potential trainers, on how to conduct training classes on software functionality. These new trainers then team teach with the vendor or project team trainer until they feel comfortable taking on the class themselves. The project team trainer or vendor then reviews and supports the trainers until they feel comfortable that the new trainers are experienced enough to handle classes on their own. Formal surveys of attendees can also diagnose trainer issues as well as content, format, and other issues and are recommended for all training classes.

Other tasks included in this step are identifying responsibility for and scheduling of the training sessions, preparing the appropriate hardware and facilities in which to conduct the training, identifying the database requirements necessary for execution of the training courses, and preparing the system database so that training exercises can be completed in class.

## SOFTWARE DEVELOPMENT

All custom software (i.e., interfaces, conversion programs, and application customizations) is coded and bench tested as part of this step. (Bench testing, as described in the *Test Design* step, is the testing conducted by the programmer to ensure that the program code executes without error and meets the requirements identified in the functional specification.) This step includes preparing a technical specification from the functional specification developed in the *Interface and Program Flow Design* and *Data Conversion Design* steps. A technical specification, usually developed by a technical analyst, is a more detailed specification as to how the program modules will be designed, coded, and linked to accomplish the functionality documented in the functional specification. Often a pseudo coding language is used in the technical specification; this language is easily translated into program code by a programmer. The technical specification also addresses requirements for the construction and bench test environment and the development and testing of common models and program skeletons. These components are then used to develop the specific software.

As previously discussed, the vendor can be used to develop much of the custom software components. Areas requiring the organization's involvement include programming to provide the vendor with interface or conversion data directly from the organization's source systems. The vendor then takes the data and restructures it into a format that is acceptable to the new application. The vendor can also provide an output interface in a format readable by the organization's destination systems, however the organization may need to develop programs that reformat the data into files that can be accepted by the destination system.

## APPLICATION DEVELOPMENT

This step of work includes loading the application software per the specifications developed during the *Business System Design* step. Tasks include loading set-up parameters, tables, files, screens, and reports. Note that in some cases, application files may be loaded automatically by the conversion programs designed in the *Data Conversion Design* step and constructed in the *Software Development* step.

If certain large files are not able to be loaded automatically, as discussed in the *Data Conversion Design* step, this step, *Application Development,* is where the data input sheets would be completed, reviewed, and manually keyed into the new system. Note that file building of this nature may not be trivial. For example, if the application to be integrated is a purchasing and/or accounts payable application, building the vendor file manually is not trivial, especially if the current vendor file maintains information on thousands of vendors (as most do). Be sure to plan plenty of time to gather and validate all the necessary file information as well as the time necessary to input the required number of files. If time constraints do exist, one approach can be used to build a very usable if not complete file. Using the vendor file as an example, sort all the vendors maintained in the current system in terms of purchase volume, current activity, and/or dollar volume. Use this ranking criteria to prioritize the vendors whose profiles are to be completed first. That way if only half of the vendor file is built by the time the system is operational, at least the half that is built may represent 80% or so of the purchases. Then as new vendors are needed, the remaining vendor files can be built as part of daily operations.

## PROCEDURE DEVELOPMENT

User manuals required to implement and operate the new application are completed in this step. These manuals are developed according to outlines generated and approved during the *Business Systems Design* step. Procedures cover areas such as user procedures, data center operations, help desk, data security and control, disaster recovery, and application maintenance.

The procedures documented in this step can range from abbreviated desktop user procedures (see Figure 47AA-10 for an example)—which focus only on how to operate the system—to full-blown policy and procedure manuals—which cover not only the procedures necessary to operate the system, but also the workflow procedures required in and around the system and the organizational policy statements regarding the particular transaction being documented. At the start of the project, a procedure strategy should be developed to identify the type, content, and scope of the procedures to be documented as part of the integration effort. This strategy can then guide the outlines developed in the *Business Systems Design* step as well as the final procedures documented in this step.

Whatever strategy is implemented for procedure documentation, two types of documents will assist in the development of procedures: vendor procedure manuals and current organizational policy and procedure manuals. Vendor documentation provides a sound basis for the development of the procedures of how to operate the system. Similar to the comments regarding the use vendor training only, system usage procedures should be customized using organizational examples. Again, trying to use a new car dealership example for how to use the system to process a certain transaction will be as useful to the user as using a real-life example from the organization.

Current organizational policy and procedure manuals provide a sound basis for developing procedure manuals that cover not only system usage but the other workflow procedures to be used with the new system as well as company policy statements regarding the transactions involved. Note that organizational policy for certain transactions may not change as the result of integrating the new system, however, in many cases, workflows will. The current documentation can assist in the design and format of the new policy and procedure manual (or improvements to it) as well as provide a checklist to ensure that the new policy and procedure manual is complete (as compared with the topics discussed in the current manual).

## TEST EXECUTION

Project team members, users, and information systems representatives will execute the tests developed in the *Test Design* step to help ensure that the system meets its specified functional performance and service level objectives. Test execution consists of following the instructions contained in the test scripts and comparing actual results with expected results (also documented in the test scripts). If the actual result does not

**Figure 47AA-10**   Sample Desktop Procedure.

---

### H1.4    DELETING AN ENTIRE JOURNAL ENTRY

The DELETE JOURNALS (JRNLDEL) screen is used to delete both the header and detail lines from the system without having to delete each item individually. To delete both header and detail journal records from the system, select the DELETE JOURNALS screen as follows:

**STEP 1:**  Place an X to the left of the JRNLDEL DELETE JOURNALS transaction on the JOURNAL MENU screen.
Press ENTER.
The Delete Journals screen (H1.4) will appear on the terminal.

---

```
OGLDDJRO                  FINANCIAL MANAGEMENT SYSTEM
JRNLDEL                         DELETE JOURNALS                    STEP

ORG ID:  ORG NAME:
JRNL ID: DESCRIPTION:

LN $ T/  EFFEC E/JOURNAL  D/C                       No        Reversal
NO # T   DATE H/SOURCE    G    CONTROL TOTAL  XLAT SJE STA ERR OOB DATE
                                        000                    00/00/00



DELETE? (Y/N):            LINE NO:
NEXT FUNCTION: JRNLDEL    NEXT KEY:
DC800003 ORGANIZATION NOT DEFINED
```

---

**STEP 2:**  Type in the journal key to identify the journal entry.
Press ENTER.
Remember, the journal key is made up of five items:
- ORG ID
- JRNL ID
- $/#
- T/T
- EFFEC DATE

The system will display the Expanded Journal Header information associated with the journal key. Detail line item information will not be displayed. Also notice a DELETE? (Y/N) promptly at the bottom of the screen. The cursor will appear to the right of the prompt. Verify that the appropriate journal is displayed.

**STEP 3:**  If this is the journal to be deleted, replace the N with a Y at the DELETE? (Y/N) field.
Press ENTER.
The system will respond with the message RECORD DELETED.
If the wrong journal has been selected, do not replace the N at the DELETE? (Y/N) field and press ENTER.

**STEP 4:**  To return to Journal Menu,
Press CLEAR.

---

match the expected result, the outcome is documented on an issue log (see Figure 47AA-11 for a sample issue log).

Issues arising as a result of differences between actual results and the acceptance criteria will be analyzed and corrective action taken. Usually issues fall into one of four categories:

- *Software Bug.* Issues of this type are those where the software functions incorrectly. These issues are usually communicated to the vendor who in turn corrects the software and provides the correction to the organization. Correction of these types of issues may not be trivial and thus time must be planned for in this step to allow the vendor an opportunity to correct the application and test the correction prior to providing new code to the organization for retesting.

- *Expected Is Incorrect.* Issues of this type are those where the software does not act as expected. This does not mean that the software is functioning incorrectly; in fact, it most probably is functioning as expected from the vendor point of view but maybe not how the organization expected it to function. For these types of issues, either the user corrects the expected result in the test script and executes the test again, or the user works with the vendor to identify another way to satisfy the test condition with the software (in the case of how the software functions is not acceptable to the user).

- *Script Is Incorrect.* Issues of this type result from errors in the test script. In other words, the actual results of the test were correct based on the way the test script was written. However, the expected results were based on how the test script was thought to be constructed, and thus the expected and actual results did not match. In these cases, the test script should be corrected to meet the condition(s) to be tested and executed again to validate the test.

- *Script Was Executed Incorrectly.* Issues of this type result from errors in executing the test script (i.e., incorrect keystroke). In other words, the actual results of the test were correct based on the way the test script was executed, but did not match the expected results because the test script was not executed as written. In these cases, the test script should be executed again to validate the test.

Note that in executing tests, unit tests should be executed and all issues resolved and retested prior to beginning the integration tests. In turn, the integration tests should be completed prior to conducting the systems tests, and the same for acceptance testing. Internal and external auditors should be notified at the start of test execution so that they can plan to observe the tests or review the documentation, if necessary, during the test effort. Test scripts, control documentation, and test results should be accumulated, filed, and stored in case internal or external auditors need to review the tests at a later date.

On completion of testing, user and management acceptance of the new application system will be obtained before proceeding with the integration project.

## TRAINING EXECUTION

This step consists of executing the training designed in the *Training Design* step. Training execution should be conducted early enough at the end of the integration project so that the training is complete prior to going live; however, training should not be conducted too

**Figure 47AA-11**    Sample Issues Log.

| Issue | Function | Test Cycle | Test Run | Test Case # | Test Cond. # | Tester Name | Software Function | Issue Description |
|-------|----------|------------|----------|-------------|--------------|-------------|-------------------|-------------------|
| 1. | Purchasing | 1 | 1 | ACQ1-11 | All | E. Smith | 2.10.3.11.8 | Detail Purchase Order not organization's form |
| 2. | Purchasing | 1 | 1 | ACQ5 ACQ7 | All | E. Smith | 2.10.3.1 | Cannot print summary purchase order |
| 3. | Purchasing | 1 | 1 | ACQ2 | All | E. Smith | None | Requisitions need to be modified to match actual test case |
| 4. | Purchasing | 1 | 1 | ACQ7 | All | E. Smith | None | Requisitions need to be modified to match actual test case |
| 5. | Inventory | 1 | 1 | INV1-INV2 | 1.INV1.04 1.INV2.04 | T. Jones | 2.9.5.2 | A/xxxxxx -Alternate Reference Number search not working in test environment. |
| 6. | Purchasing | 1 | 1 | ACQ1-11 | All | E. Smith | 2.10.8.2 | Message displayed "**Warning**" Primary vendor: (blank) when pulled up catalog item w/o vendor in catalog |
| 7. | Inventory | 1 | 1 | INV1-INV5 | All | T. Jones | None | Need a report that shows quantity on-hand, by location, by item number, but not by vendor |
| 8. | Inventory | 1 | 1 | INV1-INV5 | All | T. Jones | None | Need a report that shows vendor packaging units, and Location and Issue packaging units on same report |
| 9. | Accounts Payable | 1 | 1 | APO1 | .03 and .57 | B. Scott | 4.1.1.1 | Vendor address differed from PO address |
| 10. | Accounts Payable | 1 | 1 | APO1 | 44,52a,52b | B. Scott | 2.10.3.1 | Could not print a summary PO; see Issue #2 above |
| 11. | Accounts Payable | 1 | 1 | APO1 | 57 | B. Scott | None | The vendor was a discount vendor; another procedure would have been used. |

**Figure 47AA-11**  *(Continued)*
Issue Log Last Updated: 07/13/94 ▨▨▨▨▨ - Shaded Area = Closed Items

| Date | Assigned | Date | Age | Status | Date Resolved | Resolution/Status |
|------|----------|------|-----|--------|---------------|-------------------|
| 6/2/94 | Vendor | 6/4/94 | 41 | Open | | The custom forms have not yet been delivered. Target date: June 25, 1994. 07/02/94—custom forms delivered and loaded. Retest. |
| 6/2/94 | Vendor | 6/4/94 | 41 | Open | | The custom forms have not yet been delivered. Target date: June 25, 1994. 07/02/94—custom forms delivered and loaded. Retest. |
| 6/2/94 | Test Coordinator | 6/4/94 | 41 | Open | | Requisition will be retested. |
| 6/2/94 | Test Coordinator | 6/4/94 | 41 | Open | | Requisition will be retested. |
| 6/3/94 | Vendor | 6/4/94 | 40 | Open | | Update routine will be installed in test area by June 15, 1994. Please retest. Retested June 23, 1994. Still not working. 7/2/94—Vendor conducting further investigation. |
| 6/2/94 | Vendor | 6/4/94 | 41 | Open | | Please indicate a sample item to allow for evaluation. Sample submitted to vendor 7/6/94. |
| 6/4/94 | Vendor | 6/4/94 | 7 | Closed | 6/11/94 | Please refer to software option 2.9.3.2. |
| 6/4/94 | Vendor | 6/4/94 | 7 | Closed | 6/11/94 | Please refer to software option 2.9.3.2. |
| 6/4/94 | Test Coordinator | 6/8/94 | 21 | Closed | 6/25/94 | The PO address instead of the Billing address was used on the paper invoice for .03 and a non PO/billing address was used on .57; Will retest. |
| 6/4/94 | Vendor | 6/4/94 | 39 | Open | | The custom forms have not yet been delivered. Target date: June 25, 1994. 7/2/94—custom forms delivered and loaded. Retest |
| 6/4/94 | Test Coordinator | 6/8/94 | 39 | Open | | Retest with a non-discount vendor. |

early so users forget the training or so the training is not reinforced as the result of operating the new system.

Training courses may need to be held more than once for the same or a subset of a previously trained audience to reinforce the concepts or to allow the audience to pick up additional knowledge not clearly understood the first time around. Providing a training database and requiring all trainees to spend a certain amount of self-study time to reinforce the concepts taught in a training session also provide another avenue for additional training. Note that training examples should be available in the training database to assist the trainees in their self-studies.

Last, training does not end when the system becomes operational. Probably within the first month or two on the new system, a refresher training course will help to fill in the gaps not understood in the pre-live training or not used/reinforced in day-to-day use of the system. Also training for new hires must be considered. Will it be the responsibility of the organizational area to train their new users? Or will the organization sponsor training courses organizational-wide on the new application at frequent intervals? If the organizational area is responsible, it is important that a trained trainer conduct the training for the area and that complete training materials are used. Similarly, a seasoned trainer who is knowledgeable of how the organization uses the new application should be used to provide the organizational-wide training. Finally, training materials must be reviewed and updated as the organization expands or revises its use of the application through live operations.

## CUT-OVER PLANNING

Cut-over planning includes the establishment of the production environment and development of the plan for the transition to the new user and information systems organizations. During this step, all procedure manuals and training programs are finalized to reflect any timing changes. The old system and its operating documentation is phased out and final system documentation is assembled and distributed (unless the old system is planned to continue to operate for some time after live; see the conversion discussion regarding the no-conversion approach in the *Data Conversion Design* step). In this step, the maintenance and testing environment will be established (so that new software releases or updates can be tested before installing them into the production environment) and a process for monitoring new system performance will be planned.

A detailed cut-over schedule is developed as part of this step. Included in the schedule are what activities regarding establishing operations on the new application will be executed each day during the cut-over period. For example, if the application to be integrated is an inventory application, activities such as conducting a final physical inventory and loading beginning inventory balances into the new system must be scheduled and staffed appropriately. Also, a plan is documented for how inventory transactions that need to continue during this "time-out" for physical inventory taking will be accomplished. Further, on what day all inventory receipts will begin to be input into the new system and how the purchase orders for these receipts will be converted to the new system must be planned for and scheduled.

A detailed schedule of at least the first month of operations is also constructed during this step and includes activities like what reports will be printed each day, what batch processing will occur each evening, when the application will be available to the user on weekdays and on weekends, etc. Tasks like how to handle employees that do not use the new form must be identified, documented as to what response will be given, and responsibility for handling this situation assigned. Lastly, organizational-wide communication of the new system must be delivered to let the entire organization know what will be happening and when. This organizational-wide communication can be executed via a variety of means including meetings, newsletter articles, and memos.

## CUT-OVER EXECUTION AND PRODUCTION SUPPORT

This step covers the actual execution of the cut-over plan as well as production support and fine tuning during the initial months of the new system (especially the first period-end close). If the cut-over plan is well thought-out and documented, execution of the plan becomes straightforward. That is not to say that the cut-over does not have to be managed. In fact, it must be managed closely because many cut-over tasks are dependent on other tasks; failure to execute properly and completely any of the cut-over tasks may have severe ramifications to subsequent tasks and thus to the transition of operations to the new application. Further, not all events can be planned. In fact, most transitions to a new application do not go without a hitch. But those projects that develop a detailed, well thought-out cut-over plan are more likely to successfully mitigate any unplanned problems than those projects that cut over without a plan.

The project is not over once the cut-over plan has been executed. Much is learned in the first few days and weeks of operating the new system. Procedures, workflows, and training must be reviewed and adjusted for aspects of the application not considered during the integration project. Further, system tuning (i.e., making the system operate more efficiently from a technical standpoint) is often conducted during the first few months of an operational application. Lastly, until the application system is put through its daily, weekly, monthly, quarterly, and year-end paces at least once, these initial period-end processes may be bumpy at best.

## 47AA-3    SUMMARY

Software integration projects, by their very nature, are not straightforward. Their complexity and probability of failure is affected by factors such as the number of organizational areas affected by the application, the organization's ability to change, and the number and scope of other integration projects underway in the organization. However, the potential for success of an integration project can be greatly enhanced by securing executive commitment and support, following sound project management techniques, procuring a team that satisfies resource estimates and required skill sets, and executing the project following a step-by-step process.

The focus of this chapter is to provide organizations with a step-by-step process of how to successfully integrate software into the organization. Again, realizing that no two integration projects are the same, each of the steps described in the chapter should be reviewed prior to beginning the integration effort. The review should result in a tailoring of the steps to that which better meets the particular project's requirements. Once the tailoring is complete, project structuring and planning can begin using the tailored steps as input for the plan estimates.

Again, any integration project can be described on the outset as high risk. How the organization mitigates this risk via the structure of the project will either result in a successful project or one that was bound for failure from the start.

# CHAPTER 47B

# Groupware (New)

## 47B-1 INTRODUCTION

Groupware is fast becoming one of the most talked about topics in management circles. However, although many people have heard the term, read a few articles, or been to a product demonstration, they are still left asking "What is it?" and "What will it do for me?"

The term groupware refers to *software designed to support the work of groups —* more specifically, software designed to facilitate the collaborative efforts of work teams. The goal of groupware applications is to improve the productivity of groups.

## 47B-2 HISTORY

Computer systems have fallen into two main categories: (1) organizationwide systems that centrally process transactions and produce management information, and (2) personal systems with a wide array of tools designed to enhance individual productivity (e.g., office automation, word processors, spreadsheets, and database applications).

As defined in the chapter appendix, current trends in computing include: client-server applications, computer networking, distributed processing, downsizing/rightsizing, end user computing, electronic data interchange, PC workstations, graphical user interface, object-oriented technology, and open systems. All of these technologies share a few common characteristics: they are smaller, scalable, faster, user friendly, user accessible, and support information sharing.

Meanwhile, current trends in management philosophies suggest a focus on teamwork, flat organizational structures, participative management, employee empowerment,

---

This chapter was written by Hans Hultgren, President, Integrated Systems Group, Inc., Golden, Colorado.

workgroup dynamics, decentralized global organizations, total quality management (TQM) teams, and increased communications. In particular, the teamwork concept appears to be growing rapidly where teams are created for a specific purpose (based on their expertise, not their classification or location) and for a finite period of time.

Groupware represents the logical response to these computing and management trends. It takes advantage of the technological trends to focus on the actual work of the team. Groupware is designed to capitalize on the growing local area network (LAN) environment through facilitating group information sharing and collaboration on team projects.

## 47B-3  GROUPWARE DEFINED

Groupware is basically software designed for teams of people working together using shared information. Groupware is used to disseminate information, organize information, and support interactive or collaborative uses for information. It is modeled around, and supports, workflow processes.

The categories of groupware functionality are: mail capabilities, information sharing, document management (including interactive update), and group meeting support. (See Figure 47B-1.)

### MAIL CAPABILITIES

In the first category, mail capabilities, documents are created by one person and then "mailed" to other persons on the same system. Electronic mail (E-mail) is very popular today and typically includes enhanced features such as one-to-many mailings, reports on opened and unopened mail, ability to link up with other systems, and mail management (archiving, purging, and reporting). With advanced groupware tools, the sender can attach other documents such as spreadsheets, graphs, diagrams, and reports.

Groupware frequently includes mail-enabled applications: the mail can be initiated from within the application itself. For example, while reviewing a financial statement in a spreadsheet application, you have a question for Sue on figures submitted from the East Coast branch. Without leaving your spreadsheet application, you select the portion of the statement related to your question, initiate the mail functionality, write a quick memo, and send both documents to Sue. A message appears on Sue's PC alerting her to the incoming mail. When she "opens" the mail, she will immediately see the spreadsheet attached.

A large auditing company is using groupware to access its top experts in tax law. A person with a specific question will write a memo, attach spreadsheets and any other background information, and send it to one of the experts. The expert can then read and review the file and related information on his/her schedule and respond electronically. The response is stored and can be accessed by other employees who may have a similar question.

### INFORMATION SHARING

The information sharing begins with the basic LAN capabilities for file sharing. Beyond the typical file-server concept, groupware can allow multiple individuals to share data simultaneously. This type of software is often known as group communication

**Figure 47B-1** Groupware Functionality.

# GROUPWARE TYPE / FUNCTIONALITY MATRIX

GROUPWARE FUNCTIONALITY

| GROUPWARE TYPE | LOCATION | TIME | GROUP DELIVERABLE | MEMBERS INTERACTIVE | SHARE APPLICATION | SHARE DOCUMENT |
|---|---|---|---|---|---|---|
| MAIL CAPABILITIES | ANYWHERE | ANYTIME | NO | NO | NO | YES |
| INFORMATION SHARING | ANYWHERE | ANYTIME | NO | MAYBE | MAYBE | YES |
| DOCUMENT MANAGEMENT | ANYWHERE | ANYTIME | MAYBE | MAYBE | MAYBE | YES |
| MEETING SUPPORT Different time | ANYWHERE | ANYTIME | MAYBE | MAYBE | YES | YES |
| MEETING SUPPORT Same time / Different place | ANYWHERE | SAME | YES | YES | YES | YES |
| MEETING SUPPORT Same time / Same place | SAME | SAME | YES | YES | YES | YES |

software. A LAN allows a user to retrieve and view the same document; within a group-ware application, several people in the same application can use the same version of the document at the same time.

Each person has the ability to annotate the document by inserting notes, graphics, or spreadsheets at specific locations. This is especially useful for documentation review and peer review of draft reports or other documents. The team members can also edit the document while other team members are viewing it. An employee who is viewing his/her draft report can actually see the comments as they are attached or see the edits as they occur. Full interactive group communication is facilitated.

## DOCUMENT MANAGEMENT

The document management, includes tracking, version control, and support of the real-time viewing, annotating, and editing of documents. Additionally, the groupware application will track and log any updates and handle any data contention issues.

This functionality lends itself well to tracking systems. For example, a team member may be monitoring the status of several audits or other projects. Typically, these projects will center around an audit or project folder containing all the original data and related materials. Traditional tracking systems might keep track of where the folder is, whether it is on schedule, and any issues related to it. Groupware will accomplish these same functions; however, it can also maintain the entire folder online with all of its attachments. In this scenario, any team member could view the most current version of the audit, project plan, or software design at any time.

Groupware also coordinates a team's access to global data. For example, the team may be interested in market activity in Sweden. The groupware application could be designed to read a financial news wire, look for anything related to Sweden, and then ship that section of the news to a team member's attention.

## MEETING SUPPORT

The last category is *meeting support groupware*—software used to enhance the productivity of a meeting. This type of groupware focuses on transforming the typical meeting, where participants talk about work to be done, to one where work is actually completed. This is accomplished through the ability to solicit ideas from more than one person at a time, automatically capture all meeting information, and allow participants to voice opinions anonymously. Each person in the meeting has a PC, which is used for submitting recommendations, making comments, prioritizing, or any other type of communication.

There are inherent inefficiencies in the way meetings are typically run. These inefficiencies translate to large costs for a typical company where, on average, professionals may spend between 30 percent and 70 percent of their time in meetings. Many meetings do not allow for everyone to "get their say." The "20/80 rule" applies to meetings: 20% of the people do 80% of the talking. By allowing multiple people to comment at the same time, the people who do not normally participate in meetings are given the opportunity. Ideas and input from those who are afraid to speak in front of others can be captured by having them anonymously submit comments. Controversial ideas that normally would not be discussed can be communicated. Participants need not be embarrassed or worried that their ideas might be seen as ridiculous. (This is particularly noteworthy because most paradigm shifting ideas would probably fall into this category.)

Meeting support groupware reduces the frequency of "Groupthink," where all members of a group pocket their concerns with a particular idea in support of the perceived "group opinion." This is especially important when a team is faced with making a hard decision (a budget crunch, how to downsize, elimination of a division, etc.). Meeting support groupware makes the most of meetings by making them more productive, more flexible, and shorter.

Meeting support groupware applications vary, depending on which of the following types of meeting they are designed to support:

Same time–same place meetings, where people interact face-to-face.

Same time–different place meetings, where people meet through the groupware system from several locations.

Different time meetings, where, regardless of location, people carry on a meeting over a period of time but are not required to interact in real time.

In a same time–same place meeting, the subject matter has dictated that a face-to-face interactive meeting is required. In this case, the key focus is facilitating the meeting (not the technology). Many people find that, without the nonverbal cues and other interaction that occur in a face-to-face meeting with people applied to a specific task, people's attention will wander.

In a same time–different place meeting, several people may be at other locations. In this event, groupware strives to "emulate" a same place meeting as much as possible. Often, the concept of a "virtual meeting" is employed: video screens allow people in various places to interact as if they were face-to-face. This type of meeting calls for people to sit at PCs in front of large screens at different locations. The screens then create the illusion that all team members are in the same room.

With different time meetings, groupware concentrates on managing and tracking the meetings. An agenda may be created, specific people assigned, and deliverables identified. The groupware can then track the progress of the team and help to keep the meeting moving.

Typical uses of meeting support groupware include: group conferencing, status reporting, project management, group discussions, brainstorming, global brainstorming, document draft review and editing, candidate or request for proposal (RFP) review, strategic planning, organizational changes, auditing, and employee surveys.

For example, a person presents annual plans, a budget, a marketing plan, or some other document to a group of peers or team members who then simultaneously provide edits, ideas, comments, and constructive criticism. Comments are later reviewed in private by the presenter with no knowledge of who wrote them and no requirement to respond to or challenge the comments. All ideas have the same weight because no one knows who submitted them.

## 47B-4   CURRENT INDUSTRY STATUS

Groupware products vary greatly, depending on the functions they are designed to support. Several products that support mail capabilities, including several word processing applications, are available.

Within the categories of information sharing and document management capabilities, Lotus Notes is a complete product that addresses these functions and more. Notes is also an application development tool that allows the user to create custom applications to suit specific needs.

There are three key competitors in the area of meeting support groupware: Vision-Quest (Collaborative Technologies Corporation), GroupSystems V (Ventana Corporation), and TeamFocus (International Business Machines Corporation).

## 47B-5 CONCLUSION

Groupware is a growing and viable new software direction that can translate into strong benefits for any organization. Specifically, organizations moving toward a workgroup structure should consider implementing groupware. A review of the shared data requirements, cooperative efforts, and document tracking tools will serve as a basis for analyzing the benefits of a move to groupware.

Operations that require frequent meetings to perform—ongoing planning, prioritizing, brainstorming, and other cooperative efforts—may find strong benefits from the meeting support groupware applications. A review of the time spent in meetings, the extent to which the meeting deliverables are produced through an iterative process, and the need for creative and free-flowing ideas will provide the information necessary to evaluate meeting support groupware applications.

Software tools are designed to automate some process. This automation can provide strong benefits if the process is strong; however, automating a bad process will usually result in a bad system. Organizations that do not support the team concept and the open sharing of information will not realize the benefits of groupware applications.

## APPENDIX: DEFINITIONS

*Client-server applications.* Applications developed on a LAN server architecture for the support of specific workgroup activities. The processing can occur on an individual's personal computer/workstation or the server. Typically, the environment where applications are developed or customized by the people connected through the server is user friendly.

*Computer networking.* The linking of local area network (LAN) and geographically dispersed or wide area network (WAN) computers through direct or dedicated lines. Applications are typically stored on the server computer at the heart of the LAN/WAN. Designed to support the sharing of software and peripherals.

*Distributed processing.* The concept of moving portions of the actual computer processing from a centralized processor to local computers. Typically designed to maximize performance and minimize costs associated with processing and telecommunications.

*Downsizing/Rightsizing.* The process of moving software applications to the most efficient hardware platform. Typically involves conversion of applications from a large system to a smaller one. In many cases, the costs are quickly recovered and considerable savings are realized. Initially referred to as "downsizing" because most of the efforts centered on moving from a mainframe to a minicomputer (midrange) platform; currently referred to as rightsizing.

*End user computing.* The concept of moving the development of software applications to the employees actually using the systems. Typically involves end users' developing queries or custom reports on their own computer.

*Electronic data interchange.* The process of transferring business documents between two organizations that are geographically dispersed. Typically, EDI occurs with requisitions, purchase orders, and invoices sent between two companies that have a customer–supplier relationship. The two companies do not need to have the same type of systems or software. (See Chapter 50.)

*PC workstation.* Powerful personal computers used to run application software at the local level. Typically, their capacity includes specific applications that support a particular company function. The use of workstations has greatly grown as lower costs of these systems have made them accessible.

*Graphical user interface (GUI).* A type of user interface characterized by the use of graphics, icons, pop-up menus, and the mouse-driven "point-and-click" interface. There is typically consistency in the look and feel of all applications running under a specific GUI environment (MAC, Windows, OS/2, etc.).

*Object-oriented technology.* System software and application software developed to view all data elements, programs, screens, and reports as "objects." These objects are viewed in their relationship to each other, which organizes the software so that the time spent on maintenance and modifications is greatly reduced. For example, a change to a field length typically requires multiple changes to all programs, processors, screens, and reports. With object-oriented systems, the change is made one time and all objects (programs, processors, screens, and reports) that relate to that object (changed field) reflect the change.

*Open systems.* The extent to which differing hardware, systems software, and application software can work together. Open systems goes one step beyond data sharing to the universal compatibility level.

# CHAPTER 47C

# Graphics in Business (New)

## 47C-1  INTRODUCTION

What comes to mind when someone mentions the word *graphics?* Do you envision pie charts and bar charts? Company logos or a drawing of some sort? All of these and much, much more encompass the term *graphics*. This chapter briefly explores the purpose of graphics, various graphics elements, and some of the current software tools that support graphics for the business world. The chapter may be viewed as a valuable complement to Chapter 35 of the main volume ("Internal Management Reports"), indicating the capability of computer technology.

## 47C-2  PURPOSE OF GRAPHICS

The creation of any business document involves three key elements:

1. *Objectives.* The document answers the question, "Why is this document being created?" The intent is to understand what is to be accomplished by the document (e.g., impart knowledge, persuade, or entertain).

2. *Audience.* The document answers the question, "Who is the intended audience of this document?" Not only are the specific recipients determined, but, more importantly, such information as their existing knowledge base, attitudes, position, and reasons for viewing the document contributes to its wording and presentation.

---

This chapter was written by Melissa W. Breeze, Manager, Ernst & Young, Denver.

3. *Environmental Constraints.* Two questions, "In what time frame does the document require creation?" and "What tools are available to support document creation?" are answered.

When these three elements are combined, decisions are made on the nature of the resulting document. Is a brief memorandum presenting the results of a process all that is required, or is a more substantial report detailing the process and its results necessary? Each set of document objectives, intended audience, and environmental constraints results in a different solution.

Why are graphics created? For two major reasons:

1. *Achieving effective information transfer.* Everyone has heard the old adage, "A picture is worth a thousand words." It's true! A simple graphic may instantly, clearly, and cleanly convey information that would otherwise require substantial text to describe (and may not be as clearly understood by the intended audience).

2. *Obtaining/Maintaining audience attention.* If a document's intended "audience" is a file drawer, forget the graphics. If, however, human beings make up all or part of the intended audience, you may want to utilize means that may improve the probability of their viewing the document and increasing their corresponding attention level. A document that is "pleasing to the eye" or "attractive" is much more likely to get and maintain its audience's attention.

When determining the extent to which graphic elements should be included as part of a business document, the document's objectives, intended audience, and environmental constraints must all be considered.

## 47C-3   GRAPHICS ELEMENTS

Most people probably think of a "picture" of some sort when they think of graphics—a type of data chart (e.g., a pie chart or column chart), an organizational chart, or perhaps a cartoon. However, if you view graphics as all elements that can help effect information transfer and/or get and maintain audience attention, the possibilities expand. Graphics elements can then include:

- *Fonts.* When discussing fonts, we need to address three components:

  1. *Type*—the specific name of the font. For example:

     CG Times

     Courier

     Univers

  2. *Size*—the height and width of the font characters. Sizes for some fonts are described as "characters per inch" (cpi); others are described in "points" (the bigger the point number the larger the resulting character). For example:

     Courier 10 cpi

     Courier 12 cpi

     Univers 12 pt

     Univers 14 pt

**3.** *Appearance*—the style of the font characters. For example:

Underlined

**Bold**

*Italicized*

**Shadowed**

~~Strike Out~~

- *Character Symbols.* The • or "bullet" is probably the most universally used and recognized character symbol. However, most word processing software provides the user with a variety of other character symbols. For example, ✓ and ☐ may be used in place of a bullet. Other examples are:

- *Frames/Borders.* Horizontal and vertical lines used alone or in combination can "frame" textual or pictorial material and thus draw attention to it. For example:

> A shaded "text" box allows you to bring attention to a specific message or piece of information. It can also be used to interrupt a document's visual flow and thus revive the audience's attention level.

"Tables" are another way of framing information so that it is more clearly presented, as shown in the following example.

| *Market Share\** | | |
| --- | --- | --- |
| *The Top Three Presentation Graphics Products in Three Categories, in Terms of U.S. Units Shipped* | | |
| DOS | Macintosh | Windows |
| Software Publishing Corp. | Microsoft Corp. | Microsoft Corp. |
| Harvard Graphics | PowerPoint | PowerPoint |
| WordPerfect Corp. | Deltapoint, Inc. | Micrografx, Inc. |
| DrawPerfect | DeltaGraph | Charisma |
| Lotus Development Corp. | Aldus Corp. | Lotus Development Corp. |
| Freelance | Persuasion | Freelance for Windows |

\* "The CW Guide: Presentation Software," *Computerworld,* Jan. 25, 1993. Copyright 1993 by CW Publishing, Inc., Framingham, MA 01701. Reprinted from *Computer World.*

- *Shapes.* Using common shapes to present information pictorially is a frequently used business graphic technique. Organization charts and flow charts are examples of this graphic technique. A sample organization chart appears on page 228.

**Sample Organization Chart**

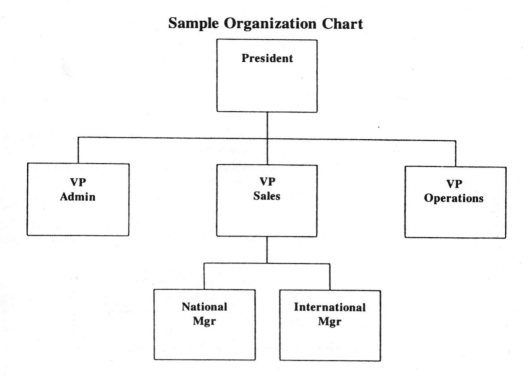

- *Data Charts.* Data charts can concisely and persuasively illustrate numeric data. Some of the more common types of data charts are described later in the chapter.

- *Illustrations.* These can range from elementary school variety stick figures to cartoons, professionally developed works of art, or objects and creatures "drawn" on the computer screen. (See below.) Sources of illustrations range from original work to commercially available "clip art" (see section 47C-4).

- *Color.* The use of color has become widespread on the business scene during the very recent past. With the ever increasing cost-effectiveness of color printers and copiers, color is fast becoming an everyday component of business documents. As with other graphics elements, the use of color should be governed by a document's objectives, intended audience, and environmental constraints.

## 47C-4    SOFTWARE TO SUPPORT YOUR BUSINESS GRAPHICS NEEDS

Creation of today's business documents may be accomplished by using a single type of tool (e.g., word processing software) or by combining output from multiple types of tools (e.g., word processing, spreadsheet, and presentation graphics software). The graphics contributions that various types of software tools can make are presented below. An emphasis is placed on presentation graphics software.[1]

### PRESENTATION GRAPHICS SOFTWARE

The following popular packages are primarily geared toward creation of data, text, and graphic (pictorial) slides for hard-copy output:

| | |
|---|---|
| Aldus Persuasion | Freelance Graphics |
| Charisma | Harvard Graphics |
| DeltaGraph Professional | Microsoft PowerPoint |
| DrawPerfect | Softcraft Presenter |

All these packages perform a similar core set of tasks and typically have the following capabilities:

- *Presentation Management.* These packages provide a central slide creation and organization scheme that supports achievement of a consistent look across a presentation. Templates or masters or both may be used. The use of common slide backgrounds is also usually supported.

- *Text Charts.* Direct or imported text entry for preformatted word/text charts is supported by these packages. Functionality usually includes automatic text wrap, text justification, freeform labels, and bullet charts with user-defined bullets. Many of the packages also provide a spelling checker. Examples of two common text charts—a title chart and a bullet chart—appear on page 230.

- *Data/Business Charts.* The following chart types are commonly supported (see Figure 47C-1 for some examples and descriptions):

    Plain, stacked, overlapped, and clustered bar charts and column charts.

    Projected and shadowed 3-D bar charts and column charts.

---

[1] The "full featured" nature of today's software demands only a cursory examination here. Readers are encouraged to increase their graphics awareness by further investigating the graphics-related capabilities of their existing software tools and the many available product offerings.

**Everything You
Wanted to Know About**

**Graphics and Business**

**(But Were Afraid to Ask)**

Sample Title Chart

**Types of Text Charts**

- **Title Charts**
- **Simple Lists**
- **Bullet Lists**
- **Two Columns**
- **Three Columns**
- **Freeform**

Sample Bullet Chart

2-D and 3-D pie charts.

Line and scatter plots.

Area charts (unstacked, stacked area total, and stacked 100 percent area).

High-low-open-close charts.

Figure 47C-2 provides suggested data chart types, depending on what your data are intended to illustrate.

Additional data/business chart functionality usually includes semi-log and log-log scaling,[2] interactive chart editing, and WK1 (i.e., Lotus format) file importation.

- *Clip Art.* Importation of vector clip art is a common capability of presentation graphics software. In addition, these packages normally include a library of clip art images. Some examples of clip art are shown on page 233.

- *Annotation and Illustration.* Basic drawing tools support creation of lines, polylines, boxes, and circles for chart annotation and diagram creation. The ability to move an object to front and back or to resize it is also typical.

- *Electronic Presentation.* These packages normally support creation of "screen shows." In addition, most offer stand-alone runtime players that support "on the road" runtime versions.

- *Hard-Copy Presentation.* With these packages, you can print a single slide or an entire presentation. Many include communications software for transmitting to slide generation service bureaus.

- *Multimedia Capabilities.* Current presentation graphics software varies greatly in its ability to support multimedia functionality (e.g., sound, video, and animation). However, such capabilities are gradually becoming standard features.

---

[2] Logarithmic scaling can be used to show the relative change of large variation in data and to compare data expressed in different magnitudes. A log chart also shows a rate of change and compresses large variations within a series. Because of the independence of X and Y axes, you can chart either a semi-log graph (usually the Y axis is scaled) or a log-log graph (both the X and Y axes are scaled).

**Figure 47C-1**  Common Data Charts Types.

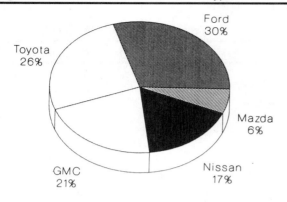

**Pie charts** are most often used to show parts relative to a whole. In this example, the total number of trucks sold is broken out by percentage of each type sold as represented by a piece of the pie.

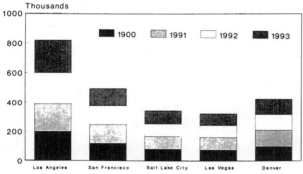

**Column or bar charts** are commonly used for comparing separate groupings. The above example charts the number of participants by city in an ongoing survey. Each year is represented by a different pattern (or color if available). Both the total and breakout by year can easily and simply be displayed.

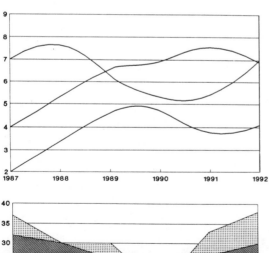

**Line charts** are quite useful if trend information is to be shown. With the capabilities of current charting software, straight-line values can be smoothed into curves, at option of the user.

**Area plot charts** are often used to show the contribution which many items make to a total over a period of time. The above example could illustrate product category sales over time with each product category being represented by a different color line.

**Figure 47C-2**    Suggested Common Data Chart Types by "What You Want to Show."

| What You Want to Show | Suggested Chart Type* |
|---|---|
| Change in volume | Area/Area with 3-D overlap effect<br>Line with 3-D overlap effect |
| Change over time | |
| Over a few time periods | Bar (horizontal or vertical)<br>Bar/Line combination<br>Line (zigzag or curve) |
| Over many time periods | Area<br>Area/Line combination<br>Line (zigzag or curve)<br>Line with 3-D overlap effect<br>High-Low-Close with area style |
| Emphasis | |
| On a part of a whole | Pie with cut slice |
| On volume | Area/Area with 3-D effect |
| On one of several series | Bar/Line combination<br>Line (zigzag or curve) |
| On sum of one series in relation to another | Proportional pie |
| On continuity and fluctuation of minimum/maximum data | High-Low-Close with area style |
| Parts of a whole | |
| At a specific time | Pie/Column |
| At 2 different times | 2 Pies/Columns<br>2 Stacked Bars |
| Over a few time periods | Stacked Bars<br>100% Bars |
| Over many time periods | Area<br>Stacked Bars<br>100% Bars |
| Relationship between two series | |
| Over a few time periods | Bar (vertical or horizontal)<br>Bar/Line combination |
| Over many time periods | Line (zigzag or curve) |
| Relationship between two (or more) series | |
| That differ widely in magnitude | Dual Y axis<br>Dual Y axis with log scaling |
| That use different units of measure | Dual Y axis |
| Comparison of two series with the same X axis classification | Paired Bar |
| Correlation | Paired Bar<br>Point Chart |

**Figure 47C-2**   *(Continued)*

| What You Want to Show | Suggested Chart Type* |
|---|---|
| Running totals | Area |
| | Bar |
| | Cumulative Line |
| Stock/bond prices | High-Low-Close |
| One series over another and frequency distribution | Histogram |
| Relative or percent of change | Logarithmic |
| Trends | |
|    Statistical trends | Line (trend) |
|    Over a few time periods | Line (zigzag, trend, or curve) |
|    Over many time periods | Bar (vertical) |

* Harvard Graphics® Reference Manual.

## Clip Art Samples

## WORD PROCESSING SOFTWARE

Many of today's word processing packages, while providing extremely full text-related functionality, also support an ever increasing graphics capability. Fully integrated graphics control and high-powered drawing tools are quite common. In many cases, individuals are using their word processing software to integrate the result of output created in other tools (e.g., spreadsheets, presentation graphic software, and business illustration software). Examples of popular word processing software include:

| | |
|---|---|
| Ami Professional | WordPerfect |
| Microsoft Word | WordPerfect for Windows |
| Word for Windows | WordStar |

Many current word processing packages users would be surprised at the graphics-related capabilities their existing tool provides.

## SPREADSHEET SOFTWARE

Spreadsheets are designed to handle a variety of tasks, including: analysis and model building, consolidation and linking, charting, worksheet publishing, interoperability, and applications development. Examples of popular spreadsheet packages include:

| | |
|---|---|
| CA-Supercalc | Microsoft Excel |
| Lotus 1-2-3 | Quattro Pro |

These packages, and others, offer varying levels of charting capabilities. The types of charts offered, the existence (or nonexistence) of slide-show capability, and a user's ability to customize the charts with titles, notes, multiple typefaces (i.e., fonts), clip art, colors, and shading should be reviewed when assessing a spreadsheet's ability to meet all or some of your graphics needs.

## INTEGRATED SOFTWARE

Most integrated software packages include, at a minimum, word processing, database, and spreadsheet capabilities. Others also offer one or more of the following capabilities: business charting, vector drawing, graphics importing and editing, and telecommunications. Examples of the latter type of software include:

| | |
|---|---|
| Eight-In-One for Windows | Microsoft Works |
| Framework XE | PFS:WindowWorks |
| Lotus Works | WordPerfect Works for DOS |

On the plus side, these integrated software packages can offer affordability, all-in-one convenience, and easy data sharing. What you will tend to give up is an overall richness of features. The individual parts are unlikely to offer the same sophisticated and complex functionality as their counterpart stand-alone packages. However, depending on your requirements, including graphic-related ones, an integrated package might more than meet your needs.

## DESKTOP PUBLISHING SOFTWARE

These products are aimed at users who develop business publications. Their functionality includes: text formatting, graphics handling, layout creation, and printing. The sophistication and corresponding capabilities of desktop publishing packages vary greatly. Examples of current desktop publishing products include:

| | |
|---|---|
| Avagio | PagePlus |
| Express Publisher | PageMaker |
| Microsoft Publisher | Ventura Publisher |

These products, and others, will allow you to create complex layouts by automatically wrapping text around pictures, linking text frames, and jumping stories to noncontiguous pages.

   A key component of this type of software is its ability to import text and graphics from other sources (e.g., word processing software and presentation graphics software). With such functionality, you can create newsletters, business forms, brochures, and a variety of other publications-related materials.

## BUSINESS ILLUSTRATION SOFTWARE

Unlike professional illustration software, business illustration software caters to nonartists. These packages typically offer routine vector drawing tools, simple image manipulations (e.g., rotate and flip), a few text effects, limited color handling, a library of clip art, a variety of font-related capabilities, and the ability to import and export files in a standard format(s) (e.g., .PCX). The following packages are examples of this type of software:

| | |
|---|---|
| Arts & Letter Apprentice | KeyDraw! Plus |
| ComputerEasy Draw | Windows Draw 3.0 plus OLE |

## MISCELLANEOUS

A discussion of graphics would not be complete without mentioning two types of hardware: scanners and printers. Scanners are hardware devices that allow preexisting graphic images (e.g., photographs and any printed matter) to be "read" into a computer system and then "placed" in an appropriate software tool (e.g., presentation graphics and desktop publishing software) where they can then be manipulated. Available devices run the gamut from gray-scale hand-held devices (do not attempt to use after too much coffee!) to gray-scale flatbed scanners to color flatbed scanners. Depending on your graphics needs, an appropriate scanning device can prove invaluable. Some potential uses for a scanner are:

- Your company's logo for use on reports, presentations, and similar documents.
- Preexisting art work for use in a presentation (e.g., product renderings, cartoons, drawings).
- Proposals to potential clients.

Without a printer that supports your graphics output, your work may be for naught. Fortunately, there is a full range of products from which to choose. Whether you require monochrome or color capability, there is a printer that will meet your needs.

## 47C-5  CONCLUSION

A significant amount of business communication, including written documents, involves persuasion. Graphics elements, when appropriately used (i.e., the document's objectives, intended audience, and associated environmental constraints are clearly defined), can help present information effectively and compellingly. With the graphics capabilities provided by today's software products, only your imagination (and perhaps your wallet) will limit your ability to create documents that transfer information effectively and obtain/maintain your audience's attention.

# CHAPTER 48

## Financial Forecast Modeling: Converting Decisions and Plans to Cash and Value (New)

The financial forecast which follows is based on assumptions which are deemed to be reasonable. It is not intended to depict events and financial outcomes which will happen; in fact, events and financial outcomes occurring as illustrated in the forecast are considered highly unlikely. This forecast is based on conditions as of the date herein. Any subsequent change in conditions would affect assumptions used in the generation of the forecast, and could result in events and financial outcomes that are materially different from the forecast events and outcomes contained herein.

—"Statement of Limiting Conditions"
on a recent financial forecast

In the long run, we are all dead.

—J. M. Keynes

The author of this chapter is Tim Cranston, Senior Manager, Ernst & Young, Denver.

## 48-1    INTRODUCTION

In a 1986 planning meeting, a company chief financial officer expressed concern that the company could not continue financing its expected growth through debt. That company currently is enjoying its seventh consecutive year of more than 20% growth, has borrowed all its external capital needs, and has paid substantial dividends in each of the last four years. Another company president found herself arbitrating a heated dispute between her highly experienced marketing and operations executives over the need to expand or reconfigure the plant to accommodate expected growth. Both executives were soon gone, and the president resigned soon thereafter facing a reduced backlog and plant overcapacity. In a third situation, a manufacturing company purchased a stronger and slightly larger wholesale distribution company in a highly leveraged transaction. During the year following the merger, the new company experienced first rapid growth, then Chapter 11 bankruptcy.

These examples have at least four things in common: (1) Knowledge and judgment about the business and markets were exercised, based on management's view and experience. (2) Planning was performed, which was illustrated in part in prospective anticipated financial results. (3) Decisions based on the plans and forecasts were made, resulting in favorable or adverse consequences. (4) Finally, the forecasting process failed to provide the information necessary to assist managements in making the right decisions.

This chapter focuses on financial forecast modeling, starting with what it is, why it is important, its uses, types, and analytical tools. After a discussion of forecast model preparation (together with a sample financial forecast made up of several templates that are critical to good financial forecasting), several financial modeling packages are described, together with some of the essential features and uses of each. The chapter concludes with a discussion of forecast modeling as a strategic tool—the imperative that forecasting models be sufficiently complex and complete so as to effectively link corporate decisions to corporate and shareholder value.

Chapter 5 of the main volume provides a brief description of modeling. This Chapter provides greater detail for those interested.

## 48-2    FINANCIAL FORECAST
## MODELING—DEFINITION AND IMPORTANCE

The real world of business is a highly complex system of infinite transactions among economic actors. Because of this complexity it is impossible to analyze or understand, much less predict, the socioeconomic interrelationships that underlie these transactions. Economic and financial "theories" or "models" must thus be used in any serious attempt to understand and predict the transactions that result from these interrelationships. Models are simple illustrations of the far more complex reality. Forecasting models are usually computer-produced spreadsheets showing the relationships between various business activities and showing future projections. The projections are determined by using econometric models that utilize complex simultaneous regression equations to relate economic occurrences to areas of corporate activity, time series models that try to establish a pattern from historical data, and judgmental models determined mostly from experience and common sense.

## FINANCIAL FORECASTING

Management constantly exercises judgment as to the direction and change magnitude of all material activities of a business, including marketing, orders, purchasing, inbound logistics, production/processing, outbound logistics, collections, and support functions. Financial forecasts report these activities in quantities and dollars, and configure them into basic financial statement format (income statement, cash flow statement and balance sheet), together with supporting schedules (ratio analysis, fixed charges coverage, "common size" statements, valuation analysis, return on capital analysis, etc.) Financial forecasting models are brought to bear on the planning process to understand and illustrate the effects of business decisions on future possibilities, learn how to cope with them, exploit their opportunities, mitigate against their adverse effects, and value their prospective operating results.

It is important for managers to understand that forecasts are only approximations. Most quantitative models use assumptions that are only rarely met in the real world. Forecasting requires considerable judgment, knowledge, experience, and common sense. In models based on cause-and-effect relationships, forecasters must exercise judgment about such exogenous factors as competing products, substitute products, leap-frog technologies, and changes in fiscal and monetary policy. Third, many believe that the more data they have and use, the more accurate the forecasting model will be. This belief is one of the most common errors in statistical applications. Few would argue that, because during the 1980s the capital markets rose in every year that the National Football Conference won the Super Bowl, and fell in every year that the AFC won, we should make our investment decision for the year on the Monday following the Super Bowl. Some forecasters become so wedded to a forecasting model that they come to believe it is the best application for all modeling requirements. (Later in the chapter various modeling packages are outlined, together with some of their individual characteristics and uses.) Finally, one of the most common myths is that complicated models perform better than simple models. Often, however, capturing in the model all sorts of exotic variables is expensive, cumbersome, and distracting. As mentioned earlier, models are illustrations of a more complex real world and should therefore be as simple as possible yet still able to capture the essential elements of that world. The forecast modeling process should start with simple algorithms, and then use increasingly complex ones until the planning requirement is met.

## IMPORTANCE OF MODELING

Referring to the opening quotes, if according to Keynes the long term does not matter, and if today's illustration of possible future outcomes is "highly unlikely" to be an accurate depiction of actual future outcomes, why should we even attempt to prepare financial forecasting models?

Forecasting the future is a fundamental tool in any business planning process. Ignoring the potential future financial effects of today's decisions would be like going on a trip without a map to an unknown destination. Forecasting models help business planners at the beginning and end of each planning cycle: They help planners determine which of the myriad planning options are realistic. Then, once the plan is set, the forecasts capture the planning information in a quantitative format that helps planners establish the tactics and action plans required to meet the plan objectives.

Forecasting is a difficult job in the face of turbulent economic conditions. Businesses must find ways to keep abreast of the effects that such changes are likely to have on their operations and financial results. Financial forecasting, together with economic analysis and other tools, helps determine the long-term objectives and the strategies required to accomplish these objectives. Business people often dismiss the need for forecasts. However, every decision a company makes is based on assumptions about the future. Investment decisions, determining working capital requirements, staffing new projects, introducing new products, entering new markets, and a host of other decisions cannot be made without some estimate of future events and their effects on the business as represented in financial forecasts.

Furthermore, business managers with effective financial forecasting and economic models can take corrective measures either to exploit opportunities or mitigate against business failure in the face of rapidly changing business conditions. These changes, in turn, require that the forecasts be revised to incorporate the new data and assumptions. Revising forecasts in the face of changing conditions can help managements not only measure the effects of such changes on their businesses, but also lead them to re-evaluate their competitive position and revise their strategies, tactics, and action plans accordingly.

## 48-3   USES OF FINANCIAL FORECAST MODELS

Financial forecasting models are used to assist in the planned employment of virtually every asset and resource of the business:

- *Revenue forecasts* capture current and prospective customer information.
- *Expense budgets* capture the resources and factors of production required to produce the revenues.
- *New product development* is determined from analysis of the markets and the estimated realizable revenues from those markets.
- *Plant expansion* is anticipated from analysis of the growth trends.
- *Wage and human resource levels* and increases are determined from the anticipated business conditions and market demand.
- *Merger and acquisition* opportunities are evaluated using forecasts.
- *External capital requirements,* levels and types are planned based on company needs and the estimated effects on the company as illustrated in company forecasts.
- *Working capital requirements* are identified in company forecasts.
- *Income tax planning* is greatly facilitated through forecasting.
- *Debt amortization* is structured with creditors based on debt service capability as illustrated in company forecasts.
- *Dividend policy* and other aspects of corporate governance are determined based on company needs as reflected in forecasts.
- *Regulatory changes* are quantified in forecasts.
- *Performance and needs of business units* are measured and evaluated based on forecasts and their realization.

There is an iterative cycle between forecasting and each of the above activities. For example, as part of the planning process, financial forecasting models help identify a need for plant expansion; then, when the expansion is completed and other changes occur, revised forecasts may be needed to fully address the changes introduced by the increased plant capacity.

## 48-4   TYPES OF FINANCIAL FORECASTING MODELS

### QUALITATIVE

Often in business, quantitative information does not exist to help business planners in the forecasting process, or the cost of collecting the data is prohibitive. Under these circumstances, a qualitative forecast may be the only methodology available. The most common form of qualitative forecast is the Delphi method.

The Delphi method is a systematic procedure for obtaining consensus among a group of experts. The Delphi method uses a group of selected experts to fill out exhaustive questionnaires anonymously. These questionnaires may require qualitative or quantitative information, and the experts may choose to exercise their best judgment qualitatively or quantitatively. Their answers are analyzed statistically, and each expert is then provided with feedback on the results. These same experts are subsequently polled again and again in an iterative process until some acceptable consensus is reached. Usually "consensus" is determined using some statistical convergence, but often practical concerns such as time and cost require that the analysis be concluded before the acceptable consensus is achieved.

### QUANTITATIVE

Since forecasting is a combination of science and art, most forecasting models apply a combination of hard data and human judgment. These data and judgments are commingled into hard quantities and amounts. Most financial forecasting models are classified under two basic categories:

- Data-based time series.
- Mathematical (diffusion) models.

Data-based time series models depend on the availability of a identifiable series of values or quantities at discrete points in time in the past. Various tools and techniques are used to extrapolate events, outcomes, quantities, and values into the future using these time-related series of historic data values. As an illustration, annual revenues of a company for the past five years, as well as the respective year in which each revenue amount was realized, constitute a time series. The goal of a forecasting model is to provide a rigorous basis for predicting the values of this time series in future years. There are several simple and complex tools used in such prediction, and these tools are discussed next.

Diffusion modeling is used in those circumstances, such as new market penetration or new product introduction, in which data in traditional time series models are not available or do not exist. Diffusion models are used either when several time series observations are available, or when no or limited data are available. In simple diffusion models in which several data points are available, three parameters need to be constructed based on three known quantities. For example, three initial input variables may be number of initial purchasers, diffusion rate, and total potential purchasers. These inputs are derived from such parameters as initial number of persons who recognize a need that the product can satisfy, a rate of increased acceptance, and total potential market for services which the product can satisfy. In the no-data diffusion model, users are required to specify three inputs: Initial number of purchasers and two constant parameters often described as coefficients of innovation and imitation. These three inputs are used to generate a forecast of product sales over time. An example of a potential application of diffusion modeling is in estimating sales of 1.8-inch disk drives. Given the market acceptance and rate of innovation in two prior generations (3.5-inch and 2.5-inch drives), it is possible to derive reasonable estimates of product life cycle, market demand, appropriate coefficients of change and substitution, and, thereby, projected product revenues.

The principal difference between diffusion and time series modeling is that diffusion modeling is a deductive attempt to reflect how a process operates, while time series modeling empirically attempts to find the best fit of a series of data points.

Because almost all financial forecasting commonly performed by modeling professionals is based on known and historical data that are readily accessible, the remainder of this chapter highlights data-based time series financial modeling and its tools and techniques.

## 48-5  TOOLS AND TECHNIQUES

*Trend analysis* examines financial data over several historic periods and analyzes them in order to observe trends that appear to be present. There are many types of trend analysis, including

- *Absolute average change* in which the average period-to-period historic change is calculated and used to extrapolate into the forecast period.

- *Average percentage change* calculates the period-to-period percentage change and uses this average to extrapolate into the forecast period.

- *Weighted average percentage change* is similar to the average percentage change method, but provides more weight to recent periods than to early periods.

- *Moving average* methods are similar to simple average methods except that the moving average methods involve using several periods to form the basis from which the average is calculated. For example, a five-year moving average uses the most recent five years and does not consider previous periods. *Smoothing* is a variation of the moving average method. For example, in a triple three-year moving average approach, historic information from the past five years would be gathered. These five years would provide three three-year moving averages. These three three-year moving averages would be averaged to provide an incremental value to add to the most recent period. *Exponential smoothing* is another variation of the moving average approach, but is no longer commonly used because of the use of the more sophisticated approaches which are outlined next.

- *Decomposition* methods forecast future quantities and values by searching for and incorporating certain types of variation. Decomposition takes into account such factors as overall trends (average, moving average, etc.), seasonality, cyclicality, and irregularity. Using decomposition, a future value at a given time (Y) results from the multiplication for the four factors—trend, seasonality, cyclical trend, and irregular variation. *Multiplicative decomposition* uses several methods to estimate the four parameters in the four factors just described. These parameters are usually calculated using regression methods (see below). *Winters' decomposition* uses exponential smoothing to describe a series that is assumed to have a linear trend with seasonality.

- *Regression and correlation* involve forecasting based on linear or curvilinear relationships between dependent and independent variables calculated by linear or multiple regression analysis, as further described below.

- *Simple linear regression* methods involve, for example, the use of least squares estimation to fit a straight line into the selected data in the time series. The forecast is nothing more than the extrapolation of the line into the forecast period. Typically a time series does not show trends that readily can be fit using a straight line. Linear regression does not adequately illustrate the time series data and does not yield reasonable estimates of the future. When this occurs, quadratic regression may be satisfactory.

- *Multiple regression* techniques calculate a dependent variable by measuring the impact of several factors on that variable. Multiple regression is generally considered to be superior to linear regression because in the real world outcomes are usually a function of several different factors rather than just one factor. A critical aspect of multiple regression is than it assumes that the relationship between the dependent variable and each of the independent variables is linear. To the extent that this relationship is polynomial rather than linear, the forecasting process can be grossly inadequate. However, statistical models are available to transform quadratic relationships into linear ones, and to assess the integrity of such modeling.

- *Autoregression* is generally thought to be far superior to linear and quadratic regression. Autoregression techniques assume that what happened in the immediate prior period is the best predictor of what will happen in this period. A first-order autoregression calculates a value (Y) at time (t) as an additive combination of a constant term (B), a second constant term [(B1 × (y(t − 1)) (the value of the series at time (t − 1)), and a random error term (e). Autoregressive models may use several prior periods in predicting values in the forecast period, for example,

$$Y(t) = B + B(1)[(y(t - 1))] + B(2) \times [(y(t - 2))] + B(3) \times [(y(t - 3))] + e$$

In this model, the value of the series, Y(t), is a weighted combination of the series at the three immediately preceding periods.

- *Box-Jenkins* method, developed by George Box and Gwilym Jenkins, is a significant development in time series analysis. Derived from autoregression, Box-Jenkins involves three stages: identification, estimation, and diagnostic checking. Identification involves determining whether the time series may be represented with a moving average model, an autoregressive model, or a combination of both.

Estimation involves approximating the model's parameters, typically using iterative techniques. Diagnostic checking determines the adequacy of the forecasting model's outputs. Box-Jenkins models are also known as ARIMA models, with three parameters which correspond to different aspects of the model: p (moving average), d (differencing, which allows time series that do not exhibit clear trends to be transformed into series that do exhibit such properties), and q (autoregression). A complete discussion of ARIMA is beyond the scope of this chapter; however, many financial forecasting modeling packages, including some of those presented later in this chapter, have built-in templates that incorporate standard Box-Jenkins and ARIMA methodology.

*Mathematical algorithms* are another tool used in financial forecasting models. Once trend analysis establishes certain key forecast values (such as revenues), mathematical algorithms allow the forecaster to derive other forecasted values expressed as a function of those other values that were determined in the trend analysis. To use a common example, if trend analysis has calculated forecast prices and product quantities shipped, forecast revenues will be the product of the two. Virtually every software package described later in this chapter is capable of accommodating all sorts of complicated mathematical algorithms.

*Fundamental research* is a forecasting tool that investigates external data from various sources, including databases, reference books, competitive intelligence, economic and industry forecasting firms, surveys, and interviews. Information derived from these sources are used in other forecasting tools. They are also used to verify results of the other tools.

*Simulation, or sensitivity analysis,* is a technique used whereby alternative outcomes are analyzed to test the validity of the model, its inputs and outputs, and its sensitivity to changes in certain key variables. Financial forecasting models often contain alternative scenarios that present three or more different prospective outcomes. Sensitivity analysis illustrates how even a small change in a variable, such as cost-of-sales percent, can have an enormous impact on forecast results and business value. Many models highlight such impacts, often in the form of a matrix presentation of changed variable and resulting outcome.

*Financial ratios* are a forecasting tool, like mathematical algorithms, used to derive forecasted values from other forecasted values already derived from trend analysis, algorithms, or other ratios. A common financial ratio that can be used in forecasting is the inventory-to-cost-of-sales (COS) ratio. For example, if forecast cost-of-sales is calculated to be $100 million, and the normal relationship between inventory and COS is 25%, then forecast inventory for that period would be $25 million. *Forecasting modeling professionals should be extremely cautious when applying financial ratios.* A small change in even one ratio, for example, COS-to-sales ratio, can have an enormous impact on future profitability, debt service capability, and corporate value. Many of the failures of the highly leveraged transactions during the late 1980s resulted from stakeholders financing transactions without an understanding of the extreme vulnerability of their capital position to even slight changes in the business and the effect of those changes on financial performance.

*Goal seeking* allows the financial modeling professional to start with a desired solution and to move backward from that desired solution to derive or seek solutions to the rest of the model. For example, the modeling professional may assume that to obtain equity capital, a 40% internal rate of return must be offered. If the model is calculated with that requirement as a given, solutions to the rest of the model must be derived in order to reach that 40% goal, for example, sales growth rate must rise, or the equity infusion must be extremely small. In some goal-seeking exercises, it may not be possible to solve the rest of the model, or the values obtained may not be realistically achievable. Forecasting modeling professionals should exercise care to analyze the model thoroughly, seeking variables whose solution is either unrealistic or simply not achievable.

*Optimization* drives the model to seek the best solution for the variable selected. The most common optimization tool is linear programming, which seeks the optimal solution given a series of constraints. An example of optimization is an international manufacturing firm using comparative advantage to maximize product output given various limitations of, and cost differences between, the factors of production.

Finally, no list of tools would be complete without mentioning the critical tool of forecasting models: *common sense*. Good judgment and circumspection are the most important aspects of forecasting, and make the forecasting process more an enjoyable art than a mechanistic exercise.

## 48-6  PREPARING FINANCIAL FORECASTING MODELS

It is said that there are more approaches to business forecasting than there are approaches to curing the federal deficit—and a commensurate level of vehemence on the part of the proponents of each approach. Financial modeling professionals should develop forecasts that are appropriate for their company's circumstances and appropriate for the purposes for which the forecasts are to be generated. The forecasting process should be a function of the uses to which the forecasts will be put, the level of accuracy required, and the strategic and financial impacts on the business if the forecasts are inaccurate.

Preparing financial forecast models involves several actions and steps, including but not limited to the following things:

1. Establishing the goals of the forecasts: As mentioned earlier, forecasts can be put to a number of uses, including assistance in resource allocation, setting performance criteria, evaluating strategies, obtaining financing, and a host of purposes. What are the business goals, and how can the model be designed so as to meet the goals of the business without providing too much extraneous details?

2. Identifying the key issues to be addressed by the model: Should the model be designed to seek an optimal solution, to highlight financial or operating constraints, to illustrate the sensitivity of the business results to a few key variables, or to provide a benchmark against which future results will be judged? Also, how flexible must the model be?

3. Identifying the target audience: Who are the users, and how sophisticated are they? Are they from within the firm or are they outside parties? How much confidential or proprietary information can be included in the assumptions?

4. Selecting the information needs and model specifications: What special circumstances or unique information does the model need to capture, and what format requirements do these circumstances dictate? Does capturing this information meet the goals outlined in Step 1? Once the data requirements have been set, how

will gathering the data affect the model design? What conversions must be performed in order to roll the data into the model in a compatible format? What special templates and features will respond to the Step 1 goals (sensitivity analysis, optimization, what-if analysis, valuation analysis, etc.)? What special matrices and schedules must be incorporated into the model?

5. Selecting the modeling software: Do the applications and data conversions require sophisticated financial modeling languages? Can the applications be addressed effectively by a simple spreadsheet package? Do people understand how to use the software selected? What training must be completed?

6. Gathering the data: If the data being gathered is costly and time consuming to collect, can the model requirements and uses be modified, or can the model's tools and techniques be revised so that more accessible data can be gathered without sacrificing output integrity?

7. Developing the model and related algorithms: Are proper documentation procedures being performed, and is debugging being continuously performed so as to establish and maintain model integrity? Are proper checks and balancing equations being implemented?

8. Integrating the inputs with the model to obtain preliminary forecasts: Now that the data is finally being entered, did the design and prototyping steps, above, correctly anticipate issues of consolidation and compatibility?

9. Preparing documentation: If the model designer and operator walk away tomorrow, could other professionals run, modify, redesign, and rerun the model?

10. Integrating the forecasts with company strategic plans: Are the results achievable? Does the business need more capital or other production factors in order to achieve the forecast? Based on forecast results, is the strategic plan of the business difficult or even impossible to execute?

This last step, integrating the forecast with the company's plan, is critical. For example, if a company's growth strategy does not include an increase in plant capacity (or new capital to finance it), but the forecasting model clearly shows that additional plant and capital will be required, then the plan has to be modified, sometimes dramatically. The forecasting process, in turn, must begin all over again, starting with Step 1, above. This iterative process is one way in which companies "keep their eye on the ball," establish realistic plans, and develop forecasting processes that have a high degree of internal integrity and external credibility with bankers, vendors, customers and other parties on whom the company's survival depends.

The forecasting process can be one of the most rewarding or misleading business processes that a company undertakes. The following can help forecast modeling practitioners in their craft:

- Know and understand whence the business came, the critical data points in the time series, and the conditions affecting the business, including the economic and environmental conditions, competitive factors, relations among suppliers and customers, and regulatory matters.

- Continuously monitor the forecasting process, seeking new information that may have an impact on the model design and execution.

- Identify the assumptions of the forecast in clear, straightforward documentation, review these assumptions with top management and outside experts, and periodically test these assumptions as new information is developed.

- Strive for just the right amount of accuracy. Don't try to count the wings on the angels on the head of the pin if all you need is the number of pins. Use whole numbers, or thousands, or millions, whenever possible.

- Prevent the occurrence of hybrid language used for communication between people of different speech. In other words, avoid jargon.

- Use simple forecasting tools on personal computers wherever possible. Complex techniques on mainframe systems do not necessarily enhance the integrity or accuracy of the model.

- Challenge the plan, forecast and procedures. Test the assumptions. Check the results. Audit the system. Evaluate periodically the entire forecasting process and related systems.

## 48-7   FINANCIAL FORECAST MODELING PACKAGES

The selection of a software package should be based on (1) how well will the package satisfy our needs, (2) the cost, (3) the level of clerical support and, (4) the amount of maintenance required. There are two types of microcomputer-based software packages for financial planning: modeling languages and spreadsheets. modeling languages are used as a tool to create customized models. Most of the spreadsheet packages are easy to use, fast, and are capable of "what-if" scenarios. Spreadsheets offer some program logic capability and many built-in financial, statistical, and mathematical functions. The following is a list and description of some of the financial planning packages currently available.

*Smart Forecast II* is a relatively easy to use forecasting package that can greatly simplify statistical forecasting projects. This package tries to focus the users attention on the forecasting task rather than the statistical analysis involved. Its user interface and help system are structured to assist persons who may not be experts in the forecasting field. People with virtually no forecasting experience and only modest computer familiarity can learn how to use this package. Data is manually entered or imported from a spreadsheet, database, or word processor. The user makes forecasts from the data by choosing among five main forecasting methods (simple moving averages, linear moving averages, single exponential smoothing, double exponential smoothing, and Winters' multiplication and additive exponential smoothing). Alternatively, the user may execute the package's automatic mode, which applies all five of these methods and chooses the one that, according to its calculations, is the most accurate. The program also provides options for autocorrelation and crosscorrelation analysis, time series decomposition to make seasonal adjustments, multiseries simultaneous forecasts for forecasting up to 60 well-related variables as a group and individually, and regression analysis for forecasting dependent variables in relation to as many as 20 other independent variables. The system also has an interactive graphical forecasting (eyeballing) mode that allows the user to manipulate or adjust a forecast to reflect specific known factors, inside information or educated guessing.

*Autobox Plus* offers both automatic and user-defined ARIMA forecasting methods. The program uses standard Box-Jenkins methodology and offers intervention deduction and transfer function capabilities. It includes modules for exponential smoothing, trend curve, moving average, and basic regression analysis. Autobox is designed for ARIMA-based modeling and forecasting. It can report descriptive statistics on data samples containing fewer than 300 observations. The user has the choice between manual and automatic forecasting modes. The automatic method is based on a system that will determine the optimum model specification for a given time series. Using Box-Jenkins criteria, it incorporates diagnostic procedures for testing sufficiency, invertibility, and necessity in the identified model. The more sophisticated user will be impressed by this program's ability to provide full transfer-function modeling for more than one input series. With the data simulation module, the user can simulate time series data based on one of three general classes of models: univariate ARIMA, transfer function, or vector ARIMA.

*Forecast Pro* is designed for the business person and automatically chooses the best forecasting technique and recommends variable transformations to improve the forecast's accuracy. After choosing the best forecasting technique, it explains in layman's terms the reasons for its decision. The program uses three statistical methods: the Holt-Winters family of exponential smoothing, Box-Jenkins (multiplicative seasonal model), and dynamic regression (for multivariate analysis). A permanent record of all your interactions with the computer (audit trail) are displayed after each stage of the forecasting process. The audit trail shows the results of the regression analysis (mean, standard deviation, and others), judgment criteria for accuracy of fit, and recommendations for further transformations. Data transformation recommended can include inverse, inverse square root, logarithm, and square root.

*Lotus 1-2-3* is fast, easy to use, and, as a result, very popular. It is capable of standard deviation, variance, and multiple "what-if" analysis, as well as "if-then-else" and "minimum/maximum" logic; has sorting capability; and provides financial, statistical, and database functions. It detects simultaneous equations (circular references) and rearranges the calculation order automatically to avoid these circular references. Recent versions also have goal-seeking and optimization capability. Furthermore, if more sophisticated analysis is required, several add-on packages for Lotus 1-2-3 are available.

An add-on package, *Forecast! 1-2-3,* contains two worksheets that allow the user to perform two broad statistical procedures—time series analysis and regression analysis. The time series worksheet allows the user to analyze up to 150 periods of historic data with equal time intervals between each data point and to generate forecasts based on that information. Manipulating data to define trends and analyze residuals, adjusting for seasonality, performing decomposition analysis, and exponential smoothing are easily accomplished by following examples in the user manual. The multiple-regression worksheet permits the user to determine statistical relationships between one dependent variable and up to 10 independent variables. The user can create a new variable from existing independent variables or from a formula. Both worksheets can display data, trends, and residuals on-screen. Worksheet screens are standard, and although not difficult to read, are more meaningful if they are customized.

A second add-on package, *Add a Stat 1-2-3,* provides programs for linear regression, t-tests, chi-square, Poisson, analysis of variance, and error bar plots. When performing any of these tests, the user must enter pairs of data in ascending order. Otherwise, data must be entered into a separate worksheet, sorted, and then re-entered into the main worksheet.

A third add-on package, *Multifit 1-2-3,* performs multiple regressions, trend analysis, and linear exponential smoothing. Unfortunately, the benefit of this package as a forecasting tool is minimized because the program is capable of projecting values only one period into the future. The value of using the multiple regression analysis is also moderated by the program's limitation of only being able to use three independent variables to describe a dependent variable. However, Multifit's ability to produce a matrix of the correlation coefficients among all of the factors is an attractive feature.

Screen and summary reports used in both *Add a Stat* and *Multifit* packages can be confusing because they require the user to page through several screens to view all the information, and they include a great deal of extraneous data. Each package includes graphics capabilities, but the number of steps involved to produce a graph reduces the positive contribution it makes to analyzing test results.

Recent versions of Lotus 1-2-3 allow the user to link several spreadsheets so as to organize and consolidate data. Given enough memory in the microcomputer, these versions can link up to 256 spreadsheets, each with 256 columns by 8,102 rows. Built-in desktop publishing (DTP) features are also available.

*Microsoft Excel* is one of the most powerful spreadsheet programs available for microcomputers with features like "what-if" scenario manager, report manager, simplified database cross-tabulation, and a spelling checker. *Excel* is similar to *Lotus,* in that it allows the user to display and link multiple spreadsheets together. It has built-in auditing tools to check the spreadsheet for formula or data error and custom applications capability to allow a user to create user-defined menus, dialogue boxes, and on-line help. *Excel's* excellent graphics capability includes hundreds of built-in chart types, as well as powerful customization capability. It has over 131 built-in spreadsheet functions, including "what-if" analysis, database, statistical, and financial functions, and an outline function that allows the user to collapse a detailed spreadsheet into summary values. One of its most powerful features is that it interfaces with *Microsoft Word for Windows* word processing software. With this feature, the user can establish an automatic link between a word processing document and a spreadsheet. If the user changes the spreadsheet, the changes will be incorporated in the word processing document. The combined *Excel/Word* software products produce an efficient and uniform package.

A new add-in for *Excel* called *Analysis ToolPak* lets you perform regression analysis, moving averages, moving averages, flexible number generation, and linear algebra on ranges of data.

*CA-Compete* is a multidimensional modeling and viewing tool specifically designed to help solve business problems quickly, realistic, and with greater accuracy and flexibility than two-or even three-dimensional spreadsheets. *CA-Compete* looks and works like a spreadsheet, but is object based, that is, it uses names you define to identify cells in the model. This package gives you the power tool model with up to 12 dimensions or categories of data with easy to use commands. You can create flexible forecasts and perform sensitivity analyses using "what-if" questions. The program offers 128 built-in functions allowing you to perform ratio analysis, variance analysis, trend analysis, and offers a goal-seeking function that performs backward "what-if" analysis. It provides a wide range of activity/cost drivers (such as scale, complexity, experience, and capacity utilization) that can be applied to model your own business. This package has a forecasting function that can provide a regression or interpolation of past data to forecast on a simple or compound basis. The statistical functions include averaging, exponential smoothing, regression, standard deviations, and variances. *CA-Compete* can import from and export to other spreadsheet, dBase, ASCII, and script files. This package is well suited for financial planning and budgeting, product/segment profitability assessment, competitor benchmarking, financial forecasting and tracking, salesforce management, acquisition analysis, human resource management, pricing decisions, contingency planning, and many other projects.

*SuperCalc* has built-in financial, statistical, and database functions. It can hold multiple spreadsheets in memory. This package has a feature to help the user audit and debug the spreadsheet, and its enhanced graphics package can create three-dimensional charts. *SuperCalc* is fully compatible with *Lotus 1-2-3* and the versions of *SuperCalc* developed for midrange and mainframe computers.

*Context MBA* performs most of the "what-if," logical, statistical, and financial functions of the other packages. Its greatest strength is that it allows the user to download data from corporate databases and public information service bureaus into the spreadsheet without having to retype the data. Two of its limitations are that (1) its maximum spreadsheet cell capacity is 95 columns by 999 rows, and (2) its response time is somewhat longer than that of other spreadsheet packages. Also, *Context MBA* does not perform goal-seeking, solve simultaneous equations, or provide loan, depreciation, or tax functions; nor does it offer any other programming logic capability. *Context MBA* does, however, provide a database management system with sorting capability and a communications package. It also allows for text, table, and graphics output. *Context MBA* provides the capability for all three forms of output to reside on the same screen or printout. Graph types include pie and bar charts, line graphs (two-dimensional only), scatter plots, and area diagrams.

*MicroFCS,* a Thorn EMI microcomputer package patterned after its first mainframe computer financial modeling package, *FCS-EPS,* performs "what-if" and sensitivity analysis, has goal-seeking capability, solves simultaneous equations, executes selected programming functions, provides financial, statistical, and mathematical functions, allows several microcomputers running this product to be integrated into the same network for such activities as consolidation, and can be integrated with the microcomputer and mainframe versions of EPS. *MicroFCS* includes a full-screen data editor, screen-formatting capability, a report generator, programmable function keys, and user-defined functions and commands. Its reporting capabilities include tables and text and, to a limited extent, graphs. Graphs can only be directed to the screen, since there is no provision for directing graphics to a printer or plotting device. *MicroFCS* does not perform such functions as optimization or risk analysis.

*MicroFCS* has a mainframe version, called *FCS,* which provides a flexible modeling language with English commands for use by nontechnical management. It has hundreds of built-in financial, statistical, and mathematical functions, and also allows the user to perform customized functions. Its data management capability includes the creation and maintenance of hierarchical and relational databases and flat or sequential files. Perhaps its most powerful feature is its reporting capability which, with over 50 report specifications, provide the user tremendous flexibility. Its powerful graphics capability includes three-dimensional plotting.

*IFPS (Interactive Financial Planning System)/Personal* performs "what-if" analysis, goal seeking, sensitivity analysis, optimization, risk analysis, financial functions, and consolidation. Perhaps its strongest feature is that, because *IFPS* and its mainframe counterpart, *IFPS Plus,* are installed in several thousand locations, its service, support, training, and reference documentation are of extremely high quality.

*Encore!Plus* is designed for professionals who have significant modeling experience. Its eight interactive sections, with over 50 commands, 12 conditional operations and 19 logic functions, make it one of the most powerful microcomputer packages available today. *Encore!Plus* provides a programming language to aid in application development, special menu screens with option-processing, and commands that allow the user to automatically create custom menus and batch files. Its spreadsheet, containing 500,000 cells, has the capability of multiple windowing and hierarchical consolidation. The spreadsheet function includes data-input screen capability and regression and goal-seeking algorithms. Various tables and schedules, such as U.S. tax tables, regression algorithms, loan amortization schedules, various statistical and depreciation calculations are also imbedded in the package. Its powerful report capability allows the user to produce formalized, customized reports. Its graphics package provides on-line display capability and Monte Carlo risk analysis.

Scores of software packages are available for virtually every size of computer. Since the introduction of microcomputers, the pace of introduction of new forecasting applications has accelerated rapidly. The final selection of a package that is right for a given application will depend on (1) the degree to which the package satisfies the business objective, (2) the cost of the package, (3) the level of sophistication and training required of the users, and (4) the amount and frequency of programmer maintenance required.

## 48-8  FINANCIAL FORECAST MODELING AS A STRATEGIC TOOL

In his book, *Creating Shareholder Value* (Free Press, 1986), Alfred Rappaport argues that the only way to judge whether business strategies succeed or fail is to determine whether they generated or failed to generate economic returns to shareholders. Managements choose from among alternative strategies by assuming that the strategy that produces the greatest sustainable competitive advantage will also create the most shareholder wealth. This "shareholder value approach" calculates the economic value of the shareholders' investment by estimating future cash flows and discounting these cash flows by the cost of capital.

The role of the financial forecasting professional is to link the strategic plans with "economic value" by translating the planning process into financial forecasting terminology, principally income, balance sheet and cash flow forecasts, together with supporting schedules. This critical forecasting role can be exciting and provide great value to the management decision-making process. But it can also be fraught with errors, as highlighted by the three examples summarized at the beginning of this chapter.

Any financial forecasting model that fails to contain algorithms, templates, and schedules that show all the complex linkages and interactions among operating strategies, financial strategies, working capital requirements, "free cash flow," discount rates, business value, and shareholder value is almost certainly not going to give top management all the information it needs to execute the plan. Too many forecasts simply contain forecast income or net cash receipts. Some of them might also contain a balance sheet forecast.

The problem with these forecasts is that they do not provide enough of the essential information about the execution of the operating plan and the feasibility of the financing plan. Some simple forecasts, for example, fail to realize that the revolving line capacity will be exceeded under the parameters of the plan. Other forecasts carry credit risk which is not matched by the interest rates and overall debt burden assumed in the model. Still others do not provide enough internal rate of return to attract equity in the amounts assumed in the forecast. It does not take a Monday morning quarterback to analyze the failure of many of the late-1980s leveraged buyouts. Many of the problems that only later surfaced could have been anticipated at the time of the transaction if sufficient care had been given to such things as likely variability of costs, sensitivity of financial variables to key operating variables, unusual working capital needs, required implementation of presumed synergies, and other situations commonly addressed in complete forecasting models.

The appendix to this chapter shows a typical financial forecasting model that highlights some of these issues. Analyze this model to determine the effects on shareholder value of such changes as:

- A 1 percentage point change in cost of sales.
- An inability to obtain subordinated financing. (Also, what is the new weighted average cost of capital?)
- A requirement, due to the inability to obtain subordinated financing, to put in a like amount of additional equity. (Also, what is the new weighted average cost of capital?)
- An inability to use all tax loss carryforwards.
- A change in days-in-receivables by 10%.

Ultimately, it is not enough for a forecasting professional to ask simply if the numbers make sense. A good forecaster will anticipate the needs of management, develop models to support those needs, continuously challenge the assumptions both of the strategic plan and of the forecast model, and seek to provide high-integrity output that shows management whether a given set of strategies is likely to add value to the shareholders. A good forecaster, along with strategic planning professionals and top management, will constantly ask the following questions:

- To what extent can the business fund its proposed strategies from internal sources, how much additional debt or equity capital will be required, and how accessible will that capital be?
- For a selected strategy, how sensitive is value to internal and external business factors not contemplated in the "most likely" scenario?
- Which combination of strategies will generate the most total value?
- How would alternative strategies affect the creation of shareholder value?

Successful planning requires sound analysis for formulating business strategies. Successful forecasting requires sound analysis for valuing those business strategies. Forecasting professionals who develop models that link the formulation of business strategies with the valuation of those strategies will sit on their company boards in the decade ahead.

## 48-9  SELECTED REFERENCES

Krajewski, Lee J., and Larry P. Ritzman, *Operations Management.* (Reading, MA: Addison Wesley, 1990).

Pearch II, John A., and Richard B. Robinson, Jr., *Competitive Strategy.* (Homewood, IL: Dow-Jones Irwin, 1991).

Raskin, Robin. "Statistical Software for the PC: Testing for Significance." *PC Magazine,* March 14, 1989, v8, n5.

Ellis, Dennis, and Jay Nathan, *A Managerial Guide to Business Forecasting.* (Flushing, NY: Graceway Publishing Company, 1990).

## APPENDIX: SAMPLE FINANCIAL FORECASTING MODEL

The following financial forecasting model illustrates the interactions of a fully integrated forecast. A forecasting professional who has all the "templates" shown would readily see many of the pitfalls and errors that commonly surface in modeling. For example, the "revolver line of the Liabilities section of the balance sheet, and the "Marketable Securities" line of the Assets section, iterate until the balance sheet balances. However, does the Company have sufficient revolver capacity throughout the forecast period to handle this Revolver (last page)? If not, what initial capitalization structure (or future capital infusion) might be required in order to make the forecast feasible? Is such capital available? What would be the effect on the corporate and shareholder value of the modified capital structure, and what would be the yields to the potential investors of each class of security? Do those yields match the yield requirements of such potential investors? Out of all the feasible capital structures, which one maximizes shareholder value? Integrated modeling such as the example shown on the following pages helps focus management attention on making the right strategic decisions, and right operating decisions, and right financial decisions, to increase the probability of success in an environment in which "good enough" is no longer good enough for survival. (While some of the exhibits are similar to certain of the figures in Chapter 5 of the main volume, it was considered desirable to illustrate in one chapter a sample of a complete model.)

# INCOME STATEMENT ASSUMPTIONS

| | | 12/31/89 | 12/31/90 | 12/31/91 | 12/31/92 | 12/31/93 |
|---|---|---|---|---|---|---|
| Sales growth rate | | 4.32% | 4.03% | 4.76% | 4.84% | 4.84% |
| SGA: variable as % Sales | | 7.7% | 7.3% | 6.7% | 6.4% | 6.2% |
| Other Op. Exp. (Savings)—absolute amount | | (1.0) | 7.0 | 9.0 | 9.0 | 9.0 |
| Depr. Exp.—abosolute amount | | 2.8 | 2.9 | 3.0 | 3.1 | 3.4 |
| Amort. of Organization Expense | | $0 | $0 | $0 | $0 | $0 |
| Other Non-Op. Exp.—absolute amount | | $0 | $0 | $0 | $0 | $0 |
| Combined Federal and State effective tax | | 34.0% | 34.0% | 34.0% | 34.0% | 34.0% |
| Other taxes | | $0 | $0 | $0 | $0 | $0 |
| **INTEREST RATE ASSUMPTIONS:** | | | | | | |
| Marketable Sec.: Interest rate | | 8.0% | 8.0% | 8.0% | 8.0% | 8.0% |
| Revolver: Interest rate | | 12.0% | 12.0% | 12.0% | 12.0% | 12.0% |
| Debt 1: (Senior, 7 years) Interest rate | | 12.0% | 12.0% | 12.0% | 12.0% | 12.0% |
| Debt 2: (Bridge Credit A) tied to assets | | 13.0 | 13.5 | 13.5 | 13.5 | 13.5 |
| Debt 3: (Bridge Credit B) | | 13.0% | 13.5% | 13.5% | 13.5% | 13.5% |
| Debt 4: (Seasonal Borrowings) Interest rate | | 11.5% | 11.5% | 11.5% | 11.5% | 11.5% |
| Additional unanticipated borrowings | | 14.0% | 14.0% | 14.0% | 14.0% | 14.0% |
| NOL beginning balance | | 0.0 | (9.9) | (10.8) | (10.8) | (10.8) |
| NOL Utilization | | (9.9) | (0.8) | 0.0 | 0.0 | 0.0 |
| NOL Adjustment | | (9.9) | (10.8) | (10.8) | (10.8) | (10.8) |
| Preferred Dividends absolute amount | | 0.0 | 0.0 | 0.0 | 0.0 | 0.0 |
| Common Dividends absolute amount | | 0.0 | 0.0 | 0.0 | 0.0 | 0.0 |
| Non-Cash Expenses (Goodwill) | 115.5 | 2.9 | 2.9 | 2.9 | 2.9 | 2.9 |
| Deferred tax additions | | 0 | 0 | 0 | 0 | 0 |

# INCOME STATEMENT

| | Actual | | | | Forecast | | | |
|---|---|---|---|---|---|---|---|---|
| | 1986 | 1987 | 1988 | 12/31/89 | 12/31/90 | 12/31/91 | 12/31/92 | 12/31/93 |
| Revenues | 461.6 | 473.1 | 532.5 | 555.5 | 577.9 | 605.4 | 634.7 | 665.4 |
| Cost of Goods Sold | 396.1 | 402.5 | 470.7 | 489.9 | 509.6 | 535.5 | 562.0 | 589.2 |
| SGA: Pre-Depreciation & Interest | 47.6 | 52.7 | 48.2 | 42.8 | 42.4 | 40.3 | 40.9 | 41.2 |
| Other Operating Expense (Saving)/Synergy | 0.0 | 0.0 | 0.0 | 1.0 | (7.0) | (9.0) | (9.0) | (9.0) |
| EBDIT | 17.9 | 17.9 | 13.6 | 21.8 | 32.9 | 38.6 | 40.8 | 44.0 |
| Depreciation | 1.8 | 4.4 | 4.4 | 2.8 | 2.9 | 3.0 | 3.1 | 3.4 |
| Amortization of Goodwill & Org. Costs | 0.0 | 0.0 | 0.0 | 2.9 | 2.9 | 2.9 | 2.9 | 2.9 |
| EBIT (Operating Profit) | 16.1 | 13.5 | 9.2 | 16.1 | 27.1 | 32.7 | 34.8 | 37.7 |
| Interest Income | 0.8 | 0.8 | 0.0 | 0.0 | 0.0 | 0.0 | 0.0 | 0.0 |
| Interest Exp: Revolver | 6.7 | 0.0 | 0.0 | 9.1 | 17.7 | 21.0 | 22.5 | 23.6 |
| Interest Exp: Debt 1 (Sr.) | 0.0 | 0.0 | 0.0 | 10.2 | 9.5 | 8.0 | 6.6 | 5.1 |
| Interest Exp: Debt 2 (Bridge A) | 0.0 | 0.0 | 0.0 | 1.4 | 0.7 | 0.0 | 0.0 | 0.0 |
| Interest Exp: Debt 3 (Bridge B) | 0.0 | 0.0 | 0.0 | 5.2 | 0.0 | 0.0 | 0.0 | 0.0 |
| Interest Exp: Debt 4 (Additional) | 0.0 | 0.0 | 0.0 | 0.1 | 0.1 | 0.1 | 0.1 | 0.1 |
| Other Non-Operating Expense | 0.0 | 0.0 | 0.0 | 0.0 | 0.0 | 0.0 | 0.0 | 0.0 |
| EBT (Earnings Before Taxes) | 10.2 | 14.3 | 9.2 | (9.9) | (0.8) | 3.5 | 5.6 | 8.9 |
| Tax Provision | 0.0 | 0.0 | 0.0 | 0.0 | 0.7 | 2.2 | 2.9 | 4.0 |
| Net Income | 10.2 | 14.3 | 9.2 | (9.9) | (1.5) | 1.3 | 2.7 | 4.9 |
| NOL Carryforward Utilized | | | | 0.0 | 3.7 | 3.7 | 3.7 | 3.7 |
| Net Income after NOL | 10.2 | 14.3 | 9.2 | (9.9) | 2.1 | 5.0 | 6.4 | 8.5 |
| Preferred Dividends—absolute amount | 0.0 | 0.0 | | 0.0 | 0.0 | 0.0 | 0.0 | 0.0 |
| Common Dividends—absolute amount | 0.0 | 0.0 | | 0.0 | 0.0 | 0.0 | 0.0 | 0.0 |
| Retained Earnings: Beg. | | | | 1.9 | (8.0) | (5.9) | (0.9) | 5.5 |
| Retained Earnings: Additions | | | | (9.9) | 2.1 | 5.0 | 6.4 | 8.5 |
| Retained earnings: Ending | | | | (8.0) | (5.9) | (0.9) | 5.5 | 14.0 |

0 = yes  
1 = no

| | 1987 | | 12/31/89 | 12/31/90 | 12/31/91 | 12/31/92 | 12/31/93 |
|---|---|---|---|---|---|---|---|
| Cash Interest Expense: | | | | | | | |
| Interest Expense: Revolver | 0 | | 9.1 | 17.7 | 21.0 | 22.5 | 23.6 |
| Interest Expense: Debt 1 | 0 | | 10.2 | 9.5 | 8.0 | 6.6 | 5.1 |
| Interest Expense: Debt 2 | 0 | | 1.4 | 0.7 | 0.0 | 0.0 | 0.0 |
| Interest Expense: Debt 3 | 0 | | 5.2 | 0.0 | 0.0 | 0.0 | 0.0 |
| Interest Expense: Debt 4 | 1 | | 0.0 | 0.0 | 0.0 | 0.0 | 0.0 |
| | | | 25.9 | 27.8 | 29.0 | 29.1 | 28.7 |

INCOME STATEMENT: COMMON SIZE

|  | Base 1988 | Fiscal 1989 | Latest 12 Mos. 4/90 | 12/31/89 | 12/31/90 | Forecast 12/31/91 | 12/31/92 | 12/31/93 |
|---|---|---|---|---|---|---|---|---|
| Revenues | 100.0% | 100.0% | 100.0% | 100.0% | 100.0% | 100.0% | 100.0% | 100.0% |
| SGA: Pre-Depreciaiton & Interest | 10.3% | 11.1% | 9.1% | 7.7% | 7.3% | 6.7% | 6.4% | 6.2% |
| Other Operating Expense (Saving)/Synergy | 0.0% | 0.0% | 0.0% | 0.2% | -1.2% | -1.5% | -1.4% | -1.4% |
| EBDIT | 3.9% | 3.8% | 2.6% | 3.9% | 5.7% | 6.4% | 6.4% | 6.6% |
| Depreciation | 0.4% | 0.9% | 0.8% | 0.5% | 0.5% | 0.5% | 0.5% | 0.5% |
| Amortization of Goodwill & Org. Costs | 0.0% | 0.0% | 0.0% | 0.5% | 0.5% | 0.5% | 0.5% | 0.4% |
| EBIT (Operating Profit) | 3.5% | 2.9% | 1.7% | 2.9% | 4.7% | 5.4% | 5.5% | 5.7% |
| Interest Income | 0.2% | 0.2% | 0.0% | 0.0% | 0.0% | 0.0% | 0.0% | 0.0% |
| Interest Exp: Revolver | 1.5% | 0.0% | 0.0% | 1.6% | 3.1% | 3.5% | 3.5% | 3.5% |
| Interest Exp: Debt 1 (Sr.) | 0.0% | 0.0% | 0.0% | 1.8% | 1.6% | 1.3% | 1.0% | 0.8% |
| Interest Exp: Debt 2 (Bridge A) | 0.0% | 0.0% | 0.0% | 0.2% | 0.1% | 0.0% | 0.0% | 0.0% |
| Interest Exp: Debt 3 (Bridge B) | 0.0% | 0.0% | 0.0% | 0.9% | 0.0% | 0.0% | 0.0% | 0.0% |
| Interest Exp: Debt 4 (Additional) | 0.0% | 0.0% | 0.0% | 0.0% | 0.0% | 0.0% | 0.0% | 0.0% |
| Other Non-Operating Expense | 0.0% | 0.0% | 0.0% | 0.0% | 0.0% | 0.0% | 0.0% | 0.0% |
| EBT (Earnings Before Taxes) | 2.2% | 3.0% | 1.7% | -1.8% | -0.1% | 0.6% | 0.9% | 1.3% |
| Tax Provision | 0.0% | 0.0% | 0.0% | 0.0% | 0.1% | 0.4% | 0.5% | 0.6% |
| Net Income | 2.2% | 3.0% | 1.7% | -1.8% | -0.3% | 0.2% | 0.4% | 0.7% |
| NOL Carryforward Utilized | 0.0% | 0.0% | 0.0% | 0.0% | 0.6% | 0.6% | 0.6% | 0.6% |
| Net Income after NOL | 2.2% | 3.0% | 1.7% | -1.8% | 0.4% | 0.8% | 1.0% | 1.3% |

BALANCE SHEET ASSUMPTIONS

| | 12/31/88 | 12/31/89 | 12/31/90 | 12/31/91 | 12/31/92 | 12/31/93 |
|---|---|---|---|---|---|---|
| Minimum Operating Cash (% of Revenues) | | 0.83% | 0.83% | 0.83% | 0.83% | 0.83% |
| A/R as a % of Revenues | | 18.10% | 16.70% | 9.90% | 9.90% | 9.90% |
| Inventory as a % of COGS | | 22.20% | 22.20% | 22.20% | 22.20% | 22.20% |
| Gross PP&E additions | | 2.8 | 2.9 | 3.0 | 3.1 | 3.4 |
| Land additions | | $0 | $0 | $0 | $0 | $0 |
| Prepaid & Other (% of Revenues) | | 5.37% | 5.37% | 5.37% | 5.37% | 5.37% |
| Days in Accounts Payable (Sales) | | 75.5 | 75.5 | 75.5 | 75.5 | 75.5 |
| Accrued Expenses as a % of Revenues | | 0.0% | 0.0% | 0.0% | 0.0% | 0.0% |
| Other Current Liabilities as a % of Rev. | | 6.59% | 6.59% | 6.59% | 6.59% | 6.59% |
| Change in Deferred Income Tax | | $0 | $0 | $0 | $0 | $0 |
| Other Liab. & Accrued Interest | | $0 | $0 | $0 | $0 | $0 |
| Depr. Exp.—Actual (for Accum. Deprec. & CF) | | 2.8 | 2.9 | 3.0 | 3.1 | 3.4 |
| Interest only on any financing (1 = yes, 0 = n) | | 0.0 | 0.0% | 0.0% | 0.0% | 0.0% |
| Debt 1: Long-term debt balance, end of year | 85.0 | 72.9 | 60.7 | 48.6 | 36.4 | 24.3 |
| Debt 2: Long-term debt balance, end of year | 10.0 | 0.0 | 0.0 | 0.0 | 0.0 | 0.0 |
| Debt 3: Long-term debt balance, end of year | 40.0 | 0.0 | 0.0 | 0.0 | 0.0 | 0.0 |
| Debt 4: Long-term portion (Seasonal Borrowing) | | 0.0 | 0.0 | 0.0 | 0.0 | 0.0 |
| Additional unanticipated borrowings | 0.0 | 0.0 | 0.0 | 0.0 | 0.0 | 0.0 |
| Preferred absolute amount | | 0.0 | 0.0 | 0.0 | 0.0 | 0.0 |
| Common & Trees. absolute amount | | 0.1 | 0.1 | 0.1 | 0.1 | 0.1 |
| APIC absolute amount | | 23.3 | 23.3 | 23.3 | 23.3 | 23.3 |

Deal Structure:

| | |
|---|---|
| Cash retained in company | 0.0 |
| Revolver | 31.0 |
| Debt 1 (7-year term) | 85.0 |
| Debt 2 (Bridge Credit A) | 11.2 |
| Debt 3 (Bridge Credit B) | 40.0 |
| Debt 4 (Add'l. Borrowing Needs) | 0.0 |
| New Preferred Stock | 0.0 |
| New Common & Treasury Stock | 0.0 |
| New APIC | 0.0 |
| | 167.2 |

Current Portion:

| | |
|---|---|
| Debt 1 (Sr.) | 0.0 |
| Debt 2 (Bridge A) | 1.2 |
| Debt 3 (Bridge B) | 40.0 |
| Debt 4 (Add'l.) | 0.0 |

|  | Base | | | Pro Format | Forecast | | | | |
|---|---|---|---|---|---|---|---|---|---|
|  | Fiscal 1987 | 11/30 1988 | Adj. | 1988 | 12/31/89 | 12/31/90 | 12/31/91 | 12/31/92 | 12/31/93 |
| **Assets** | | | | | | | | | |
| Minimum Operating Cash | 5.8 | 9.9 | 0.0 | 9.9 | 4.6 | 4.8 | 5.0 | 5.3 | 5.5 |
| Marketable Securities | 0.0 | 0.0 | 0.0 | 0.0 | 0.0 | 0.0 | 0.0 | 0.0 | 0.0 |
| Accounts Receivable (Net) | 34.0 | 75.1 | 0.0 | 75.1 | 79.3 | 83.0 | 85.7 | 88.6 | 91.7 |
| Inventory & Other | 76.5 | 94.7 | 0.0 | 94.7 | 108.8 | 113.1 | 118.9 | 124.8 | 130.8 |
| Total Current Assets | 116.3 | 179.7 | 0.0 | 179.7 | 192.6 | 200.9 | 209.6 | 218.7 | 228.0 |
| Fixed Assets: | | | | | | | | | |
| Furniture & Fixtures | 27.0 | 32.5 | 0.0 | 32.5 | 35.3 | 38.2 | 41.2 | 44.3 | 47.7 |
| Accumulated Depr. | (2.4) | (3.6) | 0.0 | (3.6) | (6.4) | (9.3) | (12.3) | (15.4) | (18.8) |
| Net PP&E | 24.6 | 28.9 | 0.0 | 28.9 | 28.9 | 28.9 | 28.9 | 28.9 | 28.9 |
| Org. Costs/Intangible | 0.0 | 0.0 | 0.0 | 0.0 | 0.0 | 0.0 | 0.0 | 0.0 | 0.0 |
| Goodwill | 0.0 | 21.9 | 93.6 | 115.5 | 112.6 | 109.7 | 106.8 | 104.0 | 101.1 |
| Other Non-Curr. Assets | 23.5 | 28.6 | 0.0 | 28.6 | 29.8 | 31.0 | 32.5 | 34.1 | 35.7 |
| Total Assets | 164.4 | 259.1 | 93.6 | 352.7 | 364.0 | 370.6 | 377.9 | 385.6 | 393.7 |

| | Base | | | | Forecast | | | | |
|---|---|---|---|---|---|---|---|---|---|
| | Fiscal 1987 | 11/30 1988 | Adj. | Pro Format 1988 | 12/31/89 | 12/31/90 | 12/31/91 | 12/31/92 | 12/31/93 |
| **Liabilities** | | | | | | | | | |
| Accounts Payable | 60.5 | 110.1 | 0.0 | 110.1 | 114.9 | 119.5 | 125.2 | 131.2 | 137.6 |
| Revolver | 0.0 | 0.0 | 31.0 | 31.0 | 90.2 | 113.9 | 122.8 | 129.4 | 134.4 |
| Curr: Debt 1 (Sr.) | 0.0 | 0.0 | 0.0 | 0.0 | 12.1 | 12.1 | 12.1 | 12.1 | 12.1 |
| Curr: Debt 2 (Bridge A) | 0.0 | 0.0 | 1.2 | 1.2 | 10.0 | 0.0 | 0.0 | 0.0 | 0.0 |
| Curr: Debt 3 (Bridge B) | 0.0 | 0.0 | 40.0 | 40.0 | 0.0 | 0.0 | 0.0 | 0.0 | 0.0 |
| Curr: Debt 4 (Add'l. Need) | 0.0 | 0.0 | 0.0 | 0.0 | 0.0 | 0.0 | 0.0 | 0.0 | 0.0 |
| Existing Note | 51.6 | 87.5 | (73.6) | 13.9 | 10.8 | 7.7 | 5.7 | 4.6 | 2.9 |
| Other Current Liab. | 19.3 | 35.1 | 0.0 | 35.1 | 36.6 | 38.1 | 39.9 | 41.8 | 43.9 |
| Total Current Liab. | 131.4 | 232.7 | (1.4) | 231.3 | 274.7 | 291.3 | 305.7 | 319.2 | 330.9 |
| Debt 1 (Sr.) | 0.0 | 0.0 | 85.0 | 85.0 | 72.9 | 60.7 | 48.6 | 36.4 | 24.3 |
| Debt 2 (Bridge A) | 0.0 | 0.0 | 10.0 | 10.0 | 0.0 | 0.0 | 0.0 | 0.0 | 0.0 |
| Debt 3 (Bridge B) | 0.0 | 0.0 | 0.0 | 0.0 | 0.0 | 0.0 | 0.0 | 0.0 | 0.0 |
| Debt 4 (Add'l. Need) | 0.0 | 0.0 | 0.0 | 0.0 | 0.0 | 0.0 | 0.0 | 0.0 | 0.0 |
| Total Long-Term Debt | 0.0 | 0.0 | 95.0 | 95.0 | 72.9 | 60.7 | 48.6 | 36.4 | 24.3 |
| Deferred Tax and Other | 3.7 | 1.1 | 0.0 | 1.1 | 1.1 | 1.1 | 1.1 | 1.1 | 1.1 |
| Additional Borrowing Needs | 0.0 | 0.0 | 0.0 | 0.0 | 0.0 | 0.0 | 0.0 | 0.0 | 0.0 |
| Total Liabilities | 135.1 | 233.8 | 93.6 | 327.4 | 348.6 | 353.1 | 355.4 | 356.7 | 356.3 |
| **Equity** | | | | | | | | | |
| Preferred Stock | 0.0 | 0.0 | 0.0 | 0.0 | 0.0 | 0.0 | 0.0 | 0.0 | 0.0 |
| Common Stock | 0.1 | 0.1 | 0.0 | 0.1 | 0.1 | 0.1 | 0.1 | 0.1 | 0.1 |
| APIC & Treasury | 23.3 | 23.3 | 0.0 | 23.3 | 23.3 | 23.3 | 23.3 | 23.3 | 23.3 |
| Retained Earnings | 5.9 | 1.9 | 0.0 | 1.9 | (8.0) | (5.9) | (0.9) | 5.5 | 14.0 |
| Total Owners' Equity | 29.3 | 25.3 | 0.0 | 25.3 | 15.4 | 17.5 | 22.5 | 28.9 | 37.4 |
| Total Liab. & Equity | 164.4 | 259.1 | 93.6 | 352.7 | 364.0 | 370.6 | 377.9 | 385.6 | 393.7 |

# CASH FLOW STATEMENT

| | 12/31/89 | 12/31/90 | Forecast 12/31/91 | 12/31/92 | 12/31/93 |
|---|---|---|---|---|---|
| Net Income | (9.9) | (1.5) | 1.3 | 2.7 | 4.9 |
| Add: Depreciation Expense | 2.8 | 2.9 | 3.0 | 3.1 | 3.4 |
| Amort. of Goodwill & Org. Costs | 2.9 | 2.9 | 2.9 | 2.9 | 2.9 |
| Funds from Operations | (4.3) | 4.3 | 7.2 | 8.7 | 11.2 |
| | | | | | |
| Working Capital Increase/(Decrease) | | | | | |
| Minimum Operating Cash | 5.3 | (0.2) | (0.2) | (0.2) | (0.3) |
| Accounts Receivable | (4.2) | (3.7) | (2.7) | (2.9) | (3.0) |
| Inventory | (14.1) | (4.4) | (5.7) | (5.9) | (6.0) |
| Accounts Payable | 4.8 | 4.6 | 5.7 | 6.1 | 6.3 |
| Accrued Expenses | (3.1) | (3.1) | (2.0) | (1.1) | (1.7) |
| Other Current Liabilities | 1.5 | 1.5 | 1.8 | 1.9 | 2.0 |
| | | | | | |
| Increm. Working Cap. Invest. | (9.8) | (5.3) | (3.2) | (2.1) | (2.7) |
| Sales of/(Additions to) Gross PP&E | (2.8) | (2.9) | (3.0) | (3.1) | (3.4) |
| Additions to Land | 0.0 | 0.0 | 0.0 | 0.0 | 0.0 |
| | | | | | |
| Non-Op. Sources/(Uses) | | | | | |
| Other Assets | (1.2) | (1.2) | (1.5) | (1.6) | (1.6) |
| NOL Utilized | 0.0 | 3.7 | 3.7 | 3.7 | 3.7 |
| Deferred Taxes | 0.0 | 0.0 | 0.0 | 0.0 | 0.0 |
| Total Non-Op. Sources/(Uses) | (1.2) | 2.5 | 2.2 | 2.1 | 2.0 |
| Non Cash Interest | (0.1) | (0.1) | (0.1) | (0.1) | (0.1) |
| Common/Preferred Dividends | 0.0 | 0.0 | 0.0 | 0.0 | 0.0 |
| Cash Flow before Debt Principal | (18.2) | (1.6) | 3.1 | 5.4 | 7.0 |

|  |  | Forecast |  |  |  |
| --- | --- | --- | --- | --- | --- |
|  | 12/31/89 | 12/31/90 | 12/31/91 | 12/31/92 | 12/31/93 |
| **Debt Financing/(Repayment):** |  |  |  |  |  |
| Curr: Debt 1 (Sr.) | 12.1 | 0.0 | 0.0 | 0.0 | (0.0) |
| Curr: Debt 2 (Bridge A) | 8.8 | (10.0) | 0.0 | 0.0 | 0.0 |
| Curr: Debt 3 (Bridge B) | (40.0) | 0.0 | 0.0 | 0.0 | 0.0 |
| Curr: Debt 4 (Add'l. Need) | 0.0 | 0.0 | 0.0 | 0.0 | 0.0 |
| Debt 1 (Sr.) | (12.1) | (12.1) | (12.1) | (12.1) | (12.1) |
| Debt 2 (Bridge A) | (10.0) | 0.0 | 0.0 | 0.0 | 0.0 |
| Debt 3 (Bridge B) | 0.0 | 0.0 | 0.0 | 0.0 | 0.0 |
| Debt 4 (Add'l Need) | 0.0 | 0.0 | 0.0 | 0.0 | 0.0 |
| Total Debt Repayment/(Financing) | (41.2) | (22.1) | (12.1) | (12.1) | (12.1) |
| Pref. Stock Issue/(Repayment) | 0.0 | 0.0 | 0.0 | 0.0 | 0.0 |
| **Equity Issue/(Repayment):** |  |  |  |  |  |
| Common & Treasury Stock | 0.0 | 0.0 | 0.0 | 0.0 | 0.0 |
| APIC | 0.0 | 0.0 | 0.0 | 0.0 | 0.0 |
| Total Equity Issue/(Repurchase) | 0.0 | 0.0 | 0.0 | 0.0 | 0.0 |
| Cash Surplus/(Deficit) | (59.4) | (23.8) | (9.1) | (6.7) | (5.2) |
| Cumulative Cash Surplus | (59.4) | (83.1) | (92.2) | (98.9) | (104.1) |
| Revolver Balance | 90.4 | 114.1 | 123.2 | 129.9 | 135.1 |
| Marketable Securities Balance | 0.0 | 0.0 | 0.0 | 0.0 | 0.0 |

# DEBT & RETURN ANALYSIS

|  | 12/31/89 | 12/31/90 | Forecast 12/31/91 | 12/31/92 | 12/31/93 |
|---|---|---|---|---|---|
| **Coverage:** | | | | | |
| EBDIT/Interest | 0.8 | 1.2 | 1.3 | 1.4 | 1.5 |
| EBDIT/Interest & Pref. Div. | 0.8 | 1.2 | 1.3 | 1.4 | 1.5 |
| EBDIT/Cash Interest | 0.8 | 1.2 | 1.3 | 1.4 | 1.5 |
| EBDIT/Cash Interest & Pref. Div. | 0.8 | 1.2 | 1.3 | 1.4 | 1.5 |
| EBIT/Interest | 0.6 | 1.0 | 1.1 | 1.2 | 1.3 |
| EBIT/Interest & Pref. Div. | 0.6 | 1.0 | 1.1 | 1.2 | 1.3 |
| EBIT/Cash Interest | 0.6 | 1.0 | 1.1 | 1.2 | 1.3 |
| EBIT/Cash Interest & Pref. Div. | 0.6 | 1.0 | 1.1 | 1.2 | 1.3 |
| CF bef. Debt Prin./Debt Prin. | NA | NA | NA | NA | NA |
| CF bef. Debt Prin./Debt Prin. & Pref. | NA | NA | NA | NA | NA |
| CF bef. Debt Prin./Debt, Pref. & Com. | NA | NA | NA | NA | NA |
| Unlevered CF/Interest | 0.0 | 0.6 | 0.8 | 0.8 | 0.9 |
| Unlevered CF/Interest & Pref. Div. | 0.0 | 0.6 | 0.8 | 0.8 | 0.9 |
| Unlevered CF/Cash Interest | 0.0 | 0.4 | 0.4 | 0.5 | 0.5 |
| Unlevered CF/Cash Interest & Pref. Div. | 0.0 | 0.4 | 0.4 | 0.5 | 0.5 |
| Hist EBDIT/Interest | 0.5 | | | | |
| Hist EBDIT/Interest & Pref. Div. | 0.5 | | | | |
| Hist EBDIT/Cash Interest | 0.4 | | | | |
| Hist EBDIT/Cash Interest & Pref. Div. | 0.4 | | | | |
| Hist EBIT/Interest | 0.4 | | | | |
| Hist EBIT/Interest & Pref. Div. | 0.4 | | | | |
| Hist EBIT/cash Interest | 0.3 | | | | |
| Hist EBIT/Cash Interest & Pref. Div. | 0.3 | | | | |
| **Liquidity:** | | | | | |
| Current ratio—without revolver | 1.0 | 1.1 | 1.1 | 1.2 | 1.2 |
| Current ratio—with revolver | 0.7 | 0.7 | 0.7 | 0.7 | 0.7 |
| **Capitalization:** | | | | | |
| L-T Debt as % Common Equity | 474.3% | 347.1% | 215.9% | 126.1% | 64.9% |
| L-T Debt & Preferred as % Common Equity | 474.3% | 347.1% | 215.9% | 126.1% | 64.9% |
| L-T Debt as % of Total Cap. | 82.6% | 77.6% | 68.3% | 55.8% | 39.3% |
| L-T Debt & Preferred as % Total Cap. | 82.6% | 77.6% | 68.3% | 55.8% | 39.3% |
| Tot. Sr. Debt as % Tot. Sub. Debt & Eq. | 335.2% | 416.6% | 269.8% | 168.1% | 97.3% |
| % Initial Debt Outstanding | 76.7% | 63.9% | 51.1% | 38.3% | 25.6% |

IRR: EBIT & EBDIT Multiples

Mean EBDIT Multiple: 5

| | | EBDIT Multiples | | | | |
|---|---|---|---|---|---|---|
| | | 3 | 4 | 5 | 6 | 7 |
| EBDIT Mult. Value in Year 5 | | 132.0 | 176.0 | 220.0 | 264.0 | 308.0 |
| Add: Cash & Mkt. Sec. in Year 5 | | 5.5 | 5.5 | 5.5 | 5.5 | 5.5 |
| Less: Debt in Year 5 | | 36.4 | 36.4 | 36.4 | 36.4 | 36.4 |
| Total Year 5 Return | | 101.1 | 145.1 | 189.1 | 233.1 | 277.1 |
| IRR on Revolver + Warrants of | 0.0% | 12.0% | 12.0% | 12.0% | 12.0% | 12.0% |
| IRR on Debt 1 + Warrants of | 0.0% | 12.0% | 12.0% | 12.0% | 12.0% | 12.0% |
| IRR on Bridge Financings A & B | | 13.0% | 13.5% | 13.5% | 13.5% | 13.5% |
| IRR on Equity Less Warrants of | 0.0% | 31.9% | 41.8% | 49.5% | 55.9% | 61.4% |
| IRR on Senior, Bridge A & B, Preferred Stock | 0.0% | 12.3% | 12.5% | 12.5% | 12.5% | 12.5% |

IRR: EBIT & EBDIT Multiples

Mean EBIT Multiple: 6

| | | EBIT Multiples | | | | |
|---|---|---|---|---|---|---|
| | | 4 | 5 | 6 | 7 | 8 |
| EBIT Mult. Value in Year 5 | | 150.8 | 188.6 | 226.3 | 264.0 | 301.7 |
| Add: Cash & Mkt. Sec. in Year 5 | | 5.5 | 5.5 | 5.5 | 5.5 | 5.5 |
| Less: Debt in Year 5 | | 36.4 | 36.4 | 36.4 | 36.4 | 36.4 |
| Total Year 5 Return | | 119.9 | 157.7 | 195.4 | 233.1 | 270.8 |
| IRR on Revolver + Warrants of | 0.0% | 12.0% | 12.0% | 12.0% | 12.0% | 12.0% |
| IRR on Debt 1 + Warrants of | 0.0% | 12.0% | 12.0% | 12.0% | 12.0% | 12.0% |
| IRR on Bridge Financings A & B | | 13.5% | 13.5% | 13.5% | 13.5% | 13.5% |
| IRR on Preferred Stock | 0.0% | ERR | ERR | ERR | ERR | ERR |
| IRR on Preferred Stock + Equity Interest | 0.0% | ERR | ERR | ERR | ERR | ERR |
| IRR on Equity Less Warrants of | 0.0% | 36.5% | 44.2% | 50.5% | 55.9% | 60.7% |
| IRR on Senior, Bridge A & B, Preferred Stock | 0.0% | 12.3% | 12.5% | 12.5% | 12.5% | 12.5% |

| | Balance | 12/31/89 | 12/31/90 | 12/31/91 | 12/31/92 | 12/31/93 |
|---|---|---|---|---|---|---|
| Accounts Receivable | 0.8 | 60.1 | 63.4 | 66.4 | 68.6 | 70.9 |
| Inventory | 0.5 | 47.4 | 54.4 | 56.6 | 59.4 | 62.4 |
| Total Revolver Limit | | 107.4 | 117.8 | 123.0 | 128.0 | 133.3 |
| Actual Revolver Balance | | 90.2 | 113.9 | 122.8 | 129.4 | 134.4 |
| Revolver Surplus/(Deficit) Capacity | | 17.2 | 3.9 | 0.2 | (1.3) | (1.1) |

VALUATION ANALYSIS

## EQUITY VALUES

|  | | Forecast | | | |
|---|---|---|---|---|---|
|  | 12/31/89 | 12/31/90 | 12/31/91 | 12/31/92 | 12/31/93 |
| **Unlevered Cash Flow:** | | | | | |
| Cash Flow before Debt Principal | (18.2) | (1.6) | 3.1 | 5.4 | 7.0 |
| Add: Interest Expense After-tax | 17.2 | 18.4 | 19.3 | 19.3 | 19.0 |
| Unlevered Cash Flow | (1.0) | 16.8 | 22.3 | 24.7 | 26.0 |

**Residual Value:**

Mean Cost of Capital:    13.0%

|  | | | Cost of Capital | | |
|---|---|---|---|---|---|
|  | 11.0% | 12.0% | 13.0% | 14.0% | 15.0% |
| Perpetuity Value in Year 5 | 226.3 | 207.4 | 191.5 | 177.8 | 165.9 |

**Equity Values-Perpetuity Resid. Value:**

|  | | | Cost of Capital | | |
|---|---|---|---|---|---|
|  | 11.0% | 12.0% | 13.0% | 14.0% | 15.0% |
| Present Value Unlev. Cash Flows | 60.8 | 58.9 | 57.0 | 55.3 | 53.6 |
| Present Value of Residual | 134.3 | 177.7 | 103.9 | 92.3 | 82.5 |
| Marketable Securities—Base Year | 0.0 | 0.0 | 0.0 | 0.0 | 0.0 |
| Corporate Value | 195.1 | 176.6 | 161.0 | 147.6 | 136.1 |
| Less: Debt—Base Year | 87.5 | 87.5 | 87.5 | 87.5 | 87.5 |
| Total Equity Value | 107.6 | 89.1 | 73.5 | 60.1 | 48.6 |

279

# CHAPTER 49

# Automated Financial Accounting Systems (New)

## 49-1  OVERVIEW

Automated financial accounting systems perform everyday accounting tasks faster and with fewer errors than humans. Today's systems allow immediate input and display immediate results.

Although the most popular financial accounting systems in use by organizations are represented by packaged software, in-house developed systems can provide unique functionality not found in marketplace software. Another system option available to organizations is *outsourcing* financial applications. Outsourcing is an emerging trend supported by complex functionality, like payroll processing, or extenuating circumstances, like a short implementation time frame.

This chapter provides an overview of automated financial accounting systems, discusses the role these systems play in the organization, and identifies the features and functionality supported by these systems. The intent of this chapter is to:

This chapter was written by Sandra Borchardt, Senior Manager, Ernst & Young, Boston.

- Indicate the benefits and disadvantages of automation
- Show the impact of the financial system on an organization and its functions
- Provide a sense of how some key financial applications function.

## 49-2  ORGANIZATIONAL IMPACT

Almost all organizations, whether for-profit or not-for-profit, have some form of accounting system. Many organizations automate their accounting system to take advantage of features and capabilities not available in a manual accounting system. Automated financial accounting systems range from spreadsheets, to off-the-shelf software, to custom-built systems. These systems operate on a variety of platforms ranging from microcomputers to mainframes. In all of these cases, however, the purpose of the accounting system remains the same: to track, measure, and report the financial events of the organization.

### THE ROLE OF THE FINANCIAL ACCOUNTING SYSTEM IN AN ORGANIZATION

One role of automated financial accounting systems is that of processing the routine financial transactions that comprise the day-to-day operations of the organization. In a retail business, these transactions include cash and credit sales; in a bank, deposits and withdrawals; and in a government agency, pre-encumbrance and encumbrance accounting. In this capacity, the automated accounting system supports the accounting function within the organization.

The automated accounting system also plays a key role in measuring the overall financial performance of the organization. Financial reporting allows senior management to evaluate the organization's performance against plan or budget, and against market indicators and the performance of competitors. Management reporting supports a measurement of the profitability of products or services offered by the organization and the effectiveness of management performance. Management reporting also enables profit center managers to reflect on past performance while supporting their day-to-day operational decision making.

Communication of a range of information, from financial results to transaction status, is another role supported by the automated financial accounting system. Investors, creditors, and employees all have a stake in the financial stability of the organization; quarterly and annual reports, produced by the financial accounting system, communicate the financial results of the organization. Automated financial accounting systems also support the communication of the status of a transaction (e.g., whether or not a purchase order has been completed or an invoice paid).

It is important to note several key characteristics of automated financial accounting systems. Accounting systems do not supply all of the information about the organization, only about financial events. Thus, nonfinancial information must be secured from some other source. Accounting systems are not only applicable to businesses but also to individuals and other organizations such as hospitals, churches, and universities. Finally, during the life of any organization there may be many individuals or groups desiring information on the financial position and activities of the organization. Thus accounting systems must be flexible and capable of serving many different users of financial information.

## TYPES OF FINANCIAL ACCOUNTING INFORMATION

There are two categories of users who utilize accounting information as a basis for making decisions, those external to the organization and those internal (management), as depicted in Figure 49-1. The automated financial accounting system must be capable of serving both categories of users.

Typically, the types of information desired by external users include an overall picture of where the business stands at a point in time, the assets the organization possesses, the obligations it faces, and whether or not the organization has been successful in its profit-making activities since the last financial report. These information needs are met by the publication of general purpose financial statements, such as the balance sheet and income statement.

In some cases, more specific information is required by external users. Customers require a receipt for a cash sale or a bill for a credit sale. In many cases, customers require a quote or estimate prior to committing to the transaction. Suppliers frequently require routine documents such as purchase orders and payment transaction documents. Further, if an order is not accepted, information regarding the return must be provided to the supplier.

Stockholders receive annual and quarterly reports and possibly dividend checks and related dividend information for tax purposes at the end of the year. Organizations must provide benefit deduction information and, at the end of the year, W-2 forms to employees. Lenders require financial statements and budgets before establishing a line of credit or extending a loan. Governments require information about the organization's profits, the amount of taxes owed, sales taxes collected, and employee taxes withheld.

**Figure 49-1**  Users of Financial Information.

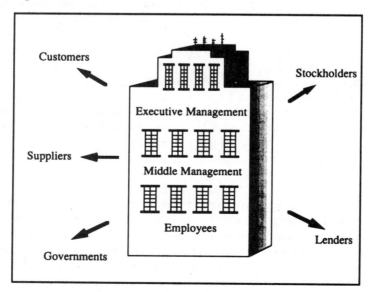

Internal users require a variety of information usually based on the level of user and how the information will be used. Executive management uses financial information along with other internal and external information to monitor and change the direction of the company and to evaluate the performance of middle management and the products/services offered. Middle management uses financial information to identify and correct situations highlighted by a significant variance and to assist in daily operations management such as pricing and purchasing decision making.

Whether the user is external or internal, the automated financial accounting system must be capable of quickly adapting to changes in regulatory or government requirements or management/organizational needs. If insufficient information is received, if the information is not timely, or if the information is not accurate, external users may levy sanctions in the form of fines or additional taxes and internal users may perform less effectively. Thus, the automated financial accounting system plays an important role in the effectiveness of the organization.

## PROCESSING ALTERNATIVES

Several processing options are available with today's automated financial accounting systems. Most systems support two types of transaction input—batch input and on-line input—and two types of transaction processing—batch processing and real-time processing. Historically, automated financial accounting systems supported only batch input of financial transactions. In this scenario, a batch file of transactions, created as an output file by an interfacing system (either an interfacing financial system or some type of keystroke data capture system), is processed by the automated financial accounting system, updating the financial records. Minimal if any editing of these transactions is conducted prior to processing by the accounting system. The majority of transaction edits take place during the update of the financial records.

On-line input capabilities allow financial transactions to be entered immediately through an interactive design that utilizes a terminal to capture the transaction keystrokes. In most systems, immediate editing features are utilized by the system to communicate keystroke errors or invalid values at the time of input; the transactions must be corrected before the system will recognize the transactions and update the financial records. Therefore, a transaction edited on-line has a better chance of updating the financial records without error than a minimally edited batch of transactions.

Updating the financial records with on-line input can occur in batch or real-time. Today, batch processing is supported by most systems for the majority of financial accounting applications. Typically, the batch processing cycle is run at night, when the on-line system is not in use. In a batch cycle, the transactions input during the day update financial records during the nightly cycle. Other system maintenance activities are processed by the batch cycle including additional input edits, updates of accounting totals for reporting purposes, system date changes, and so forth.

Real-time processing updates the financial records immediately and makes the updates available immediately through on-line screen inquiry or reporting. Because of the additional system maintenance required to update financial records, frequently real-time systems do not perform all the updates until the nightly batch cycle. Therefore, it is important to understand which reports and inquiries will reflect the real-time transactions and which will be updated during the nightly cycle.

## SYSTEM ALTERNATIVES

Automated financial accounting systems can be developed in-house, purchased as off-the-shelf software or outsourced to a company that processes the transactions on their system and provides the necessary financial reports and documentation back to the organization.

Most companies purchase package software rather than undertaking an in-house development effort for automated financial accounting systems. With the prevalence, variety, and capabilities of package financial accounting software, it is often less efficient, both in terms of time and effort, to develop an in-house application. Package software has the advantage of being tested in the marketplace, and thus most of the software problems have been identified and corrected. Also, the costs of commercially developed software are spread across the marketplace, leading to an individual site cost that is often lower than what would be expended in an in-house development effort. Because of maintenance agreements and a desire to service their client base, software companies usually offer timely software updates which meet changes in external regulatory or governmental requirements (e.g., a payroll software vendor will offer a software update to reflect changes in tax laws). Similarly, software vendors add enhancements to their software based on customer requests and competitor features, frequently at no cost if the customer is covered by a maintenance agreement, or at a minimal upgrade cost.

A third system option is becoming more popular today: outsourcing of financial applications. In this scenario, the organization contracts with a second organization to process their accounting transactions. A well-known example of this is the use of an external organization for payroll processing. Considerations for outsourcing include:

- *Risk.* Outsource companies focus on particular applications and have developed and proven procedures, controls, and software. Implementation can be accomplished quickly and is supported by the company's previous implementation experience, so that tasks are not forgotten and deadlines are realistic.

- *Control.* Outsourced applications are under the control of the outsource company. An organization is absolved of all responsibility of the application per the outsource contract. Thus the organization does not have to worry about the accomplishment of that processing. However, outsource companies have many clients and may not be as responsive to special requests as in-house staff. Special one-time or additional services not included in the initial contract may be costly. Organizations may be at the mercy of the outsource company when it comes time to renew the contract.

- *Costs.* In some cases, purchasing packaged software will be more cost effective than outsourcing, but consideration must be given to the reduction/elimination of internal staff to implement and support the application. Outsourcing may be beneficial in start-up situations where operation deadlines do not lend themselves to even the shortest package software implementation. Manually intensive or highly specialized applications (e.g., payroll processing including payroll tax filing, W-2 processing, and direct deposit handling) may be more cost effective if outsourced.

Outsourced contracts can be written in a manner that is beneficial to the organization, for instance, by basing fees on production in start-up situations or on a percentage of profits in more mature applications and establishing a payback for schedules missed by the outsource company. Finally, outsourced applications may reach a break-even point where the application has grown to a size that can be brought in-house at less cost. Figure 49-2 summarizes the relative advantages and disadvantages of custom built applications, packaged software and outsource contracting.

## STANDARD FEATURES

Common features supported by most automated financial accounting systems include:

- *On-line help.* A function that is immediately accessible by the user from a terminal and supplies the user with additional information on how the software works. On-line help can be screen-specific or field-specific. Many automated systems support both.

  *Screen-specific:* On-line help pertaining to the information currently appearing on a display screen. It allows the on-line user to press a "help" key at any screen to invoke the help function. The help session will display on the user screen presenting all functions and field-specific information necessary to complete the screen from which help was invoked. Frequently, this type of on-line help resembles pages out of the user documentation.

  *Field-specific:* On-line help pertaining to a single piece of information (i.e., a field) currently appearing on a display screen. Field-specific help can be

**Figure 49-2**   Evaluation of System Alternatives.

| | Alternatives | | |
|---|---|---|---|
| | Custom Built Application | Package Software | Outsource Contract |
| Time to implement | – – | – | + |
| Control | + + | + | – |
| Marketplace tested | – | + | + |
| Software cost | + | – | + |
| Hardware cost | + | – | + |
| Monthly contract fee | + | + | – |
| Ongoing maintenance cost | – | – | + |
| Programming cost | – | + | + |
| Operations cost | – | – | + |
| User training cost | – | – | + |

+ Advantage     – Disadvantage

invoked by placing the cursor on the field where help is desired and pressing the key that commences the help session. Field-specific help usually limits its discussion to the field from which the help session was invoked.

- *User-defined help screens* allow the user to identify acceptable field values for the organization, enter these values into a "help" portion of the system and enable users to access this user-defined help as well as the system-defined help function through the use of different function keys.

- *Menu options across the top of the screen* and *function key references across the bottom* inform the user of functions/menu choices available at the screen. Moreover, some systems display all acceptable values for a field through the use of a function key.

- *On-line inquiry* allows users to access information either by pressing a function key from the current screen or via a stand-alone menu or command option. The ability to make a database query while performing a function in the system is quite valuable. For example, during on-line input of a journal transaction, on-line inquiry can be used to verify an account in the chart of accounts database.

  If on-line inquiry is not accessible from any screen, the user must exit the current screen, access the area in the software where on-line inquiry is available, perform the inquiry, and then access the original screen and resume the activity in progress. This can mean entering and exiting several screens to accomplish a single inquiry. On its own, however, stand-alone inquiry is valuable for specific research and maintenance purposes and should be available in all systems whether or not screen-accessible inquiry is available.

**Reporting.**    Reporting capabilities of various types may be available in automated financial systems. Some of the more common features include:

- *Standard reports.*  Most automated financial systems support a set of pre-designed and pre-coded financial reports. These reports include daily transaction-type reports such as trial balances, posted batch lists, and ledgers; maintenance-type reports such as lists of database additions, deletions, revisions and audit trail reports; and financial reports such as a balance sheet, income statement, and consolidated reports. These reports usually come as is and cannot be modified by the user to reflect user-desired formats or sort sequences.

- *Report writing capabilities.*  Most automated financial accounting systems support some type of report writing capability (i.e., custom) that supplements the standard reports. Using this capability, reports can be constructed to meet the unique reporting requirements of the organization. Report writing facilities may require programming skills to develop the reports or may be quite simple to use. Frequently, a simpler report writer sacrifices the ability to customize quite complex reports. Thus, in many systems, more than one report writer facility is available, one for the everyday user and one for more complex, specialized report designs.

- *Ad hoc reporting.*  These are similar to the report writing capability discussed above from the standpoint of providing the ability to customize a report. Ad hoc capabilities differ from a report writer because ad hoc reports are considered one-time requests or infrequent requests for information. Ad hoc reporting usually supports simple selection, sorting and totaling capabilities and is usually used for database printing (e.g., print out all the expense accounts used by a cost center in the last three months).

- *Downloads.* Many systems support downloading (the process of transferring data to a smaller platform) of information into a file that is readable by microcomputer spreadsheets or other microcomputer software. This feature provides additional reporting capabilities by allowing information to be formatted and reported by the spreadsheet. Control is an issue in this instance, in that values can be changed via the spreadsheet program and thus totals represented on the spreadsheet many not equal totals in the automated financial accounting system.

**Security.** The description of security presented in this section is a short summary related specifically to software access security. Chapter 51 presents a more extensive discussion of security. Most automated financial systems have security features which allow access to be defined by one or more of the following elements:

- *Terminal/system.* This type of security allows for the definition of the devices that can access the financial system. For example, a certain terminal/printer set-up may be defined as the only system that can access the check printing facility of an accounts payable system.
- *User.* User security identifies a user sign-on and password. Automated audit trails can then be used to track application accesses by specific users, including access attempts to secured areas. In more sophisticated systems, user access records can also be used to track performance such as number of collection transactions handled by a user in a day, and so forth.
- *Application.* Application security allows access to be defined at the application level, (e.g., a user may have access to the general ledger but not to the accounts receivable application).
- *Organizational unit.* This type of security allows access to be defined by the organizational unit to which the user belongs (e.g., a user can only access financial information for his/her department).
- *Function.* Security by function specifies particular types of access, such as read only, read and input but no update capabilities, update only capabilities, and so forth.
- *Screen.* Screen security allows access to specific screens (e.g., only certain users should have access to the security definition screens in the system).
- *Field.* Field-level access allows for certain fields to be accessible for input (e.g., account descriptions may not be accessible for maintenance in the journal posting screen). Specific users may be identified to maintain the chart of accounts and descriptions via another system facility.

**Edits.** In automated financial accounting systems, an "edit" is an error message or diagnostic message generated by the software program. Most on-line financial accounting systems will support a number of edits for on-line input. These edits vary from field format edits to valid value edits.

Field format edits include edits for fields that should be all numeric (e.g., dollar amount fields), or input in a certain format (e.g., a date field format of mm/dd/yy means that January 1, 1993, should be input as 01/01/93 not as 1/1/93). Valid value edits include edits for incorrect dates (e.g., 13/34/92 would be an incorrect date) or for a predesignated set of values (e.g., the account must be defined in the chart of accounts database). On-line edits reduce the number of erroneous transactions that enter the system by forcing errors to be corrected before the system will accept the transaction and update the financial records.

Additional input edits are performed in the batch cycle. A transaction may pass all the on-line edits but may still be forced to an error correction list/file based on these batch edits. Batch edits frequently repeat the on-line edits due to transactions that enter the system in batch (i.e., from interfacing systems).

**Maintenance.**   All automated financial accounting systems support some type of maintenance facility. Single-input facilities are required to build a general ledger chart of accounts or establish an accounts payable vendor record. High volume maintenance is a feature allowing multiple records to be updated at once. High volume maintenance features are particularly valuable, for example, when establishing a new center by copying an already established center or when defining a new account for use by each center.

**Navigation.**   Navigation features (movement from screen to screen or function to function within software) differ from system to system and typically fall under one of the following formats:

- *Menus.* Lists of options appearing on a display screen that allow the user to select which part of the software to interact with. Menus assist first-time or infrequent users by displaying all available choices and allowing the user to select the choice desired. Menus can become cumbersome for the more frequent, sophisticated users, because several choices across several menus may be required in order to access a desired screen.

- *Commands.* Instructions supplied by the user which access the part of the software with which the user intends to interact. These allow more sophisticated users to type in specific characters or word sequences, which, when executed, invoke the specific screen represented by the command.

**Documentation, Support, Training, and Enhancements.**   Other software features include:

- *Documentation* including user manuals, installation guides, operations guides, and so forth.

- *Support* including client services representatives, on-site support, assistance with installation, 800 hotline support, local maintenance support, maintenance agreements, enhancement agreements, custom development services, and so forth. Support can be offered as part of the software package or for an additional fee.

- *Training* including on-site, classroom, classroom based training (CBT), and tutorials.

- *Enhancements* including software upgrades for regulated changes, user-group-sponsored changes, and so forth. User Groups are independent social organizations that meet to discuss the use and implementation of the particular package and share ideas and strategies to meet unique processing requirements. User groups also sponsor enhancements that are often acted on by the vendors.

# 49-3 TYPICAL APPLICATIONS AND GENERAL FEATURES

This section provides a general overview of the features and functionality of financial accounting software currently available in the marketplace. Although the list of financial accounting applications is lengthy, the following discussion has been limited to four applications:

- General ledger
- Accounts receivable
- Accounts payable
- Payroll

These applications were chosen because they are frequently the core financial applications employed by an organization.

## GENERAL LEDGER

A general ledger collects summary financial information from detailed subsidiary ledgers (e.g., accounts receivable, accounts payable, payroll) and based on this summary financial information, produces financial and management reports (Figure 49-3). In most organizations, the general ledger is the source of period-end financial reporting, management responsibility reporting, and external regulatory, government, and financial statement reporting.

Typically, financial information enters the general ledger in the form of a journal transaction, which may originate from many sources including an automated interface from a subsidiary system, a batch of transactions which are manually entered and subsequently update the financial accounts, a real-time transaction which is manually entered and immediately updates the financial accounts, or through the use of special automated journal features such as recurring, shell, and reversing journal transactions.

Once the financial accounts are updated, usually the result of a posting cycle, transaction reports are produced. These reports document the journal transactions input in the system and identify transactions that are incomplete, not balanced or otherwise in error.

At the end of a reporting period, usually monthly or quarterly, period-end reports are produced and certain maintenance activities are completed to ready the system to begin collecting the next period of financial transactions. At the end of the fiscal year, additional maintenance activities are performed including rolling the ending balance sheet account balances to the beginning balances for the new fiscal year, zeroing out income and expense accounts, updating the system fiscal year, and so forth.

**Figure 49-3**   General Ledger System Diagram.

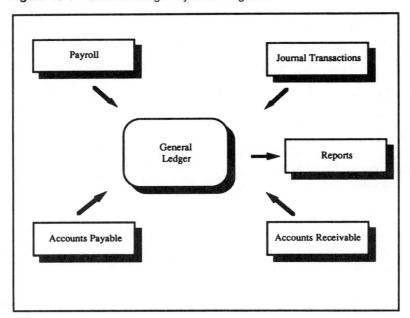

**Account Key.**   The account key is the basis for the structure of the records in the general ledger. In most automated general ledger systems, the account key is made up of entries containing at least three user definable elements: an element which identifies the company or legal entity, an element which identifies an organizational unit (e.g., department, center, division), and an element which identifies the accounting element or account. Due to additional reporting needs especially in the financial services industry (e.g., insurance and banking), many systems provide additional elements available for definition.

Defining the account key is an important process. The reporting requirements of the general ledger must be carefully considered. If the level of detail required by the reports is not collected by the general ledger through the use of the account key, the reports cannot be produced. Thus, it is important to design the account key to capture the lowest level of information required by the reports.

When deciding on the lowest level of information required by the general ledger, consideration must be given to the question of what information the general ledger should capture and report. It is easy to allow the general ledger to be the catch-all application. Careful thought must be given to satisfying a reporting requirement using other subsidiary systems or realizing that a reporting requirement cannot easily be met by the general ledger and must be accomplished elsewhere.

Consideration must also be given to the effort involved in capturing the lowest level of detail. Undue burden on the accounting department in the organization to gather and input this level of detail may offset the benefits of the information produced by the general ledger.

In most automated financial systems, detail can be summarized at different levels through the report writing facility. For example, if the center is the lowest reporting level of the organization and if centers combine to make departments, which combine to form divisions, then there is no need to capture general ledger input at the department and division levels. The reporting facility of the general ledger should allow for these levels to be reported by simply combining centers.

**Journal Transactions.**   Several journal transaction (i.e., journal) features are available in today's automated general ledgers. These include:

- *Standard journals* are the typical entries made in the general ledger. Standard journals may record an asset purchase or adjust an error. Standard journals can be received via a file from an interfacing system and processed in batch, or input on-line, and updated real-time or via the batch processing cycle. On-line features include the ability to input, edit, and balance the journal. Security features include the ability to restrict the user to input-only and another to post-only privileges.

- *Shell journals* are established for those transactions that use the same accounts but different dollar amounts each period. Utility expense and certain other month-end transactions fall into this category. A shell journal is created with the corresponding accounts. Prior to posting, the dollar amounts are input to complete the entry.

- *Recurring journals* are for those transactions that use the same accounts and the same amounts each period. Rent, loan and lease payments may fall into this category of journal transactions. As with shell journals, recurring journals are set up ahead of time with their corresponding accounts and amounts and, in many systems, can be scheduled for automatic release to the posting cycle.

- *Reversing journals*—in many automated general ledgers, standard, shell and/or recurring journals can be defined as reversing journals. For example, if the shell journal feature is set up for a monthly accrual transaction, this transaction can also be defined as a reversing journal and thus will be reversed at the start of the new period. In some systems, specific reversing dates or periods can be defined for the reversing transaction.

- *Error handling* can be accomplished in several ways. On-line edits, discussed in the previous section, identify input errors for immediate correction. Erroneous journal transactions identified during the batch cycle can be handled via a suspense account, through an error file, or dropped out of the cycle. Suspense posting posts the erroneous transaction to a user-defined account, an error suspense account. Then whenever this account shows a balance, the erroneous transaction is researched and a subsequent transaction is input to reverse the suspended balance and post the balance to the proper account.

   Use of an error file suspends the transaction prior to posting to allow the user to correct the transaction on-line. Each posting cycle will then read the error file and post all corrected transactions. Transactions not yet corrected will remain in the error file. The third type of error handling in a batch cycle is to report the transaction in error and require re-input of the entire journal.

   Both the suspense and error file methods eliminate the need to re-enter the journal and do not cause the entire batch of journals to be rejected, only the erroneous transactions. The difference is that the suspense account method posts as much of the transaction correctly as possible, thus correctly stating total balances. The error file method holds the transaction in a prior-to-posting state, thus system balances do not reflect the erroneous transaction.

**Budgeting or Planning.**   Most automated general ledgers allow for budget input and reporting, usually at the account level. Additional budgeting features available in some but not all systems include: prior and future year(s) budget reporting and comparisons; storage and reporting of original, approved, revised and other versions of the budget; and budget preparation features including what-if processing, use of last year's actuals or budget as the basis for this year's budget, increasing/decreasing of budget amounts by multiplying by a factor, and so forth.

**Allocations.**   Another feature of many automated general ledgers is an allocation facility. Allocations involve the distribution of costs and/or revenues from one organization unit to another organization unit or to corresponding products or services. Allocation features can be as simple as automatically allocating an input transaction (e.g., rent) to organizational units based on a predetermined fixed percentage (e.g., percent of total square footage) through the use of a journal transaction feature. Or allocations can be as complex as requiring statistical amounts (either input or calculated), and originating and destination organizational units and accounts.

The more complex the allocation process, the more complex and time-consuming the set-up, and thus the more prone to error the process will be. Complex allocations can also consume large amounts of system processing time and resources and the results can constitute a large number of records. It is sometimes useful to store allocation results in another portion of the database, merging the results for reporting purposes via the report writing capabilities of the system.

Other allocation features include the ability to allocate actual, budget, statistical, or previously allocated amounts; the ability to allocate based on a fixed or variable percentage; the ability to round allocations so that the final destination is given the remaining amount (i.e., so that rounding features do not result in less than or greater than 100% allocations); the ability to perform allocations on monthly, quarterly, or annual amounts; and the ability to generate allocation reports documenting which amounts were allocated from which organizational units or products/services, to which organizational units or products/services.

**Consolidations.**   Many automated general ledger systems offer consolidation features which combine separate entities (e.g., corporations, divisions, subsidiaries) for organization-wide consolidated reporting. Consolidation features include automatically generating elimination entries, allowing for consolidation of corporations with similar charts of accounts, or allowing for consolidation of corporations with different charts of accounts.

## ACCOUNTS RECEIVABLE

The accounts receivable system is the primary cash receipts system in organizations that do not require immediate payment upon delivery of goods or services. The accounts receivable application is designed to monitor cash inflows from sales and collections and provide information that will assist in managing the collection of cash held as receivables.

The accounts receivable system interfaces with the general ledger by passing summary transactions that update the accounts affected by sales and payments on account. Many organizations interface an order processing system with the accounts receivable system. The accounts receivable system passes customer credit limits and other customer demographics to the order processing system and in turn receives billing information and orders shipped from the order processing system. The accounts receivable system may also interface with a billing system if the accounts receivable system does not support the production of customer bills or statements. Lastly, an accounts receivable system may interface with accounts payables, passing customer refund information for payment by the accounts payable system. Figure 49-4 illustrates the system flows to and from the accounts receivable system.

Common features of an automated accounts receivables system include:

- *Cash application.* Most accounts receivable systems support several options governing how received funds are applied to outstanding receivables. The choice among such options is called cash application.

    Cash application based on check Magnetic Ink Character Recognition (MICR) numbers (characters printed with a special magnetic ink, like those at the bottom of personal checks, used primarily in banking, public utilities and credit card industries), amount, invoice number, oldest document, document range or customer name, are common automatic cash application features. For those accounts that cannot be supported by an automatic cash application feature, a more manual,

**Figure 49-4** Accounts Receivable System Diagram.

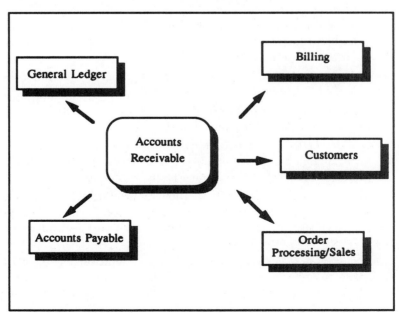

research capability is available. Lockbox features are often available including bank tape lockbox processing using the automatic cash application features of the system. Several other payment posting options may be available including acceptance of a single payment for multiple invoices, a single payment for multiple customers, partial payments, prepayments, and deposits.

- *On-line inquiry.* Many systems support on-line inquiry into the accounts receivable system including all open items, open amounts within a specific range, all debit memos, all credit memos, last payment entered, or all information on a specific invoice.

- *Aging reports.* Most systems support user-defined aging formats and aging period definition for reporting. Formats include customer summary, invoice summary, or organizational summaries by company, department, division, or sales representative.

- *Collection features.* Most accounts receivable systems support a variety of collection features including:

  *On-Line Comments/Notes:* Allows the collector to keep track of customer calls, disagreements, commitments and follow-up actions.

  *On-Line Tickler File:* Provides a reminder of commitments made by the collector and customer for follow-up and a reminder of follow-up dates based on dunning severity, notifies the collector of new invoices past due, and assists in prioritizing collection duties. Some systems also use this feature to track sales leads or, for example, to remind a user to request a current financial statement from customers.

  *Credit and Service Hold:* Provides the ability to place a problem customer on credit hold and/or service hold (as a motivator to pay) and to set credit limits by customer. Some systems support this feature automatically based on user-defined rules.

  *Small Balance Write-Offs:* Provides the ability to write off small balance amounts within tolerance limits to ensure that collectors are concentrating on the most critical accounts.

  *Collector Statistics:* Measures and reports collectors' effectiveness using automated rules or in some cases user-defined rules.

  *Collections Reporting:* Provides the ability to review collection call notes, follow-up dates, customer promises and call history.

  *Dunning Letters:* Allows for the definition of content, addressee, outstanding invoices, dunning severity levels and frequency of mailing. Many systems support numerous different types and levels of dunning letters.

- *Customer statements.* Most systems allow for printing of customer statements. In some systems, statement formats are user definable. Further, some systems allow for statements to be generated for all customers, customer ranges or only those customers over a certain age limit.

- *Customer history.* Most accounts receivable systems support the maintenance of complete customer history. This feature makes it easy to investigate discrepancies and disputes by having all past customer activity available to determine the correct response and action. Also, many systems maintain statistics on customers' paying habits and past performance, including, for example, a monitoring of past accounts receivable balances and average days to pay.

- *Other features.* Other payment features often supported by accounts receivable systems include: discounts, finance charges, adjustments, other receipts (e.g., investment income, refunds), insufficient funds and prepayment handling. Reporting features such as: payment reporting, accounts receivable and collections productivity reporting, and cash forecasting features are frequently available. Other features include linkages to rating bureaus for customer credit information.

## ACCOUNTS PAYABLE

An accounts payable system is one important cash disbursement system of the organization, payroll being the other. In its role of supporting the organized and controlled disbursement of funds to external organizations, the accounts payable system monitors the amounts due to suppliers for goods and services, issues disbursement checks and provides information for cash management purposes. Additionally, the accounts payable system should control disbursements so that cash outflows do not occur any sooner than necessary. In many organizations, the accounts payable system is also used for other cash disbursement activities such as processing customer refunds, tax liability payments, employee advances, and employee payables.

The accounts payable system can interface with a variety of systems in the organization. Some of these interfaces include:

- *General ledger.* The accounts payable system interfaces with the general ledger by passing summary entries on purchases, payments and adjustments which affect the cash, accounts payable, assets, purchases, and miscellaneous expense accounts.
- *Sales/purchasing.* The accounts payable system interfaces with the sales/purchasing system by receiving data relating to purchases and by passing vendor analysis information to the sales/purchasing system which can be used in future purchase decisions.
- *Receiving.* The accounts payable system interfaces with the receiving system by accepting documentation confirming the receipt of goods which is then matched to the purchase documentation and scheduled for payment.
- *Accounts receivable.* The accounts payable system interfaces with the accounts receivable system by accepting documentation regarding customer refunds.
- *Fixed assets.* The accounts payable system interfaces with the fixed asset system by providing asset invoice and other information for the establishment of a new fixed asset record.
- *Project costing.* The accounts payable system provides project-related expense information to the project costing system.

Other interfaces include inventory for inventory costing or cost accounting purposes and work order costing for work orders that include processing by an outside vendor. Figure 49-5 illustrates the system flows to and from the accounts payable system.

**Figure 49-5**    Accounts Payable System Diagram.

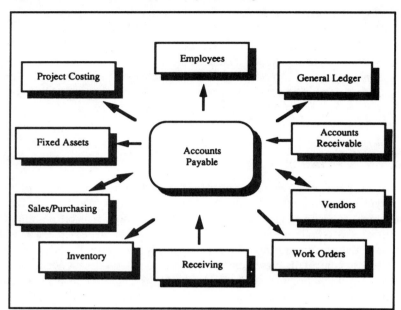

Common features of an automated accounts payable system include:

- *Invoice processing.* Automated features include using defaults from the vendor file for easy invoice processing with input of minimal information such as vendor, invoice number, date and amount. Many systems support a variety of invoice types including regular invoices, credit and debit memos, prepaid, recurring, employee travel advance and employee expense invoices. When processing an invoice, many systems allow for allocation of expenses to multiple organizational units (e.g., divisions, departments, centers).

- *Check writing.* Features include supporting multiple check forms, multiple bank accounts, multiple currencies, multiple payment methods (e.g., automatic and manual checks, electronic funds transfers, wire transfers, etc.), separate remittance advice, and payment voiding. Check printing features include printing checks in any sequence—by vendor number for easy filing or by ZIP code for low-cost mailings. Check stock control features include recording the checks used and issuing a warning prior to running out.

- *Reconciliation.* Features include bank tape processing or cleared check input. Reporting features include calculation of average float days per vendor so that payments can be adjusted to optimize cash management.

- *Cash management.* Features include determining how much to pay and when to pay. Forecasting features include identifying cash needs. Reporting features include cash management, aged payables, and other reports.

- *Payment optimization.* Allows for identification of open invoices due for payment and the ability to hold payments, create partial payments, or allow everything to be paid. Other payment optimization features include automatic calculation of the discount amount and determination of when and if a discount should be taken.

- *IRS 1099 reporting.* Features include complete tracking and reporting of 1099 expenditures and all return/amount types the federal government requires, and provisions for flexible IRS 1099 generation and reporting allowing compliance with federal reporting requirements.

- *Vendor analysis.* Includes the maintenance of statistics on all vendor and payable activity such as invoice amounts by period, invoice volumes, discounts taken or lost, and number of exception invoices. These features can frequently assist in negotiating better discounts and prices, and resolving problems efficiently.

- *Other features.* Includes the ability to order from one-time vendors without storing that vendor's information permanently; supports the tracking of unlimited vendor addresses and contacts (e.g., order address, payment address, inquiry address); produces vendor lists, labels, and customized form letters; and supports invoice matching (e.g., four-way matching requires purchase order, invoice, receipt and requestor acceptance documentation before payment is scheduled; three-way matching requires purchase order, invoice, and receipt documentation before payment is scheduled). Other features include automatic tax liability calculation and tracking of sales taxes paid to vendors.

## PAYROLL

The payroll system in the organization is very important because good employee relations require payroll disbursements to be reliable and timely. However, today's payroll function is quite complex resulting from multiple classes of employees, the proliferation of deductions, special employee arrangements, governmental reporting requirements, and management's need for cost information. Further, because the payroll function is a major cash disbursement function in the organization, cash management and control are important to the payroll process. Thus, it is no wonder that payroll departments find that they need a sophisticated, automated system capable of recording, processing, and reporting on large volumes of complex transactions.

Payroll systems are designed to streamline the employee payment process, to reduce the costs associated with payroll administration, and to provide organizations with maximum flexibility to define their unique payroll processing requirements. Inputs to the payroll system include:

- *Time records.* Documents that record an employee's time. This information is used in the calculation and preparation of the paycheck. Sick days, vacation days and overtime hours are captured on the time documents as well.

- *Payroll adjustments.* Includes additions, deletions, and adjustments of various kinds to employee payroll records. Examples include salary or wage rate changes, terminations, new employee additions, address changes, departmental transfers, tax exemption changes, and deduction authorization changes.

Outputs of the payroll system include employee paychecks (or direct deposits to employee bank accounts), employee earnings statements, various reports required by governmental authorities, and various reports useful to payroll, personnel or management staff.

The payroll system interfaces to the general ledger by passing summary earnings and deduction transactions to the general ledger. Other information required by the payroll system may be interfaced from another system (e.g., sales activity, the basis of compensating a sales staff, is passed to payroll from the sales system). In turn, the payroll system may provide information to an employee benefits system or labor distribution system. Figure 49-6 illustrates the system flows to and from the payroll system.

The basic features and capabilities of an automated payroll system include the following:

- *Hours worked.* Input of hours worked can be accomplished via an interface from a time and attendance system, via on-line input or in aggregate for the entire pay period, by day or by job.

- *Earnings.* Features include managing salaried, hourly, and daily earnings as well as jury duty, personal leave, vacation, sick leave, holidays, overtime, bonuses and downtime. Also many payroll systems support distributions to different pay groups on different schedules.

- *Deductions.* Control features include limit amounts, start dates and stop dates for each deduction. Other features include identification of employer-paid, employee-voluntary, or employee-involuntary deduction categories and taxable, tax-exempt, or FICA-exempt categories.

**Figure 49-6**    Payroll System Diagram.

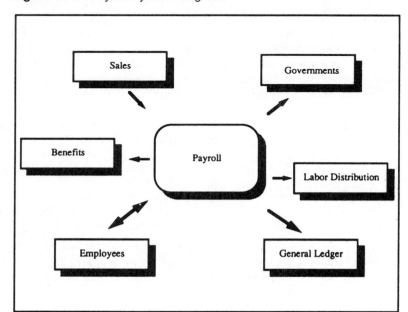

- *Taxes.* Features include withholding calculations for all United States (at the very least) federal, state, county, and local taxes, providing updates for these calculations per regulatory changes, and providing tax reporting on magnetic media where required. Both employee and employer tax calculations should be supported.

- *Payroll processing.* Features include control of organizations to be paid, the pay and deductions to be calculated, the dates, the labor distribution, and the month-end accruals. Pay frequencies supported include on-demand, daily, weekly, bi-weekly, monthly, and quarterly.

- *Check writing.* Features include supporting multiple check forms, multiple bank accounts, multiple currencies, multiple payment methods, (e.g., automatic and manual checks, direct deposit, electronic funds transfers, and wire transfers), separate remittance advice, and payment voiding. Check stock control features include recording the checks used and issuing a warning prior to running out.

- *Other features.* These include tracking of labor costs, distribution of labor costs to one or multiple organization units, automatic reversal of voided checks, historical retention of check and adjustment data, automatic bank tape processing for check reconciliation, and automatic W-2 preparation.

## 49-4   THE 1990s—FUNCTIONALITY AND NEW FEATURES

Companies selling automated financial accounting software have added so many features and so much functionality to their systems that it is difficult to determine the precise advantages of different vendors' systems. Thus, when selecting automated financial accounting software, an organization should first assess their unique needs and match these needs with the corresponding features and functionality provided by available software packages.

For example, modules desired by an organization may include general ledger, accounts payable, fixed assets and capital projects. Many software packages may not offer a capital projects module. Thus the organization should first look to packages which provide software for all these modules then evaluate whether each module can support the organization's unique needs. Similarly, if the organization has a need for encumbrance accounting, multi-currency functionality or support for the accounting standards of a foreign operation, software systems that meet these needs should be evaluated first.

It should be noted that automated interfaces between modules such as general ledger and accounts payable are usually standard in packaged software purchased from a single vendor. However, if the functionality of a module of the system does not meet the organization's needs, the value of the standard interface diminishes extensively. Although purchasing software from one vendor streamlines training, installation and maintenance, an organization should not be hesitant to purchase modules from multiple vendors if these modules best meet the organization's needs. However, custom interfaces will have to be built to automatically link the modules. (Many software systems have facilities that assist in interfacing to "foreign" modules.)

Some of the newer features include:

- *Platform-independent software.* For larger organizations, there is a growing need for software that runs on multiple platforms existing in different locations of the organization. For a smaller organization, the ability to update a platform, grow to a larger platform or select platform-specific software is also important. In the past, software was selected first, then the platform was selected based on the options available for the selected software. Today's vendors recognize the need for platform-independent software and are working to that end.

- *Graphical user interface.* "User-friendly" has taken on a new meaning in the 1990s with the advent of GUI ("gooey") interfaces. Steven R. Anderson, in an article in the *Hewlett-Packard Journal* [1990], discusses the three basic principles of these interfaces: (1) Selecting from a list of alternatives (e.g., a menu) is easier than remembering all of the alternatives; (2) Choosing alternatives by direct manipulation, such as pushing a button on a mouse or dragging an icon, is often preferred over typing in text commands; and (3) Using metaphors from the real world (e.g., a trash can) can ease understanding. Tools important to GUI interfaces include the mouse, menus, graphical icons, and overlapping windows.

- *Client-server architecture.* Although consensus on the definition of client-server architecture may not be easy to come by, this phrase relates to a networking capability where the "server" is the central facility that services all the nodes or workstations (i.e., "clients"). The server and client can exist on the same or different platforms with the server issuing the host commands, commands which are invisible to the client. For example, the server may coordinate the use of software among several users or clients. (See Chapter 47 for a further discussion of computer hardware trends.)

In the 1980s, vendors of automated financial accounting systems made great strides to match the features and functionality of their competitors. Therefore, the 1990s present an opportunity for striking new features, features forced by the need to distinguish one software vendor from another.

## 49-5  SELECTED REFERENCES

Anderson, Steven R., "Creating an Effective User Interface of HP IVIBuild," *Hewlett-Packard Journal 41:* 5, 1990, p. 39.

Bochenski, Barbara, "Client/Server Products: Every Which Way But Easy," *Computerworld,* December 17, 1990, p. 53.

For additional references on the subject of Automated Financial Accounting systems, see the following magazines or journals:

*Computers in Accounting*

*Management Accounting*

*Journal of Accountancy*

*Corporate Controller*

*Datamation*

*Financial Accounting Systems*

*Information Systems Management*

*Information Week*
*IBM Systems Journal*
*Macworld*
*PC Magazine*
*PC World*

Specialized Industry Magazine or Journal References:

### Banking

*ABA Banking Journal*
*Bankers Magazine*
*Banking Software Review*

### Healthcare

*Computers in Healthcare*
*Healthcare Computing and Communications*

### Insurance

*Best's Review Life/Health*
*Best's Review Property/Casualty*
*Insurance and Technology*

## SOFTWARE DIRECTORIES

*ICP Software Directory*
*Data Sources*
*DataPro*
*Dataworld*

## AVAILABLE ON CD-ROM

*Computer Select* (with a listing of journal/magazine articles and data sources software directory)

## PUBLICATIONS

Filed in libraries under the library call number: HF5679

# CHAPTER 50

# Electronic Data Interchange (EDI) (New)

## 50-1  INTRODUCTION

Electronic Data Interchange (EDI), has become one of the most talked about technologies. An increasing number of articles are being published in various magazines and newspapers exhorting the benefits of EDI. Corporate executives are hearing from many of their colleagues how EDI is helping to streamline corporate information and business processes. Many executives are exposed to EDI through initiatives of their suppliers or customers (or both). Yet, EDI is not new. What is new is the increasing acceptance of EDI as a standard way of doing business.

    EDI, similar to Just-In-Time (JIT) manufacturing, Total Quality Management (TQM), Business Process Redesign (BPR) and many other *acronym-based* business strategies is becoming a way of life for competitive organizations. Successful firms are coupling these strategies to gain further competitive advantage and strength.

### WHAT EXECUTIVES SHOULD KNOW ABOUT EDI

Any corporate CEO, CFO, or high level executive should have a working knowledge of technologies or business strategies that will change the way business is conducted. EDI is one of the few technologies that is also a new strategic business approach. EDI crosses all corporate boundaries, requires profound organizational change and enhanced customer/supplier relationship management, and can change the traditional "paper-based" process flow. In some instances, EDI redefines legal transactions, elimi-

---

This chapter was written by Jeffrey L. Sturrock, Sr. Manager, Ernst & Young, Dallas.

nates historical data retention methods, and can change asset and liability boundaries. A corporate executive need not become an expert on EDI, but generic knowledge of capabilities, opportunities and issues is a prerequisite.

## 50-2 EDI DEFINED

Electronic Data Interchange (EDI) is the computer-to-computer exchange of information in a standardized format. There are three key parts to this definition:

- Computer-to-computer exchange, more precisely defined, is the application-to-application (i.e., purchasing application to order entry application) exchange of data with no manual intervention.

- Information is any data that is *necessary* to conduct business, and is typically interchanged in the form of a legal business transaction (i.e., a purchase order or an invoice).

- Finally, an important part of the EDI definition requires use of standardized and commonly accepted data formats for the structured definition of interchange data.

EDI is not FAX, nor Electronic Mail (E-Mail), nor Electronic Order Entry, nor distributed computing although each of these has an appropriate place in corporate MIS strategies. Information interchange techniques can be placed in roughly four categories (see Figure 50-1). Person-to-person interchange techniques, such as the telephone, facsimile, or paper mail are intended for interpersonal communications. Person-to-application interchange techniques such as electronic order entry or captive terminal applications are used for person-to-computer data entry. Application-to-person techniques such as batch reporting or automated error suspense notification are automated computer-to-person

**Figure 50-1**

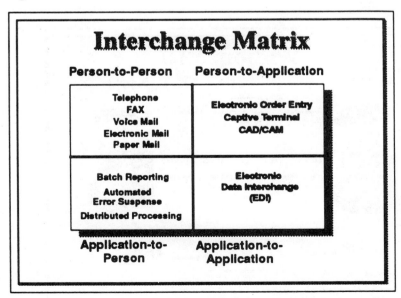

communications. EDI is one of the few application-to-application (computer-to-computer) communication techniques, offering automated, integrated information interchange without manual intervention.

Several recent surveys have indicated that although corporations have become computerized over time, there is still an enormous amount of manual processing performed. Estimates indicate that approximately 80 percent of all information traffic between corporate traders is printed from one compute and re-keyed into another computer for processing (see Figure 50-2).

EDI allows corporate traders to bypass this *print-send-enter* process that has traditionally caused delay, errors, and increased overhead costs. Simply stated, EDI allows companies the ability to conduct business in a paperless environment and manage the information flow in a much more effective manner (see Figure 50-3).

## EDI AS A CORPORATE STRATEGY

Although EDI appears to be an MIS technology, it is actually much more. EDI has a greater impact upon the underlying business departments and processes than it does upon the MIS department.

Today's global marketplace is increasingly more competitive in nature and calls for new corporate approaches. In a recent international quality survey conducted by Ernst & Young, three interesting factors should be noted:

- Technology is playing a much greater role in meeting customer needs.
- Global corporations are looking more to streamlining processes and providing information, rather than simple process automation.
- Cycle-time and other indirect indices are being used to measure success.

**Figure 50-2**

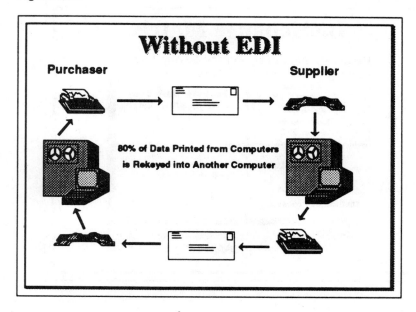

Without EDI

Purchaser                                      Supplier

80% of Data Printed from Computers
is Rekeyed into Another Computer

**Figure 50-3**

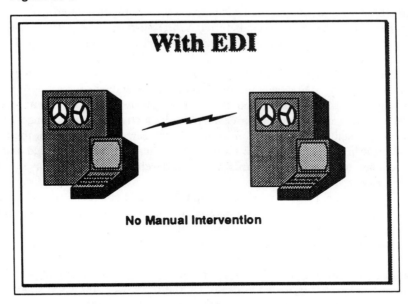

These findings indicate that today's corporations are taking a more strategic and leveraged approach to global competition, where information, cycle time, and value added processes are as important as yesterday's "bottom line" indicators. In each of the areas mentioned, the survey indicated that the Japanese employ these new approaches significantly more often than did the other respondents from Canada, Germany, and the United States.

The global market leaders (private and public) use EDI daily. The U.S. EDI market is predicted to double for the next five-to-ten years, while conservative international market predictions are even greater. While EDI is not the reason these companies are successful, each of these organizations realize that inter-enterprise information sharing is important. Much of this information is shared between various functional areas within a corporate structure. If EDI is properly integrated with corporate information systems and underlying business processes are re-engineered, then executive decision makers can make competent trading management conclusions.

EDI is just one of many tools that support corporate priorities. Coupling of EDI with other strategic tools such as bar coding, Just-In-Time (JIT) manufacturing, Computer Integrated Manufacturing (CIM), Computer-Aided Design (CAD), and Evaluated Receipt Settlements (ERS) offers the greatest benefits to the implementor.

## 50-3    A BRIEF HISTORY OF EDI

EDI actually has been in existence for over 20 years. The term EDI was coined in the mid 1970s. In EDI's early existence, data was exchanged between companies using mutually defined proprietary formats on media such as magnetic tape, punch cards, and so on. During the mid-to-late 1970s, several pioneering industry sectors began to mold EDI into a formal industry-wide strategy.

One of the first industries to take the lead in the area of EDI was the transportation sector. The rail and ocean mode carriers were being inundated with a large volume of paper necessary to move goods through the transport chain. Often, more than 15 or 20 different pieces of paper were required to move a single shipment from shipper, through the various transport points, to the ultimate consignees.

As the transport industry began to automate and computerize, they recognized that much of the data on each piece of paper was redundant. Accordingly, the transport industry formed a group called the Transportation Data Coordinating Committee (TDCC) that was responsible for developing an electronic data exchange format standard for the member transport companies. By the early 1980s, most of the transactions required to move goods through the transport chain had been modeled and electronic interchange data format standards had been developed. These format standards were call *transaction sets.*

Other industry groups in the United States and abroad were also developing industry specific standards for data interchange during this time. It became evident that cross-industry data exchange was a necessity. The definition of industry specific format standards would not allow different industry sectors to communicate effectively.

In 1979, the American National Standards Institute (ANSI) chartered the Accredited Standards Committee on EDI – X12 (ASC X12), to begin establishing cross industry, or *generic* EDI standards. Today there are over 100 ANSI standards that define a full range of data formats supporting the effective interchange of data throughout the entire business life cycle (see Figure 50-4). Essentially, initial request for quotation to final payment can now be performed electronically using the X12 EDI standards.

Likewise a set of international EDI standards called EDIFACT (EDI for Administration, Commerce, and Transport) is being developed for international trading needs.

**Figure 50-4**

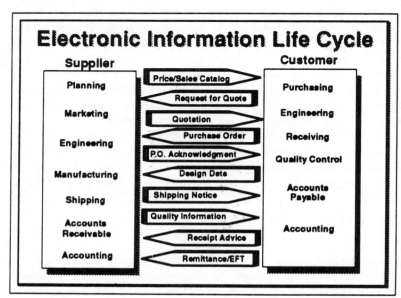

The EDIFACT standards are developed under the auspices of the United Nations and the International Standards Organization (ISO).

It is estimated that there are some 25,000 to 35,000 companies world wide using EDI to reduce costs and increase quality services to customers, and that this base is doubling each year.

## 50-4  THE BENEFITS OF EDI

Although there are immediate savings associated with the implementation of EDI, the greatest benefits can be gained through the integration of EDI into corporate information systems coupled with the redesign of underlying business process. Consequently, EDI changes the way companies do business. Some areas where EDI has helped provide the greatest level of benefits are:

- Decreased transcription and input errors.
- Increased ability to support manufacture-to-order through the electronic interchange of quote, design, and order data.
- Enhanced Just-In-Time (JIT) processes at both the supplier and customer interface points.
- Decreased overhead and indirect costs associated with paper processing.
- Enhanced cash flow through electronic cash management and Electronic Funds Transfer (EFT).
- Increased information availability without increased overhead costs.
- Increased competitive advantage through value-added information and technology services.

The ultimate savings and cost avoidance potential of each of these items is dependent upon the level and degree of EDI integration into corporate information systems and the redesign of underlying business processes. Simple emulation of paper-based business processes will only magnify inherent errors, while process re-engineering will truly offer added value and benefits. EDI "cost savings testimonials" of major companies are detailed weekly in major, popular publications.

While each of these "testimonials" are impressive, EDI was just one part of the solution that allowed each organization to achieve the stated benefits. Early EDI implementations that simply *emulated* manual paper processes showed little or no benefits. Sophisticated EDI users state clearly that strategic use of EDI with the redesign of underlying business processes changes the way they do business and offers the greatest benefits. In addition to changing base business processes, EDI is now being used in areas other than purchasing and invoicing. Some of the potential EDI business scenarios include:

- Planning data can be passed from customer to supplier to support Just-In-Time (JIT) processing.
- Request for Quote (RFQ) and Response to RFQ can be negotiated electronically.
- Invoices can be eliminated through the reconciliation of electronic purchase orders to electronic advanced ship notices and to physically received goods.

- Suppliers can manage customer replenishment levels through receipt of demand and consumption data.
- Computer Aided Design (CAD) data can be passed between customer and supplier via EDI during product design and development phases.
- Payments can be made through EDI and Electronic Funds Transfer (EFT) and can include remittance information for final supplier account reconciliation.
- Waybills, bills of lading, and freight bills can all be exchanged, reconciled and paid electronically.
- Price/sales catalogs, product information and product specifications can be exchanged via EDI.
- Quality reporting and parametric data can be exchanged electronically and automated into firm-wide quality programs.

These are just a few of the uses of EDI. Many executives contemplating the use of EDI, however, wonder what benefits are offered by implementing EDI. In a survey conducted by The American National Standards Institute, Accredited Standards Committee on EDI–X12, the top 500 EDI users in the United States cited *improved relations* and *competitive advantage* as the top two EDI benefits realized.

The majority of North American EDI users never performed a cost justification prior to EDI implementation. New EDI users, however, want to know what the "bottom line" benefits are from the use of EDI and business process redesign. Following are a few case studies where companies have implemented successful EDI programs in conjunction with business process redesign, other technology tools and organizational change.

## EDI BENEFIT CASE STUDIES

There are a number of case studies that support the claim that changing business through the use of EDI is beneficial. The majority of the Fortune 500 firms use EDI. All of the top 5 have been using EDI for some time. Many of the recent Malcolm Baldridge Quality Award recipients have used EDI for some time including Motorola, Federal Express, and General Motors (Cadillac Division). These case studies have been taken directly from press articles.

**Texas Instruments.**   Texas Instruments (TI) has one of the most successful EDI programs in the world. EDI is used throughout all of TI's operating divisions including semiconductor, defense and aerospace, and consumer products. TI uses EDI throughout the entire business cycle including purchasing, order entry, invoicing, and so on. Today, TI has over 1,700 EDI trading partners using 50 different EDI transactions around the world. TI's underlying strategy includes the use of EDI, redesign of business processes, integrated application systems and organizational change. Some of the benefits from TI's efforts include:

- One division bypasses the field sales office on 80 percent of incoming orders via EDI, offering TI sales and marketing representatives time to service the customer rather than shuffling paper.
- Through the use of EDI, bar code and warehouse automation, TI enjoys 98 percent on-time delivery in several product lines.

- Several operating areas report reduction of up to 80 percent in returns caused by administration errors.
- Order processing time has been reduced from 4 days to 1 day for many products.
- Entry and processing costs have been reduced by sending 70 percent of purchase orders (i.e., approximately 4,000 line items per day) via EDI.

**Ford Motor Company.**   Ford Motor Company has been an EDI user for over 10 years. In the past several years, Ford has employed EDI, bar code, JIT techniques, integrated systems design, and business process redesign to implement a number of successful business initiatives. Some of the areas of use and associated benefits are:

- The invoice has been eliminated in several areas through the use of EDI, all but eliminating historical accounts payable organizations. Payment is made to the supplier on receipt of goods after reconciliation with the original purchase order/release and the physical (bar coded) receipt record. This process reduced the matching process from 4-way to 2-way, reduced headcount requirements some 40% and substantially reduced billing/payment errors.
- Ford suppliers are also benefiting through improved cash availability and predictability, same day accounts receivable update and improved customer relations.

**Hanes Hosiery.**   Hanes Hosiery has implemented EDI in conjunction with bar code, automated package identification, systems integration and business process redesign in support of its "Quick Response" (QR) program. Hanes has EDI links with over 70 trading partners and has seen the following benefits:

- Reduction in customer lead time from 22 to 14 days.
- Reduction in order processing by at least 1 day.
- Decreased distribution center inventories by 14 percent.
- Total, end-to-end, manufacturing cycle reduction from 25 days to 10 days.
- Higher sales growth, better inventory management, increased return on investment, better customer service, and enhanced information.

**Military Traffic Management Command (MTMC).**   The U.S. Army's Military Traffic Management Command (MTMC) that is jointly staffed and industrially funded manages movement of 1.4 million freight shipments valued at $800 million per year. MTMC has established electronic bulletin boards to interface between MTMC, brokers, carriers and internal shippers to access rates, identify operations problems, issue traffic management advisories, and assist in rate filing. Some 2.3 million government bills of lading can be handled through this system. Through elimination and reduction in data entry, mail and processing, MTMC will save some $11.8 million per year in costs.

There are numerous other EDI success stories; however, all EDI successes hinge upon the use of EDI coupled with other technologies, business process redesign, integrated systems and organizational change. EDI users cite the intangible benefits of competitive advantage, enhanced customer service, enhanced quality and increased productivity as primary benefits, but as described above, the "bottom line" benefits are substantial.

## 50-5    THE MECHANICS OF AN EDI SYSTEM

Technically, EDI is not difficult. A simple EDI implementation can be performed with a microcomputer, software and a modem. Conceptually, there are five base components to any EDI system: Hardware, business application software (e.g., purchasing and accounts receivable systems), translation software, telecommunications facilities and EDI standards (see Figure 50-5). EDI can be performed on any type or size of hardware, from a PC or Macintosh, to mid-range computers, to large mainframe computers. Business application software, such as purchasing systems, are the author or recipient of the EDI business transactions (i.e., purchase order and purchase order acknowledgment). Translation software is used to format the business application proprietary data language into a common EDI business format language, understandable by the intended trading partner recipient. The standards, as mentioned above, offer a common electronic language easily comprehended by the world-wide business community.

A typical EDI transaction example might include the following steps (see Figure 50-6):

• A purchaser's buyer enters a purchase order into a purchasing system.
• Periodically, individual purchase orders (POs) are batched to the EDI translator software.
• The translation software reformats the PO data into a common EDI standard format and stages the data for communication to the supplier.
• Communications software sends the EDI standard data over the public telephone lines or via a Value Added Network's (VAN's) electronic store-and-forward mailbox facilities to the intended recipient.

**Figure 50-5**

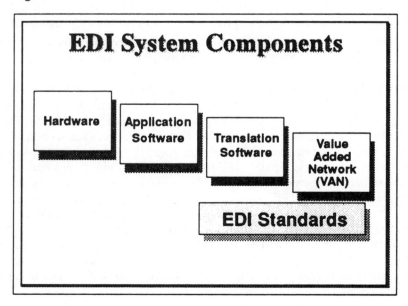

**Figure 50-6**

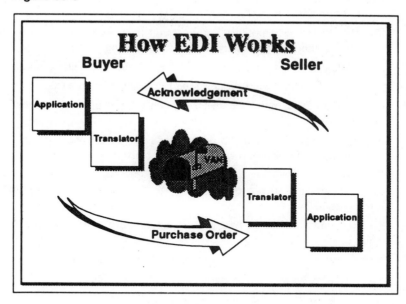

- The recipient's (supplier's) translator software reformats the PO data from the EDI standard format into an internal proprietary format, and batches the PO data to the supplier's order entry system.

- The supplier's order entry system evaluates the PO data and generates an internal order on the order entry system.

- After evaluation, validation, and review, a sales representative confirms the conditions of the purchaser's order on the order entry system.

- The order entry system generates a PO acknowledgment which in turn starts an EDI reply to the original purchaser.

Although EDI is not technically difficult, the implementation of EDI can be logistically difficult. To enjoy the benefits described above, effective planning is necessary to fully integrate EDI into the corporate information systems structure. Some business and technical issues must be considered and addressed.

## TECHNICAL ISSUES AND CONSIDERATIONS

- Are the in-house applications capable of sending and receiving EDI transactions, or are application changes necessary to fully integrate EDI into the information processing flow?

- What hardware platform should support EDI processing?

- Should data interchange with the source application occur in a batch or transaction-based processing mode?

- Are software checkpoints in place to validate (and correct) incoming EDI data prior to application input?
- Has all data for each potential transaction been identified to support business data requirements both in-house and for the trading partners?
- Has all identified data been mapped correctly into the EDI standard format?
- Should translator software be developed in-house or purchased?
- Have all data flow management tools been implemented to support EDI operationally?
- Should data be communicated directly over switched telephone communications facilities or through third-party, Value Added Network's (VAN's) store-and-forward mail boxing facilities?
- Are hardware and software tools in place to support data communications requirements?
- Are operational fall-back, troubleshooting, and error recovery contingency plans in place?
- Are proper security measures implemented to protect internal systems?

## BUSINESS ISSUES AND CONSIDERATIONS

An EDI implementation typically requires some level of business process redesign and organizational change. EDI implementation planning requires representation from all functional areas of the corporate business environment. An effective EDI implementation is best directed by a corporate-level steering committee with representation from upper management in all functional areas (e.g., purchasing, planning, manufacturing, and accounts payable). It is essential that the chosen project leader have a good understanding of all functional areas, and have the delegated authority to carry out necessary changes in support of EDI.

Some business issues that must be considered during an EDI implementation include:

- Are all business processes executed in an efficient manner in support of functional business requirements?
- What data is necessary to complete a functional business event, and when and where is certain data needed?
- What functional business transactions are candidates for EDI?
- What other technological tools should be integrated with EDI?
- What trading partners are candidates for EDI?
- What organizational changes will be precipitated by EDI implementation?
- Is a realistic roll-out implementation plan in place?
- Have review processes been set up to evaluate the benefits and payback from the EDI implementation?
- Are all audit, legal, and security procedures in place to support a paperless EDI process?

• Have internal personnel and external trading partners been informed and educated concerning potential EDI implementation impacts?

These are just a few of the technical and business questions that must be considered prior to EDI implementation. Like any corporate program, strategic implementation planning can provide an excellent tool in addressing these issues. Actual EDI implementation can take from 4 to 60 weeks. The current industry average for EDI implementation is 32 weeks.

## 50-6   IMPLEMENTING EDI

The decision by corporate management to implement EDI can be a decision that affects all aspects of the corporate culture. EDI is not just another MIS *bells and whistles* technology; EDI is a premeditated business strategy utilizing technological tools to support the corporate business priorities.

There are several steps that can enhance the EDI implementation process.

• Learn more about how EDI can work for specific needs.
• Obtain executive management consensus and commitment.
• Organize for an EDI implementation.
• Develop an EDI strategic plan.
• Perform process and technology assessments and analysis.
• Design a corporate-wide EDI system and program.
• Develop a deployment strategy that includes trading partners.

## 50-7   SUMMARY

EDI is a tool that can be an enabler for strategic business objectives. While EDI is not technically difficult, it does require an understanding and a commitment by executive management. EDI by itself is not an answer; however, coupled with other strategic corporate initiatives, it can become a powerful enabling facilitator. Most leading U.S. and international industries are using EDI. Information and education is readily available.

## 50-8   SELECTED REFERENCES

*The 1992 EDI Directory,* (Potomac: Phillips Publishing, 1992).

Barber, Norman F., *Organizational Aspects of EDI: A Project Manager's Guide,* (Electronic Data Interchange Association).

Emmelhains, Dr. Margaret Ann, *EDI: A Total Manager's Guide,* (New York: Van Nostrand Reinhold).

Kutten, L.J., Bernard D. Reams, Jr., and Allen E. Strahler, *Electronic Contracting Law, EDI and Business Transactions, 1992–1993 Edition,* (New York: Clark Boardman Callaghan).

Powers, William J., *EDI Control and Audit Issues for Managers, Users and Auditors,* (EDIA).

Shaw, Jack, and Mike Witter, *The EDI Project Planner,* (EDI Executive Publications).

Wright, Benjamin, *The Law of Electronic Commerce—EDI, Fax, and E-Mail: Technology, Proof, and Liability.* (Boston: Little, Brown).

# CHAPTER 51

# Information Systems Security (New)

## 51-1  INTRODUCTION

It is estimated that computer fraud costs American organizations between $300 million and $5 billion per year. To reduce your organization's susceptibility to fraud, a well-planned and implemented approach to information systems (IS) security is required.

Information systems security can be defined as the protection of information assets (e.g., the hardware, software, and associated data) from unauthorized or intentional disclosure, modification, or destruction. Also included under the IS security "umbrella" are the steps necessary to control access to system resources and ways in which to respond to unauthorized and/or unintentional access to systems. Information systems security should be designed to ensure the integrity, confidentiality, and accessibility, where authorized, to the organization's information assets.

## 51-2  TYPES OF SECURITY THREATS

There are a wide variety of threats to information systems security. Basically, these threats can be summarized into the following categories:

- *Intentional mischief.* Caused by theft, intentional destruction of data and other IS assets, and "hackers" (i.e., individuals who obtain unauthorized access to a computer).

- *Lack of an effective IS security policy.* Such as the failure to perform regular system back ups (i.e., saving your computer's software and data on tape or disk) or allowing system users to share their passwords.

- *Human accidents and errors.* Such as spilling coffee on a computer keyboard or tripping into a disk drive and causing loss of data. (Information systems security can't "cure" human accidents and errors. However, it can reduce the risk of and loss from them by limiting access to IS assets.)

- *Power supply threats.* Sudden lapses or surges of power that cause the loss or scrambling of data.

- *Natural disasters.* Earthquakes, fires, floods, and tornadoes fall into this category.

- *Network access.* Unauthorized access to your voice or data network.

- *Viruses.* Malicious (in general) programs that attack legitimate programs and destroy data or computer codes (e.g., the Michelangelo Virus).

- *Data "Diddling."* The unauthorized alteration of data as it is entered into a computer or the changing of data stored in the computer (e.g., changing students' grades, eliminating speeding tickets, reducing amounts owed the organization, and transferring money from one account to another).

What can an organization do to protect against these numerous threats? The next section discusses a number of proven measures that can be utilized to protect the organization's IS assets.

## 51-3 WAYS IN WHICH TO PROTECT INFORMATION SYSTEMS ASSETS

Given the large investment in and dependence on IS assets, it makes economic and business sense to protect those assets. Described below are some of the key means by which an organization can help ensure the integrity, assessability, and confidentiality of its IS resources.

### PHYSICAL SECURITY

There are a large number of physical measures an organization can implement to improve the security surrounding its systems:

- *Physical access controls.* By restricting access to IS assets, an organization can reduce the opportunity for unauthorized use and malicious harm to its computers. The computer room should be located away from public areas and protected by a security system (e.g., a key-card or combination lock).

- *Fire suppression control system.* The computer room should be protected by a fire suppression system (e.g., an automatic water or Halon system). Also, the room should have fire extinguishers and be kept as clean as possible to reduce the opportunity for fires to spread.

- *Water detection and control system.* Each year, a significant amount of water damage is incurred in computer rooms. The main causes of water damage includes burst pipes, leaking air conditioning systems, and roof leaks. To reduce the opportunity for water damage, organizations should periodically review their plumbing, air conditioning systems, and roof. Also, the computer room should be equipped with a water detection system and plastic covers for the computer equipment in the event of a leak.

- *Power supply monitoring systems.* To protect against power fluctuations and outages, organizations should strongly consider investing in an Uninterruptible Power Supply (UPS) system. UPS systems filter power supply fluctuations and ensure a constant power supply to computers. Also, in the event of a power outage or blackout, they can provide power for a limited period of time. This power can allow the organization to safely shut down its computers without the loss of data.

- *Offsite storage of backup tapes and disks.* One of the easiest ways in which an organization can protect its IS assets is to store copies of *all* of its software off-site in a protected environment. The software to be stored offsite should include copies of the operating system and other system software, application software (e.g., the general ledger), and all data, including master files and transaction details. The offsite storage facility should be located sufficiently far from the organization's data center to ensure it is not susceptible to the same natural disasters (e.g., tornadoes) the data center is. The organization needs to ensure it keeps a complete and accurate inventory of all tapes and/or disks located at the offsite facility.

## TECHNICAL SECURITY MEASURES

There are a number of technologically based security measures an organization can implement to improve the security surrounding its IS assets. These measures include:

- *Encryption.* The "scrambling" of data, based on a mathematical algorithm, that makes it unreadable to those without a "key." Encryption can be an effective security measure for organizations that transmit data between different locations.

- *Callback devices (also known as port protection devices).* A relatively effective means of controlling telephone access to an organization's computers. After calling into a system, a user must supply its identification code and password for authentification by the device. The device then disconnects the user and calls the user's preauthorized telephone number to verify the identify of the user.

- *Password.* A sequence of alphabetic and/or numeric characters which must be entered at the beginning of a computer session to verify the user's identity and obtain access to the system. Passwords can be an effective means of limiting access to a system, especially if they are frequently changed (e.g., every 60 days), random (e.g., not a person's last name or birthdate), and are not shared with others. Also, the longer the password, the harder it is to guess. (e.g., a three digit password has 47,000 possible combinations, a 6-digit password has 2 billion possible combinations.)

- *Access control software (ACS).* Mainly available for mainframe and large midrange (minicomputer) systems, can be a valuable security measure. ACS provides an additional "layer" of security on top of the application and operating system security. It also provides the ability to limit access to designated employees, monitor user violations (e.g., unauthorized attempts to access the payroll system), and report security breaches.

- *Biometric devices.* Instruments that perform mathematical analysis of biological characteristics. Today, there are wide variety of these types of devices including:
  — Voice recognition and verification systems.
  — Signature dynamics verification systems.
  — Retinal pattern verification systems.
  — Hard print geometry verification systems.
  — Fingerprint Identification.

  Biometric systems have been in use for some time now. Before selecting one of these systems, the organization should consider (1) the cost versus the benefits of the systems. Biometric devices can be very expensive. (2) The error rate should be very low. This means the system must be able to spot "counterfeits" while making allowances for normal variations (e.g., a blister on ones hand or a cold). (3) The time required to enroll people into the system.

## END-USER COMPUTER SECURITY

Microcomputer and local area networks (LANS) are becoming increasingly popular. As their popularity grows, so do the associated security risks. Unfortunately, most organizations tend to focus on mainframe security and fail to recognize the importance of microcomputer and LAN security. To increase the security surrounding these systems, a number of steps can be taken:

- *Security agreements.* Ensure that all personnel sign an agreement stating they will *not:*
  — Share their password.
  — Upload or download any software or data to the organization's computers unless instructed to do so.
  — "Pirate" (i.e., make illegal copies of) the organization's software.
- *Physical security.* Verify that the organization's microcomputers and LANs are appropriately located (e.g., in a separate computer room) and protected from power fluctuations, fire and water damage.
- *Data security.* Ensure that the software and the data on microcomputers and LANs are backed up on a frequent (e.g., daily) basis and the backup tapes or disks are stored offsite.

## EMPLOYEE SECURITY

There are a number of key measures an organization can take to limit its exposure to IS security risks. These measures include:

- *Performing background checks.* Prior to hiring an employee, an organization should perform a thorough background check of all prospective employees. The background check should include an analysis of the prospective employee's educational background and work history. Also, the organization should investigate whether the employee has a criminal record.

- *Analyzing employees' security posture.* The security "posture" of all employees should be investigated on an annual basis. This investigation should determine whether the employees' legal or credit position has changed.

- *Obtaining security agreement signatures.* All employees should be required to sign a security agreement.

- *Communicating with the Personnel Department.* The Personnel Department should immediately formally notify the IS Department of all personnel changes (e.g., employees that are leaving the organization or whose responsibilities have changed). Doing so can help guard against unauthorized access to the system by former or transferred employees.


## INSURANCE COVERAGE

Organizations should maintain sufficient insurance to reduce the exposure to losses from floor, fire, theft, and other types of disaster. The types of insurance coverage that should be maintained include:

- Computer equipment and facilities.
- Media reconstruction.
- Business interruption.
- Errors and omissions by employees.


## DISASTER RECOVERY PLANNING

Disaster Recovery Planning, also referred to as contingency planning or business resumption planning, is one of the most important aspects of IS security. A disaster recovery plan (DRP) is an organized and documented approach to responding to a disaster. A proven approach to developing and maintaining a DRP is outlined below.

- *Phase I—Assess the situation.* During this phase, the organization determines the types of risks to which it is vulnerable (e.g., fires, tornadoes, or earthquakes) and the potential impact of these risks.

- *Phase II—Analyze recovery strategies.* The key steps to be completed during this phase include determining the IS resources currently in place and then analyzing the alternatives for recovery. These alternatives can include:

  — *Constructing a backup site.* This involves building a data center in a location sufficiently far from the main data center so it is not subject to the same disasters.

  — *Utilizing a service bureau.* This option involves using the computer resources of a third party immediately after the disaster.

  — *Sharing computer facilities.* Under this option, the organization shares the computer systems and software of another organization for a limited period of time.

  — *Obtaining hot or cold site facilities from a vendor.* This option involves contracting for the use of a computer facility while the organization's own data center is being restored. A cold site is a "computer-ready" "room in which an organization can move its existing or replacement computer. A hot site is a fully operational facility with a computer and network already in place.

- *Phase III—Develop the DRP.* During this phase, the organization develops its DRP. The plan should include the following areas:
  - — An overview of the plan (e.g., the purpose of the plan, recovery, and restoration strategies, key recovery activities, and how the plan will be maintained and tested.
  - — *Emergency procedures.* The procedures to be taken to safeguard human life, limit damage to the data center, and minimize loss of data.
  - — *Response action plan.* The steps needed to respond to a disaster (e.g., how to assess the damage, notification procedures, and recovery team members and responsibilities).
  - — *Recovery operations.* A description of the major recovery tasks (e.g., the recovery logistics, off-site storage, and operating system, network, data, and personnel plans).
  - — *Restoration plan.* An approach to restoring the data center (e.g., the construction and site preparation schedule, and hardware/software and telecommunication acquisition plans.
- *Plan testing and review strategy.* An approach to ensuring the DRP is properly tested on a periodic basis.
- *DRP maintenance.* An organized approach to maintaining, updating, and storing the plan.
- *Phase IV—Test and maintain the DRP.* The objectives of this phase include:
  - — Thoroughly testing the DRP to ensure that if a disaster were to occur, the organization could recover from it on a timely and efficient manner.
  - — Developing an approach to maintaining the plan on a regular basis.

See Chapter 52 for a more complete discussion of disaster recovery planning.

## 51-4  THE CONTROLLER'S ROLE IN INFORMATION SYSTEMS SECURITY

The controller and/or chief financial officer should play a key role in implementing and ensuring employee adherence to security policies. These individuals should be leaders in implementing security policies and monitoring compliance to them. Specifically, they should:

- Communicate security policies to all employees within their span of control. This can be achieved by developing a security awareness program, requiring employees to sign security agreements, and providing security training.
- Ensure employees understand security risks.
- Assess risk on a periodic basis.
- Verify that all IS assets are inventoried.
- Ensure that backups are regularly made and stored off-site.

- Review the disaster recovery plan on a regular (e.g., annual) basis and ensure it is annually tested.
- Verify that access authorizations are appropriate.
- Investigate security violations.
- Ensure dismissed or transferred employees are removed from the system.
- Communicate a positive attitude towards security.
- Instigate period independent audits or reviews of the organization's computer security.

The controller can delegate some of these functions to a security officer or other appropriate employee. However, they should ultimately be responsible for ensuring these tasks are completed.

## 51-5  CONCLUSION

As previously noted, IS security is an extremely important area. There are numerous threats to IS assets. However, there are numerous ways in which to protect those assets. It is up to the controller to play an active role in ensuring the organization's IS assets are protected and secure.

## 51-6  SELECTED REFERENCES

### PERIODICALS

*Computerworld*

*Computers in Accounting*

*Information Week*

*Management Accounting*

*Disaster Recovery Journal*

### PRODUCT REVIEWS/INFORMATION

*Datapro*

*Data Sources*

*Gartner Group*

*ICP Software Directory*

# CHAPTER 52

# Disaster Recovery Planning (New)

## 52-1  INTRODUCTION

Management is becoming increasingly interested in the area of disaster recovery planning. Recent disasters, such as the World Trade Center bombing, Hurricane Andrew, and the Chicago flood, have contributed to this increased level of interest. As mentioned in Chapter 51, disaster recovery planning is one of the most important aspects of information security. This chapter explores a number of aspects related to disaster recovery planning, including trends related to it and a proven approach to developing and testing a disaster recovery plan.

## 52-2  DISASTER RECOVERY PLANNING TRENDS

Recent trends related to disaster recovery planning include:

- *Organizationwide Focus.* In the past, disaster recovery planning was viewed as strictly an information systems department issue; this is no longer the case. Now, senior management, as well as the board of directors, is keenly interested in the plans that are in place to ensure efficient and effective recovery from a natural or manmade disaster.

- *Legal Requirements for Disaster Recovery Planning.* Your organization may be required to have a disaster recovery plan for the following legal reasons:

    **1.** Industry. For over ten years, banks have been required to have disaster recovery plans and to test and revise those plans periodically.

2. **IRS Audit.** In the unfortunate event that your organization is audited by the IRS, you may be required to produce financial and business records going back three years or more. If you cannot deliver these records to the IRS because they were destroyed in a disaster, good luck!

3. **Contractual.** Your organization may be contractually obligated to have a disaster recovery plan. Increasingly, companies are requiring their suppliers to have a current and tested disaster recovery plan in place, to ensure they will not be stranded without supplies for an unreasonable amount of time.

4. **Common Law.** Your organization may be required to have a disaster recovery plan in place under common law. Organizations may have fiduciary responsibilities and "duties of care" to their customers, shareholders, and/or bondholders. If an organization does not exercise "good business judgment" and develop, test, and maintain a disaster recovery plan, it may find itself in court in the event of a disaster from which it did not quickly recover and from which it suffered significant losses.

- *Nonmainframe Disaster Recovery Planning.* Organizations are becoming increasingly reliant on personal computers, local area networks (LANs), and midrange computers. Historically, these mainframe alternatives were not included in a disaster recovery plan. However, with the increased use of nonmainframe computing environments, organizations have begun to include them as an integral part of the overall recovery process.

- *Business Continuity Planning.* In the past, disaster recovery plans covered only the information systems (IS) portion of the business. This is no longer the case. Organizations must now plan how they will recover *all* of their operations, not just the IS portion, in the event of a disaster; hence the term business continuity planning (BCP). Business continuity plans are designed to provide an organization with an approach for recovering all aspects of its operations. (This chapter focuses on how to recover from a disaster in the IS area.)

Additional trends on the horizon include the need to have a global disaster recovery plan that addresses an organization's worldwide operations, alternatives to the traditional hot and cold sites (see Chapter 51), and increased user involvement in the development and testing of the disaster recovery plan.

## 52-3   AN APPROACH TO DEVELOPING A DISASTER RECOVERY PLAN

Described below, and depicted in Figure 52-1, is a proven approach to successfully developing a disaster recovery plan. It is divided into five phases:

Phase I—Assess the environment in which the organization operates.

Phase II—Analyze recovery strategies.

Phase III—Document components of the disaster recovery plan.

Phase IV—Develop the disaster recovery plan.

Phase V—Execute, evaluate, and maintain the disaster recovery plan.

**Figure 52-1**   Approach to Developing a Disaster Recovery Plan.

| Phase I | | Phase II | | Phase III | | Phase IV | | Phase V |
|---|---|---|---|---|---|---|---|---|
| Assess the Environment | → | Analyze Recovery Strategies | → | Document Components of the Plan | → | Develop the Plan | → | Execute, Evaluate, and Maintain the Plan |

## PHASE I—ASSESS THE ENVIRONMENT IN WHICH THE ORGANIZATION OPERATES

The objective of this phase is to determine the types of risks to which your organization is subject and the potential impact of those risks on your IS operations.

The key steps involved in this phase are:

1. Determine what risks the organization will most likely confront (e.g., fire, tornadoes, earthquakes, or terrorism).
2. Determine the potential impact on IS operations of the risks to which your organization is subject. To complete this step, the organization should accomplish the following tasks:

Identify the functions performed by the organization.

Determine which functions are critical to the success of the business.

Estimate the impact on the business if it could not perform critical functions for one hour, one day, two days, one week, one month, and so on.

At the end of this phase, the organization should have a reasonably good assessment of the risks to which it is subject and the potential impact of those risks on the business.

## PHASE II—ANALYZE RECOVERY STRATEGIES

The key objectives of this phase are to define the IS resources currently in place, analyze recovery alternatives, and select an alternative that best meets your organization's goals.

The key steps that comprise this phase are:

1. Define your organization's IS resources. These resources most likely will include a centralized computer, a variety of personal computers and LANs, application and system software (e.g., operating systems and database management systems), and the data center.
2. Evaluate recovery alternatives.

To accomplish the second step, the main activities are:

• Define the evaluation criteria, such as these listed in Figure 52-2. Some of the criteria on which to make a recovery selection decision include: cost, subscriber-to-site

**Figure 52-2**   Key Recovery Site Evaluation Criteria.

| | |
|---|---|
| • Cost | • Site communication capabilities |
| • Subscriber-to-site ratio | • Site vendor-consulting capabilities |
| • Site location | • Site support staff capabilities |
| • Site security | • Availability of site office space |
| • Site fire and water protection features | • Location of nearest airport |
| • Site data storage capacity | • Site backup systems |
| • Site vendor's financial stability | • Annual hours available for testing the plan |

ratio (i.e., the number of hot site or cold site subscribers per facility), location of the hot or cold site, the level of security surrounding the site, the amount of data storage available at the hot or cold site, the communication capabilities at the site, the availability of professional consultants to assist your organization with planning for and recovering from a disaster, the amount of support personnel available to assist your organization in the event of a disaster, the availability of office space and supplies at the site, the financial stability of the site vendor, the number of hours per year your organization can use the site for testing its disaster recovery plan, the location of the nearest airport, the vendor's approach to protecting its site (e.g., whether the vendor has a fire control system and what flood or water damage control system is in place), and the type of backup system in place in the event of a disaster at the site.

• Determine the recovery alternatives that should be analyzed. During this activity, the organization needs to determine which recovery alternatives it will analyze. The options may include hot sites, cold sites, warm sites, mobile sites (i.e., hot sites located in a mobile trailer), or a contingency agreement (i.e., an agreement between your organization and another to serve as a recovery site in the event of a disaster at one of the locations).

• Assess the alternatives. The purpose of this activity is to assess the costs and benefits of each alternative. Using the evaluation criteria identified above, the organization completes a detailed assessment of each alternative.

• Select an alternative. Based on the assessment performed in the previous step, the organization selects the recovery alternative that best meets its needs.

Prior to signing any contract for recovery-related services, it is important to complete a number of activities:

• Ensure the contract includes all oral promises made by the vendor.

• Avoid automatic renewal clauses.

• Ensure the contract provides your organization with sufficient time to test the recovery plan.

• Have an attorney and an IS consultant familiar with recovery-related services review the contract prior to signing it.

## PHASE III—DOCUMENT COMPONENTS OF THE DISASTER RECOVERY PLAN

During this phase, the disaster recovery plan components are clearly documented. The key steps of this phase are:

1. Develop the timeline for recovery. During this activity, the organization defines its recovery time targets for each major function (e.g., the mainframe must be recovered within 48 hours and personal computers must be replaced within one week).

2. Develop recovery "scripts" (i.e., action plans) for each major function. The scripts should include: tasks to be completed, who specifically will be responsible for each task, the timing of the task, where the task will occur (e.g., at headquarters or the hot site), and how to complete the task.

3. Develop the recovery schedule. The objective of this task is to develop the precise schedule of events that will occur in the event of a disaster.

## PHASE IV—DEVELOP THE DISASTER RECOVERY PLAN

The objective of this phase is to prepare the disaster recovery plan. A sample recovery plan is shown in Figure 52-3.

The key components of this phase are:

1. An executive overview of the disaster recovery plan (i.e., an executive summary of the scope and objective of the plan, and a high-level presentation of the recovery strategies).

2. Emergency response procedures. An overview of the procedures that should take place in the event of a disaster (e.g., shutdown of the computers, fire suppression techniques, evacuation procedures, and notification procedures).

3. Action plan for responding to the disaster. Approaches for assessing the damage, notifying employees, and activating the disaster recovery plan.

4. The approach for recovering operations. Procedures for recovering the hardware, software, and network, and for ensuring that data entry operations are resumed in a timely manner.

**Figure 52-3**   Sample Disaster Recovery Plan—
Table of Contents.

- Executive Overview
- Emergency Response Procedures
- Action Plan for Response
- Approach for Recovering Operations
- How Operations Will Be Restored
- How to Test and Maintain the Plan
- Appendices
- Glossary

5. How operations will be restored. An action plan for restoring operations at the disaster site or at an alternative site. The plan should contain an approach for constructing a new facility, acquiring new hardware and software (if appropriate), and testing the new system prior to implementation.

6. How to test and maintain the plan. A detailed approach to tests and maintenance of the plan.

7. Appendices. Relevant information on the inventory of hardware and software, employee contacts, insurance policies, software licensing agreements, network and hardware vendor support agreements, and the list of data stored offsite and instructions on how to obtain it.

8. Glossary. Definitions of technical terms used in the plan.

One final note: Be sure a copy of the plan is stored offsite in a fire and waterproof location. In the event of a disaster, it won't be destroyed if given proper protection.

## PHASE V—EXECUTE, EVALUATE, AND MAINTAIN THE DISASTER RECOVERY PLAN

The main objectives of this phase are to verify that the disaster recovery plan works as designed and that the plan is appropriately maintained. The scope of the testing should include hardware, system and application software, and the communication network.
    The key steps in this phase, which are depicted in Figure 52-4, are:

1. Develop the disaster recovery plan test objectives and evaluation criteria. Specifically, the organization needs to define what it is trying to achieve by testing the disaster recovery plan, and how it will evaluate the success or failure of the test.

2. Document the high-level approach to testing the disaster recovery plan. During this activity, the organization needs to define clearly what is to be tested and how it will be tested.

**Figure 52-4**   Approach to Executing, Evaluating, and Maintaining the Plan.

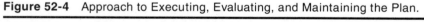

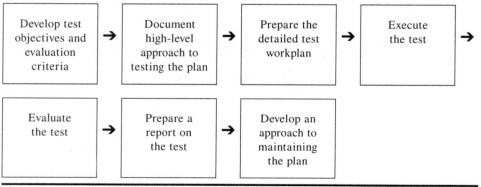

3. Prepare the detailed test workplan. The purpose of this step is to identify and document the specific steps to be taken to test the disaster recovery plan. Who will perform the test? Where will they perform the test? When will they perform the test?

4. Execute the test. During this step, the test is conducted.

5. Evaluate the test. This is one of the most important steps of this phase. The organization needs to critically evaluate what went right and what went wrong during the testing process, and incorporate appropriate changes into the plan.

6. Prepare a written report on the test. In this step, the testing team documents the scope and objective of the test and its own approach to the test. The results of the test and the changes made to the disaster recovery plan after conducting the test should be included in this document. The report should be presented to senior management, as well as to internal and external auditors, for review and comments.

7. Develop an approach to maintaining the plan. During this step, an approach to storing the plan is documented. The frequency (e.g., quarterly) with which the plan needs to be reviewed and revised is formalized.

## 52-4  CONCLUSION

Disaster recovery planning is one of the most important areas on which an organization can focus. Without an effective disaster recovery plan, an entity is extremely susceptible to natural and/or manmade disasters. An organization that has no current and well-tested plan may find itself subject to a lawsuit or at a competitive disadvantage. It is the responsibility of all senior executives, not just the director of information systems, to ensure that an organization can quickly and effectively recover from a disaster.

# CHAPTER 53

# A Brief Introduction to Client/Server Computing (New)

## 53-1 INTRODUCTION

A radical change is unfolding within the information technology arena: client/server computing. Alternatively touted as a panacea or a Pandora's Box, client/server is here and gaining momentum. The impact of client/server computing on the hardware and software acquisition and development strategies utilized by a corporation cannot be underestimated. Therefore, it is extremely important for controllers to have knowledge of client/server-related concepts and trends and the effect they may have on the organization's information technology (IT) budget and strategies.

## 53-2 THE PAST: THE TERMINAL-HOST ARCHITECTURE

Terminal-host computer systems are centralized and rely on the memory and processor of a single computer such as a large IBM mainframe or DEC minicomputer. Database

---

This chapter was written by David Bassett, Senior Consultant, Ernst & Young, Denver, Colorado.

processing, logic processing, and terminal display management are handled by the single host computer. "Dumb" terminals, tied in via local or wide area networks, serve only as input/output devices. Typically, many transaction processing activities on host-based systems are run in "batch mode" (i.e., off-line while the computer is "down"). Terminal-host systems are particularly effective in processing large volumes of transactions. For example, these systems frequently are used to run airline reservation systems and automated teller machine networks and process insurance claims. However, terminal-host systems tend to be expensive to maintain and update.

## 53-3   THE FUTURE: CLIENT/SERVER ARCHITECTURE

One of the most ambiguous terms in the computing industry is client/server technology. It has been heralded as everything from "the flavor of the month" to the "cure all" that will be the enabler of a new "paradigm" for computing. An exhaustive definition of what is and is not client/server and the various configuration topologies is beyond the scope of this chapter. However, briefly, a client/server system is different from host-based systems in that it is actually two computers processing related information concurrently and independently. The top ten elements of client/server computing are listed in Table 53-1.

Perhaps one of the easiest ways to conceptualize the client/server concept is to view computing as a spectrum of processing options. At one end of the spectrum, an individual user runs programs (e.g., Lotus 1-2-3, WordPerfect, and Harvard Graphics) on a stand-alone basis. At the other end, many users log on to a mainframe (i.e., terminal-host) system or they execute large, batch-oriented programs, see Figure 53-1.

Data processing applications may run solely on personal computers or on mainframes or midrange computers. However, a growing number of applications *execute*

**Table 53-1**   Top Ten Elements of Client/Server Computing.

1.  A client/server architecture consists of a client process and a server process that are distinct, yet interact seamlessly.

2.  The client portion and the server portions can, and typically do, operate on separate computer platforms.

3.  Either the client platform of the server platform can be upgraded without having to upgrade the other platform. ·

4.  The server can service multiple clients concurrently. In some client/server systems, clients can access multiple servers.

5.  The client/server system includes some sort of networking capability.

6.  The application logic is split in different proportions between the client and the server, sometimes all running on the client.

7.  Action is usually initiated by the client, not by the server. However, database servers can "take action" based on "triggers" (i.e., specific events), business rules and stored procedures.

8.  A user-friendly Graphical User Interface (GUI) typically resides on the client.

9.  Most client/server systems possess a structured query language (SQL) capability.

10. The database server provides data protection and security.

*Source:* Reprinted with the permission of Software Magazine, January 1993, Sentry Publishing Company Inc., 1900 West Park Drive, Westborough, MA 01581, U.S.A.

**Figure 53-1**

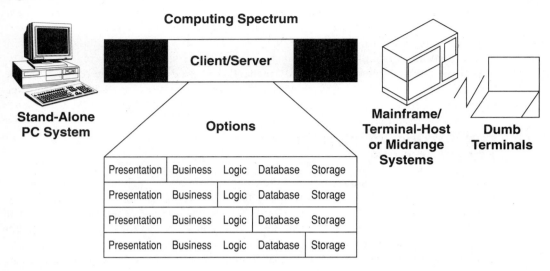

Computing Spectrum

Client/Server

Stand-Alone PC System

Options

Mainframe/ Terminal-Host or Midrange Systems

Dumb Terminals

| Presentation | Business | Logic | Database | Storage |
|---|---|---|---|---|
| Presentation | Business | Logic | Database | Storage |
| Presentation | Business | Logic | Database | Storage |
| Presentation | Business | Logic | Database | Storage |

parts of their programs on both kinds of machines; this is considered a client/server environment.

A C/S environment consists of two participating programs, one requesting service and one providing service. The one that "speaks" first is the client. Client/Server means more than running multiple programs; there must be some kind of request/service relationship between them.

One of the key reasons client/server computing is so popular is it enables "rightsizing" of midrange to large mainframe corporate systems to a potentially more cost effective computing platform. Processing data at both the client and server locations reduces the amount of information that must be bidirectionally sent over the data network. In a client/server arrangement, only required data is sent to the client. The server manages the data requested by the client. A key advantage of client/server is data can be accessed throughout the organization. Data in a relational database management system (RDBMS) can be designed to be application independent so users can access the data with a simple query tool or develop sophisticated departmental applications that access the common data. Top RDBMSs that are currently being used for client/server applications include Oracle, Sybase, Informix, Ingres, Microsoft SQL Server, and IBM's DB2.

## 53-4   INTEROPERABILITY AND SYSTEMS INTEGRATION

Interoperability refers to the capability of systems to work together. Most terminal-host based systems were designed around proprietary hardware and software architectures that complicated attempts to integrate multiple systems. There is currently a movement to "open systems" architectures where hardware, network topology, and system software provided by any vendor is interoperable with another vendor. Client/

server technology frequently is implemented where there are a variety of vendors. The movement to open systems is likely to bolster significant growth in client/server implementations as companies attempt greater systems integration.

## 53-5    GRAPHICAL USER INTERFACE

A primary characteristic of current client/server front ends is the graphical user interface (GUI) (i.e., a mouse-driven or "point & click" interface). The proliferation of GUIs is redefining end-user expectations for ease of use. A GUI requires less training and potentially can yield substantial productivity benefits, particularly in low transaction volume environments.

## 53-6    MOVEMENT TO CLIENT/SERVER

According to a recent Computerworld survey of "Premier 100" information systems executives, client/server technology and open systems are considered critical for competitive success in the next five years. The same survey also noted, however, the time frame for implementing these initiatives is at least two to four years. The survey highlighted an immediate demand for new applications and budgetary control as the highest immediate-term priorities. A summary of the ranking of various critical competitive technologies is shown in Table 53-2.

## 53-7    CLIENT/SERVER AND THE RE-ENGINEERING OF WORK PROCESSES

According to Clive Ingham of Unisys, "Some organizations are moving to client/server computing to lower costs, but those whose motivation is to re-engineer the business will realize far greater benefits. CEOs and CIOs need to understand the value of client/ server technology as an enabler for business process re-engineering." It is now becoming apparent that client/server technology can be an important component of changing business processes.

One of the key enablers of process re-engineering is systems integration through the use of client/server technology. Tom Davenport commented about the capabilities of information technology in general:

> We have had sophisticated commercial computers and data communications at our disposal for approximately 35 years. In terms of price and functionality these

**Table 53-2**    IS Organization's Ranking of Critical Technology for Competition in Next Five Years.

| | |
|---|---|
| Client/Server Technology | 45% |
| Open Systems | 20% |
| Electronic Data Interchange (EDI) | 17% |
| Object-Oriented Programming | 13% |
| Distributed RDBMS | 8% |

*Source:*  Copyright 1993 by Computerworld, Inc., Framingham, MA 01701–Reprinted with permission from Computerworld.

technologies have become incredibly useful and usable. It is time to capitalize on them fully by employing them as enablers for business process innovation.[1]

Accounting systems, particularly client/server based systems, can contribute to business process re-engineering by bringing information closer to where it has the greatest effect.

## 53-8   EXECUTIVE INFORMATION SYSTEMS

A specialized application of systems integration and client/server technology is an Executive Information System (EIS). An EIS is an easy-to-use senior management tool designed to present information from a variety of sources (e.g., internal financial information and external databases) in a variety of formats (e.g., pie charts and bar graphs). These systems are generally based on some variety of a graphical user interface (GUI) and are designed to let the user select the level of detail displayed. For example, a controller could "drill-down" through the divisions and centers to find the source of a budget variance. The EIS may have interfaces to production, shipping, and other dynamic non-accounting data. An EIS generally incorporates many information sources; therefore, a high degree of systems integration must be in place to effectively implement an EIS.

## 53-9   IMPLEMENTATION ISSUES

### PROPRIETARY ARCHITECTURES AND OPEN SYSTEMS

Implementation of a client/server system has moved from the "bleeding edge" of technology into the mainstream. One of the primary advantages of client/server can be its "open systems" independence from proprietary software and hardware. (This is both good news and bad news!) Under proprietary systems, it was assumed that an organization's network, software, and hardware would work reasonably well together. If there were problems, the single vendor would likely be able to identify the problem and recommend a solution within a reasonable time frame. Troubleshooting in the relatively "uncharted waters" of client/server and open systems environment is not quite as easy. It is critical for IT management to build a client/server system on products that have been thoroughly tested and proven to integrate well. Other steps to a successful migration to client/server are listed in Table 53-3.

### CAUTIONS

Contrary to earlier predictions, migration to client/server technology does not always immediately produce cost savings. Therefore reducing costs should not be the only consideration when contemplating migration to a client/server. For example, migrating to client/server environment can lead to an increased need for systems support, service, and administration personnel. These functions are largely centralized in a host-based

---

[1] Reprinted with permission, Davenport, Thomas H., *Process Innovation: Reengineering Work through Information Technology,* p. 40. Copyright 1993.

**Table 53-3**  Steps to Developing a Strategy for Client/Server Migration.

1. Establish business guideposts for a migration strategy to client/server and justify reasons for migration.
2. Win corporate support by demonstrating cost-effective viability and bottom-line benefits.
3. Define migration paths first with a pilot program then move to more mission-critical applications.
4. Train staff in the new architecture.
5. Choose proven products that integrate well.
6. Avoid running parallel systems wherever possible.

*Source:*  Adapted from Corporate Computing

system but can grow incrementally in a distributed client/server architecture. Clearly, other factors such as increased data access, improved ease of use, enhanced systems integration, and facilitated business process re-engineering efforts need to be factored into the migration decision.

### SECURITY AND INTEGRITY ISSUES

With host-based systems operating on mainframes and minicomputers, data security and integrity measures are relatively easy to implement and administer. Commercially available access control software (ACS) such as IBM's RACF and Computer Associates' Top Secret and ACF2 have existed for some time and are mature, robust, and effective products. In a client/server environment, security can be more difficult to monitor and increased opportunities for data loss and corruption can exist. To date, there has been limited development of enterprise-wide security systems for client/server. However, this should be changing in the near future.

## 53-10  CLIENT/SERVER ACCOUNTING

Many of the major mainframe and PC-based accounting software vendors originally had taken a "wait-and-see" strategy regarding client/server application development. Since the technology has matured, these vendors have stepped up their client/server development efforts. For example, key mainframe or proprietary system software vendors such as Dun & Bradstreet, American Management Systems, Ross, and Lawson have recently released client/server-based versions of their products. These systems will compete with such vendors as Oracle and PeopleSoft in the increasingly cut-throat client/server accounting software marketplace.

Some of the potential benefits of client/server-based accounting systems compared to mainframe/terminal-host systems can include:

- Easier to learn because of the GUI component
- Quicker and easier to modify due to the underlying RDBMS data architecture
- Scalability. Generally, the client/server software can run on a variety of hardware platforms
- Less expensive, in some cases, to operate due to the decreased system "overhead" associated with client/server environment.

Client/server based accounting packages are not a panacea. However, they have evolved to a stage where they can now be considered a viable alternative to mainframe- or PC-based software. (Please see Chapter 46 for a structured approach to defining system requirements and selecting software).

## 53-11 SUMMARY

Client/server computing clearly is a viable strategy for meeting an organization's information processing and reporting needs. In many cases, it can offer a viable alternative to the mainframe/terminal-host environment. However, as with any relatively new technology, the buyer needs to "beware" prior to adopting it. It is critical for organizations to carefully assess the financial- and human-related costs and benefits of migrating to a new computing environment. Additionally, once a decision has been made to move to a client/server environment, both the technical and human aspects of the change must be carefully monitored and managed.

## 53-12 SELECTED REFERENCES

Schwartz, David, "Oracle Applications Client/Server Overview," Proprietary ORACLE White Paper (Part No. A10545), March 1993.

"Macola Details Client/Server Product Strategy," *Accounting Today,* November 15, 1993, p. 30.

"Tempting Fate: Exclusive Security Survey," *Information Week,* October 4, 1993, p. 42.

"Client/Server Computing: The Strategic Edge for a Changing Landscape," *Information Week Special Supplement,* Spring 1993.

Davenport, Thomas, *Process Innovation: Reengineering Work through Information Technology,* 1993.

"RFP: Migrating Accounting to a Global Client/Server Network," *Corporate Computing,* April 1993, p. 112.

"Defining Client/Server Computing: Make It a Custom Definition," *Software Magazine Client/Server Special Edition,* January 1993, p. 68.

"Client/Server Architecture," *Journal of Object Oriented Programming,* February 1992, p. 40.

"PC-Based SQL: Time to Commit?," *PC Magazine,* October 12, 1993.

"Packaged Applications: When to Move to Client/Server?," Gartner Group: Software Management Strategies (File K-003-1097), December 31, 1991.

"Justifying the Cost of Client/Server Applications," Gartner Group: Software Management Strategies (File K-017-1093), December 31, 1991.

"Planning Client/Server Architecture: The Next Two Years," Gartner Group: Office Information Systems (File E-231-945), December 13, 1991.

# SUPPLEMENT INDEX